Lumbee Indian Histories

This book explores the dynamics of conflicts over racial and ethnic identities in the southern United States, focusing on the Lumbee Indians of North Carolina. During the colonial period the Lumbee were both referred to as Indians and generally treated as Whites: some owned slaves, most were just poor to ordinary farmers, half-hidden in the midst of extensive coastal and riverine swamps. From 1835 to 1865 they were legally "Free Persons of Color," a designation with a broad range of necessarily contestable meanings. Since Reconstruction the Lumbee have publicly insisted upon their legal identity as Indians, which is sanctioned by the laws of North Carolina.

This book is also a history of Native American concepts and visions of history, beginning with the contemporary period and with the perspectives of the Lumbee Indians, and working backward to the colonial period and to the major groupings of Native Americans. The fundamental question here is: what grasp upon the connections between past, present and impending future enables peoples who almost always lose to keep on struggling?

Lumbee Indian Histories

Race, ethnicity, and Indian identity
in the southern United States

GERALD M. SIDER

College of Staten Island and
Graduate School and University Center
City University of New York

CAMBRIDGE
UNIVERSITY PRESS

Published by the Press Syndicate of the University of Cambridge
The Pitt Building, Trumpington Street, Cambridge CB2 1RP
40 West 20th Street, New York, NY 10011-4211, USA
10 Stamford Road, Oakleigh, Melbourne 3166, Australia

First published 1993
First paperback edition 1994

Printed in the United States of America

Library of Congress Cataloging-in-Publication Data
Sider, Gerald M.
Lumbee Indian histories : race, ethnicity and Indian identity in the
southern United States / Gerald Sider.
p.   cm.
Includes bibliographical references and index.
ISBN 0-521-42045-8
1. Lumbee Indians – Ethnic identity.   2. Lumbee Indians – History.
3. Lumbee Indians – Government relations   I. Title.
E99.C91S53 1993
975.6′004975 – dc20   92-14644

A catalog record for this book is available from the British Library.

ISBN 0-521-42045-8 hardback
ISBN 0-521-46669-5 paperback

Culture and Class in Anthropology and History
Volume II

This is the second of three volumes on a theory of culture in history: the role of culture in the formation and transformation of systems of inequality. The first volume, *Culture and Class in Anthropology and History: A Newfoundland Illustration* [New York, Cambridge University Press; Paris, Editions de la Maison des Sciences de l'Homme, 1986], introduced a general framework for the analysis of culture, and focused on cultural processes in the context of merchant capitalism. This volume analyzes culture in the context of processes of ethnic group formation. The third volume will take up the issue of folk culture and state formation.

Dedicated in grateful memory to
Jim Chavis and Thadis Oxendine
who fought for the well-being of their people
with all their heart and wisdom, lost, and
came back again and again with more heart, more
wisdom, and more fight to win what could then be won
– and to Julian Pierce
who fought and won, even after death.

The two principles on which our conduct toward the Indians should be founded are justice and fear. After the injuries we have done them, they can not love us, which leaves us no alternative but that of fear.

Thomas Jefferson to Benjamin Hawkins,
13 August 1786

My children, my children
I take pity on those who have been taught
I take pity on those who have been taught
Because they push on hard
Because they push on hard
Says our father
Says our father

Ghost Dance song brought to the southern
Arapaho by Sitting Bull, ca. 1890

Contents

xi

Contents

Illustrations

Preface

Nearly 40,000 Lumbee Indian people now live, mostly as farmers and factory workers, in the midst of what was until quite recently the dense and extensive swamps on the inland edge of the North Carolina coastal plain, along the border with South Carolina. The Lumbee, some of whom call themselves Tuscarora, make up a bit more than a third of the population of Robeson County, with African-Americans and Whites each also approximating one-third the population of this large, tumultuous county – a county that has long played a crucial role in state and regionwide political struggles over conservative proagrarian but anti-Black agendas.

Although Lumbee (and Tuscarora) have always been one people since the time they emerged from the same colonial cauldrons that shaped the Cherokee, Creek, Catawba, Cheraw, and other southeastern Native Americans into separate and distinct peoples, their identity has often been challenged both by others, and, in different ways, by themselves.

Before 1835 the Lumbee were not ethnically categorized but had most of the legal and social prerogatives of people regarded as being of European origin, although they engaged, simultaneously, in long-continuing struggles of various forms over their social distinctiveness and their substantial communal autonomy. They hovered on, and crossed back and forth over, the boundary between being regarded as people and as *a* people.

From 1835 to 1865 they were legally classified as "Free Persons of Color," which usually meant former slaves and their descendants. "Slave" was held by the courts to be synonymous with "Negro," although it was widely known that Indians and others were also frequently enslaved.

xv

Local Whites in Robeson County knew, and testified on oath in the mid-nineteenth century, that the ancestors of the Lumbee "were never slave" but "were always free." Yet from the 1835 revision of the North Carolina constitution until the end of the Civil War, when the category was formally abolished, the ancestors of the contemporary Lumbee were legally "Free Persons of Color."

From 1865 to 1885 they had no legal designation, suffered many of the liabilities of being regarded as "non-White," and faced – and participated in creating – an exceptionally volatile social situation. In 1885 they were legally recognized as Indians by the state of North Carolina. Since then they have been struggling with the federal government for full recognition as Indians – struggles in which success and failure frequently and rapidly change places, each time with higher stakes and more serious consequences. In the course of these struggles they have come to engage in profound identity struggles with each other – struggles that also have had lives-shaping consequences.

Three specific issues are central to this book.

1. *How ethnic groups are born; how they are transformed and how they grow, change, break, or are broken apart; and how they can die.*

Hovering in the background of many treatments of ethnicity is the unannounced assumption that ethnic groups were created at the dawn of human time – or during the Neolithic age at least – and that the emergence and consolidation of state power undermined, trivialized, and ultimately homogenized ethnicity. This cannot be the case logically, and it is not what has actually happened. Were it so we would long ago have run out of the world's supply of distinctive peoples.

To the contrary: domination, particularly in the form of the expansion and consolidation of state power, not only destroys ethnic (and in a broader sense, cultural) variation, it also *creates* such variation. Ethnic groups, moreover, are far from passive in these processes of creation and destruction.

Ethnic groups often originate in relatively brief periods of cataclysmic population dislocation or conquest. But their historical career is not prefigured in their origin. Rather, it is shaped by a range of ordinary, ongoing, and inescapable struggles over the changing ways ethnicity is used to shape different kinds of lives at the local level and in society at large, over changing forms of political domination and integration, over changes in the legal status and treatment of ethnic people, and over the usually more slowly changing forms of humiliation and degradation that are so crucial to the perpetuation of domination and exploitation. All of these are interwoven, most can and do change with surprising rapidity, and only rarely are the changes synchronous. The interweaving of these diverse struggles about ethnicity creates not simply a fabric of social life, but interlocked and unstable fields of force. Think, for example, how quickly the urban riots that were so prevalent on the 1960s came and went – and not for the first time in American history.

The same social processes that create ethnic groups also create races. Although humans differ from one another biologically, "race" is no more a biological category than ethnicity. The word points to processes of social differentiation presumably rooted in biology that are rather more slow-changing than ethnicity and ordinarily even more violent. While focusing primarily on processes of ethnic differentiation, we also must address aspects of the history of Indian peoples within the United States that, more than with other peoples, demonstrate the hidden tensions between the categories of race and ethnicity. Note, for instance, how the federal government currently defines "affirmative action race and ethnic categories":

> White *(not of Hispanic origin) – a person having origins in any of the original people of Europe, North Africa, or the Middle East.*
>
> Black *(not of Hispanic origin) – a person having origin in any of the Black racial groups of Africa.*
>
> American Indian or Alaskan Native – *A person having origins in any of the original people of North America, and who maintains cultural identification through tribal affiliation or community recognition.*

In other words, "cultural identification" is necessary for the racial or ethnic identification of Indians (and unthinkable as a criterion for judging the identity of African Americans). For Indians, this identification, which presumably can be made *either* by Indian people *or* by the larger society, turns out in fact to require both.

The most important point to note here, by way of an introduction to the issues at stake, is that the historical career of any ethnic people is characteristically punctuated by breaks, by sudden and fundamental changes, and by rapid shifts in the direction and momentum of change. The social, legal, economic, and political status and situation of an ethnic people, their internal political organization, the content of their ethnic culture, their connectedness to the dominant society – all these factors and more are always and necessarily fluid.

2. The second central issue for this book is: *How Native American peoples see, claim, and seek to shape – in sum, produce – their own history.*

Preface

The phrase "production of history" refers both to basic social changes that have taken and are taking place and also to how people come to comprehend their past – how they commemorate and silence it (or parts of it), claim or deny, discover or describe one or several "pasts," in their own way or by the rules and standards of the dominant society. Above all, the production of history refers to how people try to grasp – not just to understand, but to take control of and reshape – the multiple connections between past, present, and impending future, including the terrors and the hopes that come to reside in the spaces between past, present, and future. All this, and more, is included in the concept "the production of history."

To be an Native American has very often been to suffer – really suffer – defeat in crucial, history-shaping struggles. Yet native peoples, in the face of such experiences, often continue to try to bind new and different futures to ongoing pasts. Their persistent struggles to claim and reclaim their own histories, from and against defeat, encourage an appreciative respect. These continuing struggles also raise a crucial political and theoretical issue: how *agency* (people's capacity to act both within and upon larger social forces) can be continually reborn not just from experience but against the lessons experience teaches. Hope will turn out to be created not simply in the context of struggles against the dominant society but also in the context of a people's internal struggles – the same factional struggles that have often also had such destructive consequences. The history-shaping paradoxes and contradictions of agency and hope will be a central subject of this book.

3. The third issue conjoins the first two: describing and understanding the multiple connections between the historical career of an ethnic people and their own efforts to shape, claim, and understand – in a word, to *have* – their history. In its starkest form this issue can be posed as *the complex, historically developing and changing connections between ethnicity and ethnohistory.*

At the center of these connections is the historical fluidity both of ethnic peoples and of the larger social context in which they live. This fluidity, this constant change, presents the people involved, both within and outside the ethnic group, with unavoidable and irresolvable antagonisms between their past and their present situation, and between the present and the impending future. It is precisely in the midst of these antagonisms that ethnicity and ethnohistory are transformed – often in dissimilar ways.

xviii

II

By the late 1980s the Lumbee – and three partly separate groups *within* the Lumbee who call themselves Tuscarora – were petitioning the Bureau of Indian Affairs for what is called administrative recognition as Indians, and they also put bills before Congress seeking legislative recognition. In these endeavors they have been testifying both for and against each other. It is unlikely that the situation will soon be resolved to everyone's at least partial satisfaction.

Thus this book, whether I want it to or not, is likely to be used in several current controversies. In some of these the well-being of a lot of people is directly at stake. This book is also likely to be used in ways that push aside my own sympathies and concerns, explanations, and interpretations. I have sought to deal with the multiplicity of vulnerabilities – those of other peoples and, less importantly, my own – by being as clear as possible about what I am saying and not saying, by being as careful as I can on issues that are likely to be taken up by the direct participants in the controversies, and by addressing a history of how people with and without power have used, and been used by, the methods and findings of anthropologists and historians.

The recognition that Lumbee Indians have so far achieved from the federal government has been tempered by substantial, and recently increasing, qualifications. These qualifications prevent Lumbee and Tuscarora from obtaining many federal benefits that are supposed to be available to Indians – including health, education, and housing programs. This matters, and it matters intensely: the widespread poverty, powerlessness, and substantial unmet needs characteristic of many Lumbee and Tuscarora people attest to their long history of being treated politically, economically, and socially as Indians, without being able to claim even those few forms of ambivalently effective redress from the federal government that fully recognized Indians have.

Although at some point fairly soon the Lumbee may well win the full federal recognition that they have long sought, many of their earlier struggles have ended in at least partial defeat. As in other such situations where widely shared and passionately held hopes invoke diverse strategies, none of which are fully effective, the Lumbee have had substantial, and at times bitter, internal divisions. For the past twenty years this divisiveness has been expressed in the emergence, from among the Lumbee, of groups of people who claim a Tuscarora identity and history and deny and oppose the name Lumbee.

Probably the most pressing controversy that will envelop this book is whether the Lumbee and Tuscarora are one people. Lumbee and Tuscarora, other Native American people, and government officials are all concerned with this question, and however it is answered some people will be hurt.

Indian people in Robeson County whose judgment I respect and who have seen earlier drafts of this book have urged me to address this issue at the outset. Neither they nor I think it is my place to "answer" this question, but it is important that I be clear about where I stand and what I understand.

At the level of interwoven kinship and residence, local church membership, and the cultures of concern, hope, and history, the Indian people of Robeson County – Lumbee and Tuscarora – are one people: this much, in my view, is certain. Yet the pressures they are under and the diverse and diverging claims upon hope and upon history that they make suggest they cannot simply and only be one people: Indian people, here as elsewhere, have and will continue to have substantial and at times profound divisions. The paradoxes of division and unity, the tensions and claims that fuel such splits, the contradictions that characteristically are and are not resolved – all of these are, in fact, widespread features of Native American social and cultural history.

The broader social and cultural processes within and against which native peoples have claimed their identity, or have had an identity imposed upon them, have almost always and almost everywhere divided native peoples from one another. Sometimes the groups created by such divisions have been treated as if they were distinct and separate peoples – the Seminole, for example, emerged as a separate people from the Creek Indian confederacy. And sometimes the split is simply "factional," as were the bitter and violent divisions among the Sioux during the emergence of the American Indian Movement.

The forms these divisions develop, the sorts of people who do and do not take sides, and the identities fashioned from these divisions – all change, and can change rapidly and fundamentally. The people who now call themselves Lumbee and Tuscarora called themselves Siouan and Cherokee in the 1930s and 1940s. This is *not* the same split as that one with different labels, although some of the divisive pressures have not changed significantly.

African American people in the rural southern United States (called "Black" in much of this text, to follow the local dignified self-description), under somewhat similar kinds of pressures as Indians, do not at all divide in the same kinds of ways. African American people experience and suffer from sharpening class divisions, substantially different political orientations and commitments, and different social agendas, to name but a few "dividing lines." But they do not split in terms of identity, or at least not in the ways that Native Americans do. Why? The answer seems to have something to do with substantial differences in political and social autonomy between Native American and African American people. The more fundamental splits and separations that occur among Native American peoples are also rooted in differences in the ways domination presses upon hope, and the different ways hope becomes interwoven with people's sense of history – particularly the history of their sense of "otherness"; otherness both from the dominant society and from each other.

This analysis of Indian identity struggles, from the present Lumbee–Tuscarora engagements back through the legal recognition of the ancestors of the Lumbee as a distinct Indian people within the political and cultural economy of postreconstruction North Carolina, and on back into the colonial southeast, will thus emphasize the volatile, changing, and context-specific connections between hopes and histories – histories lived and histories claimed, hopes met and hopes shattered.

One brief clarification of terms is in order: "southern" and "southeastern" have a specific use here. "Southeastern" refers to a geographic area, necessarily loosely specified, that includes the Atlantic coastal plain from Chesapeake Bay southward to Florida and along the Gulf Coast toward the Mississippi, the piedmont interior, and the southern Appalachians. "Southern" refers to an evolving historical-political matrix, which for much of the twentieth century, in the rural areas, turned on the connections between sharecropping, cotton, Jim Crow, mills, and one-party politics.

III

For the past twenty-five years I have had an active, if only episodic, part in several different kinds of Lumbee and Tuscarora struggles, beginning with the year and a half (1967–8) I lived in the central Indian town, Pembroke, with my then wife, Karen Blu. She was there as an anthropologist; I had several different positions in the community. Partly I was, and was seen as, an anthropologist, as much because of my relationship to her as for anything I myself did. I was also, and more intensely, there as an activist in what local people called "the movement" – a loose combination of voter-registration drives, civil rights struggles, and poverty programs. In this last capacity I was employed part-time for a statewide poverty program (the Mobility Project) that focused on finding jobs and homes for people being driven out of the bottom reaches of agricultural employment – sharecroppers and farm day-laborers. I was closely involved with the organization of voter-registration drives and elections and with the establishment of an Indian poverty program agency in Robeson County. Later, in the 1980s, I worked with and for Lumbee River Legal Services on the Lumbee petition to the Bureau of Indian Affairs for federal Indian recognition, especially on issues of historical origins and political and social organization. My direct involvement in these specific struggles shaped the development of my research, particularly by intensifying my sense of what is at stake in the way general analytical questions are formed. Partisanship does not change the answers social science finds – though most people who have not tried it assert it does. It changes the questions one asks. For me it shaped the two general questions that permeate this book. These questions are briefly mentioned here so that their reverberations may be heard from the outset.

The first question began as a simple pair of intellectual concerns – little more than an abstract conceptual curiosity – and led to fundamental changes in the way that I understand Native American history: *Why has Lumbee Indian identity been so contestable, been such an arena of struggle?* and *How, actually, have Lumbee history and historical origins differed from the histories of other southeastern Native American peoples, particularly those with less, or differently, contested identities?*

None of the reasons that are usually given for the contestability of Lumbee identity can withstand even a few hours of close investigation; each of these "reasons" refers to social and cultural conditions that are in fact widespread among Native Americans. To take only one of the most dramatic, in terms of the passions it arouses, both for illustration *and to dismiss it at the outset* – twenty or more years ago, some anthropologists and some local Whites in Robeson County said that the Lumbee had a contestable identity because they were either partly Black or something that was called in professional jargon a "triracial isolate." But the Seminole, for example, were substantially mixed with African-Americans, yet few if any contested their Indian identity; moreover, a great many Indian peoples have intermarried with Blacks as well as Whites, many far more than have the Lumbee, without calling their identity as Indian people into question. How then did Lumbee history differ from the history of other Native Americans so as to make their Indian identity more of an issue?

Exploring this question led to finding unexpected and profound similarities and some surprising differences in the histories of Native American peoples in the southeast. It also led to recognizing some of the complex intertwinings between the ways history is claimed and the ways it is silenced, both by those who dominate and those who are dominated.

The second general question that emerged from my activities concerned the connection between doing anthropology and doing history, not as an abstract intellectual problem about the relationships between different disciplines, but as a practical concern: *how studying the history of a people, questioning them about their history, and doing documentary research on their past affects your relations with the people among whom you live and work.*

There is a naive notion floating about anthropology that one of the ways an anthropologist can repay a people for imposing upon them is to "give them their history." Although I once shared this notion in a general and unspecific way, I am now appalled by its blind and presumptive claims to innocence in the midst of potential danger to others. For most rural people in most places in the world, including those we call tribal peoples and peasants, and people just farming and working, "history" is not just "about" power, it *is* power, and sensible people take it cautiously into their hands.

People may wish to silence aspects of their pasts, from the memory of a desire to the loss or gain of kin or land, for reasons that can include both dignity and fear, and doing history as an anthropologist among a living people often hovers on the ambivalent and ambiguous edge between a warm and intimate sharing of knowledge and a potentially violent intrusiveness.

This problem has no escape, but one transformation, which lies not in *doing* a history, for people to take up or put down, but in focusing on how histories are, and have been, embedded in the way people have built their lives and their hopes. This book is thus both an anthropology and a history of histories: it explores how people have lived and still live within and against the histories they have chosen and the histories that have been imposed upon them.

There are, in this perspective, many different kinds of histories and wide differences within each kind: histories as socially and culturally constructed concepts of the past, which often seek to bind people in different ways to different futures; histories as they come to be carved into the material and social realities of peoples' lives (the wear patterns on their houses, their tools, and their bodies; the layout of fields and forests, villages and swamps); histories in the making, that people try in different ways to shape, to claim, to shun. Hope may well spring eternal in the human breast, but it does so both from and in opposition to the histories people see and claim, the histories that pervade their lives, seen or unseen, and the historical claims that are imposed upon them.

IV

When I first moved to Pembroke, North Carolina, Mr. Barto and Ms. Geraldine Clark found me a house and made me at home in theirs. Their kindness and concern anchored life and work. Dr. Martin L. Brooks, Mr. James Chavis, Mr. Tommie and Ms. Ruth Dial, Mr. Herman Dial, Prof. Adolph Dial, and Mr. Thadis Oxendine taught me what I was then capable of learning about political organizing and Lumbee history, which they wove together inextricably. I was there primarily as a civil rights organizer, not an anthropologist, and I did no formal interviewing. They raised historical issues in our discussions about social and political goals and methods, and this merger of historical concerns with ongoing, and changing, social life permeates my work.

Horace and Barbara Locklear, Rod Locklear, Ronald and Perlene Revels, Woodrow Dial, Bruce Jones – all more my age mates – taught me about politics, companionship, and laughter. John Albert Locklear, John L. Locklear, Jr., and Clare Locklear, and Ruth Bullard Locklear have become very special friends. I lived in Pembroke from May 1967 to August 1968 and worked with Karen Blu, an anthropologist who has written insightfully about the Lumbee, and whose sociability was an important part of the field research.

In the 1980s I spent a substantial amount of time in Robeson County, in many relatively brief visits, working with and for Lumbee River Legal Services on the early drafts of the acknowledgment petition and on the possibility that Lumbee and Tuscarora might make one coordinated recognition case. Julian Pierce, the Director of Lumbee River Legal Services, was a wise and very special person to work with and to have as a friend. The intensity and fundamental gentleness of his compassion, together with his full engagement in social struggles, brought back to life the work of an older generation of Indian activists, particularly James Chavis and Peter Brooks. Julian Pierce's murder has been a tragic, unmeasurable loss for all the people of Robeson County.

The Legal Services staff – including especially Ruth Bullard Locklear, now the head of tribal enrollment for the Lumbee Regional Development Association, Derek Lowery, and Cynthia Hunt Locklear – were helpful, encouraging, and kind. Arlinda Locklear, an Indian rights attorney whom I have met only briefly but talked with at key points and on key issues, shared with me her extraordinary ability to see the interior of complex issues. To sit in on a meeting with Ruth Locklear, Emma Locklear, Bruce Jones, Rod Locklear, with an open phone line to Arlinda Locklear in Washington, and to listen to them discuss an issue, is to realize what a small piece of understanding anthropology has, and from what a narrow perspective – and this leaves out the older and quieter Lumbee, who at times leave me with the feeling that I do not know enough to understand their insights.

Wesley White read an earlier draft of this manuscript and provided knowledgeable advice on several points, and my years of research on the political history of the Indian people of Robeson County have benefited greatly by the data and insights he has shared with me.

My sons Byron and Hugh each came to Robeson County with me, and each provided their own insights into the social relations of daily life and work. It has been a special pleasure to learn from them.

Near the end of my stay in Robeson County, Stanley Diamond invited me to come to the New School and do my Ph.D. in anthropology there. I still appreciate the invitation, and the advice he and Solomon Miller gave in formulating my early analyses of Lumbee history in my doctoral dissertation.

Judy Hilkey's work on history, culture, and marxism had a substantial influence on the early theoretical development of this project, and Adelheid von Saldern's interpretations of popular and working-class culture have been particularly helpful in my recent work on culture in history.

At the center of this project is the intellectual and personal influence of Eric Wolf. Eric first put me in touch with the historians at the Max Planck Institut für Geschichte, in the mid 1970s. The perspectives of Alf Lüdtke and Hans Medick, of that institute, have come to be part of the way I think and work. The influence of several other scholars who have been part of the working group on anthropology and history, cosponsored by the Max Planck Institut für Geschichte and the Maison des Sciences de l'Homme – including especially Robert Berdahl, David William Cohen, Karin Hausen, Vanessa Maher, and David Sabean – has been substantial. From these people, and from my more recent work with Gavin Smith, now also a member of this working group, I have learned special and productive lessons about what Hans and Alf would call the "simultaneity" – the discordant concordances – of friendship and work.

Professor Rudolph Vierhaus, the director of the Max Planck Institut für Geschichte, and M. Clemens Heller and Dr. Maurice Aymard of the Maison des Sciences de l'Homme, deserve a special note of appreciation. They provided me with several residence grants, beginning before I had published much of anything at all, and without stipulating any specific project that I should work on. The freedom this gave me to work, and the learning it made possible, have shaped a major part of my intellectual life.

In the past few years, as this project came to completion, I have particularly benefited from the advice and insight of Maria Lagos, who has an insightful understanding of the dynamics of agrarian inequality. Andrea Bardfeld, Jeremy Beckett, Tom Burgess, August Carbonella, Geraldine Casey, Susan Greenbaum, Delmos Jones, Ursula Nienhaus, George Roth, and Gilbert Schrank all made important contributions. Bill Roseberry, with his characteristic mixture of excellent judgment and hard work on behalf of others, provided much useful advice.

The Wenner Gren Foundation for Anthropological Research, through the kindness of its president, Sydel Silverman, provided a grant that enabled me to make several research trips to North Carolina and to the archives in South Carolina, from 1988 to 1990. I am grateful for this aid, which has been particularly helpful for revising and expanding the analysis of the colonial period. Robert Mackintosh and Paul Begley, archivists at the South Carolina Department of Archives and History, Ms. Susan Harris, at the Pembroke State University serials collection, and Ms. Angela McCoy, legislative assistant to the House Subcommittee on Indian Affairs, all deserve extra thanks for extra work and advice. George Roth, of the BIA, was always a source of wisdom and insight, of caring and careful analyses. Dr. Stanley Knick, of the Native American Resource Center, Pembroke State University, kindly allowed me to photograph the museum displays, including the very special cover picture.

Mirella Affron, social sciences and humanities dean at the College of Staten Island, and Andrew Fuller, my department chair, have been consistently helpful and supportive, using the limited resources of a public university in ways that support both the university and the work of scholarship within it. Jane Schneider was, as always, both helpful and encouraging. Donna Jorden and Vicky Macintyre made useful editorial suggestions for the final draft. Francine Egger brought it all together – *arbeit und liebe.*

Pete Seeger used to tell a story about stone soup – about a person who started out in the middle of a field with a very large kettle of boiling water and a stone in the bottom of the kettle. As people came to look and comment, the soupmaker would agree that the soup would indeed be better if the onlooker added a thing or two and suggested that they stay to watch the result. Little by little the soup grew. I thank my friends, companions and advice-givers – for the onions, the mushrooms, the potatoes, the advice, the confrontations and the love – and hope we all enjoy the result.

This book is designed for both a general and an academic audience. To make it more accessible it has no footnotes but, rather, an extended essay on sources at the end.

PART ONE

Introductions

1

Within and against history

In 1885 the people now called Lumbee Indians (including the Tuscarora) were, after decades of turmoil, legally designated Indians by an act of the North Carolina state legislature, an act that gave them some specific entitlements, particularly schools of their own, and also a name: "Croatan." From 1885 to 1911 they were known as Croatan Indians, a name that came into strong disfavor with the people themselves, for it was shortened by the neighboring Whites to "Cro," with the implied reference to Jim Crow. From 1911 to 1913 they were legislatively designated "Indians of Robeson County," but this name implicitly raised the question "which Indians?" and in 1913 their name was changed again by the state legislature to "Cherokee Indians of Robeson County." The North Carolina (or Eastern) Cherokee protested this, perhaps because they felt it would lead to pressure to share what few entitlements and benefits they received from the federal government. In any case, the name quickly fell into disuse.

During the 1930s the Lumbee put pressure on the U.S. Congress to be federally designated Siouan Indians of the Lumber River – specifically Cheraw, although the more general name was to be the official one – and in this attempt they had the support of John Collier, the head of the Bureau of Indian Affairs. They were blocked by Harold Ickes, then secretary of the interior, who endorsed the Siouan name but raised the question of "responsibility" and eventual material support in ways that haunt the Lumbee and Tuscarora still. Ickes stated:

> It would appear . . . that the Federal Government is under no obligation whatsoever to this group of people. . . . The enactment of this legislation would be the initial step in bringing these Indians under the

> jurisdiction of the Federal Government. . . . Since the Federal Government does not have any responsibility for these people, it is not for us to say whether or not they should be classed as Cherokee. . . . North Carolina, which state is responsible for these Indians, has already designated them as Cherokees . . .

Ickes then suggested to Congress that these Indian people

> formerly known as Croatan Indians shall hereafter be designated as "Siouan Indians of the Lumber River," and shall be so recognized by the United States Government: Provided, that nothing contained herein shall be construed as conferring Federal wardship or any other governmental rights or benefits upon such Indians.

This attempt to obtain federal recognition failed for a variety of reasons, including both the issue of benefits and some substantial dissension among the people affected. In 1953 the state legislature recognized the people as Lumbee Indians, and in 1956 the U.S. Congress also enacted recognition of the Lumbee Indians, but with much the same restrictions on benefits that Ickes had earlier suggested.

All of these names had one feature in common: they were applied to the whole people. In the early 1970s about 10 percent of the Lumbee – between two and three thousand people – began to call themselves, and to be referred to, as "Tuscarora." People who call themselves Tuscarora in many cases are close kin, even full siblings, of those who call themselves Lumbee, but the division is still deep, and in some respects neither wholly new in this area, nor – as we shall see – wholly different in its origins and development from social processes that have occurred elsewhere among Native Americans.

Each of these different names came tied to a different vision and version of history, and, less neatly but still crucially, they were also tied to different visions and versions of the path to the future.

"Croatan," the first official Indian name, referred to an origin in intermarriage with the settlers of the Lost Colony of Sir Walter Raleigh. Raleigh had planted this colony on the Outer Banks – the coastal island chain off northern North Carolina – in 1586; when he could finally send ships back to resupply the settlers, in 1590, they were gone and the word "Croatoan" was found carved on a tree in the empty settlement. At Croatoan (also called Croatan) there were presumably friendly Indians, and the Indian people of Robeson County were claimed – both by the sponsors of the legislation to give them the name 'Croatan' and by some of the people themselves – to be the descendants of intermarriages between these Whites from the Lost Colony and the Indians of Croatan. In the late nineteenth and early twentieth centuries, the

4

central political effort of Indian people active in obtaining the legislation that gave them this name was aimed at securing and controlling special Indian schools. Education was the specific and preferred way forward.

The name 'Cherokee Indians of Robeson County' did not refer to an origin intermixed with historically important Whites, but to a history that claimed the Cherokee came down from the mountains to fight against White people (and perhaps also against some coastal Indians) and stayed to settle in the Robeson County area, intermarrying with local Indian people. This is a history with not only a different content but also a profoundly different orientation: against, not emerging from, White people and that "civilization." The political activities of the proponents of this vision seem to have been less focused on the sorts of developments that lead to increased integration with the surrounding White society (such as institutionalized education), and more contained within the Indian hamlets and locales of Robeson County.

The name Siouan Indians of the Lumber River, popular in the 1930s and almost legally institutionalized, is the most historically accurate, as we shall see. But in practice – that is, in its association with a number of interwoven paths to the future – it was perhaps the most problematic and divisive of all the names. This name emerged from a number of anthropological and historical investigations, and from the memories of families and the migration histories of influential people in the Indian community. It became wrapped up with two widespread and intensely popular social movements. One movement sought, both through the mechanisms of Franklin Delano Roosevelt's programs for farm reclamation and support and through the Bureau of Indian Affairs, to develop a large cooperative farm for Indians. The second, related movement developed and intensified Indian associations, including longhouses and local "Red Man" lodges that, in conjunction with the cooperative farm and with sufficient assistance from the Bureau of Indian Affairs, might become the nucleus of a "reservation," but would, in any case, be the basis for a more politically, economically, and culturally autonomous communal life.

All this was strongly opposed by local Whites, who saw their control over Indian labor and their other forms of profiteering from keeping people poor and dependent threatened. It was also opposed by a few influential Indian people who were against the idea of being reservation Indians, or were against emphasizing this particular Indian identity, either because they had another identity in mind or feared the social and economic consequences of being too specifically Indian.

In the early 1970s a substantial number of Lumbee began to call themselves Tuscarora and to organize politically, both in opposition to

5

White domination of the county, and, later, to seek recognition from the state and the federal government as Tuscarora. Whereas many people – but not, by far, all – who call themselves Lumbee still hold to the origin tradition that became socially significant with the name Croatan, rooting their history in the Lost Colony and in that particular intermixture with Whites, those who call themselves Tuscarora find their origin in the Tuscarora Indians who, in the early colonial period, lived in northeastern North Carolina. After these Tuscarora rose up against the European colonists in the early eighteenth century and were savagely attacked by the colonists, not all the Tuscarora survivors fled north to join the Iroquois confederacy. Some in fact fled south and settled in and near Robeson County.

The split between Lumbee and Tuscarora cannot be reduced to any single cause or any simple package of several causes. In some ways it restates key aspects of earlier splits, first between Croatan and the Cherokee Indians of Robeson County, then between these Cherokee and the Siouan Indians of the Lumber River movement. In some ways it *partly* reflects strategic differences, loosely connected to different visions of historical origins – a strategic split between accommodation to the White-dominated "power structure" (as the Indians call it) and open opposition. But as might well be expected, there are Lumbee who completely oppose the local power structure, and Tuscarora who make a variety of accommodations to it. In some ways the split is *partly* one of class: poorer, more rural Indians in the county have tended to ally themselves with the Tuscarora – although a great many remain Lumbee, and the Tuscarora have a number of at least moderately affluent adherents and sympathizers. This split, and the earlier ones as well, brings us back to the issue of how people live the histories they both claim and turn away from.

II

Superficially, what seems to happen when different historical origin claims become interwoven with different strategies for coping with domination is what anthropologists following the lead of Malinowski have called "history as charter." In this analytical perspective, people invent histories, either "mythic" (supernatural) or presumably "real" (secular), to justify or legitimate their group interests and group claims. This is a drastic simplification of how histories actually develop and get used – for two major reasons:

1. It makes history too much of an intellectual phenomenon, a matter of ideas and words, slighting the direct material expression of history

6

    – the multiple ways people's history becomes carved into their bodies and lives.

2. It makes the connection between history and the interests of the group appear seamless and smooth, when actually a people often must antagonistically confront not only other people's versions of their history but also their own.

The settlement patterns of Indian people in Robeson County, the kind and condition of their houses and farm equipment, the land they use – the often too wet or too sandy fields many tried to farm – the wear patterns on their houses, pathways, tools, hands and faces, and in the midst of their villages and hamlets the proliferation of well-kept churches and small schoolhouses: all this and more represents a history of land loss, of the emergence and decline of sharecropping, of socially significant spaces and distances, of specific ways of being Indian in this particular region, and also a history of people building their own lives in their own ways – their own houses, their own churches, part of their own schools (which were initially built by the county to local standards for non-White schools and were continually rebuilt by the people themselves) – and doing all this in the midst of economic and political domination. The landscape thus expresses, simultaneously, both the imposed histories of changing systems of production and the claimed histories of daily life and work in families and communities. And all of this coexisted with histories expressed in legislation and large-scale economic trends: the names and identities, with or without benefits, that were legislatively granted; the legislative acts that gave separate schools (and prisons), and that opened the Indian college to Whites and then Blacks; the factories that were, in the 1970s, increasingly planted in these fields.

When, in the 1960s, an intense effort was made to register Indian voters and to mobilize these new voters against White domination of county affairs, it became necessary to encourage people to claim something new while they were still enmeshed in the remnants and the force-fields of the old. To get people, particularly sharecroppers, out of their utterly vulnerable homes in middle of their landlord's fields first to register to vote (which was often seen as a defiant act by those who had the power to impose severe penalties), and then to bring them out again to vote against the White power elite – to do this was to mobilize people to turn against the history that they still lived within: to turn against its physical weight and ideological force, to turn against the forms of meaning it encouraged, the forms of meaninglessness it generated.

7

To urge people to claim a different reading of the past and a different vision of the future is to mobilize people to accept a new history that still does not fully make sense, that moves against the still strongly flowing currents of power and of present history. To say that this new, emerging sense of history simply "legitimates" new claims is to turn away from all the tensions, gaps, pressures, fears and hopes that live in and between people's multiple, uncertain senses of the past and of the impending future – the multiple, coexisting histories that people live within and against: the histories of their own dreams and hopes and fears, and the histories of power – of what they know has been, and still could be, done to them.

III

The continuing Lumbee and Tuscarora struggle to be socially considered Indian – to claim a name and an identity in opposition to the names and identities imposed upon them – and to be legally and legislatively treated accordingly, presents some of the central social and cultural paradoxes of Native North Americans in an especially heightened and visible form.

The volatility of Lumbee identity in the larger society, and the association between name-identity changes and internal strife together seem to give Lumbee history its unique form and interest. But serious and controversial identity issues, external and internal, are more common among Native Americans than is usually recognized. In basic ways the Lumbee are only an intense and revealing instance, with some special features, of far broader processes and issues.

Native American peoples have been forced to claim and to continually negotiate not only their public identity but also their public "presence," and they have done so, from colonial times to the present, in ways that create substantial internal struggles. When, for instance, the people who came to be known by the Europeans as the Cherokee were first encountered – and at the time of this encounter they were not even a single, separate people – they were said by the Europeans to be "poor hunters and worse warriors." A great many native people in the southeast, to whom such images stuck, were shipped as slaves to the Caribbean Islands. In claiming a different presence and place on the colonial frontier, and by having a different identity and social position imposed, the Cherokee became, in the midst of substantial and destructive internal turmoil, both one people and a very different kind of people from what they had been. As will be discussed in Chapters 10 and 11, the expansion and consolidation of the colonial frontier

8

profoundly reorganized all the native societies in the southeast, creating different kinds of native identities and social systems, with substantial antagonisms within and between them.

What is different about such historical experiences as those of the Cherokee, and what is fundamentally similar in comparison with the Lumbee, turns out to be a much more complex issue than it first appears to be. Indeed, one of the central projects of this book as a whole is to situate Lumbee history within a broader field of the southeastern Native American encounter with the Euro-American onslaught and by so doing to clarify both the Lumbee instance and the impact of the encounter on native societies.

The politics of identity are always deeply enmeshed in very broad nets – force-fields of hope, anger, concern, despair, and more. To suggest the breadth and power of these forces, consider this: the teenage Indian suicide rate, while varying substantially from year to year, has always been several times greater than the teenage White suicide rate – in some years 100 times greater – throughout the mid-twentieth century. Yet we cannot easily attribute this simply to poverty, oppression and cultural slander, for the teenage Black suicide rate is *lower* than that for Whites. Poverty, domination and humiliation press different peoples in fundamentally different ways. Such examples as this are important to keep in mind when considering the struggles that form within and against identities, to highlight the seriousness of the issues and to suggest their complexity.

IV

The fluidity of their situation, the constantly changing pressures on them, the difficulty of developing a strategy for coping even in part with these pressures, and especially the importance of maintaining at least some significant aspects of their own ways, their own social relations, their own values, in the midst of this turmoil – all this often confronts Native American peoples with *an unavoidable and irresolvable antagonism between their past and their present.* This antagonism is usually forced on Native Americans by their vulnerability in a larger society that simultaneously insists both on the "otherness" of dominated peoples and on their compliance with a larger set of constantly changing standards, laws, and practices.

This antagonism between past and present, which is also expressed as an antagonism between the present and the future, is not simply a matter of ideas and values but becomes inscribed on the material

9

realities of daily life. I think, for instance, of the Robeson County court-house as it was in 1967, with its three water fountains, with the signs over each that earlier had said WHITE, NEGRO, INDIAN, gone almost, but not quite, beyond recognition. Imagine yourself a middle-aged Black man (for we must, to understand the situation of Indian people in the south, also be clear about the processes and pressures through which African-American and White identities are socially constructed, nego-tiated, and contested) living in one of the smaller towns of Robeson County, in the courthouse because you were, say, seeking a tax reduc-tion for your home and wanting a drink of water on an intensely hot summer day. Standing in the courthouse, trying to decide which foun-tain to drink from, with all sorts of people standing around and moving about the lobby – White lawyers and judges, other Black folks, including teenagers with their then new-found Black power ideas, Indians – all perhaps watching what you did. In such situations you are confronted not simply with three water fountains with their no-longer-legible but all-too-clear signs, and with deciding which one to drink from, but also with the nearness and simultaneously the distance of the past, the ten-tativeness and the conditionality of the impending future. The man I saw stood momentarily in front of the water fountains and then walked away without drinking at all. It was not an intellectual game, seeking to situate one's public self in the uncertain connections between past, present, and future: not at those appalling stakes.

"History," in such instances – both claimed history and imposed his-tory – is far from being a "charter" for present or desired social rela-tions. It is also far from seamless, running unbroken from past to present, punctuated by dramatic incidents and episodes that sometimes alter its direction. Rather, the disjunctions – the breaks and the gaps that par-ticularly characterize the history of dominated peoples (and in some ways form part of every history) – shape how history is imposed, claimed, and understood. And these breaks, these points where the past rubs antagonistically against the present, the past and the present against the foreseen future, are often the loci both of terror and of hope, of bitter struggles over meaning and over meaninglessness.

A special instance of this antagonism between past and present, which often takes shape not in dramatic political struggles and incipient con-frontations but, rather, in the ordinary moments of daily life, is the antagonism between continuity and tradition. For an Indian sharecrop-per, for example, to sit down at the end of the day on the porch of a battered and worn frame house at the edge of a hot, dusty field – the same, or a very similar house that his or her parents, grandparents, or even great-grandparents lived in – to sit there, as they did, tired and worn from a day's labor in the fields, watching the children play in the swept-dirt yard: all this is not "tradition" but continuity, which can be the antithesis of the creativity, the expressive flamboyance, and particularly the autonomy of the ceremonies and celebrations that become known as traditional.

Until quite recently it had been a rare country Indian couple in Robeson County who could take their household – themselves, some of their children, a cousin or so: a carful, if they had a car – and go, for example, to what the more affluent, tradition-engaged Indians call a powwow: a costumed dance display, perhaps with some traveling or visiting troupes, along with traveling craft-sale displays by Indian people working the powwow circuit. A dollar or so per person admission, a soda apiece for the kids, an "Indian" souvenir: a five- or ten-dollar evening, in sum, when in the late 1960s people were getting less than five dollars a *day* for a day's labor chopping cotton. Continuity often cannot afford public tradition; such tradition can well be an assault on and a felt humiliation to those bound to continuity – all the while glorifying it. The opposition between continuity and tradition, while at times socially significant, is of course far from total: there are some forms of tradition, often religious, that merge with, rather than confront, continuity.

To understand the complex connections and oppositions between tradition and continuity we will need to look closely at the forms of social relations, particularly among dominated peoples, to which the word "tradition" refers – relations that often turn out to express claims for autonomy or partial autonomy in the midst of poverty and powerlessness much more than they express continuity with a real or imagined past.

The potential antagonism between continuity and tradition has one shape now but had a different shape earlier. The history of this antagonism began to take its current shape in the trade relations and the wars along the moving frontier where forms of Indian social and ceremonial life – from the far-ranging Iroquois militarism to the eagle-feather headdress of the plains – which are now held up as the most traditional, came into being. These forms often came into being in contexts where collusion with, and resistance to, external domination were deeply and tightly interwoven. The paradoxes and the tensions of this situation were particularly prominent in the situation of the emerging leaders (the "chiefs") in colonial Indian societies, and in many ways these paradoxes have persisted unresolved to the present.

There is one profound antagonism that at first seems to be of a different kind than the ones we have been considering. This is the fundamental opposition between work and production.

11

By work I mean that actual labor of fashioning something necessary or desired in the continuation of social life. For southeastern Indian societies in the colonial period, for example, work was hunting deer for food and for skins, raising crops, building dwelling places and ceremonial houses, making and maintaining paths or roads from place to place and all the prayers and songs and ceremonies that went with these activities – of which, of course, were also deeply embedded in other kinds of social relations than those that we would call work.

Production refers to the larger system in (and against) which work takes its shape and its pace, a system that includes both the work to produce goods and the cultural, social, political, and economic relations through which surpluses are formed, transferred out of the control of the people who did the work, and transformed. The transformations of the appropriated products of work often come back to haunt the people who did the work: it was, for instance, profits from the deerskin trade and from Indian-captured Indian slaves that helped to finance colonial European wars against Native American peoples.

Systems of production impose requirements and demands upon work: to produce, to continue the example from the colonial southeast, deerskins to trade for the guns that were essential to Native American survival; to produce, to take a current example, a major part of the crop for a landlord. In both the colonial and the modern cases the external, imposed demands of "production" pervade and shape the work process – and even the landscape itself – writing the history of domination in the tools people work with, the proportions and locations of forest and field, the shape and sag of houses, the patterns of wear in paths, hands and faces, and the relations of cooperation and conflict within work itself. But it is not a history written simply from above: with the same tools, on the same landscape, and in the midst of the same imposed forms of cooperation and conflict, people seek to, and do, shape their own lives and their own material realities.

This antagonism between work and production *has* a history, but it also seems not to be as directly about *making* history as were the conflicts we considered above. Yet a closer look, by means of an example of one of the many places where the history of work and the history of production come together, will first lead us to the point where silence enters into the discourse, and then will slam us, full force, back into the motions and immobilizations of historical process.

Indian and Black farmers in Robeson County, as in large areas of the southeastern coastal plain, must have roadside drainage ditches dug and maintained over substantial distances in order to continue to farm their swampy fields. They exert what political pressure they can muster to get this task done by the county government, for they cannot afford to do it themselves. If successful, they can then watch as the county takes Indian and Black prisoners from their own and neighboring communities, patrolled and worked by shotgun-carrying White guards, to do the grueling work, essential to the small farmers, but work that will mostly benefit the larger, White farmers, who have the equipment and resources to build the feeder ditches from their extensive fields to the main drainage lines.

Enemy and ally change places so rapidly in such instances that often the outcome – particularly for Native Americans less firmly connected than Blacks to larger cultural and social identity-formation and assertive movements – can only be silence, a silence that becomes embedded in identity itself. The issue here is the formation of social situations so interwoven with complex and rapidly shifting alliances and enmities, with needs and with doubt, that thay cannot readily be given voice, by us or by the people involved, but neither can people easily live with the ensuing silence.

When driving down the state highways of North Carolina in the late 1960s or early 1970s, one occasionally came to township boundaries marked by a roadside sign: "NO PRISON LABOR BEYOND THIS POINT." Usually this indicated what we might somewhat simplistically call a union town – a town where labor does not want to be undercut by prison workers and has the clout to keep prison labor from being used. To be an Indian in Robeson County is not to have had that option: if prisoners did not dig out the ditches, they would not have been dug. Moreover, it was not easy to get the county to do this work in Indian-settled areas: even prisoners cost money to work, and the demand for their work was strong in the predominantly White sections of the county.

It has been, in important ways, an expression of Indian political skill to get such work done in the Indian areas, and in the two or three decades after World War II it seems to have been done most efficiently and effectively in the core areas of the Indian regions of the county – places where the Indian population was substantial, community institutions strong, and the Indian leadership effective in delivering votes and mobilizing people.

Yet the process of learning crucial negotiating skills needed to get the county to do this work included the process of learning not to say too much – to oneself, to the Whites in power, or to other Indian people in the community – about who the workers were, where they came from, how and why they came to be there and the conditions under which they were worked. Such silences may have devastating consequences, particularly when they are extended to the recently emerging and intensifying class inequalities among native peoples.

We have pointed to two fundamental antagonisms in the historical processes shaping the formation and development of Native American societies – between the past and the present (with the special instance of the contradiction between tradition and continuity), and between work and production. And we have now, if too briefly, pointed to a third, which we can find in the gulf that lies between silence and situation.

This is *not* a gulf between silence and voice. To call it such would be to imply, from our safe distance, that the Indians could have talked publicly about this, or more than talk, that they could have created a discourse with its own potential or actual confrontational momentum. But to call it a gulf between silence and situation is to recognize that they knew they were silent, and why, and that they also knew that their silence was not fully determined for them, not completely imposed. It was, perhaps, both imposed and chosen.

The poorer farm Indians, out in the county, had a phrase, current if not common in the late 1960s: "Out here it's root hog or die." They were talking about what had to be done to get a living – talking with an extraordinarily powerful mixture of intense pride (they could survive on anything) and equally intense self-denigration (in so doing they became like hogs, forcing a living from the earth with their faces pushed in it).

It is a very old idiom, by North American standards: Davie Crockett used it in 1834 and referred to it then as an "old saying." It is, indeed, a long-standing paradigm for hard-pressed rural people. The ambiguous mixture of pride and self-critique hidden in the structure of this phrase, with its implication of necessity, anger, and doubt, defines what I mean by the contradiction between silence and situation. Silence, people say, can speak louder than words. It can also be, as in the example of the prison labor, particularly intimate with both vulnerability and dignity.

There is a fourth antagonism, which here can be named only by its surface appearance. It seems to be a fundamental feature of Native American social systems, one of the most powerful indicators both of the penetration of domination and of the struggle to resist, and it has been a central feature of Native American social systems from the contact period to the present. Yet it is treated in much of the literature as if it were simply incidental: literally, a matter only of incidents and episodes.

14

Although the label is at times too dramatic, this feature can still best be termed "civil war."

At times such civil war takes on the appearance, at least in much of the anthropological and historical literature, of war between neighboring and different groups: for examples, the Iroquois destruction of the Huron in the seventeenth century; the Choctaw assaults on and decimation of the Chickasaw. In few of these cases does the notion that we are dealing with warfare between previously completely separate groups bear close inspection. In other instances we are more clearly dealing with warfare completely within the "same" people – such as the brutal and bitter civil war of the Choctaw, at its peak in 1748–50, or the civil wars that broke out among the Cherokee throughout the eighteenth and early nineteenth centuries. And such conflicts persist to the present: instance the recent brutal strife among Mohawk over gambling on their reservation, or the Sioux occupation of the village of Wounded Knee in 1973, which was bitterly opposed, with arms, by other Sioux, or the case we shall discuss at some length below: the militant strife between Lumbee and Tuscarora in Robeson County in the 1970s, at the point where the two were forming into distinct, or partly distinct, peoples.

Much can and will be said about the general causes of such splits, particularly as they respond, indirectly as well as directly, to external manipulations. This is the most complex antagonism: it sums up and restates all the others, as well as taking on its own dynamic of development. One of its special causal features is the contradiction between the intense need for strategy in the face of domination and imposition and the fact that no strategy could possibly work for long, if at all. To be an Indian in America is – and since the European onslaught has always been – to be in a situation where no strategy against domination could achieve, for long if at all, the results it must minimally achieve, so there must be profound dissent over its adoption and use, dissent that is both profoundly legitimate and profoundly destructive.

But the main point to begin with is that the processes that lead to such internal antagonisms among Native American peoples and that seek to cope with the effects of these antagonisms have become completely enmeshed in native social organization. To go beyond the historical evasiveness of the usual terms in which native social organization is discussed – particularly clan and kinship, religion, rank and leadership – and to look at how fundamental antagonisms emerge and become embedded within native social systems is not to create a catalog of historical horrors. Nor, certainly, is it to blame the victims for their plight. It is, rather, an introduction to the issue of historical motion *within* native North American societies – within and between kin groups, native peoples and their leaders, the customs and ceremonies of life and of hope – including, significantly, an introduction to historical processes through which such antagonisms are transcended.

The path we shall follow leads first to the politics of Native American "peoplehood" – what it takes to become and to be a Native American people – and then to the more general issue of culture in history, in a specific context where both culture and history are both imposed from above and claimed from below.

2

Toward and past recognition

In 1978 the U.S. government, through the Bureau of Indian Affairs, published a set of regulations entitled "Procedures for establishing that an American Indian group exists as an Indian Tribe." These procedures established a process through which any Indian people not previously recognized by the federal government could petition for recognition – and for the associated benefits (and liabilities). A special office of the Bureau of Indian Affairs (BIA) was created, the Branch of Acknowledgment and Research, which is informally called the FAP (Federal Acknowledgment Program) office. It was expected that over the next decade or more a substantial portion of the Indian groups in the United States who were not federally recognized as Indian tribes – possibly several hundred peoples who were not, as far as the U.S. government is concerned, "Indians" – would petition under the new regulations to have their status as an Indian tribe acknowledged. The FAP office would review the petitions and recommend that the secretary of the interior grant or deny legal Indian status on the basis of whether or not the petitioners met the government's criteria for being an Indian tribe.

These procedures for what native peoples call recognition were established by the federal government for much the same reasons (although probably with different goals) as those that have recently pressured native peoples into wanting to be recognized. In the 1970s several substantial cases, primarily for land claims, were brought to court by native peoples. The first of these cases, brought by the Passamaquoddy and Penobscot Indians of Maine, created a whole new set of possibilities for Native Americans.

Since the founding of the United States, these two Indian peoples had lost enormous amounts of their land, which was taken by the state of Maine (and by Massachusetts, while Maine was still a province of that state). However, in 1790 and 1793, in the Indian Trade and Intercourse Acts of Congress, major dealings with the Indians, specifically including land acquisitions, were forbidden to the states and reserved to the federal government.

In enacting this legislation the U.S. government was continuing policies put into effect by the British in their American colonies in 1763. These policies sought to ensure the loyalties of Indian nations and tribes for wars with other colonial powers, for trade and for other reasons, and to do this by containing or at least coordinating the rapacious predations of states and localities upon native peoples. Such policies, while attempting to use Indians and not necessarily meant primarily to protect them, gave native people definite rights in relation to the states in which they lived – rights that surprisingly had never been extinguished, even into the 1970s, probably because it was forgotten that they had such rights.

The Passamaquoddy and Penobscot thus had a solid case against the federal government: that it had failed to protect their rights when the state (rather than the federal government) took their land. For several years, while the federal government negotiated and then legislated substantial aid and monetary recompense in order to quiet these claims, the strength of the Indian case caused turmoil in land transactions in Maine, making deeds and land titles suspect.

Other Indian peoples, some with claims to very choice land (such as large sections of Cape Cod and Martha's Vineyard – the summer playgrounds of some people with a great deal of power and influence) seemed to be in a similar position, were making similar claims, and had similar potential rights. But states soon mounted a new strategy, pioneered by Massachusetts in its defense against the Mashpee Indians of Cape Cod. The question was raised: Were the Indian people in court, even if they were *individually* the biological descendants of the people who lost the land, in fact collectively *tribal* descendants and successors of the tribe (or tribes) that had been defrauded? If the native people were not still an Indian *tribe* (for the injury, if any, had been done to a tribe, not individual people), *or if they had ceased to be a tribe when their land was taken* (the "catch-22" provision!), then however unfortunate and perhaps illegal the original transaction that took their land, the descendants had (unfortunately for them) no right or "standing" in court to press their claim for redress. The Mashpee lost, on the basis that they were no longer a "tribe."

A substantial number of other issues where native peoples' claims

18

were involved suggested new possibilities both to advocates and opponents of these claims. Cases involving treaty-secured fishing rights on the northwest coast, where very profitable but declining salmon runs highlighted tensions between commercial fishing and native rights, raised somewhat similar possibilities. Hovering in the background were some potentially contentious native rights to coal, oil, water (especially in the arid west), and other natural resources. It was becoming crucial both for the government and for "unrecognized" Indian people to clarify whether a particular Indian people were or were not an "Indian tribe" or, as the government also calls them, an "Indian entity."

Moreover, even in situations where there were no potential court cases over claims, many unrecognized native peoples, in the context of the assertive ethnic movements that blossomed in the 1960s, and perhaps also in the context of the increasing economic difficulties of small rural producers in the 1970s, began seeking official recognition as Indian people both to claim an identity that they felt was rightfully theirs and also to enhance their potential for federal assistance in housing, health care, education, and business development. In some instances such endeavors were supported by the states in which they lived (at times perhaps as a cost-cutting measure, for the federal government assumes many of these responsibilities for Indians, whereas states pay more of the costs of such social services for non-Indians).

II

A large but unknown number of Native American groups – well over one hundred, at least – live, more or less collectively, more or less within a framework of their own values and institutions, and for the groups in the southern United States that I know, with their own sense of their special history, without being recognized as Indians by the federal government. Some are so recognized by the states in which they live; others are not.

The 1978 regulations specify the requirements for a successful petition – requirements that would be ironic, in view of the pressures native people have been and continue to be subject to, if so much were not at stake in success or failure. The requirements state:

> *The petition may be in any readable form which clearly indicates that it is a petition requesting the Secretary [of the Department of the Interior] to acknowledge tribal existence. All the criteria in paragraphs (a)–(g) are mandatory in order for tribal existence to be acknowledged. . . .*
>
> *(a) A statement of facts establishing that the petitioner has been identified from historical times until the present on a substantially continuous basis as "American Indian" or "aboriginal." . . . Evidence to be relied*

upon in determining the group's substantially continuous Indian identity shall include one or more of the following:
1) Repeated identification by federal authorities;
2) Longstanding relationships with State governments based on identification of the group as Indian;
3) Repeated dealings with a county, parish, or other local government in a relationship based on the group's Indian identity;
4) Identification as an Indian entity by records in courthouses, churches, or schools;
5) Identification as an Indian entity by anthropologists, historians, or other scholars;
6) Repeated identification as an Indian entity in newspapers and books;
7) Repeated identification and dealings as an Indian entity with recognized Indian tribes or national Indian organizations.
(b) Evidence that a substantial portion of the petitioning group inhabits a specific area or lives in a community viewed as American Indian and distinct from other populations in the area, and that its members are descendants of an Indian tribe which historically inhabited a specific area.
(c) A statement of facts which establishes that the petitioner has maintained tribal political influence or other authority over its members as an autonomous entity throughout history to the present. . . .
(d) A copy of the group's present governing document, or in the absence of a written document, a statement describing in full the membership criteria and the procedure through which the group currently governs its affairs and its members.
(e) A list of all known current members of the group and a copy of each available former list of members based on the tribe's own defined criteria. The membership must consist of individuals who have established, using evidence acceptable to the Secretary, descendancy from a tribe which existed historically or from historical tribes which combined and functioned as a single autonomous entity. . . .
(f) The membership of the petitioning group is composed principally of persons who are not members of any other North American Indian tribe.
(g) The petitioner is not, nor are its members, the subject of congressional legislation which has expressly terminated or forbidden the federal relationship.

At the center of these requirements are demands for multiple forms of continuity and multiple kinds of prior recognition. Each set of demands is more complex than it may first appear to be. The multiple forms of continuity called for – identity, residence, tribal political authority – impose requirements that few "tribes" in North America, recognized or unrecognized, could in fact meet. Such totalizing continuities are indeed as much or more an artifact both of the histories and anthropologies that have been written and of people's beliefs as they are an expression of Native American historical experiences. And popular or academic recognition of Indian identity turns out to be at least as much a matter of imposing images, like children with cookie-cutters upon the tide-shifting sands, as it is a matter of recognizing something whose dimensions, boundaries, and name are given and fixed in the material world.

In these contexts of imposed demands for continuity and prior recognition, the histories and anthropologies we write take on the possibility of becoming transformed into reality: if we have called a people Indian, then they can become so; if, in our search for more popular case studies, we have bypassed such "irregular" groups to focus on the Navajo, Cherokee, or Iroquois, then the government will be willing to share our lack of recognition of a people who want – and in some instances desperately need – their claims to be met.

In particular, generations of simplistic history and shallow anthropology are embedded in demands requiring the members of the petitioning group to be "descendants of an Indian tribe which historically inhabited a specific area." In fact, few recognized, official tribes – including the Navajo, Cherokee, and Iroquois – could meet the criteria of either descent from a specific pre-contact group or continuity in a specific area. And the requirement that they demonstrate the maintenance of "tribal political influence or other authority over their members as an autonomous entity throughout history to the present" is asking them to participate in a more brutal denial of the realities of Native American history: to the extent that they were, in fact, at least socially recognized as Indians, with some substantial material authority over their own people, they were likely to run up against the same fate as befell "official" Indians – profoundly powerful and systematic attempts to shatter just this kind of autonomy and replace it with external control. There is a small but significant body of good history and historical anthropology on just these points that somehow never made it into the popular consciousness.

Thus many Native American peoples who *must*, if you note point (c) above, each remain an autonomous people to be considered Indians, must also in the midst of their autonomy adopt the dominant society's version of their history, and the dominant society's requirements for historical continuity, in order to maintain even a shred of their autonomy.

The paradoxes continue, and are heightened after recognition. Native American lands, while falling under U.S. and state *criminal* jurisdiction, have been held to be exempt from federal and state *regulatory* laws. One implication of this is that gambling regulations do not hold on Indian land. Several tribes, including a few of the half-dozen that have just been recognized, have established high stakes bingo games that draw enormous crowds and bring revenues in some cases of over a million dollars a year, but increasingly flood the reservations with outsiders and with profound social problems. Native land areas are also exempt from certain business regulations, which can make it quite profitable to establish branch corporations there. "Why move your factory to Taiwan," the (Mississippi) Choctaw Tribal Council asks, "when you can bring it here?" And, indeed, there are several major General Motors subassembly plants now in operation on Choctaw lands.

Five of the eleven new nuclear waste dumps in the United States are slated to go on Indian land that is held "in trust" for the Indians and administered by the BIA. This may well be the mid-twentieth century version of the fur trade: use and destruction are so intimately a part of domination and integration that they come to profoundly define a substantial part of what it means to be an Indian in these United States. Plans now call for the largest toxic waste disposal plant in the South to be sited immediately upstream on the main river that flows through Lumbee and Tuscarora lands, and this was arranged while the people were putting the final touches on their petitions for recognition as Indians – petitions that, should they succeed despite the unrealistic demands upon history being imposed by the Bureau of Indian Affairs, could lead to substantial areas of Lumbee and Tuscarora land being administered by the BIA – a subagency of the same Department of the Interior that is partly responsible for locating toxic waste dumps.

Accepting our version of their past history, Native Americans come to participate in new kinds of ongoing histories, in ways that often shatter the very unity and autonomy that was demanded from them. And asserting autonomy through the dominant society's version of their history, they are dragged into the ongoing historical developments of the dominant society (including, for example, the increasing plague of cancer) with their new official status as federally recognized Indians likely to become both a source of pride and material gains on the one hand, and of increasing powerlessness on the other.

III

One way to bring together, equally, the methods and perspectives of history and anthropology is to consider both how people's pasts emerge within the present and how people themselves engage, in thought and action, the complex connections between pasts and futures.

Toward and past recognition

The starting point for this double approach will be a history of the Lumbee and Tuscarora Indians written "backward": from the present to the past. It begins, however, not at the beginning – not now – but in the period 1968–73, which was one of the major turning points: the point around which a large number of people, approximately 10 percent of those who formerly called themselves and were known by others as Lumbee Indians, began to call themselves and to be known as Tuscarora. From this point we work back into the increasing distance, paying particularly close attention to the multiple, shifting chasms that open and close between, on the one side, where people say they come from – not only their origins but their sense of the past they have come through – and how they use where they think they have come from to figure out where they want to go and how to organize themselves to get there, and, on the other side, where, "in fact," they really came from, and how, and why.

But, to label "illusion" the histories people themselves speak to, about and from, and to call what we discover "reality" would be to mock their journey before it is understood, and to diminish our task before it is begun. It is more productive to say that by this means, by this multiplex looking from the present to the past, we might be able to understand something about the social construction of hopes, and the many ways that hopes and history, realities and illusions, politics, economics, and culture are interwoven. What seem to be illusion and reality, when seen from a distance, will look different upon closer inspection.

At the end of this journey, when we have seen some of what can be shown by means of such an approach, we shall return to our starting point, 1973, and work our way forward to the present, using the first journey to try to understand the currently developing culture and social organization of the Lumbee: in particular, to understand their current relations to the federal government as they seek recognition, in terms of fundamentally problematic and paradoxical situations of Native Americans that originated in the colonial period.

Doing this historical anthropology raised difficult questions about the central method of anthropological fieldwork: the method called "participant observation." This is the method of simultaneously, and paradoxically, both participating in and observing the social life of people we hope to describe and to understand.

To participate in, and simultaneously to examine as if from a distance, the social and material relations in which we are immersed, often and fortunately generates a lot of apprehension among the people being "studied" and in the anthropologist. This apprehension raises issues of the interconnections between knowledge and caution: the people being studied are often, and rightly, quite cautious. In addition to all

23

the ethical and intellectual dilemmas of anthropology, which demand their own intense forms of caution, there are other, and more reciprocal issues at stake that are important to think about.

To *apprehend* something or someone is to know, to take control and possession of, and to have the sense to be uncertain about – to fear, to be apprehensive. All these are the minimal requirements for participation as well as observation; all these bring to the foreground senses of history that can be shared, as well as simply known or known about.

To illustrate: However accepted and accepting it might make us feel to be asked to dance the Green Corn dance with Native Americans, *their* problem is that in a world where some Indians are landowners and some are sharecroppers it is not very clear that a harvest-sharing festival can be celebrated together by such unequals. Thus the unity of a common history reasserted through such a revived dance festival may, in fact, *also* become a wedge pounded through their body politic, increasing the separation between the more well off and the very poor. For us to participate in such a dance is *not* for us to dance, or to drum, or to sing – all these are just the surface glitter, however dramatically and emotionally appealing – but to be *forced* by our commitments and our connections to sense the specter of failure lurking in the outer shadows, in our sweat and in our joy; failure not simply of the harvest but of the dance itself.

If the harvest fails, particular people will suffer and some may suffer intensely, but if the dance fails even more will be lost. The failure of the dance is not necessarily caused by a harvest shortage, but comes from the rupture of the bonds – even the partly antagonistic bonds – that bind people to each other and through each other to the material and spiritual world.

Looking backward to help us see what is hidden in the world around us, and to help us sense what might be coming in the future, and at what price, is how we and they come to understand what is implied by the success or failure of the dance – and more: it is both to understand and also to deny the understanding that either success or failure is possible only if the other is also possible, is also there, waiting.

If our own search for the complex intertwinings of history and hope, commitment and betrayal, leads us to own and to share that understanding – to dance both with and against the specter of failure – then we shall become, as they are, participants in the world we are called to observe.

Since we can choose to pick up or to put down the journey – or this book – as we will, and they are more tightly bound to confrontations they may or may not have chosen, our pathway to a common participant-observation must from the outset necessarily be both distant and different from theirs. Our pathways should take us both to increasingly profound participatory encounters and to an expanded understanding of our own concepts – particularly the basic concepts of culture and social organization. The situation of historical anthropology – an anthropology that seeks engagement with the history-shaping activities of others – thus remaps, onto the domain of our core concepts and our core sense of how we see and understand, some of the same tensions that Freud found in the psychoanalytic method of "introspection." This is the learned, and never fully successful ability of the analyst to understand the other – including the madness of the other – by looking within him or herself and sensing, simultaneously, both the fundamental similarities between analyst and patient, which form the basis of understanding, and the fundamental differences, which form the basis for realistic and productive communication. Introspection is crucial to the process of healing and risky for both sides: it provides openings, without it being clear at first to what the openings will lead.

This opening – this putting at risk of our concepts and commitments – will for us be historically shaped: not by giving our concepts an intellectual history, nor even by using such lifeless categories to grasp history, but by bringing the flow of history within the concepts themselves. To do this it is crucial to focus on those aspects of a culture that are antagonistically diverse, and to see this diversity as it may emerge not simply *between* different "subcultures" but *within* each.

This book argues that it is in the midst of such diversity – and not by following "cultural rules" or adhering to some "ensemble of values" or "set of meanings" or "webs of significance" – that people try to construct their humanity, their own sense of dignity and worth. Particularly in the context of domination and the humiliations that inevitably come with domination, the problem of establishing and maintaining personal and collective dignity in the midst both of antagonistic values and of imposed limitations on the kinds of lives ordinary people live often becomes crucial to the people anthropologists study. It must be so for anthropology as well: anthropology must go far beyond its notion of culture as ensembles of values or webs of significance, and its often naive grasp of the social-relational basis of the material world and the physical environment, to both appreciate and apprehend such struggles.

IV

Indian political activists in Robeson County, in the spring of 1968, were dancing on the pinnacles of hope. After a brutally intense effort to register and mobilize voters and to build an electoral alliance with Blacks, victory seemed possible – at times even likely – and "a *whole* new day was comin'."

I remember, still very painfully, but also with a touch of wonder about the human contact that is often possible in the midst of the tensions and the gulfs of anthropological fieldwork, sitting in the kitchen of an Indian man, a man in his fifties who, for the past six months, had been trying to teach me how to be an organizer: how to register people to vote, how to talk with them about why and how to vote and about what was at stake. He had been teaching me and showing me what he could do, for he was a very gifted organizer and proud of his skills. While we registered voters he also was, as he said, "showing you around the county" (a special introduction, publicly committing us to each other's actions), so that when I wrote about it I would have more to say, and he would have more influence in what was said. He was also learning from me, from some of the things I could do or find out – statistical analyses of voting and registration patterns for each of the thirty-nine precincts in the county, and some of what they might strategically imply; the rules and regulations that governed the welfare department, which were public information but at this time not something a local Indian would or perhaps could go in and ask to see; some of the things White politicians were planning to do, to which I had better access.

In the midst of all this work, driving around the county together evenings and weekends, we liked spending time with each other, swapping stories, making small talk. Late one night in his kitchen, after we came back from an intense meeting between Indians and Blacks active in voter registration drives – the Indians mostly in the swamps, the Blacks mostly in the small towns – a meeting out in a country church basement, where we all talked about an Indian–Black alliance, he started talking to me about, as he put it, being "non-White" in the rural south. The conversation began, actually, between several Indian men in the dooryard of the church, just after the meeting; it was about where to buy a car, where you might find both a good price and also some respect from the dealer. Back in his kitchen, with just the two of us there, he wanted to talk more about this – and not to talk with me, but this time *to* me.

For several hours, long into the night, he tried to describe, often with tears in his eyes, a lifetime of juggling: leaving his wife and children out in the hot car upon some pretext or another, to go into an unfamiliar store alone so that his kids or his wife would not hear him called "boy," or his wife "auntie." And he told me that they knew "really" why they were left in the car, but they didn't say or ask. Countless incidents: a whole adult lifetime, trying to shield his family and himself, preserving their dignity and their humanity – and doing so with some success, while everyone also knew the pretexts and knew why. A whole lifetime of struggle and negotiation, relentlessly necessary, and now in the midst of the passions and dramas of the more openly militant politics, it was not at all clear to him what had been gained, or what might yet be won in this central domain of daily life. He was showing me that this is what mattered most; this was where most of the hopes were pinned. All the posturing, all the passion, all the very specific and very serious risks we all took to get people to start to vote in new ways, all the hopes we had of winning, all the work, the relentless work of organizing, and people still had to go into unfamiliar stores, or to places that were all too well known.

It has taken me twenty years to make a partial peace, as an anthropologist, with the memory of that evening, for my own political and social commitments, which I thought justified anthropological inquiry, pale before the human claims of such encounters. He could no longer ever be what anthropologists call an "informant": an informant is, in common language, a spy or an accessory to a spying operation, an aid to viewing from a distance for purposes usually antagonistic to the interests of the people being viewed. What has come from that encounter that is relevant now is my effort to pose issues of historical motion primarily in terms of the humanity of the people involved.

This project is thus conjoined with the central political problem of the Lumbee and Tuscarora for most of the twentieth century: how to sustain and develop their humanity, their dignity, their own social goals and social relations, and ultimately their identity, reaching forward from a base in poverty and domination through the assertions and negations, the collusions and the transient confrontations – in sum, through the limits and possibilities in the politics of accommodation and of opposing accommodation.

For much of the twentieth century, for the Lumbee and Tuscarora as for other minority peoples, *accommodation* was both the political entryway for domination to come within and simultaneously a central framework for expressing and asserting autonomy and dignity. It is to the specific political and cultural economy of accommodation in Robeson County, North Carolina, that we must now turn, to introduce what formed, for Lumbee and Tuscarora efforts to realize histories and hopes, the context of the known.

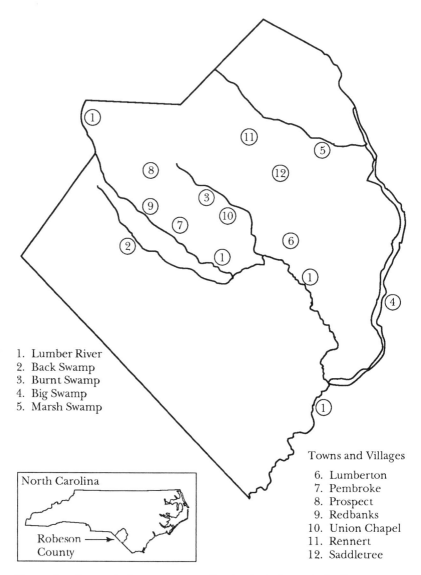

1. Lumber River
2. Back Swamp
3. Burnt Swamp
4. Big Swamp
5. Marsh Swamp

North Carolina

Robeson → County

Towns and Villages

6. Lumberton
7. Pembroke
8. Prospect
9. Redbanks
10. Union Chapel
11. Rennert
12. Saddletree

Note: Lumberton is the county seat. Pembroke is the main Indian town.
Prospect, Redbanks, Union Chapel, Rennert, and Saddletree are locales.

Map 1.   Robeson County, North Carolina

3

Elements of the known

Human dignity, the politics of accommodation, and the landscape of confrontation

I

The political history of the Indian people of Robeson County in the twentieth century pivots on the politics of accommodation. At its core a form of mobilizing support during elections, it "worked" by providing a route for channeling real and important communal and personal benefits from power-holding Whites to Indians – albeit to some Indians more than to others – while at the same time perpetuating Indian dependency and immiseration. Accommodation created both the material basis for dignity and pride – for example, new schools – and it recreated people's dependence on the interests and needs of more powerful others: it turned, at least momentarily, people who were seeking to live their lives with dignity into voters who could be "delivered" to the polls. Yet it was never just a mutual-benefits alliance between unequals: for both Indian people and African Americans it was also a moral drama in which the limits of respectability and the senses of self and of situation that were possible to hold on to, or became necessary to fight against, were given shape and form, brought forward or down.

How accommodation worked, when it did, why it was necessary, the rewards, penalties, and revulsions it brought, the reasons why it collapsed – these topics form the core of Part Two. An introductory description of it here will serve to depict the wheels and looms upon which community, opportunity, and oppression were spun, and then woven together, and will provide for the reader the common-knowledge framework of politically engaged Indians who can then be seen assembling pasts and possibilities to build alternative ways.

The roots of accommodation, like those of the poplar tree, run straight and deep into the fundamental physical geography of the county; into

29

one of the two basic Indian social institutions of the twentieth century, the schools (churches are the other); and into one of the most significant processes of the last part of the nineteenth and the early twentieth centuries: the forced transfer of land from Indian to White ownership, which left a great many Indians as smallholders, tenant farmers, sharecroppers, or just day laborers on farms. From all this came not only accommodation but, for the Indians of the county, community itself.

By 1973 there were no longer many deep swamps left in central Robeson County. Today only a few extensive tracts remain where the water stands visible all the year round and the moss and the cypress are thickly intertwined. There are many more swamps that look to the passerby like damp woods – places a bit too wet to farm, with thickets of alders or scrub oak and pine. These thin swamps can be 5 to 15 miles long, and often no more than a few hundred yards wide. Roads now cross these thin swamps easily, but still skirt the remaining deep swamps.

Interlacing the whole area are the "canals," draining the land into the Lumbee River or to one of the major swamp creeks that lead eventually to the Lumbee River. Despite their name, these canals are often little more than ditches, 6 to 8 feet across, with their banks and watercourses regularly becoming choked with weeds, brush, and swamp-alders.

In the past century these canals have reduced huge areas of swamp from thick to thin, from thin to farmland. Along with the swamps still standing, the canals divide Robeson County into a multitude of named areas: Saddletree, Rennert, Mount Airy, New Hope, Philadelphus, Back Swamp, Burnt Swamp, Raft Swamp, Moss Neck, Smiths, Union, Alfordsville, Prospect. In 1968 road directions to these places were still given in terms of the number of swamps and canals to cross before you turn. Place names change as you cross swamps that now may be no more than a 50-foot-wide stand of scrub-brush alder trees with a 4-foot creek or ditch in the middle.

From an airplane the houses and farms would look almost uniformly distributed across the landscape. Many of the named locales do not have densely settled centers, though all have an Indian church or two and one or two "stations," selling gas and some basic groceries. Almost all the locales have an elementary, or "graded" school. These different Indian locales, for the past several decades seeming like a carpet of settlement upon the land, as population density increases, are still substantially separate communities, although the boundaries are hardly visible while driving at 50 miles and hour along a macadam road. Union Chapel, for example, is 8 miles from the major Indian town of Pembroke, across two thin swamps and a few canals. An Indian man born in 1939 told me that when he was a child, during and after World War II, a trip to Pembroke down the dirt road from Chapel with mule and wagon took all day there and back. Even though the same trip now takes about ten minutes each way, the social divisions remain strong. In the early 1970s Indian people in both Pembroke and Union Chapel could still recognize each other's place by differences in speech.

Power within these Indian localities, for the first half or more of the twentieth century, was rooted in the school system. The Indian people of Robeson County were given their own school system, separate from both the White and Black county schools, by an act of the North Carolina state legislature in 1885. Called the "Croatan School District," it quickly blossomed from four to twelve to nearly thirty local elementary schools with one Indian normal school, as teacher-training institutions were called, that developed from a high school into Pembroke State College and then into Pembroke State University, a branch campus of the University of North Carolina.

All the elementary schools in Robeson County – White, Black and Indian – were governed by an all-White school board until the 1970s, and were still controlled by Whites after integration through a complex election procedure whereby the predominantly White towns, which had their own school systems and school boards, "double-voted": voted both in their own and in the county school board elections.

Although the schools were ultimately controlled by what the Indians in the 1960s were calling the "White power structure," from 1885 to the mid-1960s there was a form of power sharing between the White county school board and the local Indian communities. In each Indian community there was a school committee of three Indian men, sometimes including an Indian woman. The first committees were named by the state legislature in the same acts that created and expanded the Indian school system. Committee members were drawn from those community leaders who had been actively petitioning the legislature for their schools. Subsequent vacancies were filled with appointments by the school committees themselves, which the legislature constituted as self-perpetuating.

These local school committees, and especially the committee chairmen, had a great deal of power *within* their localities, which was based both on their role in educating the children of their communities and on their control over employment and attendance.

Teaching school was one of the very few sources of nonfarm wage income available to Indians in the county; being principal, or assistant principal, or coach, or band leader, were most of the few local occupations with substantial prestige. As the century progressed many other

31

jobs became attached to the local schools – bus drivers, cafeteria work, repair and maintenance, and so on – all poorly paid, but crucial sources of income nonetheless. People would joke with me, in the late 1960s, about how they used to go to wash their school-committeeman's car or wax his floors, hoping to get a job or to have their contract renewed for another year, and then go home, after teaching, to "chop cotton" in the fields to try to make enough money to "get by."

The school committee controlled all these jobs – or more precisely, had a piece of the power. The committee recommended hirings and firings to the county school board, which ordinarily went along unless they had their own agenda, which they developed very quickly when one of the teachers "went against" their interests. Robeson County is a big place, over 900 square miles. Not only were there three separate county school systems – White, Black, and Indian – but there were also three separate school bus systems combing the rural roadways, taking busloads of same-"color" children to same-"color" schools. In winters you could see many small children standing by the side of the roads before sunrise, waiting for a bus that might run 30 miles or more on its path. Through the light of the small fires that kindly parents or older siblings come out to kindle for their little ones you could see carloads of teachers, three, four, five to a car, running 60, 70 miles from their homes in the county to a job – teachers who once crossed the wrong line, backed a loser in a key election, antagonized a school board member or a committeeman, or maybe handled a family problem the wrong way.

The same school committees that largely decided who taught and who worked also controlled who attended their schools: precisely, which of the children in their community were sufficiently Indian to attend the Indian school. But even with all this power, further discussed in Chapter 4, there was more – much more power embedded in these committees – and this turned on the organization of county elections for county commissioner, county school board, sheriff, magistrates, recorder of deeds, and a number of less significant positions.

Out in the county votes are "delivered" on election day – literally delivered by driving people to the polls, and often by going in with them, if they cannot read, and marking their ballots. Central to the electoral process is how these delivered votes were, and to a certain extent still are, arranged. Candidates, including incumbent officeholders running for reelection, would come to locality leaders and ask for support. Usually these locality leaders were the school committee; the church-based leadership mostly stayed out of this kind of politics. Sometimes an opposition candidate would seek to develop alternative local contacts, working through other influential Indians "out in the county," such as men with a substantial amount of land, or a younger generation of men, and occasionally women, on the rise. The candidates would give the locality leaders money: some would be used to pay drivers to "carry" people to the polls, and some would be used to give people a dollar or so for voting.

Teachers, and the more prosperous landowners as well, could play an important role in this process, for reasons that have to do with the dependency of Indian sharecroppers and small farmers. To begin, many of the poorer Indians could not read well. North Carolina had laws stating, in effect, that children could be kept out of school to work on farms under the direction of their parents. Landlords often told tenants to keep their children out to work at critical times – such as during harvest, spring planting, and weeding – and poverty made parents agree to such demands, even when they did not want to comply.

In 1960 the median number of school years for Robeson County Indian men over twenty-five was 6.5, scarcely enough for basic literacy. But "reading" has only a superficial connection to the ability to read words in print. Many Indians read the Bible, for example, and discuss it with subtlety and insight in their adult Sunday school classes. A dozen or more of these same people came to me, while I was in the county, to ask me to "read" a letter they received from the social security office or the county tax office. They did not want the words but the meaning – what it was going to mean in practice – and an intercession: they wanted to know the range of possible outcomes, especially if someone with more social reach than a dark farmer in the spotlight of power made some phone calls or visited an office. The reading that six years in a segregated school ordinarily taught was about distance from power, not words on a page.

Teachers and other locally rooted elites did a lot of "reading" for people, particularly because there were no Indian or Black lawyers in the county until 1973. The baskets of corn and vegetables they were given in return were only part of the ties of alliance and grateful respect. Teachers were thus in a position to ask people to vote in certain ways. They were also in a position where, to put it gently, they could be asked to ask.

The power and importance of the locality leaders extended well beyond elections, and even well beyond their (usual) role on the local school committee. They were particularly important as channels for obtaining both individual and communal benefits from the county power structure. If, for example, a person needed help from the welfare department, it was possible to go to the welfare office directly, and some people did just this. After that was tried, or before, one could go to the local leader who "worked for" the county commissioner in the last election, and have him call the commissioner, who called the welfare department. Then you went, or went back, to the welfare department, and later you and your kin went to the polls to vote. If the school needed a new roof, the school band needed new uniforms, or the roadside drainage ditches needed clearing to keep the crops from rotting in adjacent fields, the process was the same. Individual and collective rights and benefits were primarily realizable by supporting power.

Sometimes the locality leader could deliver benefits, sometimes not; it depended on how willing the local officeholders were to "play ball" with the Indians, how much they thought they needed to whether they wanted to or not, and what kinds of resources were available to spread around the county after the demands of the primary constituents – the Whites – had been met.

The locality leaders were enmeshed in a two-way delivery system. Part of their ability to deliver the vote and to maintain their own position depended not simply on the muscle they flexed in elections but on their actual ability to deliver benefits between elections. They were thus under pressure to back the more "liberal" of the White candidates, who would be more likely to do things for Indians. They also, however, needed to back winners, so it was often safer to go along with incumbent officeholders. The choices were often difficult, the penalties for misjudgment high.

In all of this, despite the benefits that local leaders could sometimes channel to their communities and the power they could exercise over who got jobs teaching in or working for the schools, they were also in some respects completely powerless. There were several periods of intense and substantial land loss by Indians in the twentieth century about which they could do absolutely nothing. Nor could they contain the anger or the hopes of a younger generation of Indians, coming up in the 1960s, who on the one hand could see the success of southern Black militance – almost daily television fare – and on the other hand were witness to the increasing fiscal inability of the county to provide substantial benefits to Indians.

In the late 1960s, for example, two new high schools were built: one for Whites, in Lumberton, the county seat, and one for Indians, in Pembroke. The White high school was air-conditioned, important for large, internally airless buildings in this very hot and humid climate. The Indian high school had the duct-system installed, but not the air-conditioning equipment. A White county official told me that "we

34

knew that there would be all hell to pay, and a lot of it." Several of the local Indian leaders had told him (and some of his colleagues) this, in case he did not fully grasp the anger this would provoke against both him and his Indian-leader allies. But in the face of declining revenues for what was then primarily still an agrarian county, and the rising costs of manufactured goods, county officials felt they simply could not afford to air-condition both schools: they thought they could pay the political price more easily than the material cost.

It has been fashionable in anthropology to call such men as these locality leaders, standing between the powerful and the powerless, "brokers" – the innocence of that term ordinarily concealing far more that it reveals. What could not be concealed here was either the nakedness of the priorities or the crumbs of accommodation. Early in the twentieth century these locality leaders were also, we have noted, revealed as helpless when they could not stop the land loss. But at that time the Indian people who lost their land were reduced from farm owners to tenants, sharecroppers, or just smaller farmers on mostly poor land – the very people who most needed the services of these leaders, yet the sort of vulnerable people that the locality leaders could afford to serve neither well nor fully.

By the late 1960s Indian people in these small, rural communities were moving into new sorts of jobs – factory work, mostly – with new ideas and new claims. In this new context, when the leaders could make no effective deals with power they could no longer deliver their people. The " brokers," not being able to break and deliver Indians to the harness of accommodation, were themselves broken. They went down hard, some using what power and influence they could still muster to work against the emerging Indian–Black alliance. But despite all this they were not, for the most part, evil men out simply for personal gain and the devil take the hindmost. They had been a key part of the structure of hope for many poor Indians in need, and for their communities as well.

The context in which locality leaders operated – a widely known, intensely public and continuing history of denied, deniable, and minimally satisfied hopes – drove many Indian people to enclose their humanity within family, kin, local churches, and local sociability. Doing so, they partly turned away from engagement with domination, when they could, letting the locality leaders go to deal with the Whites. On the other hand, withdrawing into family and community also at times provided a context where people had their resources for confronting domination renewed, renewed in the wellsprings, whirlpools, and quicksands of family, kin group, church, and community. This is not to romanticize families or diverse forms of community: it often takes rage as well as hope, emotional distance as well as passion, and familiarity with endless struggle to immerse, or bury, one's self in the politics of "civil rights."

A crucial point emerges from this brief description of the organization and the collapse of accommodation: in the midst of all the dealing and double-dealing that has characterized the core of accommodation, it is easy to lose sight of the fact that what is ultimately at stake, *both* in accommodation and in the alternative political forms that emerged since the late 1960s, is the search for the same humanity and the same dignity that was sought, but could not be fully realized, within the confines of forcibly impoverished families, kin groups, or churches. As the viability of small farms was increasingly undermined in the 1950s and 1960s, people were pressed outward, out of a life largely contained in local farms, local schools, local churches, and local sociability. Unlike the depression of the 1930s, when failing farms also drove people out, the 1960s provided opportunities to venture outward, still within the county, but going beyond the agrarian-based locality, its leaders, its forms, its ways, to seek to earn in industry what we too casually call a "living": their livelihood and their lives, not simply an income. This search for their own life – as Indians and as people wanting to move up – was both a continuation of what people tried to have through the politics of accommodation, and also in some ways a fundamental change. Just "getting by" was no longer good enough; increasingly it was no longer even possible.

II

Robeson is a big county, very big in many ways. Diamond-shaped, it is nearly forty miles from north to south, thirty-five miles from east to west. Nine hundred and thirty-two square miles, it is one of the largest counties in the state, and for the past century or more one of the most politically important in statewide struggles. Its political importance flows from two sources: the geography of state politics, which balances diverse and often antagonistic regional interests, and the political geography of "race," settlement patterns and occupation, which make the 90,000 inhabitants of Robeson County a volatile voting bloc, capable of shifting support between, and at times awarding success to, competing statewide interests.

From east to west – from the Atlantic ocean to the Appalachian mountains, 350 miles inland – the state of North Carolina can be visualized in three broad bands, each crossing the state from north to south. The first starts at the seacoast and extends 60 to 80 miles inland. This coastal plain was, by and large, the domain of cotton, with planters, smaller farmers, and slaves populating the region and the larger planters and merchants dominating all. Inland from the coastal plain is the piedmont, from 100 to nearly 200 miles wide. Its hard-rock hills and uplands, forests, fast rivers, and small fields were the seat of small farms and small manufacturing. For the simplest schematic introduction to the regional politics of the early mid-nineteenth century: the planters had the wealth, and wanted tight control over the slaves, free Blacks, and poor Whites who produced and threatened their wealth; the piedmont had the majority of the voting population and wanted to use the wealth of the coastal plain to build bridges, roads, and railroads – to lay out and sustain the infrastructure of their interests.

Beyond the piedmont lay the Appalachian Mountains, domain of Cherokee Indians and the merchants, traders, colonial officials, and land speculators who mined the possibilities that emerged from the land, the people, and their own specific opportunism. A crucial region in colonial geopolitics, by the early middle of the nineteenth century (save for a few brief moments around the Civil War) the mountain peoples were no longer a critical force in the conflict between piedmont and coastal plain. Robeson County, lying on the inland edge of the coastal plain, along the border with South Carolina, was – and has remained so.

By way of introduction only, call the statewide conflict one between "conservatives" and "liberals." The conservative agrarian elite of Robeson County and, indeed, of the whole coastal plain, in order to generate a necessarily compliant labor force, tied to the land for labor-intensive agriculture, wanted to choke Black aspirations (to aspire is literally to breathe, as well as to hope, to underscore what was and is at stake). The piedmont liberal elite, perhaps at bottom no more decent or humane, needed a more mobile and more autonomous labor force, and in this context gave people a few more apparent benefits.

The task of the White elite in Robeson County, from after the Civil War to the early 1970s (that is, during the whole period when sharecropping developed and stayed predominant), became one of getting some of the Blacks and most of the Indians – who were as badly treated as the Blacks – to vote against what objectively might be termed their own "liberal" interests and to side with the local conservative elite, thus sending to the state legislature a relatively large and powerful delegation, and putting in pro-agrarian (and thus *necessarily* anti-Black) governors and, as we shall see, at the crucial period when the state constitution was revised, supporting constitutional forms that were substantially antithetical to their interests.

The task of Indians and Blacks active in the civil rights movement in Robeson County in the 1960s and 1970s, when agrarian interests were on the wane but the old power-wielding White, local elite were still frighteningly strong, was to break this pattern of Robeson County's support of statewide conservatives and to break the local pattern of accommodation in which it was rooted. *These were completely different – at times even incompatible – tasks.*

As the state became increasingly committed to policies supporting industrialization, the statewide political machinery during the 1950s fell increasingly into the hands of liberals, a rapid process capped by the 1960 election of Terry Sanford as governor. Out-of-power conservative state-level politicians and candidates had little access to Indian locality leaders, who were still tied to a White Robeson County elite that had made its own peace and deals with the emerging bloc of statewide liberals. The conservatives in statewide politics, generally well bankrolled, therefore offered and secured deals with the newly emerging Indian activists, who were desperate both for financial support and for a chance to have some connections to real power, if one of the state conservatives both won and also remembered his Indian supporters. By the late 1960s and early 1970s Indians were often backing statewide conservative politicians in order to get from them the funds and the "connections" to oppose both local White agrarian-based politicians and the remaining Indian locality leaders who still worked with, if not for, the local power structure and the more liberal, pro-industrialization element of the state Democratic party.

In the complex set of dealings and double-dealings that emerged, the new Indian leadership, opposed to the traditional locality leaders and the politics of local accommodations, did not, to my mind, have completely clean hands – though most had good hearts for their own people – for they were very casual about how their pattern of dealing with state-level conservatives would affect Black people. In all this, including the still powerful locality leaders, the Indian vote was far more fluid, far more volatile, and at times far more self-betraying than the Black vote. Explaining why this was so will lead us back to the fundamental geopolitical organization of county politics.

III

In the 1960s many people in Robeson County said, and all sides believed, that the county was "one-third Indian, one-third Black, and

38

one-third White." This was close to true, particularly at midcentury, but it did not measure voting potential for many reasons, including the developing differential proportions of *adult* populations, the growing differential impact of migration and migration possibilities, and differential residence and occupation patterns, with their implied differences both in vulnerability to pressure and to civil rights organization. In sum, there have been substantial differences in the ability of diverse interests to mobilize, shape and deliver White, Indian, and Black votes.

First, an obvious but important point to emphasize is that the African-American people of Robeson County are part of a large "ethnic" population that by the early 1960s was very much on the move. Support – from money to lawyers to ideas to civil rights workers to specific legislation – poured into the county while young Black people in search of jobs poured out. A declining and aging population was being politically mobilized. But after the 1968 elections, when for the purpose of state legislative elections Robeson County was merged with two adjacent counties to form one legislative district that would elect, as a district, four state representatives, there were substantial numbers of Blacks in the adjacent counties that could and did make common cause with the Black people of Robeson County. In the same period the Indian population, much less prone to migrate, was increasing – but there were no politically significant numbers of Indians outside Robeson County with whom to forge electoral alliances.

When young Black people moved north to city lights and city jobs, they still maintained their ethnic and social identity, perhaps even enhancing their ethnic self-image. When Indians moved out of Robeson County, they ceased in many ways to be regarded as Indian, or to be able to maintain ties of ethnic sociability in their daily lives – unless they went to one of a few special places, especially one neighborhood in Baltimore and a couple of spots in Michigan that in the heyday of industrial production during World War II used a lot of Indian labor. These locales still had substantial Indian communities drawn originally from Robeson County, but no longer had jobs to offer.

I talked with a couple of young Indian men who went to Baltimore in the early 1960s with a group of friends, looking for work. One day, still jobless, they pooled some of their change, bought a small bag of rice, spread it on the windowsills of their room to attract pigeons, and then scraped the rice back off the windowsills to cook with the pigeons. Still later and still jobless, they came back home to Robeson County. This – the pigeon stew and the return home – was not only necessity, but also, as they looked back to tell me the tale, a high-spirited confidence in their "country smarts," which sustained commitment to their

Table 1. *Robeson County population by ethnic category*

	1960		1970*	
	Number	Percentage of total	Number	Percentage of total
Indian	26,278	29.5	26,486	31.3
Black	26,256	29.5	21,876	25.9
Indian + Black	52,534	59	48,362	57.1
White	36,552	41	36,262	42.9
Total	89,086		84,624	

* 1970 census figures were not generally known until 1973.

current political struggles. Not being able to leave, they had to stay and win what could be won from the county where they were born, the place that was, willingly or unwillingly, home. And they thought they were going to win – although it was the Blacks, in some ways less innocently, naively, and passionately optimistic about their overall situation, who actually did win.

Second, and more important for purposes of understanding elections, while the total population (89,000 in 1960) was considered to be approximately one-third each Indian, Black, and White, making it look as if all the Indians and Blacks had to do was to join together and stick together to win what elections could give, there were multiple intervening realities. The 1960 census – the one available for the intense political activism in the period 1966–70 – showed the actual population of the county, including adults and children, to be 41 percent White, 59 percent Indian and Black (Table 1).

But the voting-age population had a different composition. Blacks and Indians had more children than did Whites; there was a substantial Black outmigration of young adults; Indians and Blacks had lower life expectancies than did Whites. Taken together, this gave an adult population composition that was 51 percent Black and Indian combined, and 49 percent White. (Voting age at this time was twenty-one.)

These figures are only an introduction to two further problems: Whites tended to turn out in much higher percentages than Indians or Blacks for elections and rarely voted for non-White candidates; Indians and Blacks not only had lower turnouts, but in an election where an Indian ran against a White some of the Black vote could be obtained for the White candidate, and even some of the Indian vote as well. When a Black ran against a White it was usually even more difficult to get

Indian votes for the Black candidate than Black votes for Indians in an Indian–White contest.

Organizing to win was, in general, harder for Indians than for Blacks. In one Black town precinct in 1968, 600 people voted and 596 votes were cast for the Black candidate, a percentage that was impossible for Indian activists to deliver. This was partly due to the remaining power of White landlords and Indian locality leaders, partly due to the relatively greater ease of splitting the Indian vote (for reasons to be discussed later), and partly due to the matter now at hand, which is the different geographic dispersion of Indians and Blacks within Robeson County.

Robeson County has six small towns, each with an official population of between 1,500 and 3,000 in 1960, and Lumberton – the county seat – which had a population of 15,000. One of the small towns, Pembroke, located in the center of the county, is almost entirely Indian. The other five small towns lie in a diamond-shaped pattern near the borders of the county, and are almost entirely White and Black. One town, Red Springs, where people lived who owned a great deal of land that Indians sharecropped, had a widely known reputation for not even allowing Indians in the town: not to live, not even to shop.

Blacks and Indians responded differently to the land loss of the late nineteenth and early twentieth centuries: Indians stayed on the land as tenant farmers; Blacks moved to the towns, increasingly settling in specific neighborhoods. Some of these neighborhoods were not actually *in* a town, for town residents had water and sewer lines, garbage collection, and street cleaning. When wages are so low that the taxes collectible (on wages or property or as direct billings for such services as water or garbage) cannot meet the cost of these minimal services, it pays to draw town boundaries to exclude substantial portions of Black neighborhoods. Voting district and school district boundaries were all, of course, drawn by analogous principles.

The Black vote, which came from compact, densely settled neighborhoods and was more readily focused than the Indian vote on specific issues and candidates, was often primarily addressed to issues that emerged in town elections, even though many of the Black town residents were not eligible to participate in the town elections. These town elections raised a very full bag of issues: mayors and boards that controlled services (and the taxes and rates for these services), that oversaw town police and controlled the town school system. Several towns had schools that were separate from the county school system, providing schooling for Whites and Blacks resident in the towns, leaving the county schools in large areas of the county substantially to the

Indians. (The county would sometimes pay tuition to the towns to enroll Black children, technically not town residents, in town schools in order to maintain segregated schools.)

When town residents voted, they voted both for their own town school board members and *also* for the members of the county school board, thus giving Whites control of the county schools as well as those in town.

Allocations from the state to the county provided the basic funds for all the schools in both the towns and the county. The county school board allocated these funds between the schools in the county and the towns. Town residents imposed upon themselves an additional tax, used for supplemental funding for their schools. This funding system was the basis for the towns' claim that they could vote in both town and county school board elections, which gave the Whites effective control over the allocation of both countywide funds apportioned between county and town and of town funds apportioned between White and Black schools. One Indian teacher told me, in 1967, that she was allocated $24 *a year* for all school supplies for the thirty children in her first-grade class – paper, crayons, pencils, chalk, and everything else. Other Indian teachers told me, for example, that they had a movie projector in their school, and could borrow films from the county school board's central office, but they had no shades for their classroom windows.

Against this double voting by the towns, the Indians primarily had to use legal challenges – the state legislature rejected attempts to change the system legislatively, and the Indians lacked the voting power to change the balance of power in the school boards. Black people in Robeson County were more affected by the allocation of educational funds within towns and so had to focus their attention on town elections. This attention was further held by a range of other serious issues they confronted as residents of, or adjacent to, towns. Yet they also played a crucial role in county elections.

IV

In 1965, under the influence of President Lyndon B. Johnson, a voting-rights act was passed by Congress – an act that removed any special restrictions (beyond citizenship, age, residence, and certain criminal convictions) for registering to vote or for voting. It is important to note that these restrictions – especially the literacy test and the poll tax – were *not* universally prohibited in the new civil rights act: they just could not be used in counties where less than 50 percent of the adult population were registered to vote, or where less than 50 percent had

voted in the previous presidential election. It was unclear, for it seemed
legally permissible, whether the poll tax or the literacy test would be
reinstated once registration or voting figures reached 50 percent: this
created extra pressure to win what could be won as quickly as possible.

Between 1965, when the Voting Rights Act was passed, and the spring
of 1968, there was a massive increase in the number of Indian and
Black voters and a dramatic, dream-inspiring shift in the composition
of the electorate. In 1965 there were approximately 4,000 Indians and
3,100 Blacks registered to vote; even together they were substantially
outmuscled by the 11,900 White voters. In three years the number of
Indian and Black registered voters nearly doubled, the product of extraordinarily intense efforts; White enrollment rose only 13 percent.
When the voter registration books were officially closed, exactly three
weeks before the May 1968 Democratic party primary, there were 13,408
Indians and Blacks registered and 13,401 Whites.

As the total voter registration fast approached the legal "magic marker"
of 50 percent of all the eligible voters in the county, neither the poll
tax nor the literacy test were brought back, although a few right-wing
politicians made some very scary demands about this.

A few interpretive comments on this might be in order, impelled less
from necessity in the argument here than as a reflection upon, and a
reaction to, the intense fear that we all felt then about that possibility.
It is absolutely inconceivable to me, now, that after several hundred
years of putting Black and Indian people to the wall, *power-holding*
Americans would wake up one morning in the early 1960s feeling that
it was wrong to treat people that way, and so decide to make the election rules a bit fairer. Rather, segregated elections were part of a system
whose reproductive center was segregated schools. The non-White
segregated schools – if I may be permitted to resurrect functionalist
anthropology to make a simple point – were devices designed primarily
to produce field hands: people who would sit in a cabin broke and
often hungry for half the year for a chance to chop cotton the other
half. A non-White school system does not educate Black people, or
Indians, or Hispanics, even though the people who work in them may
try, and at times succeed. Such schools, for the most part, take young
human beings and produce the social-structural and cultural victims of
the future.

In agrarian societies such schools took brains and produced hands:
field hands, not even very employable as factory workers in high-
technology plants. In the early 1960s this system, *on the national level,* was
breaking down: first because Black people were struggling effectively

against it, and second because it was no longer useful. The mechanical cotton-picker and the emergence of modern industry and a modern army made such schools an obstacle to "progress" – to new ways of incorporating people into larger social systems; to new ways of *using* people. On the local level, however, the entrenched agrarian elite did not want to be muscled aside from their privileged places and their continuing need for field hands and for exceedingly cheap domestic labor. They still had a lot of power: power to create and power to destroy.

It is important to keep in mind that when national trends and movements such as civil rights and integrated eduction rub against the grain of local power, some of the most heart-wrenching dramas are played out not in the arenas of demonstrations, marches, and symbolic entrances and expulsions, but in the daily life and hopes of ordinary, usually quiet people, called upon by others and by their own feelings to make high-risk decisions in situations where no one but themselves pays the price for losing. The fact that the "new way" is often not, at some deep level, really about meeting their needs and their hopes is just plain appalling.

The state of North Carolina has had, since the early 1960s, an effective policy of attracting industry by offering a reasonably educated, nonunionized, very low-wage labor force. Whatever one thinks of that policy, consider it at the time when it was being put into place, in the middle and late 1960s, before most of the present factories were up and running, while the agrarian-based elites still both called the tunes and paid very close attention to those who danced out of step. Look at the local changes this policy of industrialization and civil rights was creating through the eyes of a middle-aged Indian couple – for example, a family sharecropping on a White-owned farm, whom no one else will employ if they are evicted, asked to vote for an Indian or Black or "improving" White candidate, or even just asked to register to vote. Or consider Black parents, the husband working as a mechanic for a White-owned garage, the wife as a domestic, offered the possibility of enrolling their children in the White high school, under the first "integration" plan, which allowed parents to "choose" the schools they wanted their children to attend.

All the terrible risks these exceptional, ordinary, very vulnerable people took by voting, or by sending their children to formerly all-White schools, all the turmoil they endured to live the dream, some making it, others losing badly, and twenty years later their children, themselves now married and supporting families and often their surviving parents, were earning $3.70 or so an hour, the standard nickel or dime more than minimum wage that factories in the county pay for working on the line, even to people who have worked there five or ten years. This is $148. a week, before deductions.

V

In 1968 North Carolina was still so solidly in the Democratic party that the crucial elections were not the regular elections in November between Republicans and Democrats but the Democratic primary in May, which determined the candidates for the November election. Technically the primary election was for all parties, but at this time and place the Republican party primaries were not at all relevant. Whoever the Democratic candidates were, they won – at least at this time. In 1967, when a Republican party organization was forming in the county, its organizer went to the county manager to ask for a meeting room and was offered a telephone booth. Five years later, in 1972, a Republican actually won the governorship of North Carolina, the first to do so since 1901.

When voters register they can declare their party affiliation: Democrat, Republican, or Independent. Even those Indians (and others) who planned on voting Republican in the fall election would usually register as Democrats in order to vote in the spring party primary – at first for the candidate they would rather have win; later, with more sophistication, for the candidate they thought would be easiest for the Republicans to beat.

A few descriptive comments about how the primary election was organized in 1968 and an introduction to some incidents during the election will convey a sense of the organization of political power, and will show some of what underlay the diverse developments that emerged from the electoral battles over civil rights.

In 1968 the state senator from Robeson County (to the North Carolina not the federal, legislature) was Hector McLean. Through a combination of legislative rules and usual practices, state senators ordinarily have enormous powers. Much of the state budget for roads, schools, hospitals, prisons, and public welfare is allocated to the counties, rather than spent directly by the state, although the legislature keeps an eye on how the county uses these funds. When the senator and representatives from a county unanimously introduce a bill in the state legislature, applicable to affairs within the county, the rest of the legislature almost automatically gives its assent under the "home-rule" tradition. As the leader of the county delegation, the state senator – Hector McLean – had a great deal of power to shape this legislation: its wording, its

45

provisions, what was brought forward and when. He also had the power to nominate the judges who presided over the county courts – judges who presided, indeed, over a wide range of individually and socially significant cases.

Hector McLean was also the president of Southern National Bank, the largest and most socially powerful bank in the county, which not only held mortgages on a great many farms, houses, and businesses in the county – White, Black and Indian – but which itself also owned substantial tracts of land, much of it acquired through foreclosure, farming it mostly with Indian and Black tenants and White managers.

Hector McLean's first cousin was Dickson McLean, who held three significant positions in the county. To begin, he was one of the senior partners in McLean and Stacy, the most prestigious law firm in the county. In 1968 he was also the county attorney, and sat in on all the county commissioners' meetings, offering advice about what could and could not be done and handling the legal suits against the county. Indian activists said that Dickson McLean never lost a case before a judge appointed by his cousin Hector. Undoubtedly this was factually untrue, but it gives some sense of the power he was thought to wield.

Further, Dickson McLean was also the chairman of the Robeson County Democratic party. All voter registration and the conduct of all the primary and regular elections – including the act of voting and counting the ballots – was overseen by a board of elections. This board was composed of three people, two appointed by the party having the most votes in the preceding presidential election, and one appointed by the other party. As chairman of the county Democratic party, Dickson McLean appointed two of the three members of the Board of Elections and the Republicans appointed the third. This board employed a registrar of voters, who maintained the registration books. It also appointed, or refused to appoint, the local registration officials who in each of the county's thirty-nine precincts could also register voters (or disappear when most needed); and in *each* of the thirty-nine precincts, during primary and regular elections, this same board appointed three people to supervise the voting process in the precinct, count the ballots, and report the results. A description of one of the more bitterly contested elections in 1968 will illustrate some of the practical potentials of this system: the way it actually worked on a local level, whether or not the people who put it together did so for such purposes.

One of the district primary elections for county commissioner, in the spring of 1968, was particularly hard fought. A Black man was running for office with very active Indian support. Whites and Blacks were about evenly numbered in this election district; Blacks and Indians together decisively outnumbered Whites. The district had four small precincts, and the combined registration figures for the district were 1,015 Whites, 1,009 Blacks, and 781 Indians. With these figures Blacks and Indians were saying they *had* to win – both would and must; Whites were intensely concerned to demonstrate that could not happen.

White strategy, as explained to me by a White office-holder from another district in the county, was to ignore the Black vote and focus all possible pressure on the Indians. They were looking, he said, to get 500 Indian votes away from the Black candidate, and the first move was to raise the price ordinarily paid for a vote from one dollar to five. When I gaped at this figure (we had so few material resources other than our energies that it seemed inconceivable), he laughingly asked me if I had "any idea how cheap twenty-five hundred dollars is for a key election." It very quickly became much less droll.

Each precinct had one place to vote, usually a school room:

The Polling Place

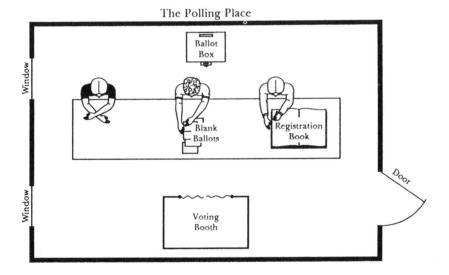

In one such room, in one precinct in the district, all the student chairs had been removed, or pushed against a wall, leaving the room open. You entered from a door near the front wall. Just to your right three tables had been lined up, stretching from nearly the wall where the door was to nearly the opposite wall, where the windows were. In front of the table was the voting booth, where people went to mark their paper ballots behind a curtain. Behind this table sat three middle-aged White men. Behind the three men was the ballot box,

47

ostentatiously locked, with a slot on top where the marked ballots were to be put. The first man behind the table, the one closest to the door, had the registration book. When you came in the door you gave him your name, he checked to see if it was in the book, and you signed, or, if you could not write, made a mark by your name to indicate that you were voting. In the middle of the table was the man who gave you the blank ballot. The man at the far end had no specific task except to watch: the law required three poll watchers.

An incident that happened not to every voter but to some, occurred especially when several Indians and Blacks were waiting at the registration book to be checked before voting. A man or a woman would come in, give his or her name, get a ballot, and then would go into the voting booth, to mark the ballot, often slowly and laboriously. They would then often fold it several times, and come out from inside the curtained, private voting booth clutching this small bit of folded paper, to face the table with the three men sitting there and the ballot box on the other side. The man in the middle would, sometimes, reach out his hand for the ballot.

At this point voters had two choices: They could hand him the ballot, and he would turn around in his chair and put it in the box behind him. Sometimes when he did this he unfolded the ballot to the point where it had only one fold remaining, and sometimes he would unfold it all the way and then fold it in half again. Or, you could ignore the outstretched hand and walk around the table, by the window, to put it in the ballot box yourself. The poll watcher at the end of the table at times would call out to the man with the registration book: "What's his or her name?" "Who does he or she work for?" – or the scariest question of all – "Who's his or her people? [kin, family]." Sometimes an Indian or Black voter came out of the voting booth and handed an open ballot to the man behind the table when he did not even have his hand stretched out for it.

If a person could not read or write, someone could go into the voting booth with him or her to mark the ballot. This ballot marker could be either a relative, a bystander, or one of the official poll watchers. Bystanders could only mark two ballots; the official poll watchers had no limits. With stories circulating from previous elections that poll watchers would say such things as "You don't want so and so to win, so we'll just put an x by their name," it was important to keep a steady supply of fresh "bystanders" near the polling place. In one polling place, with two middle-aged Indian women standing in the schoolyard, waiting to be "bystanders," a middle-aged White man drove up in his car. Charges were subsequently filed that he pulled a gun on the two women and said: "Get out of here you goddamn nigger-loving Indians." When the case went to court he was found innocent, on the basis, people said, of his known character. The Black candidate – inevitably, as can be seen now, but to our surprise and dismay then – lost.

So it went. A great many Indians and Blacks who were registered to vote between 1965 and 1968 were registered by dint of extremely hard work: driving around the county, talking to people about their problems and about the importance of voting, going back to pick them up to take a carload of people to register, finding the registrar was out and having to come back another day, and so forth. Further, one of the most effective ways of getting people to register and to vote was to talk with them about the problems they were having, and to try to explain that many of their problems were not just personal but also social: with more money in the schools their children might do better; with a more humane welfare department sick parents might have an easier time getting help. But ultimately none of the new hopes and understandings that were raised could be fulfilled. The Indians lost every election they contested in 1968, worked even harder and planned even more intensely for 1970, and lost everything again.

After the 1968 election Robeson County was redistricted for purposes of electing state representatives, combining Robeson County with two adjacent counties that had substantial numbers of Blacks and few Indians. A Black minister from Robeson county won one of the four seats; the Indian candidate finished eighth in a field of nine.

By the spring of 1970 the Indians were not only losing every election, they were coming to see that they were in even worse shape politically than Black people, and Black people still were in difficult circumstances.

Right after the May 1970 primary ended, the White superintendent of the county schools announced the integration of the Indian schools of the county, which was widely understood to mean both combining Indian and Black schools with each other, and to be the end of one of the two major Indian social institutions. He underscored the total powerlessness of Indians by saying publicly – it was quoted prominently in the county newspaper – "And there isn't anything the Indians can do about it."

49

Lumber River, just south of Pembroke

There is not a great difference between rivers and swamps. The Lumbee, or Lumber River (formerly Drowning Creek), has a surprisingly powerful current in the main channel, which since the 1970s has been periodically cleared of deadfall and tangle. Raft Swamp is a "deep swamp": big, and with the kinds of vegetation, such as cypress trees, that flourish in water that stands and flows the year around. The pine forest is a "dry island" – perhaps farmable, perhaps too sandy. This is the landscape that sheltered Indian people in the colonial period; the same swamps and dry islands in which Henry Berry Lowery and his people farmed and fought in the mid-nineteenth century and from which the Lumbee Indians publicly emerged.

Raft Swamp, a few miles northeast of Pembroke

Small pine forest, between the Lumber River and Raft Swamp

Tobacco barn and ditch

The tobacco barn was photographed in 1990, at the end of a decade when such barns were rapidly going out of use. At least as much tobacco was still being grown, but it was increasingly "bulked": dealt with through mechanization and containerization. As farm labor opportunities rapidly declined and many old-style farm folks found themselves utterly unwanted or unable to work in the emergent factories, farm labor became so cheap, while mechanization costs kept rising, that these old barns, which required enormous quantities of hand labor, were being put back to use by 1990. This particular one is closer to the road than usual, and 10 feet or so lower in height. In the foreground is a drainage ditch, draining the fields into one of the swamp streams. Such ditches, along every county road in the Indian center of the county, usually have a slow runoff and rapidly clog with vegetation. The two adjacent fields – one waterlogged, one sandy; both widespread characteristics   illustrate the problem and the triumph of Indian agriculture.

Waterlogged field

Sandy field

Hector Mclean's family house

Southern National Bank

The McLean family house in the 1950s (from a photograph in the Pembroke State University Archives); and Southern National Bank, built in the late 1960s. Hector McLean, whose ancestors were governors and state senators, was president of Southern National from 1955 to 1991. In the transformation of Robeson County from a region of great agricultural wealth and poor farm tenants to low-wage manufacturing, the McLean residence was replaced with one quite a bit more subdued, and this new bank was built, far more imposing than before. The house was torn down to make room for the bank's parking lot, and the lions were moved to the new McLean residence.

Tenant farmer's house

Indian "mobile home" community

Tenant farmer's house, home to many small-scale farmers and sharecroppers in the 1940s and 1950s. By the mid-1960s they were becoming scarce, although still used by landlords for their farm day laborers and still lived in by people too old, ill, or poor to have much choice. The "mobile home" community recreates the social density of an Indian village – but without the churches, stores, stations, and schoolhouse, and without the mix of social class.

The McLean and the tenant farmer houses are from the same historical period, as are the bank and the mobile homes.

House in field

House and trailers in field

These four photographs show some of the tensions between living within, and simultaneously against, historical pressures and processes. The church and school develop and present an *Indian* moral and social world that is constructed both within the values of the larger society and against the pressures of poverty and racism. Prospect Church is large, affluent, powerful, and Indian – with all the contradictions that entails. The Union Chapel School, by dint of much hard work from teachers and parents, gave Indian farm children an education good enough to take them out of the community, and a sense of an almost all-Indian social life strong enough to make many want to stay within. The houses show the same tensions, but

Prospect United Methodist Church

Union Chapel graded school

more subtly. Two common Indian rural dwelling patterns are shown here: the house in the back of the field, away from the road. White, Protestant, relatively affluent farmers in middle America usually build their houses much nearer the road. Indian social life is just as densely woven, but often more privately held away from general public view. The house with the cluster of half-hidden mobile homes and out-buildings expresses the same social dynamic, with the addition of kin and close neighbors: a form of living an *Indian* social life, but as just people, not with the extra work and the tension of being Indian among Whites and Blacks.

Senior Citizens, 1982 Lumbee Homecoming Parade

Redmans Lodge, Saddletree Community, 1910 (from a photograph in the Native American Resource Center Museum, Pembroke State University)

Ways of living, making, and claiming history.

Model tobacco barn, Native American Resource Center Museum, Pembroke State University

Henry Berry Lowery's cabin, 1990, awaiting restoration at the Native American Cultural Center (on land that was once the Red Banks Farm)

PART TWO

The embers of hope

Prologue

Six long-smouldering political events broke into the open or were forced underground in the four weeks between March 15 and April 12, 1973. The way people mapped and remapped the routes to and between these events will show us the different visions of history and hope, of fear and desire, that each event expressed, contained, or destroyed.

Each event emerged from its own specific historical sources, and each expressed the actions of different people setting themselves *against* their pasts, either in an attempt at outright rejection or in an attempt to transform the continuing past by bringing it within a divergent, changing present. Setting themselves in opposition to pasts riven with images and material realities of domination, people learned new lessons about what they could still do and what could still be done to them. The six events were

1. On March 15, 1973, the Lumbee Bank opened for business in its brand new and impressively large quarters in the new Lumbee Shopping Center, right in the heart of Pembroke. The bank had started two years earlier in a small, prefabricated building, as the first primarily Indian-owned bank in America.

2. Three days after the new bank building opened, on March 18, 1973, "Old Main," the oldest surviving building of what was once the all-Indian teacher-training college in Pembroke, was completely gutted by a fire that was transparently arson.

3. On the day after Old Main burned, the first Lumbee Indian to sit in the state legislature, appointed to fill the vacancy created by the death of a White representative, took his seat in the State House.

4. Four days later, on March 23, several hundred Tuscarora Indians were beaten, some brutally, by the county sheriffs and state police as

51

they demonstrated in front of the predominantly Indian high school in the community of Prospect. Since the beginning of 1973, a White-owned barn or tobacco shed or vacant farmhouse had burned, one just about every other night, all spring long. A day or two after the Tuscarora demonstration at Prospect, two weeks after Old Main was burned down, the barn burnings stopped.

5. Before the week was out, on March 29, the *Robesonian* announced to the county that another faction of the county's Tuscarora Indians had filed suit against Rogers Morton, the U.S. secretary of the interior (and thus the head of the Bureau of Indian Affairs) for their rights as Indians under the 1934 Indian Reorganization Act. They won this suit, much to the surprise of the Lumbee, in April 1975 – three months before Chief Howard Brooks, one of the leaders of the Tuscarora demonstration at the Prospect schoolhouse and one of the victims of police assault, was sentenced to a year in jail for "inciting to riot."

6. Two weeks later, on April 12, the FBI, apparently acting on a tip from an Indian, found a truckload – more than two tons – of crucial legal and historical documents taken from the Bureau of Indian Affairs offices, in a Tuscarora-owned house, back in the swamps of Robeson County. These documents had been acquired during the Trail of Broken Treaties occupation of the Bureau of Indian Affairs offices in Washington, D.C., in the fall of 1972.

All these events are closely interconnected. All directly or indirectly entail relations between the Indian people of Robeson County (including relations between diverse classes and groups of Indians then in formation), between Indians and local Whites, and between Indians and the state and federal governments. The first three incidents – the bank's opening, the destruction of Old Main, and the appointment of an Indian state legislator – bear specifically upon issues of class formation among the Indians of Robeson County, and the way that this class formation interweaves with relations to the dominant society. The last three incidents – the Tuscarora demonstration at Prospect, the lawsuit, and the discovery and repossession of the documents – are explainable in ways that highlight the tensions that were interwoven in the split between Lumbee and Tuscarora, including tensions that emerged from the relations between the Indian people of Robeson County and the federal government. The first three incidents are discussed here in Part Two, the second three form the core of Part Three.

4

Challenges to respect

On July 4, 1973, the Independence Day holiday, the Lumbee had their third annual homecoming-weekend parade down the main street of Pembroke. It was a small-town, community, I-know-the-people-marching parade, and it was an Indian parade. Churches and clubs built floats, several dozen people on horseback went before, after, and between the floats – some in ordinary work clothes, some dressed as cowboys, some as Indians – school bands in flashing costumes marched and played small-town school band tunes, expensive cars hauled dignitaries and local beauty queens. It was a parade rich enough to excite continual comment, and small and cheerful enough to go through town twice – to the end and back.

In the midst of it all was one stunning float – literally stunning: I turned away, seeing it as humiliating to Indians. It was built by an Indian church on a very large flat-bed trailer-truck, the kind of rig that hauls bulky loads on interstate highways. In the middle of the trailer was a large signboard extending the width of the trailer and 8 feet high. On this signboard, facing the front of the trailer, a "Christian" devil was painted in red, with pointed ears, horns, tail, cloven-hoof feet, trident and all, the flames of hell forming the background. Before this painted devil, a dozen real, living, adolescent Indian boys dressed as "Indians" with feathers, bare legs, and moccasins, danced in a circle.

On the other side of the signboard partition, facing the back half of the trailer, was a pulpit, Bible on top, at which stood a young Indian man in a preacher's black suit. Facing the pulpit and preacher were several rows of metal folding chairs, four across, with an aisle down the middle. On one side of the aisle were little Indian boys in sports coats

53

and slacks, on the other side little Indian girls in dresses, all neat and quiet, listening to the Bible being read to them. At the back of the truck was another signboard on which was written one word: PROGRESS. When the parade was over the Indian judges awarded this float first prize.

Of all the paradoxes, contradictions, ambivalences, doubts, and assertions that we might – and must – here engage in order to understand, the most useful starting point is the then collapsing social power of the very form of respectability this float advocated.

In the poorer country Indian churches and also for older people, the intense religiosity of church was and would remain a substantial source of dignity – but a dignity that did not by itself provide much in the way of a basis for claims upon a wider social field. Those wider social claims were then being formulated and expressed in the more prosperous Indian churches, but in a context where a substantial amount of upward mobility intermingled with religiosity.

Even in the prosperous Indian churches, however, the larger field in which claims for dignity and respectability were raised and shaped was still, in 1970, primarily an Indian field, countywide rather than locality-based. Unlike contemporary southern Black churches, both the poorer and the more prosperous Indian churches had renounced the collective social action of confrontational militance, thus addressing their expressions of respectability primarily to other Lumbee Indians and "sympathetic" Whites, rather than forcing it upon the larger society as southern Black churches had done. Montgomery, Selma, Greensboro, Birmingham: such centers of Black political activism and cultural claim became, at least for a moment, names that reverberated with the passion and moral force of an older set of names – Jerusalem, Bethlehem, Calvary. Meanwhile several of the more prosperous Indian churches sought to use new forms of prosperity to organize an integration of respectability and accommodation – an integration that became assertive in the face of White bigotry but was also deeply divisive among themselves.

When people from a victimized minority group copy the values of the dominant society, in dress, housing, or even "appropriate" behavior, it can well be a form of quiet but insistent ethnic confrontation: I am as good as you, whatever you say, and not only as good as you but *good*. It can easily, however, *also* become a form of confrontation with one's own underclass, a particularly ambivalent, painful, and at times provocative confrontation for both sides. One of paradoxes of respectability is that it can be an aggressive claim on the larger society – a claim for recognition made against a hostile or uncaring domination – and simultaneously be *respectful* of a set of dominant values and ways that are felt, particularly but not exclusively, by the poorer members of the ethnic group, to be oppressive, stifling, and destructive. Further, the religiosity of many poorer Indians – or of churches that primarily congregated poor Indian farmers – was itself a focus and a goal rather than a framework on which to erect other social claims.

Two diverse and divergent forms of respectability were being expressed and consolidated in the late 1960s. One, rooted in local social institutions – particularly village churches and schools – was being undermined by "progress": the progress of increasing relative poverty, the progress of increasing class differentiation within these villages, the progressive integration of villages into larger social institutions. The other form of respectability, the more "middle-class" form of those who were rooting themselves in the income and opportunity possibilities of the larger society and of local commercial and professional activity, was also running into a number of obstacles, including an increasingly antagonistic social and cultural split between this emerging Indian elite and the increasingly hard-pressed Indian underclass.

In fact, the first homecoming parade three years earlier, on July 4, 1970, brought to the foreground the issue of the paradoxes and transformations of respectability. In that parade the winning float was built on a similar large flat-bed trailer-truck. That float had a large tepee in the center – plains Indian in style, and never used in the eastern woodlands except as a recent symbol of Indianness, shared throughout America. It was an enormous tepee, 15 feet tall and well made. On the back of the float was a large sign, facing backward, with a drawing of a brick house, a locally powerful symbol of Indian affluence.

Brick houses were scarce among Indians until the late 1960s. The Indian doctor had one, as did a few store owners, and also, way out in the country swamps, a few of the more successful bootleggers. A few prosperous Indian farmers had them, some financed from working and managing their own farms, some in part through the labor of Indian sharecroppers. Most of the brick houses, in 1970 still scarce enough to be very noticeable, were owned by Indians who worked at jobs that were vulnerable to pressure from the local White elite: schoolteachers, people in administrative positions in poverty programs or local industry, or those with state jobs. Indeed, the term "brick house Indian" was used by Indians out in the county to refer not to house type but to a vulnerable and hence untrustable Indian elite: potential sellouts and potential antagonists to the increasingly angry claims of many of the county Indians – yet envied nonetheless. A brick house – which was usually not constructed of bricks, but simply had a facing one brick thick on the front and half way up the sides of the house – was also very much a symbol of Indian success, usually taking a great deal of hard work and thoughtful planning, as well as new kinds of opportunities.

Beneath this large picture of a brick house on the back of the float with the tepee were the words THINK INDIAN. This float won the prize, of course, and the next year a picture of this float adorned the cover of the advertising/program booklet put out for the homecoming festival. Under the photograph of the float and the sign was the caption: "The Challenge to All of Us." The words were precise – to *all*, rather than to each of us. Brick houses were not only valued goals but the material embodiment of a deeply yet ambivalently divisive process.

The precision of this caption will become more evident when we begin to consider other events in 1973, such as when the Tuscarora Indians, having left the swamps of Robeson County to join the American Indian Movement's march on Washington, and the occupation of the Bureau of Indian Affairs (BIA) office, came back to Robeson County with a truckload of crucial BIA documents and, it is said, backed the truck through the locked gates of the Lumbee Recreation Center and burned Lumbee's electric golf carts.

II

Put yourself in the place of either of two Indian women, or both, and you could taste in their tears the impending demise of the older form of respectability – a respectability founded upon the toil of hard work (the hard work of hand labor in farm and house, self-directed in the midst of imposed need), the decencies of local, mostly "fundamentalist" churches, and the rewards within family and locality that hard work and moral decency often brought.

I sat inside one of the brick houses late one afternoon in 1968, just visiting with an Indian couple, when the wife's sister came home. She came inside the door, closed it behind her and leaned back against it, crying quietly and very hard. A middle-aged woman, plainly and neatly dressed, greying hair still well in place from biweekly visits to the hairdresser, she just leaned back against the door and cried and cried. We all went to her. She looked at us and said: "They turned the belt up."

They turned the belt up. Miss, to give just her title (both married and unmarried women are called Miss) because I do not want to use her name, worked at the new athletic-shoe factory in the county. Almost a thousand people worked there – Blacks, Whites, and Indians – most for a nickel or dime more than minimum wage. (North Carolina then tied

Mississippi for the lowest average manufacturing wages in the United States.) As people got used to the pace of factory work, the managers turned the speed regulators of the conveyor belts along the production lines up a notch or two. Up with it or out were the only choices this woman had, and she knew how high the penalties for each would be, made all the worse by the hopes that had been attached to the coming of "industry."

That same spring of 1968, on an open field near the middle of Pembroke, an agent of the agricultural extension service set up several long folding tables to make one long table. On the table he put a massive sewing machine, a machine that sewed green tobacco leaves, dozen upon dozen, one after the other, onto 6-foot-long wooden sticks.

Fields of tobacco are governed by an allotment system limiting their size and are prized possessions, bringing at that time about $1,200 an acre on an allotment that averaged, for those Indians lucky enough to have one, 5 to 6 acres. This was the best money possible for a farmer, and enough to spread, like a thin layer of jam, to the edges of the community.

Tobacco leaf is picked green, first from the bottom of the plant, later in the season from the middle and then the top. At first mules, and by the 1960s tractors, drag sledges without wheels through the extraordinarily hot, dusty fields, down the rows between the 6-foot-high tobacco plants. For the first few passes down these rows people lie on their backs on the sledges, picking the bottom leaves as they are dragged down between the rows of plants. Then they kneel for a few more passes down each row, and then finally they stand on the sledge: brutal, hard, painful work, despite the money.

The green leaves are dried and cured in a series of stages, first on the farm, later by the factory. Standing in the fields are the tall tobacco-drying sheds, one of the characteristic sights of the rural south. Around each shed, 8 feet or so up the shed wall, runs a shade-roof, either all around or just on three sides of the building. Under this roof, during the harvest, women, children, and some older men work, hand-tying tobacco leaves to 6-foot lathing sticks, which are then hung on drying racks inside the shed. Hot, monotonous work, but not excessively hard, it is made more sociable by the chatter amidst the work. It doesn't pay much, but particularly for the poorer people of the county the pay is important in ways that are difficult to convey fully. It is money for new clothes for the children to wear when school opens, for church clothes, for shoes, for weddings, for unpaid doctor bills, occasionally a new, or newer, stove or refrigerator. Family money for adults and children; expressive money for adolescents. The two or three hundred dollars that a person – or, say, an older woman and a child or two, working together – could earn usually formed an absolutely crucial part of the family's annual cash income.

After the leaf-sewing machine was taken away and the farmers all went home, one older Indian woman still sat at the far end of the table, and then she laid her head face down in her open hands upon the table. This time there were no choices. She, and her way of life, were finished.

III

When Old Main – the oldest surviving building of the once all-Indian Pembroke State College – was rebuilt, after it was burned to the ground in the spring of 1973, an Indian museum was established inside the new building. One of the most prominent and attractive displays in this new and fancy Indian museum was a model of an old-style tobacco-drying shed, which after a few years was moved into a corner, its place taken by a near-life-sized model of "Henry Berry Lowrie's cabin."

A tobacco-drying shed may not seem very much like a "real" Indian artifact. It is, indeed, the same kind of wooden, tin-roofed shed that White and Black farmers also have owned and worked around. Yet it powerfully, if indirectly, represents – and momentarily re-creates, while you look – an earlier form of Indianness, or at least what a great many adults of the current generation now consider their Indian past.

To see this requires us to look again at the losses these two women, caught up in the gear-toothed jaws of mechanization, were suffering.

For the farmworker, to begin, the loss was far more than the chance to buy clothes and shoes for her children. She was losing the autonomy and the dignity of work – work that depended on her skills; work that was deeply rooted both in the familiar and the family. Even though this work was deeply interwoven with the poverty imposed upon non-White farm laborers, dignity and respect could still be claimed in its midst. In this context it is crucial to note that while there was a model tobacco shed in the museum, there was no sledge.

Ultimately, it might be argued, the absence of the sledge robs the current generation of children of an appreciation of what their parents and grandparents endured: the context in which they developed and claimed their social worth; how much they did, with how little, and at what cost. Without this context the extremely hard labor of the older generation to build their own lives and their community – its churches, its schools, its ball fields, its tiny one-truck firehouse – is at least partly trivialized. Yet the absence of the sledge is also understandable: people had worked, and worked hard, to transcend and to trivialize such brutality; to put the past behind them.

More subtly and perhaps even more significantly, in the world of farm-laboring Indian people a "homecoming parade" with its expensive floats and fancy cars, its public, assertive proclamation of "Indian," would probably have been inconceivable, not only because it was unaffordable and, earlier in the twentieth century, perhaps even dangerous, but also because a publicly proclaimed Indianness was unnecessary. Public dignity and the social expressiveness of one's ways could be found and expressed in the communities where people lived. Indeed, they had to be found and founded there, for the surrounding White society was a dangerous place to directly proclaim one's dignity and worth.

The tears of the woman caught in a production-line speedup for which she lacked the stamina were not simply tears of exhaustion and transformed anger. It was also grief, for she, too, along with the women tying tobacco leaves, was confronted with unchosen loss. The four-year-old Chevrolet sedan in the dooryard, the neat bungalow house with its small grass yard – all this dearly won participation in the values and ways of the larger society, which had become her own values and ways, depended on her ability to work in a context over which she no longer had any control whatsoever. Her own worth, her knowledge, her skills, her ties of kin and community that once could all have been mobilized for harvest help were now nearly totally irrelevant to her work. If she were fired, some of her possessions and some of her social position would also go, for while her work did not depend on her social ties, her social position was increasingly dependent on her work.

Two processes were happening almost simultaneously. People were being driven or pulled outward from their small communities: not physically removed, but the community as a possible container for a whole social life, a place in which one could earn and have a living, was becoming increasingly porous. Simultaneously, some people – not the more successful but a lot of "just plain folks" – were rapidly finding it increasingly difficult to live well and properly, by the standards they had come to hold, within a larger social field. Social scientists often talk about the costs and difficulties of such social and economic transitions as industrialization: what is often overlooked is that after the transition itself the "costs" that ordinary people bear – social, emotional, and financial – can keep rising, increasingly outpacing the returns.

In 1969 and early 1970 there was a major attempt to unionize the footwear factory where Miss —— had been working. The union lost the certification election, and the company celebrated the occasion with a picnic for all the workers who survived both the dismissals of activists and the speedup. It was humble pie, heavily sugared – the free hot dogs and soda at the picnic and the free turkeys given at Thanksgiving and Christmas – but there was a lot of it. Many of those who came to the picnic on company grounds, far from any Indian community, or who took the turkeys home in their own cars to their individual families, enjoyed themselves at what seemed to be the company's expense.

The point here is *not* that one cannot be Indian in the modern world. Considering all the changes Indian people and societies have been through, that would simply be nonsense. Rather, as the larger social context shifts, what is possible at the local level shifts also. New possibilities emerge, and some formerly possible ways of putting together a reasonable life are destroyed.

For ordinary people in small communities the larger social world often rubs anatagonistically against local ways, particularly against local values about good ways to live. Especially when ways of earning a livelihood change, how the larger society rubs against the local changes also. In these shifting frictions, which often include threatening changes in what kinds of things are certain and clear and what kinds of things are uncertain and unknowable, at least some people and at times a great many will lose much of what they have worked for, including part of their dignity and respectability and their sense of their own and each other's moral worth.

Anthropologists have often claimed that a people's culture is rooted in and expressed by their "values." Life would be easier for all of us, anthropologists included, were the world so simple. More to the point is the changing *space* between people's values and what it is possible for them to do; the changing tensions within values, within social relations, and especially between people's values and the social and economic relations people both choose and have imposed upon them.

To live in a social world requires some individual and collective autonomy and public expressiveness – even for slaves. There must be some freedom to maneuver and to achieve, some small social power to make claims on a larger field. As people were driven or pulled from their communities by the declining returns for small-scale farming and the increasing spread of wage labor jobs, they were forced or encouraged to make their social claims for dignity and worth in arenas far larger than their own villages and towns.

In more direct terms, you can't live a good life within your own community – a life of church and church socials, of a small community school and a volunteer fire department, of a network of co-involvement (friendly, antagonistic, or both) that spreads in time and space through sequences of plantings and harvests, inheritance and dowry – if you can't live within a community, although your home is still physically there, because you can no longer earn a living there, because schools are merged and consolidated, because insurance companies do not recognize one-truck fire brigades, because modern roads and mechanization and the increasingly high costs of farming have driven a wedge through even the smallest villages, splitting haves from have-nots, pulling the haves out to fancier churches in other places and to generally unapproachable ways – then the community as a whole and the ordinary people within it must be able to make some effective claims on the larger society or the whole framework in which people live their Indianness in these communities, not as Indians but as people, shatters. A politically assertive Indianness thus became increasingly more of a moral, social, and political necessity because the communities in which Indianness – and more profoundly: a sense of self – had been based began to come apart at the seams.

Just after the Democratic party primary, early in May 1970, when the Indian candidates all lost, and lost decisively, while some Blacks won, the White superintendent of the predominantly Indian county school system announced the integration of Indian schools and capped four years of intense struggle and constant defeat with the public statement, mentioned above: "and there isn't anything the Indians can do about it."

The response of Indian political activists was intense, and it shifted the center of Indian political passions and activism out of the domain of direct electoral confrontations. The response, however, did not directly engage the emotionally and socially crucial issue of Indian schools, which left a chasm cutting across the landscape, a chasm between people's feelings and needs and the actions that were planned, a chasm from which three thousand Tuscarora Indians would soon be almost simultaneously born.

A new Lumbee Indian organization was created that May of 1970, after the lost election and the public humiliation – the Independent Americans for Progress. By the end of May they had organized and announced a "Red Power" meeting in Pembroke. It was a meeting like none other before. All through the bitter election struggles of the 1960s the meetings were small and half-hidden, held often at night in places like church basements, with a dozen or two specifically invited people present, and with serious, if not always effective precautions to keep Whites, or Indians likely to inform Whites, from finding out what was going on. The Red Power meeting, by contrast, was public – very public. Over a thousand Indians came, as did a number of White reporters.

At the Red Power there were Indian war dances performed by local high school students and a lot of speeches. The speeches called for a whole range of economic actions, some directed against White discrimination, such as boycotting businesses that did not hire Indians. Far more, and far more intensely, the speeches called for the development of an Indian-owned and Indian-managed "modern" economy: particularly an Indian shopping center and an Indian bank.

The Independent Americans for Progress moved fast and effectively during the brief period that the organization lasted. As one of the more active forms of the newly emerging and newly affluent Indian middle class – interwoven with the still-forming Indian Junior Chamber of Commerce clubs and some older, more established and formerly more conservative groups, such as the Indian Rotary Club – they had a long reach and a lot of skill at moving and turning what they could hold. By July 4, 1970 – in less than two months – they had helped organize the First Annual Lumbee Homecoming weekend, including the Homecoming parade, a Miss Lumbee beauty contest, a bow-and-arrow shooting contest, and a variety of other events. The bank took only another year to open.

IV

The new Lumbee Bank sat uneasily at the T-shaped juncture of two major divides – like earthquake-prone fault lines that run deep below the land; rupture points held together only by the enormity of the friction and the pressure holding diverging forces against each other. One divide, in the early 1970s, put reasonably well-to-do Lumbee people on one side, and impoverished, still primarily agrarian-based Lumbee and Tuscarora on the other. The other divide, the top of the T as it were, pressed Whites against Indians. These fault lines cemented together, moment by moment, the inherently explosive tensions that create and define such divides. In logically predictable but historically surprising and sudden movements, the faults cracked and people were ground against and then torn from one another.

Banks in Robeson County are only superficially "about" money. Far more deeply and for far longer they have been about land: who can own it, who can farm it, and with what kinds of equipment; more recently – by the late 1960s – what kinds of houses or homes could be built or bought on the land or in town and what kinds of businesses Indians (and Blacks and Whites not from the traditional landholding or mercantile elite) could buy or build. To explain how this worked, and why a Lumbee Bank was both possible and intensely desired by a wide range of people, it is necessary to give a brief description of the historical dynamics of agrarian credit in Robeson County.

By the early 1960s, newly affluent Indians were themselves financing Indian endeavors, from businesses to the new Indian newspaper to church construction to land acquisition, for themselves and for others. But the scale of the required investment was increasingly rising beyond their personal funding abilities, beyond the stretch of the profits they were deriving from store ownership, land speculation, large-scale tobacco or soybean farming, funeral homes, and the few other opportunities for modest accumulation. These newly affluent Indians had momentarily escaped from the control of the county's credit institutions and they were now having to go back, joining their poorer cousins in the waiting-rooms of power. They at least were waiting inside, and being called "Mister": limited gains.

From whatever point in the history of a people or of a place when access to goods or to the means to produce goods becomes even partly commoditized – becomes accessible primarily through money, rather than by kin or communal nonmonetary interchanges – controlling credit often becomes one of the most powerful and pervasive ways of continuing domination. Superficially less dramatic than torture, murder, concentration camps, and other bloody brutalities, credit consolidates its almost irresistible power by controlling time, which first entails the directed allocation of human productive activity across specified periods (for example, springtime loans to particular kinds of farmers, in amounts of substantially different scale, for the production of specific crops with specific inputs of seed type, fertilizer, insecticide, different sorts of equipment, and the like). Second and more broadly, particularly in agrarian forms of credit, credit becomes control over time by being designed with double intent: if the credit leads to successful production (that is, a good crop) both lender and producer benefit, however unequally; but if the credit is followed by failure, the producer will usually bear most of the loss. Providing credit is a long-term, as well as a short-term, strategy of accumulation.

Tables 2 and 3 introduce the social matrix from which agrarian credit continually emerges in Robeson County and illustrate the cumulative effects of its prior existence.

Social differentiation in agrarian societies takes many forms: the most profound are based on developing differentiation in access to land and to labor. Agrarian societies ordinarily have several different forms of credit actively operating at any one time, and credit is also used for a

63

Table 2. *"Soil Bank" Payments of $30,000 or more, Robeson County, 1967 (Payment for taking a portion of one's farmland out of production for one year)*

Paid to	Locale	Amount ($)
McNair Farms, Inc. (connected to Red Springs Implement Co. and to Pates Supply Co. in Pembroke)	Red Springs	297,000
Southern National Bank (Hector McLean, president)	Lumberton	148,343
D. D. McColl	St. Paul's	70,271
Ted Smith	Parkton	61,457
Earl Parnell	Parkton	42,720
Maxton Supply Company	Maxton	37,346
Lewis McNeill	Red Springs	35,934
K. M. Biggs, Inc. (a supply company and general merchant)	Lumberton	31,692
J. D. Hagler	Maxton	30,809
Pates Supply Company	Pembroke	30,267

Note: McNair Farms/Red Springs Implement Co., Southern National Bank, Maxton Supply Co., K. M. Biggs, and Pates Supply Co. have the largest dealings with Indian farmers and sharecroppers and together controlled most of the trade with, and credit for, Indian farmers.

Source: Agricultural Stabilization and Conservation Service Program, Records, Lumberton, N.C.

Table 3. *Income of farm and non-farm rural families, Robeson County, 1960*

	Rural families[a]			Rural farm families[b]		
Income ($)	Number	Cumulative number	Cumulative percent	Number	Cumulative number	Cumulative percent
Less than 1,000	4,598	4,598	33.1	2,754	2,754	39.7
1,000–1,999	2,863	7,461	53.7	1,557	4,311	62.2
2,000–2,999	1,865	9,326	67.1	932	5,243	75.6
3,000–3,999	1,427	10,753	77.4	558	5,801	84.0
4,000–4,999	902	11,655	83.8	332	6,133	88.5
5,000–5,999	811	12,466	89.7	323	6,456	93.2
6,000–6,999	482	12,946	93.1	165	6,621	95.6
7,000–7,999	320	13,268	95.4	95	6,716	96.9
8,000–8,999	213	13,481	96.9	63	6,779	97.8
9,000–9,999	110	13,591	97.8	51	6,830	98.6
More than 10,000	311	13,902	100.0	106	9,936	100.0

a. Median family income $1,822.
b. Median family income $1,459.
Source: U.S. Bureau of the Census, Census of Population, North Carolina (Part 35 C), 1960, adapted from Table 91, 93.

variety of purposes. Whenever particular forms of credit become associated with expansion, especially in landholdings, we usually also find
loss: even unfarmed land is ordinarily not unused. Less obviously, credit
for simple continuity of operation also becomes associated with loss
and accumulation.

In Robeson County there have been three main local sources of
credit (leaving aside federal crop-production loans, which work much
the same as local banks): banks, "supply companies," and landlords.
Since the mid-1960s banks made substantial loans for farm expansion,
particularly for consolidating scattered or even adjacent holdings into
large tracts and converting these tracts from crops to cattle or to machine-
intensive, high-volume cash crops such as soybeans. Further, banks seem
to have followed this policy on their own extensive holdings, accumulated
through mortgage default, tax auctions, and direct purchase. In such
transformations sharecroppers are frequently displaced and small farmers
lose substantial amounts of land.

Supply companies deal in farming supplies, everything from tractors
and other farm equipment to seeds, fertilizers, and insecticides and also
clothes and housewares. These are all available as advances against the
sale of the crop, with the land as surety for the loan. Supply companies,
along with banks, accumulate a lot of land. People say, perhaps apocry-
phally, that some of the supply companies have diluted fertilizer with
sand for farmers whose land they want; yet they have acquired extensive
holdings even without such illegal evils.

Landlords ordinarily made advances to their tenants against the income from the sale of the harvest. These advances – also made to some
day laborers against an anticipated harvest bonus – were for episodic
expenses such as medical bills or other necessities, and also in many
cases took the form of weekly or monthly advances for food and other
daily needs. This accumulating debt, sometimes settled at harvest,
sometimes not quite, was used to bind labor to a future year's work,
accumulating a stable work force for the landlord and constraining the
possibility that the tenant could find or negotiate a better deal elsewhere. Along with the general decline of sharecropping since the 1950s,
and the massive land loss by small farmers in the same period, this
miserable, life-sustaining, lives-imprisoning form of credit has also declined, by now almost to the point of disappearance, as it became less
and less necessary to bind or to sustain an agrarian labor force.

Farmers who lose their land often become sharecroppers, and then,
or directly, become farm day laborers, this last shift emerging in part
from the organization of the "soil bank" payment system.

Sharecropping – providing all the labor, half the seed, half the fertilizer, and all the equipment, in return for half the crop – was recognized

65

in culture, in law, and in practice as a form of tenancy that gave the sharecropper some slight claim on the farm, particularly its produce, if not on the land itself – more claim than day laborers had. This claim never amounted to very much, usually little more than the right to stay on the farm until the harvest was finished and to have a share of the harvest. Sharecropping agreements never formally extended beyond a year's duration, so any improvements the 'croppers made to the land were lost to them if they were "turned out" after the harvest. In many cases more enduring informal relations existed but with no further real surety than prior practice.

The soil bank payment system, designed to keep farm commodity prices up by diminishing supply, without the government having to buy and store surplus, paid the landowner for *not* growing specific produce. It clearly would, and did, have a devastating effect on sharecroppers: their income came only from the crop actually sold. To alleviate this problem, the soil bank regulations state that payments to landowners were to be shared with sharecroppers. While clearly not designed to be closely enforced, it was cause enough for many farm owners to convert their labor force from sharecroppers to farm day laborers, who had no claim on the soil bank payments.

A farm day laborer works for a daily wage, when and how he or she is told to, losing in the process not only an average of about a third or more of the already low earnings a sharecropper on an equal-sized farm could expect, but also all the autonomy and the decision-making dignity of "cropping." Croppers were, for the most part, farmers – farmers who decided how and where and when to plow and plant, weed and harvest, although some landlords were closely involved in such decisions. Day laborers were told what to do that day, paid at the end of the day, and told again the next day.

In addition to the wage and perhaps a small bonus at harvest sale, day laborers got a house – more likely a shack – to live in, minimally maintained by the landlord. A value for this housing was entered on the books of the farm; providing housing meant that the farm owner did not have to pay day laborers the minimum wage or anything near it. The house also meant (anthropologists these days are fond of talking about "meanings") that the day laborer could not get another job to supplement his or her income: if the farm owner came out to ask for a day's work and the laborer was not available, or not visibly sick, the family could be fired and turned out of their home on very short notice.

Sharecroppers were becoming day laborers for more reasons than the effects of the soil bank program. Chief among these further reasons were the cost of acquiring and maintaining farm equipment, relative to the value of the crop sold, and the availability and cost of credit to buy and maintain this equipment. As the price of tractors and harvesters produced in unionized factories rose much more rapidly than crop prices after World War II, it became increasingly difficult to meet one of the basic requirements for being a sharecropper, one of the conditions that separated 'croppers from day laborers – providing all the farm equipment. Ever the relatively more prosperous sharecroppers were increasingly in trouble, as were the small farm owners, and increasingly even the larger farm owners who borrowed too much at the wrong time in the volatile price curves of credit costs and crop returns. Sharecroppers and day laborers were also being turned out because the larger landowners, including the banks and supply companies, were substituting beef cattle, pecans, or other highly mechanized crops for the usual labor-intensive mix of tobacco, field corn, and some cotton or vegetables.

When the Lumbee Bank opened its new headquarters in the midst of a Lumbee shopping center on the main street of Pembroke in the spring of 1973, less than two years after it started in a small prefabricated building, it did indeed seem like the fulfillment of a dream: not only the specifically announced dreams and plans of the 1970 Red Power meeting, for these were fading almost as fast as they were realized, but the end of a nightmare. Almost every Indian family I knew or talked to in the county could tell stories of kin, close or distant, who had lost land to supply companies or banks or large-scale White landlords; could tell stories of years upon years of toil for minuscule recompense, the good years going to pay accumulated debts, the poor years calling forth intense attempts to secure further credit. Not all the stories were of loss; there were many of pride – pride in a community that pooled its resources to keep Whites from buying Indian land at tax auction, pride in families that held together and managed. Taken together, these stories wove a tapestry of constant struggle, and the backing for each tale was often the need for, or the hard-won capacity to bypass, external credit. A Lumbee bank – the Lumbee's own bank – would change all that. Among rich Indians and poor, the pride and the hope was widespread.

The fact that banks make money for their shareholders was regarded as irrelevant, and the fact that banks are legally responsible to their depositors (most of whom would also be Indians), and responsible also to various government regulatory agencies, having thus to make "sound loans": the fact that sound loans to Indians and to Blacks and poor Whites in the context of a broader social system that often makes such loans at least *seem* rather risky – all of this was, for the moment, briefly

67

acknowledged, at least in private, but pushed aside. In the context of the horrors of the credit system Indians had been confronting, it seemed, understandably, that whatever the constraints an Indian bank could be a lot fairer and more just.

What did not get discussed at all was the way the Lumbee Bank came not only from need but also from processes of class formation among the Lumbee, which created a number of affluent Indian people with the funds to invest in such an enterprise. In addition to whatever good the bank has managed to do for individuals, it has also fed and nourished that class formation, with more ambivalent effects.

Several of the affluent Lumbee had accumulated a substantial part of their wealth from land speculation: buying land from Indians offering to sell it and reselling it later to other Indians for either housing tracts or "modern" farms. They did not force the Indians who sold to sell, and they did not ordinarily pass the land from Indians to Whites. But they were making a lot of money from the social and economic transitions that were in progress. Some of this money went back to the Indian community, partly in a visible form, to church-building funds and donations to Indian candidates; partly in a less visible form, to privately help kin and neighbors; partly in an individualized form, large, well furnished houses and fancy cars. A lot of the money that went into the Indian bank had been made from other Indians, and not all these other Indians could spare it. This growing realization coexisted, however, with a widespread pride in the fact that some Indians were "making it."

The new Lumbee Bank was, in any case, in a magnificent building: lots of brick, lots of glass, carpets, all. It gave a truly wonderful, warm feeling to see and hear Indians, even the old farmers in overalls or faded print dresses called "Mister" or "Miss." Even when the teller or officer knew the customer well, the title stayed: "Miss Ruth"; "Mr. John Paul" – a southern, country practice with a rich and special significance for people there who are not White. The bank even had two drive-in windows. Despite all the windows – the plate glass on the front and side, the drive-in windows projecting out into the parking lot – the poorer Indians, and their hard-fought struggles for respect and for the minimal means to sustain respectability, were dropping from view.

5

The fires of race

The first fire in Old Main, the oldest and for a long time the only building on the campus now called Pembroke State University, was reported by a guard at 5:40 Sunday morning, March 18, 1973. Three and a half hours later, when the fire seemed extinguished, a sheriff's investigation found that "a hasp had been pried off a rear entrance and that the fire had been set in at least seven places by arsonists." But the blaze supposedly "rekindled itself," and by midafternoon Old Main was completely gutted.

While the strong smell of oil made arson obvious it was not completely clear, particularly to those Indians feeling the loss most intensely, what sort of person might have done it and, among many possibilities, what the purpose was.

Professor Adolph Dial, a Lumbee and the head of the college's Indian Studies Program, with the circumspection of his position, expressed this widespread and continuing uncertainty by quoting an anonymous poem (in his 1975 book on the history of the Lumbee, *The Only Land I Know*, coauthored with David Eliades of the History Department):

> *Some say it was White citizens,*
> *Some say it was an inside job,*
> *Others say it was the Tuscaroras,*
> *Some say it was PSU students,*
> *Still others say it was AIM.*
> *Who did it, it is done,*
> *Like the reward for the body of Henry Berry Lowery,*
> *The reward for the burning of Old Main will probably*
> *never be collected.*

The embers of hope

A reward of $5,000 had been offered by Governor Jim Holshouser, after standing on the charred steps of Old Main, holding the hand of Jaynie Maynor Locklear while speaking to a large and angry crowd of Indians, including about 150 Tuscarora, many in "war bonnets." The Tuscarora, most of whom at that time did not finish grade school, much less attend either high school or college, were there in force to defend the remains of the building from further assault, including demolition by order of the president of the university. They were very angry and difficult for the police, also there in force, to contain. Cars with Whites along the main road in front of Old Main were rocked, coming close to being rolled over, and some were stoned as well; a White-owned building at Pates stockyard was torched, along with its oil-storage facility. And it was not just the Tuscarora who were enraged.

Ms. Locklear, an influential Lumbee, had been the leader of the Save Old Main Committee, formed in early 1972 when the college president – the first Indian president since its founder, who had been presiding over the increasing modernization of the college, its increasing integration into the statewide university system, and its increasingly White student population – had announced plans to tear Old Main down to make room for a modern auditorium. She stood there with Governor Holshouser, watching the ashes of her committee's work and dreams smoulder, in the hope that something might be done.

Holshouser had been on those same steps less than a year before: in July 1972, while running for governor as "a man of the people" and the man who would be the first Republican governor of North Carolina since reconstruction. He had come to Pembroke to support the Save Old Main Committee and had also, that year before the fire, gained the support of the most militant of the Tuscarora factions, sharing a speaking platform with both Dennis Banks of the American Indian Movement (AIM), and the Tuscarora chief, Howard Brooks. Both the Tuscarora and the representatives of AIM working with the Tuscarora in Robeson County would start calling him "Whorehouser" soon after he actually won the governorship – their courtship with power transformed when they realized the marriage ring was intended to go through their nose.

The early 1970s were a time of intense turmoil over the integration of the county school systems and over their control. The Civil Rights Act of 1964 offered "freedom of choice" to pupils in the public schools as a replacement for what had become illegal forced segregation; in Robeson County most chose to stay where they were, particularly most of the Indians. As free choice increasingly gave way to specific, federally mandated plans for integrated schools, Robeson County, in 1970, was among the last places in North Carolina to have a plan for integration.

In August 1970 officials from the Robeson County Board of Education, under threat of court action for continued evasion, were forced to go to Raleigh to meet with federal officials charged with ensuring integration. The pressure was on, but in this county there were three separate school systems: White, Black, and Indian. Local Whites first tried to use Indian opposition to integration to show that segregation was not simply White-based; when that failed it seemed as if they were going to meet the government's imposed quotas and timetables for increasing integration by mashing the Indian and Black systems together and by a few other moves, such as bringing the Black varsity ball teams up to the White schools.

As we have seen in the analysis of accommodation, schools were the center of the political organization of the Lumbee, the center both of their alliances with the White power structure and of their cultural, social, and political autonomy. This autonomy was the crucial precondition for any political alliance. Separate Indian schools were a major power base for most local Indian leaders and , because the schools were both crucial to effective Indian leadership and an opening for White control over Indian communities, they were also a significant, if infrequent, reminder of the vulnerability of local Indian leaders and their communities.

Such contradictions and ambivalences introduce the special intensity of any issue concerning schools, perhaps even more intense for the Indian people of Robeson County than for Whites or Blacks. More than being a core feature of Lumbee political organization, the separate elementary and high schools have been crucial to an Indian cultural and social life: schools and churches are the places where Indians become connected to other Indians. They are not simply the *center* of the community; in fundamental ways they *are* the community.

The same Federal integration laws and policies that were pressing on the county's public schools were being used to press changes on the University of North Carolina. This university conglomerate centered itself on an almost entirely White prestige campus at Chapel Hill and spread out to a number of essentially all-Black, primarily technical and teacher-training branch campuses and a handful of local-draw, mostly White, branch campuses, also funded to be third- or fifth-rate institutions.

Between 1969 and 1971 the university system was reorganized, drawing the branch campuses – Black, White, and Pembroke – more tightly into a common administrative net and making more funds available for branch campus development. This was the context – more "development" and less of a local, special character – in which Old Main was to be torn down and replaced. At the time, Pembroke State

College, as it was then called, had slightly more than 200 Indian students, about 2,000 Whites, and a sprinkling of Blacks. The college was first opened to Whites in the early 1950s, partly to build enrollments and partly to comply with the 1954 Supreme Court decision (*Brown v. Board of Education*) on desegregation, which in North Carolina had more impact on the smaller campuses than at the core, Chapel Hill. At the time Pembroke State began to admit Whites there were also about 200 Indian students, but they were the only students at the college. Until 1945 the college had been exclusively for Lumbee Indians; it was then opened to federally recognized Indians throughout the United States – a goal for Lumbee seeking broader recognition by Native Americans, for its own sake and in support of their efforts to pursue identity claims and program benefits from the federal government.

Integration was seen by Lumbee and Tuscarora (and by many Whites and Blacks, of course) as a profound threat to their cultural identity. Their bitter and sustained protests, from court cases to the 1973 "riot" at Prospect (discussed in Chapter 4), were supported by a wide range of people who did not usually identify themselves with Lumbee interests, including U.S. Senator Sam Ervin, the White-dominated county school board, AIM, some Black politicians, and others. The Lumbee were fighting for their survival as a political group and a political force, and their struggles were being used by others to advance their own ends. Not only were their schools to be integrated into a single countywide system, but in the intensely hard-fought elections of 1968, 1970, and 1972 they had been completely unable, alone or in alliance with Blacks, to gain a controlling or even a substantially influential position on the county school board.

II

While the college was all Indian it served as a substantial source of pride and the main source of teachers for the all-Indian county schools. The college, along with each of the community-based Indian "graded" schools and the Indian high schools, also enabled the Indian people of Robeson County to define, for themselves and for others, who was and who was not an Indian. (A "graded" school is grades 1 to 8; these schools and high schools were legislatively called the "common" or "public" schools.)

Each Indian grade school, each Indian high school, and the college, while it was all Indian, had its own "blood committee." For the graded schools this was usually the local school committee; the high schools and the college usually had separate committees. From 1929 to 1945 the college blood committee was legally chartered by the state to pass judgment on the Indianness of pupils and teachers in all the Indian schools of the county, although this was ordinarily left to local committees. All the adult Indian people in Robeson County in 1973 knew about these committees and the crucial role they played in their communities, but by then few people talked about it. With the pressure of integration transforming or destroying Indian schools, the tensions and the internal dynamics that once shaped Indian schools were fading into generalizing, community-maintaining memories.

In 1929, when the Lumbee were officially still called the Cherokee Indians of Robeson County and the college was the Cherokee Indian Normal School of Robeson County, the state legislature passed an act "to codify and prescribe the racial qualification of those seeking admission into the Cherokee Indian qualification of those seeking admission into the Cherokee Indian Normal School at Pembroke, and in the common schools of Robeson County for the Indian race" (Public Laws, 1929, Chapter 195):

> *Sec. 1. That in order to protect the Public Schools in Robeson County for the education of the Indian race only, and the Cherokee Indian Normal School of Robeson County, there shall be a committee composed of Indians who are residents of Robeson County, and all questions affecting the race of those applying for admission . . .* [to these schools] *shall be referred to the committee hereinafter named, who shall have original, exclusive jurisdiction to hear and determine all questions affecting the race of any person or persons applying for admission or attending . . .* [these schools]. *All such questions coming before the County Board of Education or any School Board in Robeson County, shall be forthwith removed before said committee for hearing: Provided, however, that an appeal shall lie from the action of said committee to the Superior Court of Robeson County. . . .*

> *Sec. 7. Persons of the Indian race of Robeson County who are descendants of those . . . who were within the terms and contemplation of chapter 51, Laws 1885, and within the census taken pursuant thereto by the County Board of Education of Robeson County . . . may attend the common schools of Robeson County for the education of the Indian race only, and no others shall be admitted to said schools.*

Seven Indian men were appointed to this committee. They were given the right not only to elect their chairman and secretary, but also to perpetuate themselves by filling vacancies, although the legislature kept control of the possibility of reappointing an entirely new committee. The autonomy of the committee from the county court system, granted in 1929, was regarded as a substantial gain, for which Indians fought very hard, and it was one of the main differences between this act and the Act for the Protection of the Indian Public Schools of Robeson County of 1921 (Public Laws, Chapter 426).

From the first Indian school system created in 1885 until the mid-1960s, effective control was maintained by *local*, not countywide, Indian school committees: appeals of their decisions, which when the Croatan School System was first created were sent to the county superior court, now went to the countywide blood committee. Local committee decisions seem usually to have been sustained when appealed. Although there has been some substantial tension between local Indian leaders and countywide Indian political leaders and issues, the two most intense struggles emerged elsewhere: within the local Indian communities, and between the Indian committees and the White-dominated county and state courts and boards.

III

The issue of who could or could not attend Indian schools in Robeson County was a matter of much concern and substantial contention. The core of the issue was the social separateness of Indian people: both the clarity of the boundaries between Indian, Black and White and the boundary between different sorts of Indians.

When cases went to court the key issue was usually the historical claims forming or denying such boundaries. Out of these controversies over school attendance the Lumbee emerged as a recognized, separate group, fighting for this recognition every step of the way. In doing so they also created another, shadowlike group of Indians, who came to be known as the Smilings.

Smiling Indians emerged in Robeson County in the first two decades of the twentieth century – as Indian residents of the county who were excluded by the Lumbee – and disappeared from view in the 1960s. While Smiling origins lie deep in the colonial period, in the same firestorms and cauldrons that gave birth to the Lumbee (and the Cherokee, Catawba, and Creek) as distinct peoples, their social emergence as a distinct people in Robeson County started with a school admissions case in 1915.

In 1913 three brothers, A. A., W. W., and W. D. Goins, who were born and lived in Sumter County, South Carolina, before moving to Robeson County about 1907, sought to enroll their children in the Indian normal school. Their sister had gone to this school and was teaching in an Indian graded school in the county. Despite their sister's position and personal history, their own children were denied admission by the Indian school committee and the case went to the superior court, where they won. The normal school committee then appealed to the state supreme court. The following excerpts from the case records bring to the foreground how history was invoked, and how it became crucial to the construction of what was called a "pedigree" – a genealogy of social and ethnic relations as well as relatives.

Plaintiff's petition, superior court:

> *10. That the order* [denying admission] *adopted by the defendant, Board of Trustees, . . . was upon the alleged ground that the plaintiffs had not proved their "Pedigrees," meaning thereby that the plaintiffs had not established to the satisfaction of the said Trustees that they were of pure Indian blood. . . .*
>
> *11. That when the sister of the plaintiffs applied for admission in . . . 1908, that the Board of Trustees . . . then called upon plaintiff's family to prove . . . that they were genuine Indians of pure blood, and that the plaintiff, W. W. Goins, at said time went to Sumter County, . . . from which place he had removed to Robeson County, and secured documentary evidence . . . the Trustees of said school [then] appointed a committee to go to Sumter County, South Carolina and make investigation* [and report] *. . . and upon said report the sister of the plaintiffs was duly admitted to said school.*

From the statement of case on appeal:

> *Upon the direct examination of W. W. Goins . . . counsel for plaintiffs asked the witness . . . "What did Dr. Furman (meaning the same Dr. Furman who was a* [White] *neighbor of the plaintiffs while they were living in Sumter County, S.C.) do toward establishing the fact that you were indian people?"* (objection over-ruled) *. . . "He traced up our origin and found out that we – our parents went from North Carolina, some of the older ones, and there were a lot of names, Oxendine, Hunt, Chavis and Goins . . . he having traced them up first give me a little light and that was what I found out about it."*
> [Oxendine, Hunt and Chavis, but not Goins, are common Lumbee family names.]
>
> *. . . Fannie Chavis, witness* [the sister who went to the Normal school, questioned by counsel:] *"I ask you to look at that paper . . . and state whether or not that was the certificate they (the plaintiffs) got from the* [White] *clerk of the court . . .* [of Sumter County, S.C.] *on which you were admitted to that school?" "It is." . . . The said paper . . . was as follows:*
>
> *State of South Carolina, Sumter County.*
> *I, L. I. Parrott, Clerk of the Court for Sumter County, said state, do*

hereby certify that the families of Smilings and Goinses of this county have been known as "Red Bones" ever since I have been acquainted with the people.

Mr. McDonald Furman, now deceased, took a great deal of trouble several years ago to establish the fact that they were descendants of the indian race, which he did to his entire satisfaction, so he has told me on several occasions.

They are looked upon as a separate race, neither white nor negro.

Given under my hand and official seal this 17th day of February, A.D., 1908.

L. I. Parrott

This certificate is given at the request of W. W. Goings.

The testimony quoted below is from the plaintiffs – the Indians who were trying to gain admission to the Robeson County Indian Schools – and their witnesses:

Willie Goins: My name is W. D. Goins; I now live in Mallory, S.C.; I was living at Pembroke . . . last year. . . . I was born in Sumter County, S.C. . . . I am entering forty-one years of age; my father is still living. His name is William Goins. We belong to the indian race of people if any to my knowledge. The reputation of my family is that our ancestors came from Cumberland County, North Carolina [just to the north of Robeson County], *but I don't know anything about it. . . . Some of the families down there were Jackson Chavis, Gibbs, Goins, and Smilings and also Chavises. We were not associated with that class of people (meaning the negroes) and we pulled out from among them and built us a new church by the name of Hopewell . . . and finally there was such a few of us we couldn't do anything ourselves and we came from there . . . up here to Robeson County North Carolina. I heard of these people (meaning the indians of Robeson County) up here and knew some of them; got acquainted* [working turpentine and timber] *in Florida and Georgia and so that was our reason for coming up here. We could not get them together down there as there was such a few of us. We tried to get a school in South Carolina but we did not succeed. My wife was Elvy Chavis before she was married. She was supposed to be an indian herself* [Chavis is a Lumbee Indian name], *she is a white woman.*

W. W. Goins: I am a brother of W. D. Goins. I was born and raised in Sumter County, S.C. My mother is there. I have been living in Robeson County, N.C. for the past eight years. I have one child of school age. . . . Dr. Furman traced up our origin and found out that we – our parents went from North Carolina, some of the older ones, and there were a lot of names, Oxendine, Hunt, Chavis and Goins. Names of the families in the Indian colonies down there were Smilings, Chavis, Goins, the Oxendines are dead. Old Bill Chavis, my great grand-father went from this [Robeson] county. Tom and Bill Chavis came from Robeson and old man Goins came from Cumberland County. My wife's name was Pauline Epps. Her father was Edward Epps and her mother was Adeline Epps. Her mother was supposed to be half white and half indian.

We had a separate school for our people. Tom Hodge [a White] gave us $20.00 a month to teach the school. Had school three months in the year. . . . The school was along with the church; not of this church we drew out from, but this other church. They hired a negro preacher and that was why we drew out. We pulled out and built a church separately. None of my family – that is my sisters and brothers ever intermarried with negroes. Since we came up to North Carolina we have associated with the indian people and always went to the indian churches; been here eight years. Our church joined the Croatan [Indian Church Association of Robeson County] *Association* before we came here. . . . They made an investigation before they admitted us. Sent Rev. Blank, Rev. Gilbert Locklear, and Rev. Bell. They went to Sumter and while there went out to my father's and stayed. My sister was admitted to the Norman school. They excluded her at first but I went Sumter and got papers from the clerk showing how we were regarded and they admitted her back into the school. She attended school five years and had been teaching in the indian schools of Robeson County for five years. My father is not here at the trial. He is sick and not able to come. . . .

A. S. Locklear: I know William Goins, father of these parties. I visited them in South Carolina once about six years ago. The general reputation I got down there was that they were indian people. They were supposed to be indians. I have lived in Robeson County all my life and I am perfectly familiar with the indian people up here. From my association, being in the home of old man Goins and his family and from the investigation I have made of the people there, my opinion is that on the mother's side plaintiffs are indians and on the father's side malungeans [i.e., Indian and White]. The Rev. William Goins is not a typical indian by feature, he is a mixture between white and indian.

The reputation among the people down in South Carolina where the plaintiffs formerly lived was that Goins, Smilings and Chavis Families had no negro blood and that these families had made every endeavor to keep themselves aloof from the negro. Did not want to associate with them in churches and in schools. I attended their church while down there. . . . After my investigation and report to the churches [here] *there was never any more question raised about their race. I also know that the* [Burnt Swamp (Indian) Baptist] *Association appointed a committee to investigate it. The plaintiffs were admitted into the Burnt Swamp Baptist Association as indian people. I saw the mother of Emma Goins and she was as indian if ever I saw one. I have made considerable search into the history of the various tribes of indians in this section of the state and they are from various tribes. They are Cherokees, Tuscaroras, and Creeks.*

Lizzie Brown: I am a sister of the plaintiffs. Been living at Pates [in Robeson County] *for five years. I was raised in Sumter County, S.C. My boy goes to the public indian school at Pates. He has also gone to the Normal. We are indians in the North, but they gave us the name of "Red Bones" down there. The reputation is that there was not any negro blood in any of my ancestors, nor my father and mother.*

Fannie Chavis: I am a daughter of Emma Goins and sister of the plaintiffs. Have lived in Robeson County 8 years. I attended the Norman about four or five years, probably more. I have taught for six years. Teach in the Indian Public schools . . . ; never have taught negroes nor have ever associated in church or schools with negroes. The reputation among the people where we lived in South Carolina is that we belong to the indian race of people. My husband's name is Eli Chavis.

Eli Chavis: I am a brother-in-law of the plaintiffs and have lived in Robeson County all my life. I belong to the indian people. I investigated the race and nationality of my wife before I married and learned she belonged to the indian race. Did not look like there is any negro blood in my father in law; none at all.

Rev. J. J. Bell: I have been a minister of the gospel about twenty seven years; I have been preaching to the indian people, I belong to the indian race. I am a member of the Burnt Swamp Baptist Association, and was one of the committee appointed by the Association to investigate whether or not the Goins were indians, and whether the Hopewell church should be admitted into the association. This was several years ago. Rev. Gilbert Locklear went with me. I stayed at the Goins house while I was there (meaning Sumter County) pretty much at night. We made an investigation; that was what the Association sent me to do. We investigated among white people mostly; I did not question the indian people very much. The general reputation of those I questioned was that plaintiffs are indians, never were slaves. . . . We reported to the association that they belonged to the indian race. . . .

Hamilton McMillan, witness for the defendants: I am a resident of Robeson County; I am now seventy eight years of age. I represented Robeson County [in the state legislature] *in 1885 and 1887. I am*

> *familiar with the Act of 1885 designating certain indians of Robeson
> county as croatan indians; I introduced the bill myself. I was acquainted
> with the indians of Robeson County at the time the Act of 1885 was
> passed designating them as croatan indians. I had been investigating
> their history for several years before that. I gave them the designation
> of croatan indians in the Act. I wanted to give them some designation.
> There was a tribe known as croatan tribe on croatan island, it was an
> honorable name and it was a complete designation. . . .*
>
> *The indians designated as croatan indians were living in Robeson
> County. . . . none of them lived in Sumter, S. C. as far as I know. . . .
> I had the Act of 1887 passed to establish a normal school for the
> croatan indians of Robeson County. . . .
> Question by the court: Do these people here call themselves croatans?
> A. No sir. They call themselves malungeans. . . .
> Q. Were they never called croatans until this Act was introduced in
> here? A. No sir.
> Q. Where were they from anyway? A. The traditions all point to their
> residence west of Pamlico Sound, beyond Cape Hatteras* [in the north-
> ern part of North Carolina].

The plaintiffs won – they were Indians of Robeson County in the eyes
of the court – but the county replied by building them a separate
school: an Indian school in the midst of their "settlement" area, but a
school for different Indians. Centered on their school and their local
church, for the next half-century they were regarded as a distinct and
separate people, called Smilings. A fourth "race," as local people called
them, was born in Robeson County.

The Smilings – the predominant family names, by the mid-twentieth
century, were Smiling and Epps; Smiling is the family name most different from familiar Robeson County surnames – lived a rather socially
isolated life in the southwestern part of Robeson County. They had the
reputation of working hard on their land and of trying, even more than
usual for poor farmers and sharecroppers, to be self-sufficient in the
cycle of production and consumption. Many seemed to stay out of cash
exchange relations (and also credit relations) as much as possible. They
often bartered, with merchants and others, from crops they produced
for goods they needed.

Several accumulated modestly good-sized farms, by local standards,
although their diminished presence in the local cash economy made it
unclear to the surrounding Lumbee if they were, in daily life, rather
poor or not. In 1958 the county built them a new school, replacing the
dilapidated building they had been using. This new school required a
substantial amount of "sweat equity" – contributory labor – by the Smiling

community. It had three teachers, counting the principal who also taught the twenty or so high school students all of their classes; the other two teachers taught grades 1–3 and 4–8.

By the mid-1960s such schools were no longer considered viable, and the "Smilings" lost their separate school, and with that much of their separate identity. While they are not now completely part of the Lumbee people, they no longer seem to have a special social identity.

The relative shortness of their collective life with a socially institutionalized identity – about a half-century from their birth to their decline as a separate Indian people within the county – highlights the centrality of domination, intersecting with specific claims and needs, in the historical formation and historical "career" of diverse and divergent ethnic peoples. The Smilings' history also raises important and revealing issues about systems of "race" and ethnic divisions in the southern United States.

In local areas throughout the south, much more often than is widely recognized or thought about, more than two "races" or ethnic groups are socially recognized – sometimes three, sometimes four, with the fourth often changing its composition and social position: note the suggestive emergence of the Tuscarora shortly after the decline of the Smilings as a separate group. It may well be that the intersection of class and culture, domination and claim, cannot often or simply be expressed, at the local level, through a social and cultural division into two races or ethnic groups. This is an issue that calls out for further research and focused analysis, for what it is likely to reveal about ethnicity and the emergence of races as expressions of the historically developing logic of domination based upon difference and distance imposed from above and claimed from below.

IV

Behind this case, and cited at key points in it, was a series of legislative acts that usually came in pairs: one act establishing a legal name and legal rights for the Indian people of Robeson County, the other concerning Indian schools.

On March 11, 1913, the legislature passed Chapter 123 of the Public laws of North Carolina, "An Act to restore to the Indians residing in Robeson and adjoining counties their rightful and ancient name, Cherokee Indians of Robeson County." The act asserted that this name shall not entitle them to "any benefits or rights" of the Cherokee Indians in the mountain counties in the western part of the state, but it continued all the benefits and rights that they had as "Indians of Robeson

County" and as "Croatans." Further, the act changed the name of the Normal School to the Cherokee Indian Normal School of Robeson County. The next day, the legislature passed Chapter 199, Public Laws, 1913, appropriating $2,250 for the Cherokee Indian Normal School, and a further $1,000 over the next two years – the first substantial amounts of money that the state had given.

Although the money was increasing, it was still not enough to run an effective teacher-training institution: and although the school was called a normal (which means teacher-training) school, it in fact awarded its first high school degree in 1912, and only four more in the next ten years; actual normal school status in the state educational system came in 1928.

Two years earlier, in 1911, the state passed another pair of laws on the same day. The first, Chapter 168, accepted the transfer of the deed to the school property from the trustees of the school to the state board of education – a school building that had been constructed largely by the labors and donations of the Indian people themselves – and instructed the state board of education to appoint "seven members of the Indian race" to the new board of trustees of the normal school, whose name was changed from Croatan State Normal School to the Indian Normal School of Robeson County. The act gave the trustees *"the power to employ and discharge teachers, to prevent negroes from attending said school, and to exercise the usual functions of control and management of said school, their actions being subject to the approval of the State Board of Education."*

The records of the normal school were, however, kept with the Division of Negro Education of the state's Department of Public Instruction; the state had its own agenda for the separation of Blacks and Indians. Indians of course knew this, and fought it: in 1931 they pressured for and act to be passed requiring the records of the Indian schools to be kept separately (Chapter 141, Public Laws 1931).

The second act passed in 1911 – on the same day that the state took title to the Indian Normal School, Chapter 215 of the Public Laws – was "An Act to change the name of the Indians in Robeson County and to provide for said Indians separate apartments in the State Hospital." It officially changed the name of the people from the now distasteful Croatan to Indians of Robeson County, gave them separate wards at the state hospital for the insane and instructed the county authorities to provide "in the common jail . . . and in the Home for the Aged and Infirm . . . separate cells, wards or apartments for the said Indians." By 1911 the separation of Indians, Blacks, and Whites was fully institutionalized – or as fully as might be done in the broader legal, social, and cultural contexts of the southern United States.

V

The focal issue in the political culture of domination and, simultaneously, assertion and accommodation, was the separateness of the Indian people of Robeson County: separateness from Blacks and Whites both in the history that was invoked and in the future that was being built into school buildings and jails, hospitals and old-age homes. But alongside this separateness came an imposed and also asserted deference to Whites and to the White power structure. The Goins case shows us witness after witness invoking past efforts for separate churches, separate schools, separate social ties, separate marriages, and separate ancestors, and yet crucial to the case and to the prior acceptance of the plaintiffs' sister by the Indian normal school committee was the testimony of two Whites: the clerk of the court of Sumter County and Dr. Furman. In the same vein – or to use a more active metaphor, artery – when the Indian ministers were sent from Robeson County to see if Hopewell Church should be admitted into the Burnt Swamp [Indian] Baptist Association, they noted that "we investigated among whites mostly."

Further complexities in the role of Whites in the social construction of Indian separateness, and the accompanying histories, are suggested in the testimony of Hamilton McMillan, who as senator in the state legislature of 1885 sponsored the legislation that accorded the Indian people of Robeson County legal recognition as Indians and also provided – actually invented, as Whites have invented *all* "tribal" names for native Americans – their first official name: Croatan. The name was a transformation of what he claimed they called themselves (both Croatan and Melungean refer to a prior intermixture with Whites; the first specific, the second general) but McMillan's new name fit with the capsule "history" that he wrote into the preamble of the act:

> *Whereas the Indians now living in Robeson County claim to be the descendants of a friendly tribe who once resided in eastern North Carolina on the Roanoke River, known as the Croatan Indians; therefore, The General Assembly of North Carolina do enact:*
> *Sec. 1. That the said Indians and their descendants shall hereafter be designated and known as the Croatan Indians.*
> *Sec. 2. That said Indians and their descendants shall have separate schools for their children, school committees of their own race and color, and shall be allowed to select teachers of their own choice, subject to the same rules and regulations as are applicable to all teachers in the general school law.* [Laws of North Carolina, 1885, Chapter 51]

It was a new kind of social separateness that began to be institutionalized in 1885, with separate grade schools and school committees, which within two years blossomed into a separate normal school and a separate miscegenation act:

> *All marriages between an Indian and a negro or between an Indian and a person of negro descent to the third generation, inclusive, shall be utterly void:* Provided, *This act shall only apply to the Croatan Indians.* [Laws of North Carolina, 1887, Chapter 254]

To understand the transformations that were occurring at the end of the nineteenth century and in the early years of the twentieth, we must see the institutionalized separateness (and, simultaneously, the essential deference to Whites and the White power structure) in two contexts: first, the loss of Indian-owned land, which undermined one of the mainstays of actual Indian autonomy; second, the fact that the Croatan people and the "Jim Crow" legislation that systematically and increasingly institutionalized both segegation and racism came into being at about the same time.

Indeed, the principal objection that the Indians had to the name Croatan, which by 1911 their mounting protests managed to have officially changed, was that local people shortened it to "Cro." Indians were increasingly asserting their autonomy at the same historical point when there was a massive intensification of segregation and the debasing humiliation that is segregation's constant servant. The two processes were deeply intermingled: increasing Indian and Black claims for autonomy and increasing repression fed off each other. The chosen separation of the Indians from both Whites and Blacks was partly an agreement with dominant White values and also an attempt to create a profound distance from these destructive ways.

To *claim* segregated facilities – schools in particular – conceals some of the assault on autonomy, but not all, for Indians were still segregated as an intensely disadvantaged people. The tensions of the twin birth of Croatan and Jim Crow were neither resolved nor concealed by Indian name-changing, nor by the few dollars given in support of "pure-blood" Indian schools.

VI

In 1913 the Indians of Robeson County, continually frustrated in their attempt to get the state to fund the normal school at any operationally effective level, turned (unsuccessfully) to the federal government for aid. In the hearings before the House Committee on Indian Affairs (in re S. 3258, Feb 14, 1913), the issue of Indian land ownership was raised, intermixed with questions and comments about their "blood," their education, and their political rights – intermixed in ways that hint at the conjunction of political disfranchisement and land loss. The

The embers of hope

conservative North Carolina Senator, Furnifold Simmons, is testifying on behalf of the Indians:

> *Mr. Burke. Are any of them full bloods?*
> *Sen. Simmons. Yes; there is one of them behind you.*
> *The Chairman. Are they voters, Senator?*
> *Sen. Simmons. They are voters now. Under our* [N.C.] *constitution, up to 1835 all freemen were permitted to vote.*
> *Under that term "freemen" the Indians of Robeson County exercised the right of suffrage. In 1835 we substituted for the word "freeman" the word "white." In 1868, when the new constitution was adopted, they came in and voted as the colored people of the state were allowed to vote. . . .*
> *Mr. Miller. They have real estate as well as personal property?*
> *Sen. Simmons. Yes, sir.*
> *Mr. Miller. They hold their property in severalty?* [individually]
> *Sen. Simmons. Yes, sir.*
> *Mr. Hayden. And they did not get it from the government?*
> *Sen. Simmons. No sir. We do not know exactly how they did acquire it. The title is now based upon possession so long that the State presumes a grant. . . .*
> *Mr. Miller. Do you happen to have anything to show the total value of their property?*
> *Sen. Simmons. I do not know, but Mr. McLean here can give you an approximation.*
> *Mr. McLean. I could not tell you the taxable property, but some of them own small farms; a large percent of them do not own real estate. . . .*
> *Mr. Burke. How did they acquire the land?*
> *Sen. Simmons. They acquired it by possession. They were there before the revolution.*
> *Mr. Campbell. Before the white man came.*
> *Sen Simmons. Before the white man came; and by reason of the fact that they had acquired some land there and by reason of the fact that the white people sustained a most kindly feeling toward them up until the close of the* [Revolutionary] *war. . . .*
> *Mr. Campbell. Would it not be more proper to put it that the land they now hold is a part of the land held by the American Indians that the white man has not yet taken from him?*
> *Sen. Simmons. That is the correct way of putting it.*
> *Mr. Hayden. That is the only example in the United States.*
> *Mr. McLean. I should say there are several thousand acres.*
> *Most of them settled on it time out of mind, They have divided those tracts up into small tracts, probably 25 or 50 or 75 acres. . . .*

84

> *Mr. Burke, questioning Mr. Locklear* [an Indian from the county, who came to witness and to testify]. *What portion of you have farms?*
> *Mr. Locklear. Well, about 25 per cent of them own small farms, anywhere from 1 acre to 25 or 50 acres.*

Forty-one years earlier, in 1872, H. W. Guion, a lawyer resident in Robeson County, testifying in the U.S. Senate on conditions in the county before the Civil War, said:

> *Well, right in that neighborhood, now, were between two and three thousand, all in one body, living by themselves. They were very innocent and inoffensive in those days, before the war; they had their own body of land together; they were very poor.*

They were poor, indeed, but still more self-sufficient upon their land than Guion liked:

> *They are a very worthless, trifling people, or they were when I knew them, seven or eight years ago. I was president of a railroad, and we were building a railroad through the county; and I wanted to get these people to dig a canal. But they were so lazy, I could not get them to work until bacon [pork] got up to 25 cents a pound, and then they would go out and work just long enough to get a little bacon and then they would carry it away.*

Throughout the south, the last two decades of the nineteenth century were, as C. Vann Woodward points out, the high point of positive relations between Whites and Blacks and simultaneously of lynching. By the late 1890s the positive sentiments and practices were nearly all gone, leaving brutality alone and victorious. To take only one of many possible markers of this profound reduction, *Plessy* v. *Ferguson*, the U.S. Supreme Court's legitimation of the concept of "separate but equal," was decided in 1896. Under the triple pressures of an extended and severe agrarian depression, the attempts of conservative Democrats to undermine populism's success by racist appeals for White unity and by pressuring Blacks to vote against White populists, and the increasingly institutionalized physical segregation, Black people were being disenfranchised not just as citizens but once again as people.

The rapidly developing new discourse on domination was punctuated by episodes of large-scale violence: in 1898, in the city of Wilmington, North Carolina, just east of Robeson County, a mob led by a former congressman torched the Black neighborhoods, killing and wounding and driving hundreds out of the city. In this context for a people to publicly assert their separateness and their differences from Blacks might seem to make some kind of cruel sense, but to appreciate the fuller paradoxes of the Croatans' situation several other dimensions, both external and internal, must be indicated.

While the whole culture behind Jim Crow pressed down brutally on Black aspirations, it also intentionally and specifically squashed Indians. In 1900 Albert J. Beveridge, an immensely popular senator, put the issue of denying Indians their rights in the most forceful way, in his Senate speech calling for the colonization of the Philippines after the Spanish-American war. Opponents of recolonizing Spain's former colony had invoked the Declaration of Independence: "We hold these truths to be self-evident: that all men are created equal, that they are endowed by their Creator with certain inalienable rights, among these being life, liberty and the pursuit of happiness." Beveridge, on the floor of the Senate, replied:

> *It will be hard for Americans who have not studied them* [the Philippines] *to understand the people. They are a barbarous race, modified by three centuries of contact with a decadent race* [the Spanish]. *The Filipino is the South Sea Malay, put through a process of three hundred years of superstition in religion* [*i.e.*, Catholicism], *dishonesty in dealing, disorder in habits of industry, and cruelty, caprice, and corruption in government. It is barely possible that 1,000 men in all the archipelago are capable of self-government in the Anglo-Saxon sense....*
>
> *... What alchemy will change the oriental quality of their blood and set the self-governing currents of the American pouring through their Malay veins? How shall they, in a twinkling of an eye, be exalted to the heights of self-governing peoples which required a thousand years for us to reach, Anglo Saxon though we are?...*
>
> *The Declaration* [of Independence] *applies only to people capable of self-government. How dare any man prostitute this expression of the very elect of self-governing peoples to a race of Malay children of barbarism, schooled in Spanish methods and ideas? And you, who say the Declaration applies to all men, how dare you deny its application to the American Indian? And if you deny it to the Indian at home, how dare you grant it to the Malay abroad?*

VII

In addition to the new kinds of vulnerability Indian people of Robeson County increasingly faced at the point when they became legislatively recognized as Indians – an intensifying vulnerability as non-Whites and a new vulnerability as Indians – the issue of separateness from Blacks also tore into the fabric of family and community relations. Earlier in the nineteenth century, as we shall see subsequently in the discussion of the Henry Berry Lowrie war, the very survival of the Indian people depended in large part on close and intimate relations with Blacks

86

and with poor Whites, rather than with the White political and economic elite, as well as a communal social organization centering on the
possession of land. When all this was lost, new kinds of family and communal tensions emerged, tensions that can be illustrated in the suit of
"Jacob Moll" against the Prospect community school committee (Croatan
District 4 in the new Indian school system), a committee headed by
Preston Locklear, Jacob Moll's wife's brother. (Jacob Moll is a pseudo-
nym, borrowed from my own family names, as the wounds of this issue
are still wide open over a century later.)

On September 3, 1888, J. A. McAllister, clerk of the County Board of
Education, which oversaw all the White, Black, and Indian common
schools in the county, wrote:

> *It is ordered by the board of education that [Jacob Moll] be assigned
> to Croatan District No. 4, and the committee of said district are hereby
> directed to receive his children into the public schools of said district. By
> order of the board of education.*

Two issues were at stake when the case went to court: the issue of the
autonomy of the local Indian school committee, which presumably had
been given the power to decide who could attend their school, and who
could teach, and the issue of whether Jacob Moll's children qualified.
Although most of the case focused on the second issue, the Indian
committee kept trying to force the issue of their rights to the foreground.

The state by this time was considering someone "Negro" if they had
"negro blood within the fourth degree." While Jacob Moll's wife was
clearly a Croatan Indian, Moll, as the North Carolina Supreme Court
stated,

> *was a slave before 1865,* [thus] *we think the charge that he was pre-
> sumed to be a negro was unquestionably correct. While they were in
> bondage there was no such thing known among the slaves as comput-
> ing degrees of removal from white ancestors.*[!] *For all purposes, the
> law regarded them all as negroes. . . . We will not consider the testi-
> mony tending to show that those persons (the Croatans) were, in fact,
> of negro descent or were formerly called mulattoes.*

Let us put aside the question of actual historical intermarriages of
Indian people with Whites and Blacks, noting that *all* Indian peoples
throughout the southeast have substantially intermixed with both Black
and White people: the Cherokee had a major dispute with the
Charlestown colony in 1715, Charlestown demanding the return of
"runaway slaves," the Cherokee saying that it was their wives and hus-
bands that were asked for; the Seminole war was fought so successfully
by the Indians because it was, in fact, based on a combined force of
Seminole and Black warriors; Scotsmen played an important role within

the Cherokee tribe, and so forth. Let us also put aside the clear historical lie that all slaves were Negro, which denies not only the very large
number of Indians who were enslaved but also a substantial number of
Whites, including the 80,000 Irish shipped off as slaves to the Caribbean after the English conquest, where the descendants of these slaves
were known as "red legs." The point at issue here is the creation of
"Indian" and "Negro" as cultural, legal, and political-economic categories, and *why* some folks, such as the Seminole and Cherokee, who were
probably neither more nor less intermarried with Whites and Blacks
than the ancestors of the Lumbee, are unambiguously categorized as
Indians, and why some folks, such as the Croatan-Lumbee, have had to
fight for this recognition. And the issue here is not just *why* but *what*
this struggle entailed.

During the Moll case, J. C. McEachin, a White witness for the Prospect
school committee's defense, testified: "The people now designated as
Croatans were called mulattoes up to the passage of the Croatan act,
but were always a separate race to themselves." "Mulatto," as some local
Whites were calling the Croatan people, means a mixture of White and
Black. "Malungeon," which Hamilton McMillan testified the people
called themselves, means a mixture of White and Indian. The name
that McMillan gave them, "Croatan," refers also to a presumed history
that combines White and Indian: Croatoan is the name of the place
Sir Walter Raleigh's "lost colony" set out to reach when, isolated from
contact with England between 1586 and 1590, they abandoned their
fortress home on Roanoke Island. John White, the governor of the
colony, went back to England in 1587, shortly after the colonists were
settled. Returning in 1590 he wrote:

> *[A]ccording to a secret token agreed upon between them and me at my
> last departure from them, which was that in any way they should not
> fail to write or carve on the trees or posts of the doors, the name of the
> place where they should be seated; for at my coming away they were
> prepared to remove from Roanoke fifty miles into the main. . . . [W]e
> passed through the place where they were left in sundry houses, but we
> found the houses taken down and the place very strongly enclosed with
> a high palisade of great trees with curtains and flankers, very fort like,
> and one of the chief trees or posts at the right side of the entrance had
> the bark taken off, and five feet from the ground, in fair capital letters
> was graven "CROATOAN" without any cross or sign of distress.*

This event, plus the fact that some of the surnames of the people
now called Lumbee and Tuscarora are the same as those of the lost
colony (but these also were common English surnames) became interwoven into the historical claims of a substantial number of Lumbee and

of White advocates for the Indian people of Robeson County, including Hamilton McMillan. The federal legislation that granted recognition (without benefits) and the name Lumbee invokes this history in its preamble:

> *Whereas many Indians now living in Robeson and adjoining counties are descendants of that once large and prosperous tribe which occupied the lands along the Lumbee River at the time of the earliest white settlement in that section; and*
>
> *Whereas at the time of their first contact with the colonists, these Indians were a well-established and distinctive people living in European-type houses in settled towns, and communities, owning slaves and livestock, tilling the soil, and practicing many of the arts and crafts of European civilization, and*
>
> *Whereas by reason of tribal legend, coupled with a distinctive appearance and manner of speech and the frequent recurrence among them of family names such as Oxendine, Locklear, Chavis, Drinkwater, Bullard, Lowery, Sampson and others, also found on the roster of the earliest English settlements, these Indians may, with considerable show of reason, trace their origin to an admixture of colonial blood with certain coastal tribes of Indians. . . .*

The Tuscarora, the most recent of a number of groupings of Indian people in Robeson County, including many who have accepted the name Lumbee, bitterly resent and resist this history, claiming descent from Indians, not Indians and Whites. But whatever ancestral history is claimed or imposed, the key issue from the end of the nineteenth century to the present has been autonomy and being able to assert and maintain some collective self-determination in alliance with, or in opposition to, the interests of politically and economically powerful Whites.

From the point where the Indian people of the county became Croatans in 1885 until the effective and widespread imposition of school integration in 1973, the major arena for publicly asserted and recognized self-determination was the schools. The Indians may have been "awarded" this form of self-determination by the legislature, but as the Jacob Moll case made evident in its long trek to the state supreme court, they had to struggle constantly to defend their self-determination against attack and encroachment. The local White power structure may not have had any legislative basis for challenging Indian self-determination, but they challenged and encroached nonetheless: J. A. McAllister, the County Board of Education Clerk (that is, the board's secretary), who wrote and signed the order to admit Moll's children, testified:

> *[McAllister] . . . said the signature was his. Thought the order had been read to the Board of Education – was not sure – the matter was discussed but no regular order was made, the Board not being certain*

they had the power to make one. No order in relation to the matter was ever recorded in the minutes – do record all the orders of the Board in a book kept for that purpose – the Board took no vote on that matter – it was done simply to try to arrange the differences between them without intending that it should be enforced as an official order.

The Croatan school committee won the case, preserving and enhancing their capacity to decide who may and may not attend their school – but it was a victory not only over the White county school board but also over kinship: a bitter struggle in the central Indian community of Prospect between Preston Locklear, the head of the Prospect school committee, and his sister (who was married to Jacob Moll), echoes of which still reverberate; a victory over his own nephews; a wedge driven into his sister's marriage. Pounding on this wedge was not simply Preston Locklear, or just the legal issue of local Indian self-determination, but a changing social reality. The days when an Indian–Black alliance was crucial to the well-being of each – an alliance that reached its high point from 1864 to 1884 – were now gone, to be resurrected in a completely different form in the civil and voting rights struggles of the 1960s. The place of this alliance was taken by a constantly challenged, institutionalized separateness, an assertive Indianness ambiguously allied with and opposed to White domination and centered on control over local schools in the Indian communities, and the Indian college that supplied Indian teachers for these schools.

Burning Old Main – and the previous threats to demolish it in the cause of modernization – along with the imposed integration of community schools, *was thus rightly seen as an attack on the Lumbee and Tuscarora's Indianness itself, an attack on history become social identity.* Tuscarora were out defending the charred exterior walls of Old Main alongside the Pembroke State College Indian alumni in the Save Old Main Committee because it was their identity as Indians, as well as that of the Lumbee, that was under assault, under threat of demolition.

6

The embers of Hope, Inc.

I

The day after old Main burned, with the acrid smell of charred wood still heavy in the air around Pembroke, Henry Ward Oxendine, the first Indian to become a state representative, took his seat as a legislator in the North Carolina House of Representatives. He was still a student in law school and was the vice-chairman of Robeson County's district Democratic Party. He had just been appointed by the district party's executive committee to fill out the unexpired term of Frank White, who died in office the week before.

There was more than smoke in the air. It was nearly three weeks since two hundred heavily armed Indians associated with the American Indian Movement took and held the village of Wounded Knee, South Dakota. AIM was in the air, and it seemed to many people in the county that Red Power was smouldering in the acrid ashes of Old Main. The local White-owned newspapers were smeared with heavy black ink across the front pages: President Allende in Chile, taking his country back from U.S. corporations; "Black September" killing three diplomats in the Sudan, including two "Americans," the Irish Republican Army blowing up British Army barracks. And right up front, along with all the other "terrorist" challenges to moderation and traditional forms of organizing rule over subject peoples, was what the *Robesonian* was calling the "tepee peace talks" out in South Dakota, which, with the defiant intransigence of the Sioux, were not unfolding the way peace talks with Indians usually did.

During this same three weeks between the seizure of Wounded Knee (February 27, 1973) and the seating of Henry Ward Oxendine (March 19), the Concerned Parents Organization – a group opposing

91

the integration of Indian schools, and the group from which the Tuscarora had emerged as a people three years earlier – was also on the move in the county, to the state House in Raleigh, and some even out to Wounded Knee to join or support the occupation.

Lumbee as well as Tuscarora were going to Raleigh. When a car caravan of forty or fifty Lumbee showed up in the state capital on March 12, they were given a number of promises: that there would be an Indian, probably Henry Ward Oxendine, appointed to the state House, that there would be public, open hearings on the Robeson County schools and that the county school board would be expanded from seven to thirteen members, with six seats "reserved" for people from "out in the county" (a proposal that was quickly dropped). The legislators making the promises and the Lumbee listening were pretending to be looking ahead to a brighter future; both had at least one eye looking back over their shoulder to the Tuscarora, who had come to Raleigh the week before in larger numbers than the Lumbee, asked for more, got even less, and left enraged.

On March 6, only one tense week after the occupation of Wounded Knee, a caravan of 150 Indians, mostly Tuscarora and their supporters, went from Robeson County to the state legislature in support of a bill to break the "double voting" of town residents in the predominantly Indian county school elections. The same night a hundred Tuscarora – perhaps some of the same people, on their way back from being rebuffed in Raleigh – drove through Lumberton, honking their horns, running red lights, and breaking the windows out of downtown stores. They were demonstrating in support of Wounded Knee and against the rebuff in Raleigh. And before they left Raleigh they promised to come back, a thousand strong, demanding at the very least to be heard on the issue of Indian control of Indian schools.

So when H. W. Oxendine went to the state House, it looked to some like the fulfillment of a dream – an Indian in the legislature, on the right side of the door that demonstrators were constantly being pushed or escorted through.

The problem was that the local White elite, who were largely responsible for putting H. W. Oxendine in the state House, had their own dreams. The day after the Red Power meeting in Pembroke, May 25, 1970 – a meeting triggered by the total, humiliating losses in that May's Democratic primary elections; a meeting drawing the largest and most emotionally intense crowd since the 1958 routing of the Ku Klux Klan – the *Robesonian* actually called for White support for the future election of one of three named Indian "leaders." The paper noted, after giving capsule biographies of each (omitting the fact that they all worked at a job controlled by Whites and that none of them had been active in the past decade's civil rights and election struggles) "each is tall, affable, and has a pleasing countenance." Henry Ward Oxendine was not on this list, but he was sufficiently affable to be appointed. Whether he was tall and pleasing or short and dark did not turn out to matter as much as the fact that he was young and very inexperienced in the struggle for Indian rights, at a time when the county was a pressure cooker with the Indians' continual losses, in the midst of the whole civil rights ferment, plugging the vent.

II

The most explosive and intense specifically political issue that spring was double voting for the county school board, which continually ensure the election of a White-dominated board. Behind double voting and adding substantially to its effectiveness, was the further practice of making "single-shot" voting impossible – and when single-shot voting was legalized, of constructing the ballot so that it still seemed impermissible.

Single-shot voting was outlawed in Robeson County in 1956. In 1958, when for the first time since reconstruction a Black ran for office – a popular minister, who tried for the Lumberton City Council – this new regulation against single-shot voting prevented his election. It worked like this:

Suppose there are, say, 1,100 Whites who vote, and 1,000 Blacks. There are four vacancies on the town council (or the county school board, or any multiposition election). In the May Democratic primary, which is the crucial election, five Whites and one Black file nominations. There are now six names on the primary ballot, and the four with the most votes will be the Democratic party's slate in the November elections – assured of victory all through the twentieth century, until the Republicans became a force in the county around 1980.

The anti-single-shot rule says that in order for your ballot to be counted you *must* vote for as many candidates as there are positions to be filled: in this instance, four positions.

Let us be generous, and say that of the 1,100 White voters 100 will vote for the Black candidate, Mr. B. B now has 100 votes. These same 100 White voters who voted for the Black candidate *each* have to vote for three more candidates, so the White candidates – W1, W2, W3, W4 and W5 – will split 300 votes. The totals so far look like this:

B	100
W1	60
W2	60
W3	60
W4	60
W5	60

Now the other 1,000 White voters, who will not vote for a Black even by mistake, come and each cast votes for four candidates. They will divide, let's say equally, their 4,000 votes among the five White candidates, who will get 800 each. The totals now look like this:

B	100
W1	860
W2	860
W3	860
W4	860
W5	860

Now it's the turn of the Black voters. Full of pleasure and hope at the chance to elect a Black person, they resist all efforts to buy or pressure their votes, and all vote for the Black candidate, who now has 1,100 votes and for a brief moment is leading the field. But they *must* each vote for three more candidates for their vote to be counted, and so they divide their 3,000 votes among the five Whites, 600 each. The final score is

B	1,100
W1	1,460
W2	1,460
W3	1,460
W4	1,460
W5	1,460

The four winners will be drawn from this list, depending on variations in their popularity. Mr. Black, or as he will now again be called, after all the work, danger, and dreams tied to the election, boy, has his 1,100 votes and his chance to try again, and again, and again.

It was never clear when the anti-single-shot regulation was repealed nor, because it seemed so blatantly unconstitutional – forcing you to vote for people you did not want to win – was it fully clear why no one tried to challenge the rule in the courts. The rule was definitely in effect in 1968, the first election that the Indians and Blacks together stood any real chance of winning, and it was still effective in the May 1970 Democratic primary, when the ballot for the state House of Representatives said "vote for four," and for the county Board of Education it said "vote for three." It remained unclear, to say the least, whether you *may* vote for four or three or, in order to have your ballot counted, you *must*.

What the anti-single-shot rule did was to make it impossible for Indians and Blacks to go for a piece of the pie – one or two non-Whites inside the power groups: one or two of the seven county commissioners, one or two of the seven school board members. To run fewer candidates (or more) than the number of positions there were to fill was to guarantee loss. During the winter of 1967–68 I explained the above figures at several Indian and Black political meetings, but I had neither the sense to realize that the situation would always be impossible, nor the sense or resources to mobilize a court case.

In the heady, optimistic days of the 1960s civil rights movements it seemed to both Indian and Black activists as if the way to deal with this situation was to go for it all: If there were four vacancies for county commissioner, put up four candidates – two Indians and two Blacks, ideally, each being voted for by both – and let the Whites run whoever they wanted, but hopefully more than four, so they would split their vote. This is what the Indians and Blacks decided to do in the winter of 1967–8. It was tried in the primary election of 1968, and again in 1970.

Not allowing single-shot voting encouraged totalizing the confrontation. The losses for Indians and Blacks in 1968 and 1970 were thus also felt to be more total – more total than just all the candidates in multi-position elections.

III

The extraordinarily intense effort at voter registration between 1965 and 1968 brought the number of registered non-White voters to numerically equal strength with the White voters, and this relative proportion held steady as the numbers drifted upward between 1968 and 1972. It was not until the mid-1970s that Indians and Blacks moved decisively ahead, but by that time the Indian and Black politics of combined confrontation had been transformed into a combination of individualism, more tentative alliance, and more separate dreams.

The registration figures presented in Table 4 are perhaps more difficult to see into than they seem at first glance. Knowing how little followed directly from them, they now seem slightly flat. But they were then the galactic climax, scary and sweet, of a long-suffering passion bred from centuries of imposed public dishonor, punctuated by glimmers of chance.

But more than just registration numbers determine elections. Both sides understood in the late 1960s that turnout would be crucial, and an intense effort was put into getting a large percentage of the Indians and Blacks to go and vote, but to do so in ways that would conceal what

Table 4. *Voter Registration, Robeson County*

	Spring 1974	Spring 1972	Spring 1968	Fall 1965
White	18,850	15,672	13,401	11,868
Indian + Black	23,474	15,524	13,408	7,110
Black	10,123	6,755	5,893	3,093
Indian	13,351	8,769	7,515	4,017

was happening until the last possible minute. Whites might then be less likely to respond with an equally intense effort, but rather would count on the historically low turnout of registered non-White voters to continue, and so themselves make only modest efforts.

In one key precinct election, in 1968, it worked like this: The polls in North Carolina opened at 6 a.m., and at 6 p.m. they closed and the doors were locked; anyone inside the polling place when the doors were closed could vote but no one else could enter. All day long, from early in the morning, Blacks and Indians were brought to houses and a church near the polling place. Three people would enter and then one would leave; four or five would enter and two would leave. Some of those who left went and voted, so all day long there was a trickle of Black and Indian votes cast. Just after 5:30 p.m., when it was too late for the Whites to mobilize, well over a hundred people "marched into the polling place," ready to vote. Some were kept there until past 11 p.m., as the poll officials invoked one challenge after another, one delay after another, but almost everyone got to vote. It was ecstasy; the election was ours.

After the voting ended, when it was time to count the ballots, they threw the Indian and Black observers out, wanting to count the ballots privately. The observers protested, they shouted, they threatened suit, they pounded on the door – ballot counting is by law public, and people are allowed to watch – so they were let back in, a few minutes later. The ballots were counted and we lost.

Later, I asked a White politician "in the know" how it was done. He said it was simple. All our ballots were on the top of the box, since we had voted last. They kicked our watchers out, scooped up a couple of handfuls of ballots, which got tossed into the drawer of the desk on which the ballot box sat, and let our people back for the count.

Story after story, dream after dream. The stories could continue, but the dreams had to give way.

Beyond such stories, and contributing powerfully to the certainty of loss, was the process of political choice, particularly among the poorer rural Indians. Large turnout or small, deceptions or none, it was in fact difficult to keep Indian voters in the combined Indian and Black camp, not simply because of the pressure that could be put on them, but also because the appeal of White candidates could be quite strong. Paternalism and a stream of small favors loom large when people go to vote. Some White officeholders did indeed extend themselves to do favors for Indian and Black people – the kinds of the favors and interventions that get noticed and talked about. It was never "pure confrontation"; not even the activists wanted that. And it was not easy to talk to someone about a relatively abstract issue such as differential funding for schools when they had a personal favor done for them, a contribution made to their church's building fund, a reckless or drunk driving charge dropped, a handshake that went with a hello by name and a direct, person-to-person request for their vote.

Underneath these politics with a personal touch lay the structure of double voting discussed above, which ensured that control of the county school board remained in White hands by permitting town residents to vote in both town and county school board elections. The reality of the voting process was that even if the combined numbers of Indians and Blacks were somewhat larger than the number of White voters, the Whites would win: numbers had to be quite substantially in favor of Indians and Blacks. Most of the Whites in the county lived in the towns, and they had to be excluded from the county elections if politics were to bring Indians any rewards.

Sitting in on an Indian strategy meeting as the 1968 May primary election drew near and the leaders struggled to keep a common strategy in the face of mounting pressure, I heard one Lumbee say to another, in all seriousness, "We have too many chiefs and not enough Indians." It was startling to hear this phrase outside the context of White corporate America – it is a bureaucratic, not a Native American, concept – and even more upsetting as we came to realize that, in the electoral context, there might never be enough Indians, or Indians and Blacks together.

But the optimism in 1968 was still intense. It belonged to individuals and to groups, and it was purchased at enormous cost in effort and in risk, making it seem even more valuable.

In the 1968 primary, we were working in close alliance in one election district with a Black man, a town resident, deeply committed to the joint project of electing combined Indian and Black slates. He had a job as a delivery man, from about 4 a.m. until noon or so, and then he

97

would come down to work on the election. On election day, with all the work we all did going rapidly down the drain, he walked into one of the polling places with his drugstore box camera and took several photographs of a variety of (what some people in power would call) "irregularities."

After that – between the primary and the "runoff" election three week later – his life and the lives of the wife and children became a hell. People called his house, not giving their names, and offered to buy the film. He said no. Then they started calling, especially when he was out on the delivery route, saying things like "tell that nigger husband/father of yours we're going to blow his nigger head off if he doesn't turn over the film."

What seemed to make the whole intensifying horror show so special was that the pictures he took never came out – the camera was broken. With the concurrence of his family, he never once said this to his callers, nor would he let any of us have the word "get out." All we could do was keep company with him and his family for the next few weeks.

I was riding with him in his car one day then, on some small errand, and we were talking about our chances for winning the runoff, about the kind of work it would take, and about the kind of opposition we were running into. We were both pretty wide-eyed, and doing what we could to make each other feel easier. He reached under the seat cushion of his car and took out a large and particularly ugly pistol to show me. He told me he took that pistol off a dead "Chinese" officer in Korea, and that "if I was good enough to fight for my country I'm good enough to vote."

I was very deeply moved – by his extraordinary bravery, by the horrible price he and his family were paying for their sense of right and wrong, by the wonder of people who could hang on to a sense of right and wrong in the midst of terror squeezing hope – and I was also completely appalled. It seemed that a sea of misplaced cliches was emerging from the sweat of our efforts and fears: the Indians using a cliche about not enough Indians; this man telling me about soldiering and voting. I wanted to yell at him – because he also had a permanent limp from a war wound that he got in a place he never knew existed before he was sent there – that he didn't have to fight in wars to qualify to vote: I hadn't; that he shouldn't have to risk ten years or more of his life in some stinking jail for shooting at a White punk, to get his civil rights; that he sounded like some introductory sociology textbook chapter on "civil rights," and it was all wrong that we should all have to go through all this. But his optimism was overwhelming: I said nothing. We had, in any case – or saw ourselves as having – few other choices, and hopes were our reward.

98

The embers of Hope, Inc.

That optimism had a history, and its history raises crucial, though in part unanswerable, questions about the basis of oppositional *power*. As difficult as it might well be to grasp the material, ideological, and social basis of dominant power, it is even harder to understand how *opposition* becomes effectively mobilized. Trapped and encouraged by the rules for challenging domination imposed by the dominant society, and trapped and encouraged by its own, context-specific rages, fears, hopes, and claims, opposition often seems so dependent on imposed conditions that we have difficulty seeing how it develops enough freedom to maneuver.

Further, it often becomes increasingly clear that having both a material and an organizational base is crucial to developing an oppositional movement, and that a mixture of hope, physical and conceptual energy, and incipient or actual violence is always not quite enough. But the crucial material and organizational basis for opposition is often riven with imposed contradictions, fragile hopes, and misspent energies. What then works, not simply to sustain opposition but to give it autonomy, freedom from determination by domination?

Part of the answer may lie in the capacity of a dominated people to attack their domination precisely in its own terms and with its own symbols. Success in such struggles, while significant, is often limited: one can ride to work as a maid in the front of the bus. This symbolic victory cannot be slighted, but it is a victory whose effects on exploitation are, at best, ambivalent: both oppositional and easing the pressure. A more effective source of oppositional autonomy seems to lie in a dominated people appropriating as their own, and refashioning, the contradictions imposed on them. To explain this leads us to the issue of struggles among and between Indians and Blacks. Very important parts of the processes whereby dominated peoples take control over their own lives, and challenge domination at least partly in their own ways and on their own terms, have their origins in the struggles and conflicts among themselves.

IV

"Hope" was incorporated in the warm and active spring of 1968: literally incorporated – organized by a half-dozen Indian activists, registered with the state as a nonprofit educational association designed to seek grants to fund Indian voter registration and "voter education," including the expenses of getting around the county to talk with the new potential voters, and to mobilize Indian people to express their interests at the polls. With the nearly total absence of discussions about class, these interests were assumed to be representable by "getting some of our own

99

in." Hope, Inc. had a broad social reach, if a restricted ethnic one: it was also going to try to do something about adult literacy training, supporting and perhaps channeling the efforts of a Quaker social action group that had been working in the county for the past two years, spreading the message of love and literacy.

When Hope was born, Reginald Hawkins – "the Hawk," as he was fondly called – a black dentist from Charlotte, North Carolina, had just announced his candidacy for governor: a first for twentieth-century North Carolina politics, and a big first. Everyone, Black and Indian, knew he was going to lose, but the spring of 1968 was the pinnacle of civil rights optimism, and at least the Hawk was going to take some White folks down with him when he went, by bringing large waves of new Black voters to the polls, who would vote for local candidates as well as for him. With the excitement his candidacy generated among Blacks and at least some Indians, with the statewide surge in non-White voter registration, and with a far larger turnout than usual expected, mobilized by his dramatic candidacy and his powerful public speeches, lots of local Black and Indian candidates seemed likely to win.

Hope, Inc. was a complexly woven net, catching multiple and diverse histories in its web. Most of all it seemed to be supported both by optimism and by realism. The optimistic pole was built from dreams and victories: the Montgomery bus boycott, the Selma marches, the Greensboro, North Carolina, sit-ins, which drew nationwide boycotts of stores like Woolworth's that in the South refused to serve Blacks at their lunch counters. The stories – true or false – that circulated about such events were full of high-spirited life: one of the four young Black men who sat down at the Greensboro Woolworth lunch counter – the actual origin, if not the first, of the civil rights sit-ins – when told by the waitress, "We don't serve niggers," replied "That's ok, I don't want a nigger. Give me a hamburger, well done." Another, who had bought some trinkets at an adjacent counter, pointed to them and said, "You just did."

A different kind of optimism was found in such stories as that circulated about Rosa Parks, the Black woman whose ejection from the bus after her refusal to get up to give her seat to a White man triggered the Montgomery bus-system boycott (and the civil rights career of the Reverend Martin Luther King, Jr., then a twenty-six-year-old pastor of a Montgomery Baptist church). The stories usually omitted saying that Mrs. Parks, at the point when she refused to give up her seat, was seated in the Black section at the back of the bus. She had just gotten up from her seat in the front of the bus to give her place to a White, as the bus filled, and had moved to sit in the back of the bus. After the White, front, two-thirds of the bus filled, Blacks already in "their" section at the back of the bus were supposed to stand, relinquishing even the "colored" seats. When she was asked to move again she refused. Her very human, very real mixture of compliance and defiance was optimistically altered, in the stories, to make it seem simply and solidly confrontational: in the stories she was sitting in the front of the bus. These were confrontations that were going to be chosen and going to be won. And wrapped around all the optimism, like bunting on a medieval war-lance, was the 1964–5 civil rights and voting rights acts, which made the confront-ations seem legal, legitimate, and there to be won.

Hope was also held up by realism, or so it then seemed: a realism of at least half-understood, half-admitted mistakes made in the recent past. Hope, Inc., for example, replaced the former Indian activist organiza-tion, "The Lumbee Citizens' Council," created in 1966. That name summed up a series of disastrous misjudgments, and it seemed espe-cially significant that the council was being left behind.

As the Ku Klux Klan came under increasing liberal attack in the late 1950s and early 1960s, it was drawing fewer sympathizers and even fewer members. Simultaneously, its agendas were rebound in a slightly softer cover: segments of the Klan and its sympathizers were trans-formed into the "White Citizens' Councils" that were to reach racist goals by somewhat more "democratic" means. The Lumbee Citizens' Council had nothing to do with the White Citizens' Councils, but the name was scary, it did not go well with Blacks, and it was a mistake to choose that name and simultaneously to seek to develop an alliance with Blacks.

The Lumbee had their own prior experience fighting the Klan. In early 1958 an Indian woman living in a mostly White neighborhood in Lumberton, the county seat, started dating a White man. Her neighbors started making some trouble, which at first she squashed by letting it be known that if the trouble continued she would sell her house to Blacks and move out: an ambivalent response, at best, as far as the Blacks were concerned. Perhaps a cross was burned on her lawn, perhaps not; social memory differs on this point. In any case, the Klan decided that they would "show power" to the Lumbee.

A small group of klansmen from northeastern South Carolina, under the leadership of "Catfish" Cole, rented a field on the outskirts of Maxton, about four miles to the east of Pembroke. At the Klan rally about 150 klansmen appeared, to face a crowd that was estimated at between 1,500 and 3,000 Lumbee, many of whom were armed with shotguns, hunting rifles, or a variety of other weapons: Indian soldiers had come home on leave from local army bases, bringing a couple of buckets of hand grenades "just in case." It was one enormous party, joyful and tense, and the state police and the sheriff's deputies stayed in their cars along the roadside near the field.

When Catfish started speaking, an Indian at the back of the crowd shot out the single light bulb over his head. These are folks who hunt for their tables, and the klansmen ran as fast as they could. But in the pandemonium that followed, not a single klansman was hit. The only person even slightly wounded was a reporter taking pictures of the armed Indians, grazed when his camera was hit. After it was over, the Indians pushed Catfish Cole's car – an aging Cadillac coupe – out of the ditch, where his wife had driven it trying to turn around and run (her husband was somewhere out in the swamps). The sheriff, who had gotten out of his car when the shooting stopped, went to the microphone and told people that if they went on home they would be there in time to watch "Gunsmoke." So the Indians "went on home," stopping by the Maxton town jail to insist on the release of a couple of Indians who managed to get themselves arrested.

One strangeness on top of the other: the Indians made it clear that the Klan was not to "mess with them," but they did not injure any klanfolk, though they easily could have; the Indians made it clear that the Klan could not "do" Indians as they had done Blacks, which was both good for the Indians, and not so good, for it made them feel superior to the Blacks, victims of an even more violent history.

The media loved it all, for all the right and all the wrong reasons: the incident made the national press; a picture of one Indian, with the captured Klan flag draped around his shoulders, made the cover of *Life* magazine. Indians had shown that the Klan was resistible, and the White bandwagon was subtly but insistently beating out the message that Indians were somehow still the noble savages, Blacks still the deserving victims. The implication was that Whites, after all, were more guiltless than the liberals thought – all people had to do was "stand up" to the Klan. How could the Indians, in the midst of both the drama and the hot flush of victory, not think likewise?

The name Lumbee Citizens' Council, in use from 1966 to 1968, crystallized some of these new, and intense, ambiguities. It also echoed one of the most powerful and appealing names and social movements in their history – the Siouan Council of the 1930s – and it was taken up while Indians were still reveling in the flush of their victory over the Klan, for six years later, in 1964, the governor had found some pretext not to allow the Klan to meet again in Robeson County: laws about "free speech" to the contrary notwithstanding, the governor understood that an even larger number of armed Indians than in 1958 would turn out to greet the Klan.

But the name also echoed the oppressive and racist White Citizens' Councils, and Indians knew that Blacks found it offensive; they knew it in their constantly repeated denials that the offense was intended. Indians were proud that they had done something more than Blacks had but also knew they were heavily dependent on Black political and organizing skills, resources, and national contacts. The most diverse values and views were being mixed together in the midst of an intense and well-earned joy and pride for what they had done: it is indeed special to beat the Klan.

Indian people felt good about what they had done; felt they had earned their victory, and did not talk much about the kinds of outcomes that would be likely if Blacks in the rural South had tried to do the same. But the situation was even more complex, for the founder of the Lumbee Citizen's Council was the one Indian medical doctor in the county: Dr. Martin Luther Brooks, who saw himself, with some justification, doing for the Lumbee on the local level what the Reverend Dr. Martin Luther King, Jr., was doing nationally for Blacks. Dr. Brooks took out full-page advertisements in the local newspapers mourning the murder of Dr. King, in the early fall of 1968, advertisements passionately acknowledging the debts of Indians to the Black-led civil rights struggles. A culture of Indian claims was being re-formed in the midst of profound cultural turmoil.

In one swift stroke, combining patient moral decency and strategic insight, Black organizers from Atlanta, working with local Black advisers, cut the ground out from under the Lumbee Citizens' Council, spelling out its organizational doom in that subtly and thoughtlessly anti-Black form, providing part of its limited success, and stimulating its transformation into a more cooperative organization. They did this by giving the Lumbee Citizens' Council, in late 1966, a substantial financial grant and some very sophisticated technical advisers for its voter-registration drive. From early 1967 until the spring of 1968 – when a new, and newly named Indian organization, Hope, Inc. replaced the Lumbee Citizens' Council – it was regional and national Black money and Black skills, intersecting with Lumbee energies and dreams, that kept the Lumbee's voter registration drive alive.

V

The support that came from Black civil rights organizations for the Lumbee Citizens' Council voter registration drive was all the more surprising considering what Lumbee political activists did in the 1964 governor's election. They did not create, but they certainly did participate in a profound reversal of the limited gains of 1960.

North Carolina seemed to be moving out of southern agrarian particularism and joining mainstream, liberal, Kennedy-style America with the election of Terry Sanford as governor in 1960. Sanford's liberalism consisted primarily in not demeaning Blacks publicly – a major boon – and in supporting those changes, such as massively increased funding for education, that benefit modern industry rather than agriculture and also give new kinds of people new kinds of chances. The Sanford years were good to many people in Robeson County. Even though the poorer farmers and sharecroppers were being increasingly marginalized, increasingly put to the wall and squeezed both in and into almost total silence, a lot of other people were finding both a modest prosperity for themselves and more hope for their children.

Governors in North Carolina are not allowed to succeed themselves. They, and their political organizations, ordinarily designate successors. Terry Sanford's successor-designate was L. Richardson Preyer, another liberal. Because Preyer was the "machine" candidate he was backed by Lumberton's White "power structure" – a label the Lumbee used. Running against Preyer was I. Beverly Lake, an extreme conservative, and Dan Moore, a middle-of-the-road candidate.

The Black activists backed Preyer, of course, but the Lumbee sided with Moore. There were two primary elections in the spring of 1964. The first eliminated Lake, who kept either of the others from winning a majority, although Preyer was ahead. In the second, three weeks later, Moore beat Preyer both in the county and in the state. The local White elite, still agrarian based, were ambivalent at best about the election of another Sanford-style liberal governor, and so mostly "sat on their hands." They did not put much money or effort into the runoff election, leaving the pro-Preyer Blacks unsupported and underfunded.

Moore poured a lot of money into the county, especially to finance Indian activists in what was then often called "the Movement." Unlike the old locality leaders, still working for and with the county power structure, the Movement could pull votes in for Moore – and, as the deal with Moore went – for whomever else they wanted on the local level. It was these funds that helped build the Movement, expanding it out of the four-precinct, nearly all-Indian corner of the county where it started in the 1950s, and making it countywide. As a countywide movement it worked in areas where the Indian population was sparse, and the need to cooperate with Blacks more intense. The Moore

campaign thus both created the material and organizational precondi-
tions among Indians for Indian–Black cooperation, and simultaneously
gave people, particularly Blacks, memories for continuing mistrust. When
the Atlanta-based Southern Christian Leadership Conference funded
the Lumbee Citizens' Council in 1966, that mistrust was laid aside – but
not quite buried – for four hopeful years.

In 1964, when Moore's campaign was financing an emergent Lumbee
activism, it looked as if the old Indian locality leaders had been forced
off their seats of power. In 1963 the county school board took direct
control of the local schools, ending the role of local school committees
but allowing them to remain functioning in a purely advisory capacity.
At the same time, the county school board was expanded, by legislative
fiat, from five to seven members, and one Indian and one Black were
appointed by Whites to the board. These two men were widely regarded by both Indians and Blacks as excessively compliant; they stood
for reelection in the spring of 1964 and won, with extensive White
support, over Indian and Black opposition. This was a bitter blow to
Indian and Black activists, for it showed that they could not even control which of "their own" would represent them.

   In the spring of 1964 the local school committees were dissolved, and
the patronage and admission powers of the locality leaders were substantially undermined. It looked, in sum, as if the Whites could still run
things mostly as they wished, but with locality leaders substantially
undermined, it also seemed as if a new kind of political activism, based
on mobilizing Indian and perhaps Black votes in new ways, might well
succeed.

"The Movement," as the activists called themselves in the early 1960s,
was trying to "advance the cause." "The cause" was a mixture of personal, political, and economic gains in well-being for each, and even
more for all "the Lums": opportunity to earn and spend money with
dignity, security and freedom from insult; a good education for Indian
children, and a chance for Indian children and adults to enjoy it –
schools with bands and sports teams, and the playing fields, uniforms,
instruments and equipment that make it all festive and special; decent
school cafeterias and libraries as well; a wide range of other desirables:
new church buildings, new Lumbee-owned businesses, Lumbee in new
sorts of political or administrative positions, a Lumbee newspaper –
all the social goods that small-town middle-class Whites have, but for
Indians, as Indians.

   The crucial point to make here is that in 1964 it looked as if these goals *could* be won for all "the Lums." The Lumbee as a people would have some, perhaps even some substantial differentiation in material well being, but no fundamental divisions. It was not until 1970 when the Lumbee – battered at the polls, losing their all-Indian schools and increasingly profoundly divided in material well-being and in opportunity – split into Lumbee and Tuscarora that the dream of advancing the cause for all fragmented into separate episodes. In 1964 it had been a very solid dream; it seemed possible, and it seemed justified by a two-decade history of modest but cumulative success.

VI

In the 1950s when the Movement was first emerging, Robeson County was organized into six electoral districts, each composed of a number of election precincts. Maxton District, in the western corner of the county, contains four precincts, each also a township: Pembroke, Smiths, Alfordsville, and Maxton. This district has a clear Indian majority: more Indians than Whites and Blacks combined. Just to the south of Maxton District is Rowland District, which is predominantly Indian, with the Indians and Blacks together constituting a majority. Red Springs District, to the northeast of Maxton, is predominantly White, but the Indians and Blacks together have a slight majority. The eastern half of the county – St. Pauls, Fairmont, and Lumberton districts – all have a clear White majority.

County commissioners are elected from these districts: one from each, except Lumberton which elects two, giving the Whites effective control even should the Blacks and Indians ever manage a solid electoral coalition. Until 1967, when they were replaced by appointed magistrates, each of the districts elected a recorder court judge, who dealt with minor offenses. Each of the electoral districts, with their specific ethnic compositions, have presented a range of political possibilities and impossibilities substantially different from the county as a whole: school board, sheriff, and judges are elected countywide. While the Indians could be denied effective political voice countywide, they had more chance on the district level, although there was less to win.

Maxton District has been the center of Indian political power and social and economic life in Robeson County. There are two different core Indian communities in this district. The most visible to outsiders is the almost entirely Indian town of Pembroke, with the college, a high school, the Indian town police and fire departments, a substantial post office and an array of small Indian-owned businesses, plus, in the early 1960s, some socially and economically crucial White-owned businesses, including a branch office of a regional bank and Pate's Supply – a large farm-supply operation. The other key Indian community, more hidden from view but perhaps more powerful, is Prospect, the core of which is simply a substantial brick church, a high school, and an elementary school, facing each other at the intersection of two rural roads.

Prospect is the center of Indian landholding, the seat of the largest Indian landlords, and the largest and most affluent Indian church, and it is surrounded by the densest network of rural Indian social and community life. In and around Prospect one can simply be an Indian the way one can simply be a person: in the absence of Whites and Blacks the confrontational or distancing defensiveness of an oppressed Indian identity falls away – much of the time, in any case – and people take steps to keep it that way. In 1967 a neighborhood of rather poor Indians raised $16,000 to buy a piece of land at tax auction to keep it out of the hands of Whites.

In 1950, in one of the rural areas of Maxton District, near Prospect, an Indian school principal had come to be increasingly disliked. The local school committee, under substantial Indian pressure, recommended his removal to the county Board of Education. The principal was well-liked by Whites, and the board responded by "shuffling the member-ship" of the local committee (as the local Indians phrased it: to shuffle is both to re-sort, as with a deck of cards, and also to move with excessive deference) – and the principal remained. A delegation of Indians, mostly from Prospect, "got together" and went to see the county commissioners. The principal resigned.

This was the start of the Movement – or as they called themselves at first, "the organization." They ran a candidate for county commis-sioner from Maxton District in 1954, and won; in 1956, with help from the Blacks in Maxton town, they put in an Indian as recorder court judge for Maxton District. In 1958 another Indian, with support from the organization, replaced the first county commissioner – and held the post for sixteen years, although one Indian on a board of seven commissioners can accomplish less than people expect.

Some of the same people active in the organization in the early 1950s were still struggling in 1973, when Henry Ward Oxendine was appointed, although by then the embers of political hope were only a dim glow and much larger fires were raging. What kept them going, through it all, not just through all the continuing defeats but through the bitter blows of the continuing White use of appointments to choose who would "represent" Indians and Blacks?

The partial victories, the changes, the growth in the scope of the

107

struggle and in the visions for the future, the improvements in material well-being for at least some in the rural South – all these were important. In addition, three further points constitute part of an answer:

First, perhaps, but least important, was simple opportunism: some people wanted to run, or to substantially support those who did, for the gain that might be gotten, for the excitement of it all, for the chance.

Second, and usually more significant, was the issue of "advancing the cause" – doing something that would in some way help those of one's own, and others in similar situations, who had been so long and so systematically denied: denied decent schools, denied a fair hearing when in trouble, denied access to even those programs they were legislatively entitled to, denied, above all, the dignity of equal participation. Many people became and stayed politically engaged as much or more for others, or at least for issues, as for themselves.

The third factor is surprising, complex, and probably as significant as the first and the second together: the *internal* political divisiveness of the Lumbee, only partly based on internal social divisions, has been an important component in maintaining the Lumbee's political struggles for a better place in the larger system.

Among a people such as the Lumbee, substantially and systematically battered by larger political and economic forces, the dramas and the issues of oppression and exploitation are so intense and the efforts to oppose, to distance, to accommodate, and even to collude, all in the hope of limited gain, are so serious in their risks, so attractive in their simple, usually small-scale victories, and so tragic in their losses, considering what is at stake, that it seems as if all the significant struggles occur between a dominated people on the one side and those who dominate on the other. But this, in fact, is not ordinarily the case. For the Indians themselves the internal struggles can be equally compelling and equally important, as *it is precisely these internal struggles that provide a substantial part of the limited autonomy of a dominated people.*

To be an Indian – as with many other proportionately small, dominated peoples – is to be in a situation where no conceivable strategy for coping with domination can possibly fully succeed in bringing even the limited rewards that are deemed minimally necessary – or not succeed for very long. Isolation, violence, accommodation, opposition, distancing, separate development, collusion, cultural distinctiveness: every strategy, every path has its intense followers, its bitter critics, and those who ignore both. Followers, critics, and the uninvolved often have at least some reason on their side. So they turn against each other, with even more passion as they come to realize their strategy might be somewhat more successful if it had more adherents, and in so doing

108

they direct their energies and their passions as much for and against each other as for and against those who dominate them.

Such internal struggles can get completely out of hand and become appallingly destructive. They can also, however, shape an emerging history – retrospective and prospective – that creates its own partial distance from domination, rooting itself substantially, if not completely, in a people's relations to each other. The Tuscarora Indian "riot" at Prospect school will help us to begin to unravel the historical dynamic of such unity and divisiveness – a dynamic that goes far beyond politics to shape and sustain a people in constant formation and re-formation.

PART THREE

"Root hog or die"

Prologue

While the basic racial-political categories that developed in the colonial and pre–Civil War South (White, Negro, Indian, Free Person of Color) were deeply embedded in the developing organization of both the economy and the state, as well as in people's ideas and beliefs, the reality these categories sought to define and control was more complex and ambiguous than any number of categories could define or express. What kept the categories open and ambiguous was specifically the fact that they had different dimensions and different shapes in the domains of the economy, the state, and popular culture, thus creating areas of tension and uncertainty in which people could and did negotiate and contest identities along with the rewards and penalties associated with those identities. As the birth and decline of the people called "Smiling" has shown, it is not simply the benefits and restrictions attached to diverse racial categories or ethnicities that come to be at issue, but the categories themselves – and the whole system of categories, which turns out to be less fixed and immutable than we usually think it to be.

The *Robesonian* – the county newspaper – carried the following story on page 1 of the May 26, 1961, edition:

Adopt 'Barbarous' as Tribal Name
INDIAN GROUP SEEKS TO FORM
A UNIFIED EASTERN NORTH CAROLINA TRIBE

A small group of Indians of Robeson, Bladen and Columbus counties is holding a series of meetings this week in an effort to organize one over-all tribe for east Carolina Indians, to be known as the Barbarous. The name, they say, comes from Indian records.

111

> *Big attendance was reported at a meeting Wednesday night in Hoke county. Further meetings are scheduled for Prospect high school tonight at 7:30, and for Waccamaw school Saturday at the same hour. The group announcing the meetings is composed of Jack Locklear of Pembroke, president of his home district "Barbarous" group, Benny Locklear of Lumberton, Willy Moore of Bladen, J. L. Jacobs and W. G. Patrick of Bolton, and Carmel Locklear of Pembroke.*
>
> *Although Locklear says that Indians here have no official tribal name, an act passed in the Congress in 1956 designates certain Indians as Lumbee of North Carolina.*
>
> *Jack Locklear said: "Because Indians in Eastern North Carolina aren't members of a tribe recognized by the U.S. Government, they are denied benefits they would otherwise be eligible for. They need to organize and we want to do it before the big National Indian Council in Chicago June 13–20.*
>
> *"More than 112,000 Indians in Eastern North Carolina are eligible to become members of the Barbarous tribe."*
>
> *Locklear explained yesterday that "benefits" does not refer to money benefits from the federal government, but to benefits which would come from being organized for political purposes.*

This clearly seems a mock. Without an explicit word, the header calls our attention not to the hopes but to the then semiliteracy of the people involved in this organization (some of whom have since become exceptionally articulate by the standards of the dominant culture). We can well guess a part of what lay behind this name-claim: These Indian people took a racist adjective in some early text, or texts – perhaps "the barbarous Indians of this place" – as a name.

We should, for the moment, ignore the various laws of the state of North Carolina to the effect that a farmer could keep children out of school to work the fields under the direction of their parents whenever he wanted, which meant that farmers often told their tenants to keep their children home to help make the crop, with the poverty and the powerlessness of the tenants constituting varieties of agreement to such demands, even when they were seen as destructive. Thus in 1960 most Indian men over age twenty-five had not completed seven years of grade school. We can also ignore the role of anthropologists at the University of Chicago, and various foundations, in setting up the conference at which the "barbarous" Indians were hurriedly trying to find a place for themselves and their hopes.

Rather, we should look more closely at the implicit claim, in this newspaper story, that the language of the Indians' discourse is confused, ignorant of the basic rules both of language and of how meaning is conveyed, while the language of domination, for right or for wrong, is clear and well-constructed. Another illustration, from a few years later (when the Barbarous Indians were gone and the Tuscarora – including many of the same people meeting at the same places – were not yet born) will not bridge this huge chasm, for it is a mirage, but rather may make it disappear.

By 1968 many of the smaller White farmers of Robeson County were in deep trouble. The costs of farming and the costs of achieving modest middle-class aspirations were outstripping returns on the sale of the crop. One farmer in such circumstances had divided his farm, bringing in a second sharecropping family. To explain what this meant, for him and for the sharecroppers, a few introductory points about the share-cropping system in the mid-twentieth century South must first be made.

Sharecroppers ordinarily provide all the labor on a farm, and all the tools and equipment as well. They pay for half the seed and half the fertilizer, and when the crop is sold they get part of the proceeds, which in the 1960s was a "stated half."

A stated half: many times farmers would take the crop to market, sell it, come back and say what it sold for and what would be deducted from the sharecropper's half for seed, fertilizer, and the "advances" – the credit extended from landlord to tenant for groceries, doctor bills, and so on. Some tenants kept, or had their school-children keep, their own records.

Some landlords were scrupulous and straightforward, taking the sharecroppers along to the sale of the crop, showing receipts, and so forth. From such high ground the rivers of truth ran down into a swampland of domination and imposed need. In 1967, in the southeastern part of the county where not many Indians or rural Blacks lived, a nine-year-old son of a sharecropping family drowned in the farmer's pond while his parents were out doing fieldwork. This happened in June. The landlord paid for the burial with an advance against the 'cropper's share of the harvest. In the post-harvest settling up the landlord deducted $200. from the 'cropper's share for the cost of the funeral. This cost seemed unbelievably high, considering the quality of the burial, and the parents went to the funeral director to ask. He showed them the bill to the farmer, $175., and said that the farmer had agreed to pay after the harvest. The farmer had turned a $25. profit on burying his sharecropper's child.

To return to 1968, and to the farmer who divided his farm (also in the southeastern part of the county), this farmer had a smallish farm, say 110 acres, with one 'cropping family working it. By bringing in a second sharecropping family, each of the two families would be working approximately 55 acres, with more intense labor than possible or necessary on a larger unit. With the extra labor, the total output on the

113

farm would go up, perhaps 10 to 20 percent, from which increased output the landlord's "half" would rise. The total income of the first family of sharecroppers would, of course, be something like 55 or 60 percent of what it had been previously, and the second, new family would earn about the same amount.

In this context, in the early summer of 1968, the situation of the two families was desperate. They were short of food. One of the two families I went to see had an open loaf of bread, a half jar of jam, and some tea bags as the only food in the house. The other family were eating unripe pecans, and the children were having trouble controlling their bowels.

An attempt was made to get these families food relief, in the form of what was then called "surplus commodities," from the county welfare department. In order for the families to get these provisions, the landlord would have to sign "a paper" stating that they had earned less than a certain amount – about $1,500. – the previous year. *One of the families was White, one was Indian. What the landlord said, when he refused to sign, was: "If you give these niggers free food they won't work."*

I remember, most of all, two feelings when I heard those words. The first and strongest blended helplessness and rage. The other feeling was even more complex: I realized that landlord had a much clearer understanding of "race" than I did – he at least knew that it had hardly anything to do with the color of your skin or where your ancestors came from. And for all the brutality of "race relations" I never fully understood just how violent it all was until I saw that if they were going to be starved and bludgeoned into niggers, I was, inescapably and by the very same violence, made White; neither one without the other. Whatever we thought or felt about the whole process, whatever our wishes or desires, the only possible escape was to track that violence to its source and take it apart.

The present here is constructing, in the midst of its brutalities, pasts – pasts that deceptively claim to be about places of origin and the humanity of one's ancestors. The present here is also seeking to construct a future – a future that has a great deal to do with the claims that a declining agrarian capitalism could still make and enforce upon vulnerable people.

In both these instances – the Barbarous Indians and the unfed niggers – ethnicity does not simply emerge from history; history is created within ethnicity. For ethnicity is *never* innocently and simply just there; it always makes claims and these claims always seek to shape connections between pasts, presents, and impending futures.

If impoverishment and domination shape ethnicity and ethnicity, when seen as a process, creates and claims histories, then oppression creates history through culture as well as class. The beat of police clubs on the newly emergent Tuscarora in front of the Lumbee school at Prospect should imprint upon us the realization that the connections between oppression and history, culture and class, are all built on foundations of materialized power. In the chaos power creates and in the order power imposes, the victims – as well as those who oppress and those who, for the moment, just wait – form and assert new ideas about historical continuities and discontinuities.

The history Part Three addresses is centered on three instances of ethnic and racial transformation: the emergence of the Tuscarora from the midst of the Lumbee, in the 1970s; the decision, by the federal government in the 1930s, that Lumbee (then calling themselves Siouan) were an Indian race – and the simultaneous decision not to support them as Indian people; and the multiple ways that the post–Civil War violence in Robeson County led the legislature of the state of North Carolina to agree that the ancestors of the Lumbee were socially, politically, racially, and historically Indians.

7

Prospect and loss

On Saturday afternoon, April 7, 1973, an anonymous telephone call to the Robeson County sheriff's office led the sheriff, two deputies and several FBI agents to a house between Maxton and Prospect where, in a boarded-up back room, they found over 4,000 pounds of Bureau of Indian Affairs documents – treaties, interoffice memoranda, comments on claim cases. Some of it was just paper, neither historically nor currently useful; some of it might well have been of great potential use to native peoples who feel that, even within the narrow confines of imposed treaty rights and law, they have not received their due. Another 4,000 – or more – pounds of documents in two other hiding places were soon discovered, and all of it was shipped back to the BIA.

The *Robesonian*'s recounting of the event neatly sums up the characteristic mixture of wished-for rights, hoped-for access to powerholders, an "Indian grapevine" that spreads the word and marks the spot of impending trouble with amazing speed, and the incipient but usually unrealized violence that colored Tuscarora politics:

> *After knocking at the doors and at every window, the agents then, according to the warrant, were authorized to enter the home* [of Dock "Pap" Locklear] *for the search for the documents.*
>
> *FBI agents removed a piece of plywood that had been nailed over an opening in the rear of the house and discovered a room, approximately ten feet square and some six feet deep in documents, files and papers that had been allegedly stolen from the B.I.A. offices.*
>
> *Agents and deputies then began the ordeal of removing the documents and had about half the load of files out of the house when Keever Locklear, a close friend of Pap's, arrived and protested what he called "an illegal search."*

> *Keever Locklear insisted that the agents had "violated the Constitution" by breaking into a man's home while he was not there to defend his property.*
>
> *Locklear was informed of the federal warrant and the authorization the FBI had obtained in the search for the stolen documents, and then was told that since it was not his property that the FBI had no further discussion with him about the matter.*
>
> *Shortly thereafter, the Rev. Elias Rogers, Chief of the Eastern Carolina Tuscarora Indian Organization, arrived and joined Locklear in the protest.*
>
> *Rev. Rogers insisted that the FBI bring the Secretary of the Department of Interior and the Director of the Bureau of Indian affairs down to Maxton to claim their documents and that the FBI had no authority to remove the papers from private property.*
>
> *Dock "Pap" Locklear arrived and at the insistence of the other two, chased law enforcement officers out of his house and dared them to set foot on his property, brandishing a pistol and a shotgun.*
>
> *"Pap" Locklear then ordered the FBI agents and deputies off his property and during a heated argument, reportedly leveled his gun at an FBI agent and then swung the shotgun until it was reportedly pointing at Robeson County Sheriff's Deputy Garth Locklear.*
>
> *Deputy Locklear fired a warning shot and "Pap" Locklear retreated into his home.*
>
> *After about a 30 minute stalemate, he surrendered to authorities, still protesting that his Constitutional rights had been violated by the agents entering his home without him being there and without his permission.*
>
> *At the time "Pap" Locklear surrendered, Keever Locklear and the Reev. Elias Rogers had already been placed under arrest and were enroute to the Robeson County Jail.*

[None of the Locklears here are related, although all are Indians.]

Who might have informed the sheriff? Understanding why it is impossible to guess requires explaining how the documents came from the BIA offices to the swamps of Robeson County, and what happened to the people who loaded them on the truck in Washington, D.C., after they brought the documents "home."

American Indian Movement activists and organizers came to Robeson County in October 1972, six months before the documents were found, as the vanguard of the "Trail of Tears" – the cross-country caravan to Washington, D.C., to seek treaty-justice. Several Tuscarora joined AIM on the trail, which turned into a seizure and an extended occupation of the national BIA offices.

Tuscorora – and their Lumbee congeners also, of course – can be amazingly resourceful people: however bad things are in Robeson County it is breathtaking to travel from Robeson to any of the surrounding areas on the southern coastal plain and see what a difference the presence and the possibility of intense struggle has made. In any case, while the federal and D.C. police were pounding on the front door of the Washington, D.C., BIA offices, trying to get their hands on the occupying Indians, Tuscarora were loading documents into a rented truck pulled up to the back door.

When they came back down to Robeson County, they did two things. First, they stopped their truck (and the small cavalcade of cars with it) at the county school administrative offices, where the school board meets, and demanded a meeting with the superintendent of the county schools to discuss Indian control of Indian schools. On the way to Washington the month before, the Tuscarora had had another of their semiconfrontational, presence-announcing demonstrations, driving through Lumberton, running red lights, honking horns, and making their presence felt. Few if any people in the Lumberton "power structure" were willing to talk to Tuscarora at this point, and the sheriff – we may guess – when he went to eject the Tuscarora from the school office building, was a bit concerned about his image as the upholder of law, order, and whatever else small-town southern sheriffs in the early 1970s may have regarded themselves as upholding. They were very forcefully ejected. At that point, *as rumor has it,* they drove out in the county, backed their truck through the locked gates of the Lumbee Recreation Center, and burned some of the Lumbee's electric golf carts. Then they went and put the documents away.

Shortly after they returned from Washington the Tuscarora – at that point calling themselves the Eastern Carolina Tuscarora Indian Organization (ECTIO) – held an election for chief. Elias Rogers, leader of the "moderate" faction, which included Keever Locklear and Carnell Locklear, won. The major issue in the election was whether the courts or confrontations would be the most effective strategy. Howard Brooks, leader of the more militant faction, walked out after the election, forming his own Tuscarora group and taking about a third of the Tuscarora with him. On December 15 he was elected chief of his group, which had no fixed name as yet, but was occasionally referred to as the Tuscarora Council.

Chief Howard, in his postelection speech, said that the main issue was Indian schools, and that "we may need a Wounded Knee here in Robeson County" – a possibility that aroused serious concern among Whites and many Lumbee. Tensions between the two factions of Tuscarora were high, and stayed strong all the following spring. In

March 1973 – four months after the Tuscarora split, and a month before the tip that led to the repossession of the BIA documents – guns were fired into Carnell Locklear's home. He had just been elected secretary of the ECTIO, and Tuscarora supporters of Chief Howard Brooks were indicted for the shooting.

There were, in sum, a lot of people with angry memories of Tuscarora that spring: Whites, Lumbees, and other Tuscarora. Almost everyone then active in politics, in the broadest sense of the term, was angry at someone else – someone *other*, and in most cases someone becoming *more other* – and most of the key players could mobilize a lot of force on very short notice.

This split into two separate groups, after they came back from the BIA, was the culmination of a fairly bitter division among the Tuscarora since their formation in the spring of 1970, and an expression of a deeper and long-standing tendency toward intense, and often partly institutionalized, factionalism among the Lumbee. The "moderate" position, led by Keever Locklear, Rev. Elias Rogers, Carnell Locklear, and an allied group, perhaps more intransigent, led by Vermon Locklear and his wife Leola, emphasized legal battles for their rights. The more militant group, led by Chief Howard Brooks, focused on demonstrations and confrontations.

The moderate faction, emphasizing legal action strategies, was hampered by an unrealistic sense both of their rights and of what was possible, constantly seeking to conjoin rights the law provided with rights they thought they ought to have. They were also hampered by the enormous cost of attempting to secure these rights in court or by administrative appeal: they were mostly very poor farmers and sharecroppers and they were continually digging in almost empty pockets for the collections to pursue their rights. Yet they won some startling victories.

The more militant faction confrontationally demanded their rights, and they were encouraged and supported by the successes of both Black militance and the American Indian Movement. Although they had less success than others in Robeson County, their presence seems to have been a substantial factor in the negotiations powerholders became willing to enter into with other factions, other tendencies.

This chapter focuses on Tuscarora militance, which, although only one tendency among the Tuscarora people while they were united, came to define the public appearance of the Tuscarora. The next chapter centers on the legal maneuvers of the Tuscarora, which sprang from and were interwoven with the remembered history of Lumbee attempts to obtain federal assistance as Indians and to secure what they came to see as their Indian rights.

119

II

After Henry Ward Oxendine was appointed to the state legislature, the *Carolina Indian Voice,* a Pembroke-based, Lumbee-owned and staffed weekly newspaper, editorialized on Lumbee politics:

> There are a few stars, but no supporting cast. The average . . . Indian does not care anymore what the stars do. They understand, instinctively, that they are not welcome to comment or participate in the decision making process. . . . The Tuscaroras (both of them – Howard Brooks' Tuscarora Council and the Eastern Carolina Tuscarora Indian Organization) are the only political group that seems to rely on and involve the grass roots people in their activities. We applaud them publicly for this, to us, intelligent approach to politics.
>
> In the status-quo middle-class Lumbee camp, we have not observed a people attitude. We have observed, over and over again, the same people calling the shots and formulating "stradegy" as they call it. Rep. Henry Ward Oxendine is a fine, sincere man, but he is not necessarily the choice of the people. He was appointed by two people, and cheered on by another handful of political pros. . . .
>
> So, we conclude, politics, as do Gospel Sings, belong to the people.

During the week of March 18–23, 1973, beginning the day after Old Main burned, and at the same time as Henry Ward Oxendine's entrance into the state legislature, Chief Howard Brooks's Tuscarora Council sought to gain access to the Prospect Elementary School in order to have a public meeting: they wanted to talk about Indian control of Indian schools and about keeping Indian schools all-Indian. While the Prospect community is the seat of rural Lumbee power, it was also the center of the Tuscarora's growing membership, although their members came more from the poorer, outlying farms than from the rich lands of Prospect itself. The Prospect school committee, all Lumbee, denied them free use of the building, by a vote of three to two, but said they could have access for a $20. fee. The Tuscarora angrily claimed that other organizations had free access to the school and that they had helped to build the school with their labor and their donations. The school committee told Young Allen, the White superintendent of the county schools, about its decision, and reported that the Tuscarora said they were coming to the school despite being denied free access. By 6:30 p.m. on the evening of the announced meeting – Friday, March 23, 1973 – a confrontational standoff was developing rapidly: the sheriff, his deputies and the state police were lining the road in front of the school, with their guns, their helmets and their extra-long nightsticks.

Across the road, clustered in front of Prospect's main church, were

150 to 200 Tuscarora, rallied by Chief Howard; Vernon Bellacourt, the national director of AIM; and Golden Frinks, a Black activist and the field secretary of the Southern Christian Leadership Conference. Militance was reviving the Indian–Black coalition – at least for the moment – after electoral alliance had failed.

It was a cold evening, despite the hot words of Frinks, Bellacourt, and Brooks from the steps of Prospect United Methodist Church, and despite the fires built for warmth. By midnight, with Chief Howard promising to stay until they gained access to the school, and saying that Governor Holshouser had promised to meet with the Indians to mediate the dispute, the crowd of supporters had thinned to about sixty and Fred Miller, a representative of the U.S. Justice Department's Community Relations Division, who was serving as a negotiator, observer, and moderating influence, had gone back to his motel. The police came across the road. What followed was, in the words of the Indians, a "police riot," although it was Chief Howard who was booked for incitement to riot.

Fifty-eight Indian people were arrested, some shotguns and machetes were confiscated, and a substantial number of Indians, subsequently charged with such offenses as public obscenity, were hurt.

Perhaps it was the intensity of the issue at stake: Indian schools for Indian children. Perhaps it was the burning of Old Main, which seemed both such an appalling loss and such a victory for the university administration that wanted it torn down. Perhaps it was the nightsticks and blackjacks, the arrests and the jailings: most Tuscarora were, after all, middle-aged, quiet, church-going folks, completely unaccustomed to violence despite their bravado, and completely lacking in the kinds of supportive training – practical and emotional – in civil disobedience and passive resistance that Black activists were getting. Perhaps it was the indictments hanging over peoples' heads: Chief Howard was brought to trial two years later for inciting a riot, and was given a one-year sentence. Perhaps it did not fully turn on what happened that evening and in the weeks before. But that night in the spring of 1973 seemed to be a major shift in the course of events. Tuscarora membership, in both factions, went into a slow but noticeable and steady decline, and the barn burnings stopped completely.

III

In the forty nights before the "Prospect riot" forty barns had burned – tobacco barns mostly, plus an occasional empty house, an attempt or two to burn parked and empty school buses, and a couple of classroom fires. Not counting a few old barns, widely said to have been burned by their owners for insurance purposes, all the new barns that were torched belonged to Whites. McNair Farms, a large "farm supply" corporation in an adjacent county, with extensive business operations in Robeson, lost three barns on one of their tracts of land in the county, a tract still known as "the Bullard farm" – Bullard being an Indian name. D. H. Wilkerson, a wealthy White, lost two barns in the midst of rural Prospect, on land that "had always been Indian land." Maxton Supply Company lost three barns in the same area. John McArthur lost two; Gus Speros, a nouveau riche White contractor from Maxton, who was elected to the state legislature with wide Indian support (for he had built several Indian churches, billing only his costs) lost his tobacco barn the night after he legislatively blocked ending double voting for the county school board. Every night, or every other night, a barn or two went down – from mid-February until the end of March.

Many people in Robeson County suggested that it was probably Tuscarora, or Tuscarora supporters, who did it. Both Tuscarora and Lumbee had a lot to be enraged about, and in their continual losses in the battles for their schools they were increasingly desperate.

On the March 15, the week before Old Main burned, the state legislature took two actions that, in the midst of the continually burning barns, continued White control over the county schools.

First, they killed a "compromise" plan to create two school districts in the county – one for Lumberton, one for the rest of the county. At that point there were six separate school districts: one for Lumberton, four small-town districts, each with their own, essentially White/Black schools, and the county district, which included the rural areas of the county and the Indian town, Pembroke. Merging the six districts, which all voted in the county school elections, into two completely separate districts would have withdrawn Lumberton's vote from the county school board elections and given the Indians a chance: on that basis it was opposed and blocked by Whites from the small towns.

What the legislature then did – that is, the county's delegation, coming to the full legislature under the "home-rule" practice, where the whole legislature ordinarily supports what a delegation requests for its own county – was to expand the county school board from seven to eleven members. The additional four members were to be elected from the county alone, giving Indians and Blacks some representation, if not control. The legislature, at the suggestion of the county's delegation, appointed two Indians and two Blacks – people that powerholders thought they could work with – to the four new seats, creating incumbents for the following elections.

122

In the week before this happened there was a frenzy of activity as the Indians tried to win something more from the legislature. The Indians were supported by the Reverend Joy Johnson, a Black legislator from the town of Fairmont, who had won his seat in the 1970 elections. But Rev. Johnson was not getting support from the other members of the county's delegation – either Gus Speros or Luther Britt, the State Senator from Robeson County and a member of one of the largest landholding extended families in the area. All Rev. Johnson could do was push for a compromise, and it seemed to the Indians no compromise at all.

The day before the legislature acted, about one hundred Indians, mostly Lumbee, demonstrated at the state capital. They met with the county's delegation and were told that Henry Ward Oxendine was likely to be appointed to fill the unexpired term of Frank White – but this was not what they came to hear, and their disappointment with the expansion proposal, which was passed the day after they went home, was intense. The disappointment was further increased because they felt that unlike the previous Tuscarora attempts to regain control of the schools, this time they were acting "responsibly."

One week before the Lumbee demonstration another hundred or more Indians – mostly Tuscarora – had come to the legislative caucus room to hear the "options" for ending, changing, or continuing double voting discussed. They were extremely distraught by what they heard. Returning from Raleigh, a motorcade led by chief Howard drove through Lumberton, honking their horns, running red lights, and smashing the windows out of twenty-eight stores, demonstrating both against double voting and, as he subsequently told reporters, in support of the Indian occupation of Wounded Knee.

Chief Howard also told reporters, the morning after, that "another Wounded Knee" might be needed in Robeson County. That night he led another motorcade to Lumberton and was met by a serious show of police force. Diverted, the motorcade drove more or less quietly through three smaller towns – Fairmont, Maxton, and Pembroke – and the following day Chief Howard announced the end of motorcade demonstrations.

The struggle over double voting in the spring of 1973 was the last small glow of hope for Indian control over their own schools. In the past three years they had increasingly lost not only control but also the distinct and separate Indian schools themselves.

Further, in the spring of 1973 all the excitement and all the drama of the Tuscarora involvement with AIM was fast fading. When AIM came to the county only six months before, in the fall of 1972, and set up a regional office, it had seemed as if the whole Tuscarora search to have their Indian identity acknowledged and accepted was succeeding.

123

Here, as if from a dream, were the most Indian of Indians, come to make common cause with their Tuscarora brothers and sisters. They demonstrated together, they spoke on platforms together, and a substantial contingent of Tuscarora went to Washington, D.C., with AIM: all to increasingly little effect, although while it was happening in the fall and winter of 1972 it seemed to be a major counterassault for the losses suffered when the schools opened at the end of the summer of 1972.

IV

The schools had opened quietly in 1972, with almost all the pupils reporting to the schools where they had been assigned by the county board's "pupil assignment" (integration) plan. The quiet orderliness of the opening, however, was widely understood to express the utterness of the defeat of Lumbee and Tuscarora, particularly in its contrast to previous openings.

The year before, in 1971, a substantial crowd of Indian parents had shown up at Prospect school on opening day, to defiantly bring their children who had been assigned to other schools and to protest the assignment of two Black teachers to Prospect, the one remaining all-Indian school in the county. Seven parents were subsequently convicted of various "misdemeanors" in the district court at Lumberton.

Angus Blue, Jr., faced the most serious charge: "interfering with an officer," and he drew a six-month sentence. The judge had offered all seven parents suspended sentences, in return for guilty pleas, but they all contested and all drew prison sentences. Blue was the first to be tried:

> *Deputy Sheriff R. J. Locklear testified that he was attempting to disarm Lewis Barton, who had a hatchet, but someone [Blue] seized him around the throat from behind. He didn't get the hatchet, he said, because a long knife was pulled on him when he was released by Blue.*
>
> *"Angus told me to put my gun down but it had not been out of the holster," he said. . . .*
>
> *Curlie "Bossy" Barton was next and Deputy J. G. Locklear testified that Barton was wearing a hatchet on one side and a knife on the other; that R. J. Locklear did not pull his gun, but that Deputy Bill R. Locklear did pull his.*
>
> *R. J. Locklear said that he saw the weapons and the knife pointed at him.*
>
> *Danford Dial, principal of the school at the time, stated that he did not call the officers but did call Supt. Young Allen to report the incident, and presumably Allen called for help.*

Lewis "Bunk" Barton was third. Mrs. Annie Belle Gerald, a black teacher assigned to the school, testified that she and Mrs. Beta Ashley, the other black teacher involved in the case, had gone to [Principal] Dial's office after receiving threats in their classrooms, where Barton entered and threatened them with an upraised hatchet.

She quoted Barton as telling them to go back where they taught before, and if not "I will check your brains.". . . Homer Barton was fourth and was convicted on testimony, by Deputy Bill R. Locklear, that Barton had pulled a knife on him and that was when the deputy had pulled his gun.

Mattie Bell Locklear was next. Mrs. Gerald testified that Mrs. Locklear led a group into her classroom and told her to get out and not come back.

Mrs. Ashley testified to the same treatment of herself. [Deputy] J. G. Locklear testified that Mrs. Locklear was using foul language and was so upset he feared she might have a stroke.

When Peggy Barton came to trial, J. G. Locklear testified that she used foul language, and ordered the teachers to get "the niggers and whites" out of the school.

He said he reminded her that she was reputed to be a God-fearing woman and that she replied with a blasphemous curse.

He said that she was moving back and forth between the group of woman protesters and the men protesters. . . .

J. G. Locklear testified in the case of Retha Mae Locklear, stating that she used foul language and referred to "the niggers and whites" and that she claimed that the whites hadn't paid any taxes in seven years in support of the school.

Mrs. Gerald and Mrs. Ashley, who are still employed by the R.C. Public Schools, said they have now been assigned to Rex-Rennert School [an Indian elementary school, out toward the margins of Indian territory] *where they will report soon.* (*Robesonian*, September 22, 1971, pp. 1–2)

Of all the upsetting aspects of this incident – the agitation, the desperation, the attack on Black people in particular – the hatchets and knives people brought to this encounter are especially appalling, for they indicate just how corrosively intrusive are the dominant society's fantasies about Indians: if it takes "tomahawks" and "long knives" to be an Indian in the eyes of power, then Indians will take them up, waving them both at helpless people and at armed police. Indians were farmers long before Europeans ever arrived, and in different ways have been farmers since: "the savage" is a European fantasy forced upon peoples too desperate to have much choice about the illusions they used to armor hope in the face of almost certain loss.

125

V

Danford Dial, who resigned as principal of Prospect school in the early fall of 1971, the day after this incident, with Indians making threats against his life, had been one of the major Indian heroes of the school struggles in the fall of 1970, just one year earlier.

The school year that began in 1970 was the first after the integration of the county school system had been announced. Over 500 Indian children defied the pupil-assignment plan and showed up at the school they attended the previous year. But the chairman of the county school board declared school property out of bounds for any "unauthorized persons," including children not at their assigned schools, technically then committing the criminal act of trespass by going to the schools they went to before. So were their parents who brought them. Further, he asked the federal courts in Fayetteville to force the Lumbee to comply with the federal integration order. He was under a lot of pressure from agents of the federal government itself to take such firm action, whether he wanted to or not.

Just before the schools opened, state education and federal civil-rights officials had come to the county to hear Lumbee complaints about integration, which for them meant the loss of their schools. After hearing the pleas and speeches, the federal official replied that they would "make no exceptions for any particular minority group in carrying out the plans for school integration" (*Robesonian*, August 25, 1970). He said that the Lumbee could try the courts but he also pointed out that, on the basis of cases elsewhere, they were not likely to succeed. And the federal officials capped the meeting by saying that if the school officials did not carry out the integration plans, they would be "personally subject to legal action."

After this show of force, on the evening of the day that the school board's chairman issued his "unauthorized persons" warning, more than four hundred Lumbee met at Prospect school and "passed the hat" for the legal battle. The first pass of the hat raised $900 of the needed $2,000; the second brought the total to $2,200.

But the show of government force was taking its toll, and people were pinning their hopes on help from outside. The week before the fund-raising meeting an estimated three thousand Indians had gathered at the Oxendine school, in Pembroke, at a meeting to discuss their schools. Sen. Sam Ervin, Jr. – later to draw national attention for his role in the Watergate hearings – sent a telegram to Danford Dial, who read it to the crowd:

> *No greater tyranny is being practiced upon the people of the South in general and the Lumbee Indians in particular than the tyranny*

> *being practiced upon them by the Department of Health, Education and Welfare. Let me assure you that I shall continue my fight to protect the people of the South in general and the Lumbee Indians in particular, against this tyranny.*
>
> *While the telegram was being read, there was such silence in the audience "you could have heard a pin drop," said* [Lewis] *Barton, Lumbee writer and historian. The instant it was finished, there was thunderous applause, which was long sustained. (Robesonian, September 4, 1970)*

The possibility that some relief might come from the federal government itself was heightened when Dr. Helen Schierbeck, a Lumbee Indian and the head of the Indian Education Office of the U.S. Department of Health, Education and Welfare, asked the National Congress of American Indians to intercede with the Department of Justice and the White House on behalf of the Lumbee, with the request publicized in local and area newspapers.

As with many peasant and town protest movements in early modern Europe, where "the crowd" called on the king for justice, this turn for help outward and upward was associated with a dramatically intensified focus on local needs, locally specific strategies, and highly localized forms of mobilization. Indeed, the call for help from above – from people with more power and authority than local elites have – is rarely as blind or naive, in action or concept, as it is made out to be. This call for help from the most powerful authorities, coupled with an active, public presence of a lot of people, all usually discordant and often at least potentially violent, is a phenomenon that early modern historians have often termed "king and crowd" riots – except that a far broader range of powerholders than just "kings" are often called upon, and a far broader range of local actions than simple "crowd riots" are often brought forth. Closer inspection of such phenomena show them to often be well-focused, if not well-planned "squeeze plays" against local authorities.

When the larger powerholders who were called on turn against the people, as they almost inevitably do, they often confront people with more physical, organizational and ideological resources than those who called for their help. It might be useful to develop more clarity about such political engagements – which seem in general to be too easily dismissed as transient or naive through such labels as "king and crowd riots" – for what may be at stake in the general type is understanding forms of intense political engagement by people who at some deep level know they are very likely to lose, lose brutally and with substantial physical cost. In such contexts the grand authorities – kings and presidents and departments of justice – may be called forth more as mirrors for than sources of hope, and the ignorance of these grandiose authorities, rather than of ordinary folks, may be crucial to whatever localized success such protest may achieve.

Be that as it may, the Lumbee did not seem to notice, and certainly did not publicly comment on, the fact that Sen. Ervin and his ilk were transparently using the Lumbee for their own posturing on much larger stages. Many Lumbee waited for help that never came; some would begin to mobilize for the court suit that, five years later, broke double voting; and many, not willing to wait, transformed themselves into Tuscarora in this fall of 1970.

VI

In early 1974 – with an indictment for inciting to riot hanging over his head, the court case against integrating Indian schools lost, the attempt to break double voting for the school board by pressuring the legislature (which seemed the last slim hope for some special Indianness about the schools) also having failed, the Tuscarora movement split and in decline – Chief Howard wrote a letter for public circulation, to explain the origin of his opposition to the Lumbee. It centered, surprisingly, on the congressional legislation that seemed to recognize the Lumbee as Indians: "In 1956, there was a thing called the *Lumbee Bill* which had terminated our people from Federal assistance."

He was referring both to the general federal policy, elaborated by President Richard Nixon in 1972, of terminating the special status of reservation Indians, which was so devastating in its effects, and also to the 1956 Act for Congressional Recognition of the Lumbee. That act stated:

> *Be it enacted by the Senate and the House of Representatives of the United States of America in Congress assembled, That the Indians now residing in Robeson and adjoining counties of North Carolina, originally found by the first white settlers on the Lumbee River in Robeson County, and claiming joint descent from the remnants of early American colonists and certain tribes of Indians originally inhabiting the coastal regions of North Carolina, shall, from and after the ratification of this Act, be Known and designated as Lumbee Indians of North Carolina and shall continue to enjoy all rights, privileges and immunities enjoyed by them as citizens of the State of North Carolina and of the United States as they enjoyed before the enactment of this Act, and shall continue to be subject to all the obligations and duties of such citizens under the laws of the State of North Carolina and the United*

> States . . . *and shall continue to be subject to all obligations and duties of such citizens under the laws of the State of North Carolina and the United States.* Nothing in this Act shall make such Indians eligible for any services performed by the United States because of their status as Indians, and None of the statutes of the United States which affect Indians because of their status as Indians shall be applicable to the Lumbee Indians. (Public Law 970, June 7, 1956; emphasis added)

Chief Howard wrote, commenting on this act and other problems and issues:

> *We . . . have school problems. Up until 1956, and 1913, the state of North Carolina billed* [built; passed legislative bills?] *to the Indian people, 27 Indian schools. In 1956, when the act of the Lumbee Bill passed, H.E.W. integrated and took away these schools* [he is referring to the College being integrated, first to Whites and then later to a few Blacks, starting in the early 1950s and more intensely following *Brown vs. Board of Education* in 1954]. *This is not what the facts are about now. The fact that we are up against now is "Federal Recognition" as Tuscarora Indians. This fight will never end until that day comes when the Federal Government will give us our historic name as Tuscarora Indians. . . . We have suffered here under tremendous police brutality here in this county simply because they do not want to see anything historical happen to Indian people here. . . . One of the things that has happened since the enactment of this piece of filth (as I call the Lumbee Bill) is that it deprived us of every chance we have of becoming historical people, unless this struggle continues.*

The idea that the Lumbee act was a betrayal of their rights as Indians – rather than the victory it seemed to many at the time – was shared by both Tuscarora groups. However bitter the split between the Tuscarora became, they still agreed on this. And they turned out, much later, to be at least partly right, although in the early 1970s the Lumbee did not have any idea of the magnitude of the problems this act would cause.

Over and over again, particularly for the Tuscarora, the major problem was finding a successful strategy not only in the midst of loss but also under the intense pressure of the sense that worse losses were to come. The impossibility of finding some successful strategy kept pounding wedges between people. This, and some glory chasing, was what split the two Tuscarora groups apart, and it was also the driving force in the separation of Tuscarora and Lumbee.

The Tuscarora emerged out of the Concerned Parents' Organization, meeting in Prospect in the fall of 1970. These were people who at that point called themselves Lumbee, and who had raised $2,200 – only to see their money and their court case very quickly lost. That defeat, coming after a string of electoral defeats, and seething in the cauldron of need, rage, hope and despair, was the birth of the Tuscarora – a people who could hardly afford further court cases or the assertive, economically and culturally expressive nationalism of the Lumbee Homecoming festivities, which began in the summer of 1970, parade and all.

The Lumbee shopping center, the Lumbee bank, the recent modestly affluent past now being celebrated: all the futures that were being claimed in parades and banks and fancy big stores in Pembroke, the Indian town, that took checks and credit *cards* but did not give credit as credit was once widely given in the small, rural, Indian "mom and pop" stores, by the storekeeper writing the amount on your page in a school copybook kept on the counter – all of this, the paraded past and the glittering future, and justice as well, was completely beyond the reach of most of the people who began to call themselves Tuscarora. And the small rural stores were closing, for a substantial part of their cash business, which helped them to carry the credit accounts, was now going to the Indian shopping centers in Pembroke and the better prices and wider range of goods that could be had there.

In that same circular letter, explaining his position in early 1974, Chief Howard wrote "[Our] past should have been revealed to the entire nation in this struggle." It was his strategy and his hope, particularly after the split with Rev. Elias Rogers the previous fall, but the past wasn't revealed. Nor would it be when, fourteen years later, two Tuscarora Indians, Eddy Hatcher and Timothy Jacobs, seized the offices of the *Robesonian* to call attention to the plight of their people. What did reveal – and invoke, and create – the past, partially and to a more limited audience, were the court cases, turning on both "justice" and the peculiarities of precedent.

8

The original 22

On March 29, 1973 – less than a week after the Prospect "riot" – the *Robesonian*, which noted on an interior page that Chief Howard's Tuscarora had given up trying to get access to Prospect and had moved their meetings to Union Elementary School, announced to the county – on page one, with a substantial headline – that the other Tuscarora group, the Eastern Carolina Tuscarora Indian Organization, led by the Reverend Elias Rogers, Keever Locklear, and Carnell Locklear, had filed suit against Rogers C. B. Morton, the secretary of the U.S. Department of the Interior and thus the head of the Bureau of Indian Affairs.

Rev. Rogers said that the suit, *Maynor* v. *Morton*, was filed on behalf of "all Indians in Eastern Carolina, including those who consider themselves Lumbees, as well as other groups." Specifically, however, the suit sought to gain the rights of Indians for the descendants of the twenty-two Indian people in Robeson County that the federal government had recognized in 1936 as being *persons* of "one-half or more Indian blood" under the provisions of the 1934 Indian Reorganization Act. These were the people that Indians in the county referred to as "the original 22."

Shortly after the Tuscarora split in the fall of 1972, the Eastern Carolina Tuscarora Indian Organization, which had two and at times three of the surviving seven "original 22" as members, asked the Bureau of Indian Affairs for assistance in forming a tribal organization, and for "clarification" of their rights to other benefits – particularly education, health care, and housing – that Indians were entitled to under the Indian Reorganization Act. It was a highly charged, surprising move. The ECTIO may have been the more "moderate" group, but here they

131

began to formulate a claim on the history of the original 22 that would turn into a powerful and effective confrontation.

On January 10, 1973, the deputy assistant secretary of the Department of the Interior wrote them that by the government's interpretation, the 1956 Lumbee act – which ended with the clause "Nothing in this Act shall make such Indians eligible for any services performed by the United States because of their status as Indians, and None of the statutes of the United States which affect Indians because of their status as Indians shall be applicable to the Lumbee Indians" – *terminated* the rights of the Tuscarora, encompassed within the Lumbee act, to any federal assistance.

The Tuscarora sued, on the basis that they were not Lumbee in 1936 – the original 22 were recognized simply as Indians, and indeed no one was a Lumbee in 1936, the name not coming into use until 1953, with state recognition. They felt, and the suit claimed, that an act that gave the name Lumbee to the Indians of Robeson County could not possibly terminate their rights, and with the support of the Native American Rights Fund, they were in court, going after Rogers Morton, Nixon's secretary of the interior.

The suit was presented on a broader terrain than the simple denial of rights to the descendants of the original 22. Among their lawyers were Arlinda Locklear, the first and one of the best Lumbee attorneys, and Tom Tureen, whose successful defense of the rights of the Passamaquoddy Indians of Maine established a whole new basis for Indian rights cases: the active responsibility of the federal government for ensuring the rights of Indians. In the "statement of facts" of their case against Morton, these lawyers asserted:

> The Indians of Robeson and surrounding counties have been sorely ignored by the Department of the Interior. Indeed, the Department has treated them with the same contemptuous disregard that it has shown practically all of the Indians who live east of the Mississippi. . . .
> [T]he policy of nonrecognition has been seriously damaging. It has meant that the federal government has not protected the land of eastern Indians and as a result eastern Indians, who constitute 25% of the Indian population in the United States, possess only 2% of United States Indian land. It has also meant that non-recognized eastern Indians have not benefitted from the special health, education and welfare programs which the federal government provides other Indians, and, in the South, it has condemned Indians to suffer the same, if not worse, abuses that southern whites have heaped on those of African ancestry, by denying them the opportunity to prove their separate identity.

> *Thus it is not surprising that over the years plaintiff Maynor and thousands of other Indians from his community have been obsessed with ending this discrimination. This case involves two such efforts, each of which was at least partially successful, and the Department of the Interior's claim that the participants in the second of these two efforts undid the achievements of those who took part in the first.*
>
> *The first effort in question was undertaken shortly after the Indian Reorganization Act, 25 USC 460* et seq., . . . *was passed in 1934. . . . This statute, which was the cornerstone of the New Deal for Indians, was primarily designed to strengthen tribal governments, and Indians who lived on reservations were automatically covered by its provisions. In addition, however, the Act was also open to any non-reservation Indian who could prove that he possessed at least one half Indian blood (25 U.S.C. 479). This was and is the most stringent eligibility standard which the federal government has ever applied to any Indian program* [which ordinarily require demonstrating one-quarter "Indian blood"], *but it nonetheless represented a significant breakthrough for Indians such as plaintiff Maynor, who until then had never had a statutory mechanism available to them for establishing their eligibility for any federal Indian benefits. Furthermore, while the IRA provided few substantial benefits for individual Indians, it did give such individuals special standing to petition the Secretary* [of the Department of the Interior] *to establish a reservation for them, and thereby grant them access to the full range of Indian services.*

The Indian Reorganization Act (IRA) of 1934 was designed, in part, as a remedy for the appalling suffering that had been imposed on Indian people – in general by the European and Euro-American onslaught, more specifically by the Dawes Severalty Act of 1887. The Dawes act, also known as the General Allotment Act, was designed to "civilize" and assimilate Indians by pressuring them to individualize their landholdings. Each Indian family was to be allotted, in severalty (individually) and from the tribal reservation lands (the lands already "reserved" for Indians) a specific parcel of land, to which they would eventually get title. The balance of the land was to be opened for settlement by U.S. citizens.

The amount of land lost by native peoples as a consequence of this act was staggering: From an already inadequate and intensely circumscribed base of about 155 million acres in 1880 (much of this being land that Euro-Americans did not want or could not use) native peoples were reduced to 70 million acres by 1934. This act had even more deadly consequences than land loss: as a result of allotment, the landholding unit became the individual Indian or the family. The clan, the extended kin group, the tribe or tribal section, the village – whatever had been the collectivity whose fundamental material basis was its possession and management of its lands now had that basis completely undermined. Of the 70 million acres that remained in Indian hands in 1934, 30 million acres were in the possession of tribal units, primarily in the arid southwest, and 40 million acres were held individually.

The appalling poverty and the often near-total collapse of native peoples' ability to minimally provision themselves with the most basic material necessities of life – increasingly characteristic features of native peoples' situation in the late nineteenth and early twentieth centuries – were thus brought about by two main causal forces: loss of land and the widespread disintegration of native social institutions that bound people together. The U.S. government responded to the massive intensification of helplessness and dependency that its own policies created by, at best, ignoring the plight of native peoples and, at worst, by further manipulations and impositions – in ration supplies, in the inadequate provision of alternative productive means, such as providing completely inadequate tools and supplies for farming and then claiming that Indians have an ideological or cultural resistance to agriculture. All this just exacerbated an already impossible and destructive situation.

In 1928 the Brookings Institution, a Washington, D.C., policy research organization, called attention to the life-destroying immiseration of Native American peoples in a report authored by Lewis Meriam. Nothing significant was done about it until Franklin Roosevelt came to the presidency; he appointed John Collier, an anthropologist and "New Deal liberal," as commissioner of Indian Affairs. Collier was pivotal in the design and development of the 1934 Indian Reorganization Act.

One of the central issues that the act was designed to address was precisely the shattering of native social institutions induced, or massively exacerbated, by the Dawes Severalty Act. This intended remedy was to have new destructive consequences in general, and to raise further specific problems for future Lumbee and Tuscarora attempts to gain recognition and a material basis for their collective identity.

As a precondition for acquiring material benefits through the IRA, the act required, and to a large extent imposed, liberal models of "tribal" organization: a tribal constitution, elected rather than kin-based leaders, and specific tribal membership rolls and membership boundaries (that is, each tribe would have to delineate who could and could not be a member, and provide a specific list of members to the BIA).

As part of the need to address the previously imposed disintegration of native social institutions, and the consequent individualization and atomization of native social life, the Indian Reorganization Act had to face the problem of how to deal with individual Native Americans not directly or tightly connected to "tribal" social institutions, or at least not connected in ways that the Bureau of Indian Affairs recognized.

This created a lot of conceptual and administrative difficulty for Collier, who on the one hand did not want to simply abandon individual Indians to their suffering, and on the other hand found it difficult even to define who an Indian was unless that person was connected to some form – even an imposed form – of tribal social organization.

The Indian Reorganization Act applied to:

> *All persons of Indian descent who are members of any recognized tribe now under Federal jurisdiction, and all persons who are descendants of such members who were, on June 1, 1934, residing within the boundaries of any Indian reservation,* and shall further include all other persons of one-half or more Indian blood. (Emphasis added)

Collier wrote a memorandum on September 22, 1935, concerning this statement of eligibility, stating that the members of recognized tribes presented no problems of administrative identification (although members of unrecognized tribes might well be considered individual Indians, since the tribe itself had no official standing in the BIA), but

> *the provision that "all other persons of one-half or more Indian blood" shall also be eligible under the Act confronts the Indian Office with an administrative problem of some complexity.*
>
> *This memorandum outlines the policy which the Indian Office will pursue in determining whether or not an applicant . . . meets the requirement . . . as to degree of Indian blood.*
>
> *Determination of the degree of Indian blood is entirely dependent on circumstantial evidence; there is no known sure or scientific proof. Nor has any legal standard of universal applicability been set up by statute for the determination of who is, and who is not, an Indian. These circumstances would seem to require that the Office of Indian Affairs establish a useful and practical definition of the . . .* [unclear word: term?]*, and fix upon a method of ascertaining blood degree which will admit of some administrative latitude.*
>
> *There will be few cases which will not be marked by some measure of reasonable doubt. We hold that it is proper to resolve this reasonable doubt favorably or unfavorably to the applicant in accordance with factors not strictly biological, but which may fairly be considered indicative of an Indian heritage.*
>
> *The evidence upon which a determination of blood degree may be made divides naturally into five classes (1) tribal rolls . . . accepted* [by

us] *as accurate . . . which record the percentage of Indian blood; (2) testimony of the applicant, supported by family records, . . . showing blood degree; (3) affidavits from persons who know the applicant['s] . . . family background; (4) findings of a qualified physical anthropologist based on examination of the applicant; (5) testimony of the applicant and supporting witnesses, tending to show that the applicant has retained a considerable measure of Indian culture and habits of living. . . . burden of proof on applicant.*

. . . [U]sually, however, investigation of the applicant's claim will be required. . . . Where the available evidence is insufficient to establish degree of blood, the Commissioner may appoint as a member of the [investigating] committee a competent physical anthropologist to examine the applicant.

. . . In reviewing the findings of the investigator or investigators, the Commissioner of Indian Affairs will exercise administrative discretion in determining what comparative weight shall be given to the various kinds of evidence. Where the genealogical or biological data still leave doubt as to the applicant's claim, the commissioner will consider whether or not the attitude of the applicant and his manner of living tend to show the inheritance of Indian characteristics.

It is a stunning document, breathtaking for its mixture of bureaucratic arrogance, reasonableness, and naiveté – and, it is hoped, humbling for anthropologists to contemplate. It was penned less than fifty-five years ago by a man who, however misguided, was not a racist or even a biological determinist, though he does, at the end, refer ambiguously to the "inheritance" of Indian characteristics. The then-current anthropological theory told him you could tell about "race" by measuring skull shapes, skin color, and an assortment of body parts. Two hundred and nine Indian people from Robeson County had applied for "recognition" to qualify for the benefits and to come under the provisions of the act, and on behalf of John Collier off to Robeson County went a Harvard professor, Carl Selzer, complete with borrowed measuring tools and camera.

On July 30, 1936, Selzer wrote to Collier:

I have the honor to submit the following report dealing with the degree of Indian blood of the so called "Robeson County Indians" of North Carolina.

All the data contained in this report were collected in June 1936 in Robeson County, North Carolina in my capacity as a member of the "Eastern Siouan Indian Commission." In accordance with instructions received, separate racial diagnoses were made for each person with the purpose of determining whether the applicants examined did or did

> *not possess one-half or more Indian blood. No distinctions or designa-*
> *tions were made as to tribal affiliations of the subjects. These diagnoses*
> *were based solely on the manifestations of physical characteristics of*
> *known racial significance as interpreted by the science of physical and*
> *racial anthropology.*

The letter continues, thanking Professor E. A. Hooten, chair of the Division of Anthropology at Harvard, for the loan of anthropometric and camera equipment, and Major Dunham of the Army Medical School for a supply of serum for blood group tests.

Selzer tested all – and only – the 209 individuals who applied to the BIA for recognition; of these he recommended acceptance of twenty-two as having "one-half or more Indian blood." In several cases full brothers and sisters of those accepted were rejected: it would have been a farce were so much not at stake.

So the origins of the "original twenty-two" Indians lie, in part, in two acts of domination: the Indian Reorganization Act and the measurements and blood tests of "racial anthropology." There is, however, far more to the Indianness of the original twenty-two and their kith and kin than this, which was just a small part of their ongoing struggles for land, for rights, and for recognition.

II

The Lumbee Recreation Center, with its nine-hole golf course, fishing lake, swimming pool, and extensive picnic grounds was built with a government grant in the mid-1960s. It quickly became the focus of intense controversy between more and less affluent middle-class Lumbee, and a source of bitterness for many poorer Lumbee – who got to see the place on a rare, free church trip but ordinarily could not even think of affording the steep annual membership or even the single-use fees. And it turned into a point of strong contention between Lumbee and Tuscarora – Lumbee claiming that it was Tuscarora on their way back from the BIA occupation in 1972 who backed their truck full of BIA documents through the gates of the Recreation Center and burned the Lumbee's electric golf carts. For many, however, the Recreation Center was – or was also – a source of pride; another instance of Lumbee success in acquiring the material benefits of middle-class Americans, another instance of Lumbee success in dealing with and obtaining benefits from government programs.

The land the Lumbee Recreation Center was built on in the 1960s had been, since the 1930s, the site of bitter conflict. The land was the last

remnant tract from two failed destroyed Depression-era rural resettlement programs for "the Siouan Indians of Robeson County" – Pembroke
Farms, composed of a number of individually owned neighboring farms
built on a tract of land, and an Indian cooperative farming group, the
Red Banks Mutual Association, that used a single large tract of land
leased from the federal government through Pembroke Farms.

The land of Pembroke Farms and the Red Banks Mutual Association,
mostly acquired in the 1930s, had barely been fully settled by Indians
in 1943 when the federal government started to take the project apart.
In a letter to James E. Chavis, whom the government referred to as
"Secretary of the General Council of Indians of Robeson County" (March
22, 1945), J. B. Slack, the regional director of the Farm Security Administration, stated:

> *All of the land on Pembroke Farms Project which has been developed
> into farm units is being offered to present occupants wherever they can
> qualify. . . . The additional land, priced in accordance with its fair
> market value . . . was offered to the present occupants on the basis of a
> 40 year loan at 3% interest. . . . After each family was given ample
> time to reach a decision relative to the purchase of additional land
> under these terms, the remaining land, consisting almost entirely of
> woodland, was divided into various sized tracts. These tracts will be
> offered to the public in the near future . . . it may be purchased by
> anyone who can meet the terms under which it is offered.*

The General Council of *Siouan* Indians (not the "General Council of
Indians," as the farm security director called them), the sponsors of the
Pembroke Farms project, protested the sale of these "surplus" lands
as strongly as they could – with petitions, with telegrams, with letters
to Washington. In October 1945 William Zimmerman, the assistant
commissioner of Indian affairs, wrote to Stott Noble, the assistant ad-
ministrator of the Farm Security Administration, that

> *the recent sale of approximately 3,000 acres of alleged surplus lands*
> [from a total holding of just over 9,000 acres] *was a mistake. I
> believe that these lands should have been held for . . . future use. . . . The
> opportunity to provide additional land for this Indian group within
> easy access of the present school will probably not come again for many
> years. In view of our general supervision of Indian affairs I hope that
> in the future your administration will take no steps looking to the sale
> of other land or the dispossession of any of the present project clients
> without first giving this Office an opportunity to consult with you.
> Although I should be very reluctant to assume any direct responsibility
> for this project, it may be that the Indian Service could be helpful.*

In 1943 the Farm Security Administration was the subject of congressional hearings and under pressure by an increasingly conservative

Congress, suspicious of all the Depression social programs. These hearings elicited a capsule economic history of the Robeson County projects:

> Name – *Pembroke Farms, N.C. (RI-NC-22)* . . .
>
> Justification – *Pembroke Farms was initiated by the Resettlement Administration in 1936 for the purpose of providing sufficient suitable land and homes for Indian families of the Siouan Tribe.* [Note how the people are, and are not, Indians, "real" Indians with a historically sanctioned Indian name – Siouan Indians – as the government finds it convenient.] *The government has made development loans to 75 farmers and by means of long-term payments these Indians will eventually own their property and continue to be self-sustaining.*
>
> Description – *The project consists of 9,297 acres of which 4,804 acres have been developed into 65 individual farm units. As of March 31, 1943, the project was fully occupied. The land was purchased in 1936, 1937 and 1940. The dwellings constructed on the family units consist of five and seven rooms each. Outbuildings consist of stock barns, poultry houses, smokehouses, combination cow barns, smokehouses and poultry houses, hog houses, and new privies. Each unit has a well and a hand pump.* . . .
>
> *The project has a combination grade school and community building. There are also three large drainage canals which are for the use of the entire community and which are connected with a system of drainage ditches.*
>
> *In addition, the Government made a loan to the Red Banks Mutual Association for the development of a cooperative farm in 1938. The association has 16 members and has rented 1,720 acres of land from the Government on a 99 year lease. The occupants are all Indian families.*
>
> *In the cooperative area, on a site known as the Red Banks Tract, facilities such as tobacco curing barns, mule barns, machine sheds, grain bins, warehouses, and tool sheds have been constructed. These buildings are for the use of the 15 members of the cooperative association living in this area.*
>
> . . .
>
> Ownership of land – *As of March 31, 1943, there have been 64 farms sold* [to their Indian occupants], *at an average selling price of $4,947. The average unit investment on the farm units by the Government was $6,428. Deeds are being prepared and will be delivered to the families soon. The land being farmed cooperatively will be sold to the Red Banks Mutual Association.*
>
> Family progress – *The families on this project in 1942 had on the average a gross income of $2,315, a net income of $1,585, and a net*

> worth of $1,857 which was an increase of $677 over 1941. These
> families canned 358 quarts of fruits and vegetables per average family
> [it is continually surprising what the federal government knows
> about the people in its charge, and how, and in what forms it
> knows this]. *On the average they produced 998 gallons of milk in*
> *1942, a 36% increase over 1941; 1,624 pounds of pork, a 38%*
> *increase over 1941; 783 dozen eggs per family, an increase of 44%*
> *over 1941; and chickens, 559 pounds, an increase of 53% over 1941.*
> *In addition to the above products, the Red Banks Mutual Association*
> *which operates a part of the Pembroke project with 15 families partici-*
> *pating, had a gross income of $35,587, a net income of $6,203, a net*
> *worth of $8,454, and paid out $586 in dividends to members. This*
> *income was from the sale of beef, pork, cotton, lespedeza seed, and other*
> *agricultural products.*

These production and income figures make a startling contrast to
the figures collected when the government surveyed the area only eight
years before, in the context of feasibility and planning studies for the
establishment of Pembroke Farms and the Red Banks project.

Throughout the early 1930s, but with particular intensity after the
passage of the Indian Reorganization Act and the establishment of
several Depression farm and land projects, Joseph Brooks, the leader of
the Tribal Council of the Siouan Indians of Robeson County, and James
Chavis, council secretary, had been pressuring the Bureau of Indian
Affairs for land – not a "reservation": Jim Chavis told me, in 1968, "That
would have set us back a hundred years." They wanted land for Indians,
Indian-owned land. Even the White county officials were worried about
how many Indians had pellagra, and other nutritional diseases, for lack
of enough land to grow food.

In 1935 John D. Pearmain, Indian rehabilitation specialist of the
Resettlement Program, came to Robeson County to survey and to report
on Indian farms and farming – what would today be called a "needs
assessment" study. His survey included several interviews concerning
the current circumstances of the Indian people in the county, from
which I have selected four: James Chavis and Joseph Brooks, two major
Indian leaders of the 1930s; Ulysses Chavis, James Chavis's brother, who
was also his tenant, and Leonard Bullard, who along with Ulysses Chavis
typifies the circumstances of ordinary Indian sharecroppers and small
farmers in the midst of the Depression. While James Chavis and Joseph
Brooks were in somewhat better circumstances than was usual for Indians, the differences were rather small – and neither benefited from
the resettlement program they worked so hard to bring.

In the quoted reports that follow I have included much but not
all of the repetition, particularly of income figures, in the original

documents, because one gets from this a sense of the government agent himself wrestling with the difficulty of the Indian people's situation. I have also included much, but not all, of the description of the houses, to illustrate how Indian people then lived – the past the brick houses seek to transcend. I must also add that including all the details from the following four reports makes me uncomfortable, because of their intrusiveness upon the privacy of the people interviewed. They are included, finally, primarily for the younger Indian people of Robeson County today and those in similar situations, who may find it significant to reflect on the difficulty of their grandparents' adult lives – how much they did, politically and socially as well as personally – with how very, very little.

> Name   *Ulysses Chavis*
> Section   *Pembroke Township, Robeson Co., N.C.*
> Occupation   *1/3 cropper (farms on his brother James Chavis' place, but his brother wants the farm himself in 1936)*
> Age   *32 years*
> Family   *Wife and four children, ages 7, 6, 4, 2 (6 people on place)*
> Farm   *28 acre farm – 15 acres tilled – 13 acres woodlot – farm rather run down when bought two years ago by James B. Chavis. The man who had it previously "stuck fire in it," i.e. hurt the soil by burning the fields over repeatedly (and the place showed it. JDP)*
> Crop acreage
> *5 acres cotton, made 711 lbs. (got [he kept] 1/3 of seed)*
> *0 acres tobacco (had no allotment)*
> *3 acres corn, produced 85–90 bu.*
> *3/4 acres of oats*
> *Income of 1/3 cropper:*
> *His 1/3 of all cotton, including his 1/3 of seed,*
> *brought*..*$30.50*
> *uses his one third of corn on place* .... - - -
> *Worked outside for wages 12 days on tobacco,*
>   *in the field, $1.25 per day (12 hours)* *15.00*
> *Also 5 weeks grading tobacco at 5.50* *27.50*
>   *Gross Income for year, cash received* *$73.00*
> *Moving Dec. 1st. Has had no success getting another place, has been trying ever since 1st of September – would like to get a place with 20 acres of good tilled land with a "provision of tobacco"* [an allotment] *(2 ½ acres). . . . could handle 25 acres of tilled if he had a place for small grain [wheat] as well as the 8–10 acres of cotton. Has small garden 1/20 acre – owns one cow (dry) 3 small pigs – 22 chickens.*
>   *Interviewed 11/3/35 on his place by JDP.*

Name *James E. Chavis – Secretary, Siouan Tribal Council*
Section *Pembroke Township, Robeson County, N.C.*
Occupation *Farm owner (his brother, Ulysses Chavis, running his farm as a 1/3 cropper this year, but next year James E. Chavis will operate his own place. . . . Also teaches school at Pembroke. Gets some $83. per month while teaching (3 months); says he has been working almost 30 years to have a place of his own. Bought his present place two years ago. Paid only $1,000. for it understanding that the land was not so good as other, more expensive places. Says he never could have saved enough to buy it without the teaching job.*
House *Has 3 room house; 7 people in it – (2 families); House in pretty good shape; needs a 4 room house to cost about $550.*
Age *Aged 39.*
Family *Has wife and one child. Was one of 9 children; all but 3 are grown and married.*
Farm *See under Ulysses Chavis. Says he himself can get a living off his farm but that his brother did not have enough of a money crop to support his family. (Ulysses Chavis' total cash taken during 1935 was $73.50 from crops and labor.)*
REMARKS
Newcomers (white farmers) driving Indian sharecroppers from farms. Says trouble in this part of the country is that the landlords hereabouts have gone to the NW part of the state where the farms are smaller, but good tobacco farms, and gotten the farmers to move in here [as sharecroppers]. *(This is confirmed by John Strickland and A. C. Locklear and two (white) plantation overseers, J. R. Moore of Fletcher Plantation, and W. R. Beeson. . . . JDP) Says landlords who have done this hereabouts are Paul McNeil, brought in 8 families in 1934 from NW part of state, H. B. Ashley brought in several also; W. R. Beeson, Supt., Pates Supply Co. Farms, a division of the John F. McNair Corporation (land corporation) – McNair "a million dollar merchant and landowner" owning thousands of acres – "3 to 5 miles at a stretch in one block on one road" – "Have been bringing in farmers from outside and squeeze the local men out." Do this "to drive a better bargain. . . . "*
Rehabilitation *Says as far as he knows (he is Secretary of Siouan Tribal Council) only two Indians out of about 3,000 families have received Rehabilitation loans to help them buy a mule, seed, equipment, etc., though more applied. Says that on a 1/3 croppers farm, if the government bought it, 3 farm owners could be put on the same land, and would each do as well as the tenant (who only got 1/3 of all he raised of tobacco and cotton); says that each of these new owners on his*

own 1/3 of the land would get more off it than the present 1/3 cropper does now, because as owners they would each "take better care of the land they owned", i.e. would not only farm it better, but would also plant crops like wheat (for flour) that no sharecroppers plant now, or plant only occasionally. (Note: Wheat has to be planted in the fall, and most of the share croppers are not told by the landlord until about December 1st whether or not they are to be allowed to have the farm for the succeeding year, so they do not plant wheat for the most part, and therefore have to buy their flour on credit, at exorbitant prices. See elsewhere for confirmation by different individuals of excessive prices charged on credit accounts *by company and other stores. [JDP]) . . .*
    Interviewed 11/8/35 and again on 11/10/35 by JDP.

Name   *Leonard Bullard – age 39*
Section   *Philadelphus Section, Robeson County, N.C.*
Occupation   *Tenant Farmer – 1/3 cropper – landlord gets the cotton seed* [an arrangement where the tenant gets half of the cotton crop but the landlord gets all the cotton seed; roughly equivalent to the returns on 1/3 the whole].
Family   *Wife and two adopted children (girls age 13 and 14) – 4 on place*
House   *Has new house built by landlord last winter – 4 rooms cost about $200.00 – size of house 24 × 24 feet – it took four men 5 days to build house – all rough lumber – metal roof – 1500 ft of lumber on the four outside walls – 2 rooms "ceiled" and 2 rooms "unceiled." Also 2 men one day on chimney – total labor on house about $50.00 (three men at $1.00 per day, one man at $3.00 per day and two masons one day) – $50.00 for lumber and $50.00 for metal roof – about $200.00 in all. (Roof leaks already)*
Farm
Works 23 acres:
8.0 acres of cotton (cleared $80.00 out of cotton, from his 1/2)
0 acres tobacco
15.0 acres of corn – used all corn on place
Income   *Has been close to 20 years on same place with same landlord. Cleared $80.00 last year after picking and selling and paying his bills – had 1/4 acre garden (enough) – no cow – one mule – four small pigs – 20 or so chickens – took in about $20.00 on outside labor helping barn tobacco elsewhere.*
Expenses   *Clothes and all other purchases has to come out of the $80.00 plus $20.00 noted above as his cash income for the year ($100.00 total).*

143

Remarks

*The 23 acres of tilled land is about as much as he can tend himself –
he has been in pretty good health, except his back has bothered him the
last four or five years – has never been able to save any money – the
two adopted girls help to pick cotton, also his wife – this year he hired
$1.12 worth of help (1 day).*

Interviewed 11/8/35 on his farm by JDP

Name *Joseph Brooks – Delegate, Siouan Indians of Lumber River.*
Section *Pembroke Township, Robeson County, N.C.*
Age *31 years old*
Family *Wife and 3 small children; six in household (one girl of 19,
a relative boarding with them)*
House *Four room house – frame – matched pine inside, 5 to 6 inches
wide, wood floor (single thickness – as are all the houses visited) 2 stack
chimney (rather, 2 fireplaces in the one central chimney) and stove flu
separate, tin roof, living room and kitchen 16 ft. × 18 ft. each, 2
bedrooms . . . porch . . . outside of house sheaved with "German" siding;
house built in 1926; . . . says same house could be built today for
$400.00; A. C. Locklear says it would cost $500.00 today . . . house
set on wood blocks; no plaster; two bedrooms are unfinished inside;
living room and kitchen – walls and ceiling are finished with "ceiling";
house two feet above the ground as are most or all of the houses visited.*
Income *Had 3 acres of tobacco and not on government contract;
sold $488. worth of tobacco net, after tax had been paid at .06 cents
per lb; no cotton; 1 acre of corn, well fertilized, produced about 32
bushels; has 4 hogs; 40 chickens, bought 2 tons fertilizer at $26.50 per
ton; 200 # soda cost $3.00, 2 bags . . . fertilizer $3.12; paid out $40.00
for outside labor* [income less costs = $388.88].

Interviewed Thursday 11/7/35 at his place.

III

The year that the Indian Reorganization Act was passed, 1934, was a
year of intense struggle for the Indian people of Robeson County, who
were trying to become recognized by Congress as Siouan Indians of the
Lumber River. This movement, centered in the rapidly growing Siouan
Lodge organizations, was led by Joseph Brooks and James Chavis. It was
running into trouble in its appeals to congress, not just for the usual
reasons, but also *because* of the active opposition of another Indian faction
whose most influential member was the Reverend D. F. Lowery.

144

The original 22

On February 12, 1934, E. J. Britt, attorney and leading member of one of the largest landholding families in the county, wrote to North Carolina's Senator Josiah Bailey, who had been helping James Chavis and Joseph Brooks, and the substantial and passionate following they had mobilized, with a bill for congressional recognition as Siouan Indians. Britt, along with D. F. Lowery, opposed recognition of the Siouan Indians:

> A number of the Indian people of Robeson County came to see me on Saturday and desire to enter a protest to a Bill that has been introduced in Congress, changing the name of the Indians of Robeson County. . . . There was a good delegation of these Indian people who came to see me on Saturday, who represent the best element of their people, and they say that at least 90% of the best element of the Indians of Robeson County are opposed to the passage of this Bill. They are satisfied with their present status and hope to remain as Cherokee Indians of Robeson County.
>
> I hope that you will see to it that the Bill is not passed, or . . . that you will hold the matter up until a delegation of the best class of Indians can be heard on the matter.

Reverend Lowery wrote to Senator Bailey himself, on the same day, trying to account for the mass support for the bill and against his position. He wrote on letterhead of his church

> A Big Church   A Big Sunday School
> A Big Epworth League   A Big Welcome For All
> The First M.E. Church

> The Bill to change our name from Cherokee to Siouan is not what the people want. It has a big following thinking it will bring lands and money. If the provision was read to our folk and they knew about it they would be all off.
>
> The big mass meeting was because it was announced that our Representative Clark was to speak. Had he been present and explained the meaning of the provisions on the bill he would not have gotten very many votes for its passage.

When the Siouan bill failed, later in 1934, it was the collapse of a lot of hopes, a lot of dreams and a substantial amount of support that the Indians had generated in Washington, including within the Bureau of Indian Affairs. Indeed, the 1936 testing and registration of the original 22 as *individual* Indians, under the protection of the Indian Reorganization Act, was one outcome of that collapse of the attempt to get federal recognition for the *group*, for Siouan was not just a name, not just an identity, but a real group. In the early 1930s, the Siouan Lodge had developed and sustained countywide Indian leaders, local councils

145

with local leaders, regular local and mass meetings, celebrations and festivals, membership rolls – a whole panoply of tribal institutions satisfying to its substantial membership and impressive to outsiders.

The Siouan Lodge movement, and the pressure it brought to bear in Washington both for new gains and for redress of prior grievances (particularly the setbacks of 1912–22) emerged from and transformed a smaller movement in the late 1920s and early 1930s to have the Indians of Robeson County federally designated as Cheraw. In fact, Senator Burtan K. Wheeler, chairman of the Senate Committee on Indian Affairs, in his report on the Siouan Indians of Lumber River, January 23, 1934, began by proposing an amendment substituting the word "Siouan" for "Cheraw," in the Cheraw bill that died in the Indian Affairs Committee in the summer of 1932. That Cheraw bill, as the secretary of the Department of Interior pointed out in his comments, "provides for the enrollment of the Croatan Indians of North Carolina as Cheraw Indians, and would permit their children to attend Government Schools" – particularly the federal Indian college at Carlisle, Pennsylvania, where several Indians had gone in the early twentieth century, until they were rejected for being insufficiently Indian after World War I. Too Indian for the White colleges in North Carolina, not Indian enough for the federally supported Indian colleges, they were confined to the still poorly developed normal school in Pembroke, unless they could afford to go, at their own expense, to Tennessee or beyond.

IV

The Siouan bill was steadily dying, albeit with some flutters and flourishes, as Senator Bailey and the other members of the North Carolina congressional delegation withdrew their support, being willing to give some easy assistance to Robeson County Indians, but not wanting to get unnecessarily embroiled in local controversy. Yet, the passion for recognition and for land was intensifying dramatically.

In early 1935 William Zimmerman, assistant commissioner of Indian affairs, wrote to Fred Baker, superintendent of the Sisseton Indian Agency and a former member of the commission to enroll the Eastern Band of Cherokee (descendants of those who escaped the forced removal westward), sending him to Raleigh and Pembroke "for the purpose of making a preliminary investigation of the feasibility of setting up a land purchase and work relief project for the rehabilitation of the Siouan Indians of North Carolina."

Commissioner Zimmerman's letter to Baker contained two key points. First, he suggested that the U.S. government might provide land for the

Indians of Robeson County, but would hold title to the individual plots of land, which was exactly the policy of the Dawes Severalty Act: it had, in general practice, the advantage of inhibiting the sale of plots of land to Whites, and the massive disadvantage for Indians that as long as the government held title the land could not be used to secure crop-production loans, making it impossible for the Indians to compete in the market with White-owned farms, and making it almost necessary to just rent most of their land to local White farmers (at a price set by the government).

Second, the letter noted that Joseph Brooks had visited the Office of Indian Affairs, seeking help: particularly land. Brooks was asking for 20–40 acres a family (less than former Black slaves were supposed to be given after the Civil War – they got "40 acres and a mule"), although he also asked for pasturelands, suggesting the possibility of a collective enterprise. Brooks also asked for Indians to be consulted in the whole process, and Fred Baker was told to contact him.

Baker's report, submitted July 10, 1935, strongly endorsed the project:

> *I visited the town of Pembroke . . . which is almost in the exact center of the Indian population and met Mr. Joseph Brooks, the tribal delegate of the so-called Siouan group, at whose instance and suggestion the investigation was to be made. A series of group meetings at various centers of Indian population were arranged for during the following week. . . . Some seven public meetings were held which were attended by the Indians in each neighborhood. It is estimated that at least four thousand Indians were present at these gatherings. I explained the object of my visit fully and frankly and at each meeting the Indians present were called upon to express their views as to the proposed project and as to the problems confronting them as a people. It may be said without exaggeration that the plan of the government meets with prac-tically the unanimous support of all of the Indians. I do not recall having heard a dissenting voice. They seemed to regard the advent of the United States government into their affairs as the dawn of a new day; a new hope and a new vision. They hailed with joy the offer of the government; many of the old people could not restrain their feelings, – tears filled many eyes and flowed down furrowed cheeks . . . as the old people expressed so deep a longing to have a piece of land on which they could live in peace without fear of ejection by a landlord. Inquiry revealed that only about fifteen families out of every hundred owned any land; that eighty-five percent of the Indians were tenants or "share-croppers."*

Baker goes on to describe the system of sharecropping, and to show how difficult it was to live within its strictures. He noted that a few years earlier the county health officer, partly under pressure of Indian complaints, began to pressure landlords to allow tenants a bit more land for their own vegetables in order to reduce the widespread incidence of pellagra among Indians. He found that credit for foodstuffs given by landlords or merchants during the growing season was restricted to minuscule levels and was very costly when available. Some of the problems he saw; some he heard about through intense complaints:

> Underneath all of these complaints I could detect at times hot resentment and at other times a supplication and a prayer that the general government come to the rescue of this suffering people and take measures to break the bonds which shackle them to a system of land tenure unworthy of a free people. Over thousands of these Indian people there hovers constantly the fear of being given notice on December 1st that they will not be given a renewal of their lease the following year. Many publicly recounted this experience and their pathetic story of wandering about seeking a refuge and a haven for their families.

After considering the impact of "resettling" Indian families on the local White farmers' labor needs, Baker recommended a project for only two hundred Indian families. Clearly he was a decent man, but he was also a liberal, and did not contemplate more fundamental and more adequate solutions.

> The present Indian population is pressing closely upon the tillable land now available for their use. . . . They do not have the same opportunities held forth to them as members of the white race in the South. I find that the sense of racial solidarity is growing stronger and that the members of this tribe are cooperating more and more with each other with the object in view of promoting the mutual benefit of all the members. It is clear to my mind that sooner or later governmental action will have to be taken in the name of justice and humanity to aid them.

The bill for recognition as Siouan Indians had just failed, owing to the opposition led by Rev. D. F. Lowery, who was clinging to the Cherokee name and history. As Superintendent Baker was proposing to help the Indian people of Robeson County *as Indians*, in an all-Indian project, he had to deal with the issue of origins:

> Some writers on the subject have maintained that they belong to a branch of the great Siouan family, a linguistic group named after the well-known Sioux or Dakota Indians. An effort has been made during the past two years to have this name, "Siouan," officially recognized by the Congress of the United States as the proper name of this tribe. Legislation to accomplish this object was introduced in the Congress but it met with opposition on the part of a minority of the tribe and failed of passage. Officially, then, under the laws of the State of North Carolina they are known as "Cherokee Indians of Robeson County." Having

> served as a member of a commission to enroll the Eastern Band of
> Cherokees of North Carolina I am constrained to doubt the correctness
> of this designation. Their connection with the Cherokee Tribe must
> have been extremely remote in the past. That they possess Indian blood
> is beyond question.

There is a profound tension evident in this conjunction of identity
struggles and political-economic situation: First, being Indian – indeed
being any non-White – worked to exclude them, as a people, from
either the political or economic resources necessary to obtain and to
hold on to land. (Poor Whites had a similar difficulty gaining access
to land ownership, but they faced a substantially different dynamic of
domination, exclusion, and inclusion.) The problem of land acquisition
was not simply cost: Land, as Baker made clear near the end of his
report, was widely available; the current price was about $15 an acre for
unimproved land (land that had usually been logged, but was not fully
cleared), plus the costs of clearing and ditching: *"there is right at hand
great areas of excellent land in Robeson and adjoining counties available for
their settlement provided some plan is worked out to clear, ditch, drain and make
it ready for the growing of crops. Less than half of the land in Robeson County
alone is in cultivation, and the same may be said of adjoining counties."*

If Indians were excluded from access to land in substantial part because
of their Indianness, it did not really matter which Indians they were; it
was sufficient that they were Indian, or more broadly, that they were
not White. If, however, the government was to help them redress their
situation, then their position would be far more secure if they were
recognized as a specific group – indeed, a specific "tribe" of Indians.
The government, particularly in this period, conceived of itself as
having specific obligations to specific tribes of Indians, and other than
placing substantial aspects of its Indian administration in one bureau,
did little for Indians in general. In sum, it did not matter at all what
kind of Indians they were when they were squeezed off their land or
prevented by a variety of socioeconomic obstacles, particularly access to
credit, from acquiring land; it turned out to matter a lot what specific
kind of Indians they are if they were to get any help redressing this
situation.

While Baker was proposing to help them just as Indians, the fragility
of their position without a historically specific, and even *also* a historically famous identity, was evident in the internal government discussion of the Siouan bill during the year before Baker wrote his report.

Harold Ickes, secretary of the Interior Department, wrote to Senator
Wheeler on the subject of the Siouan resurrection of the Cheraw recognition bill, on January 10, 1934:

> As directed by Senate Resolution no. 410, dated June 30, 1914, a careful investigation was made of their condition. . . . The report shows, among other things, that until 1835 these Indians were recognized as citizens of the State of North Carolina, but were disfranchised in that year and placed upon the footing of free persons of color. Later in 1885 their civil rights were restored and they are now recognized as citizens of the State.
>
> . . . It would appear from other facts set forth in the document referred to that the Federal Government is under no obligation whatsoever to this group of people. We believe that the enactment of this [recognition] legislation would be the initial step in bringing these Indians under the jurisdiction of the Federal Government. Certainly it would have the effect of providing educational facilities for some of them at the expense of the Government. . . .
>
> . . . I do not favor the bill in its present form. . . . I do believe that legislation to clarify the status of these Indians is desirable. Therefore, it is suggested that all after the enacting clause be stricken out and the following be substituted therefore:
>
> That those Indians in Robeson and adjoining counties, North Carolina, who were formerly known as "Croatan Indians," shall hereafter be designated "Siouan Indians of the Lumber River," and shall be so recognized by the United States Government: Provided, That nothing contained herein shall be construed as conferring Federal wardship or any other governmental rights or benefits upon such Indians.

Appended to this letter was a report by the distinguished and scholarly anthropologist, John R. Swanton, written in 1933, entitled "Probable Identity of the 'Croatan' Indians," which surveys the history of Indian peoples in this region and concludes:

> The evidence available thus seems to indicate that the Indians of Robeson County who have been called Croatan and Cherokee are descended from certain Siouan Tribes of which the most prominent were the Cheraw and the Keyauwee, but they probably included as well remnants of the Eno and Shakori, and very likely some of the coastal groups such as the Waccamaw and Cape Fears. It is not improbable that a few families or small groups of Algonquian or Iroquoian connection may have cast their lot with this body of people, but contributions from such sources must have been relatively insignificant. Although there is some reason to think that the Keyauwee Tribe actually contributed more blood to the Robeson County Indians than any other, their name is not widely known, whereas that of the Cheraw has been familiar to historians, geographers and ethnologists since the time of DeSoto, and has a firm position in the cartography of the region. The

> *Cheraw, too, seem to have taken a leading part in opposing the colonists during and immediately after the Yamasee uprising. Therefore, if the name of any tribe is to be used in connection with this body of 6 or 8 thousand people, that of the Cheraw would be the most appropriate.*

V

While the struggles with the federal government in the 1930s turned on the intersection of identity and land, those at the end of the nineteenth and the early twentieth century were focused on the connection between identity and schools.

In 1885 the state recognized the Croatan Indians in the same bill that gave them the first benefits of this recognition: a separate school system. That precise conjunction was carried to the U.S. Congress in a search for federal recognition and, especially, federal assistance for education. It was intensely fought until 1914 and decisively lost. By the time it was lost the whole struggle for identity and education was deeply embedded in a historical vision of the Indians of Robeson County as having Cherokee origins.

Multiple histories intersected destructively throughout this period and on into the 1930s. These multiple histories went deeper than the issue of whether the people now known as Lumbee and Tuscarora have a Siouan, a Cheraw, or a Cherokee origin. As we shall see in Chapter 11, this way of posing the question of origins profoundly misunderstands the actual history of all southeastern Indian peoples. The life-shaping issues embedded in the controversies over Lumbee history centered on issues of land, education, and identity in the context of land and education.

To illustrate, in 1967 White county officials decided to redig the Back Swamp drainage canal, and to assess farmers along its drainage network for the costs. Back Swamp begins just below Red Banks, on the western edge of the center of the most dense Indian settlement, and meanders south and east, passing south of Pembroke. It was an explosive issue: at the height of the early harvest season in 1968, when a day away from farm work meant a noticeable loss of income, there were 500 Indians in and around the county courthouse, protesting the plan to redig the canal: "This land," as one Indian told the court, to cheers and substantial applause, "was our fathers'."

Explosive, but multifaceted. On the one hand, better drainage meant better crops: fields waterlog quickly in this exceedingly flat terrain. On the other hand, there was the memory of events when the Back Swamp drainage canal was first dug. In 1912, when Back Swamp was surveyed in preparation for its ditching, the main channel was 50 to 1,500 feet wide, with substantial portions of the water surface being over 1,000 feet wide, plus an additional extensive watershed of tangled undergrowth. By plantation standards it was far too wet to farm. The survey claimed "it is impossible to cultivate much of the land in the district," but it was implicitly referring to White methods of commercial cultivation, for many Indians were farming small plots scattered about on the higher ground. There were, moreover, a substantial number of good, working Indian farms at the edges of the wetland.

After the ditching between 1914 and 1918 Back Swamp was a 16-foot channel, with another 16-foot right-of-way on each side. As the land was cleared out, so were many Indian landowners.

Some swampland is underneath standing water and thus cannot be farmed, but much of the land in Back Swamp, and elsewhere in Robeson County, is not swamp but "swampy." This means that the land is not under water but is "wet" – in some spots soaking wet after a rain, or between rains; in other places it is just too wet for crops to do well. Looking across a field of corn growing in swampy land you would see some spots bare of crop, some where the crop was stunted and "doing poorly," and some where it was "just fine." The boundaries of such a field would likely be very irregular, the margins defined by where the land is, in ordinary years, too wet to plow. Around this field there would be growing not the cypress trees characteristic of the standing-water swamps, but ash and alder and perhaps pine, if that side of the field were sandy.

Draining the land means both creating newly farmable land by getting rid of standing water, and, what is more important for understanding Indian land loss, removing wet spots in land that was already farmed. To drain the land, a major channel is dug about where the center of the swamp channel naturally ran, and the farmers on each side are assessed both an initial and an annual cash payment for the cost of this ditch. They not only have to pay this, they also have to "tie themselves into" the main ditch if they are going to get any benefits: they have to dig, or pay to have dug, channels around and sometimes into their fields, and they have to dig channels from their fields to the main ditch, which might be a half a mile or more away.

For farmers with small plots of land, much of which may be devoted to "subsistence" agriculture – farmers who are, in any case, often only imperfectly connected to crop markets – the extra cash costs of such drainage projects are often devastating. During this first ditching of Back Swamp, in 1914–18, a large bank in the county seat advanced farmers the cash for the drainage assessment, which had to be paid, with their land as security for the loan, and a substantial number of Indian farmers soon became sharecroppers.

This was the second time since 1885, when the Lumbee were recognized as Indians by the state, that they suffered through a period of rapid and widespread land loss. In 1890 a large lumber company from South Carolina began buying substantial tracts of land in central Robeson County, with the promise to resell it at a low per-acre cost when they were through logging. As the company continued to buy land over the next decade or so, it built narrow-gauge railroads into the swamps to haul the timber out, and dug its own drainage canals to facilitate the work. When it resold the land, by then largely cleared and partly drained, it did so at $5 per acre, a good price by current standards, but in blocks of no less than 100 acres and for full cash payment at the time of sale. The White-owned banks refused to extend credit to Indians or Blacks.

In the midst of this land loss it is somewhat surprising that the struggles in this period for recognition from the state and from the federal government did not raise the issue of land but of schools. In the context of trying to find White legislative support for their schools, Indians shifted from the aging Hamilton McMillan, a member of the state legislature who sponsored the initial Croatan legislation and who was a strong advocate of the notion that the Indian people in Robeson County were the descendants of the "lost colony," to A. W. McLean, who was their active supporter in their appeals to Congress, in 1912–14, and who had been very influential in 1907 in helping them attain substantially increased funds for the normal school from the state. Angus McLean strongly held the notion that the Indian people of Robeson County were descended from the Cherokee; he testified in Congress to that effect in 1913, in congressional hearings into the status and needs of the Indian people of Robeson County.

These hearings came at the end of two years of an active search for federal support for Indian schools, and particularly for the normal school, which was poorly funded by the state. In 1911 U.S. Senator Simmons had introduced a bill to appropriate $50,000 for normal school construction and $10,000 annually for maintenance. The bill passed the Senate, and generated widespread interest and large public-support meetings in the county, but it subsequently failed in the House, despite the support of the representative from Robeson County.

In 1912–13 Senator Simmons and Representative Godwin tried again, this time first introducing a bill to recognize the Indians of Robeson County as Cherokee, which the state had done in early 1913. The state passed a bill that was sponsored by A. W. McLean, over the opposition of the Eastern Band of Cherokee. The House Committee on Indian Affairs held hearings for a similar Federal bill, and McLean testified in support of the measure.

The Reverend D. F. Lowery, the first person to actually graduate from the normal school program, who began teaching in the normal school in 1905, the same year he graduated, was a political protégé of McLean. He was also head of the Indian delegation that went to Washington in 1913 with McLean, seeking funding for the schools and recognition as Cherokee. Thus D. F. Lowery's opposition to the Siouan bill in the 1930s originated in the struggles for education and Cherokee recognition early in the century. His continuing insistence that his people were Cherokee undermined the possibility of a significant resettlement program being developed and then left the Indians more defenseless when the Red Banks–Pembroke Farms project was gutted.

After both claimed histories – the Cherokee and the Siouan – failed to get federal legislative support, Rev. Lowery, by then an old but still powerful man, was an active and important supporter of the state and federal legislation that in 1953 and 1956 recognized the people as Lumbee, a name with a Siouan linguistic structure (the double "e" ending) but no specific historical reference other than the one attached as preamble to the state's recognition – the old "lost colony" idea that first appeared with the Croatan recognition.

VI

The general theme is ancient, and far more widespread than Robeson County. Struggles that are lost – such as the Cherokee recognition and education bills – seldom stay lost, nor do they often return in productive ways. Rather, they reemerge in ways that can undermine newly rising struggles: the Siouan-recognition–land acquisition movement of the 1930s, in this instance. And these new struggles often fight issues that might have been more effectively fought at an earlier time: the passionate struggle for land, the mass meetings, the intensifying involvement with each other that Fred Baker pointed to in the 1930s – none of this, or only tiny glimmers, shone in the dark days at the beginning of the century, when the land was being lost and the struggles focused on the schools.

This is not – not at all – to say what people should have done, or what they could have done. It is, rather, to open the complex issue of how history lives and how people live their history.

One of the strongest impressions that emerged from living with and among Lumbee and Tuscarora, and from working with and for them

154

in several of their struggles, is the intensity with which people's sense of their history is privatized – privatized and encapsulated within family, kin group, neighborhood, and church association. Rural people in general seem to emphasize the very local and the very particular as a crucial aspect – but not at all the whole – of their sense of history, and Lumbee and Tuscarora do this with passionate force.

Histories and historical controversies matter in the way that they separate and enclose small groups of people intimately connected to each other. Such connections may be friendly, antagonistic, or both, but the sense of history – or histories – that emerge in their midst and on their pathways constitute an important part of a whole range of sharings and of contestations that shape the dynamics of all significant intimacies. It may be that the privatization of such microhistories turns people away from larger social and political agendas; it may also be that it gives people strength, direction, and the resource of experience for larger encounters. This varies, and it varies rapidly in time and in space.

People such as the Lumbee and Tuscarora, who construct their sense of history both in the face of continual threats of loss and in the context of continuing struggles, some of which they win, invoke history both by choice and by necessity. In the struggles many feel they must fight, history matters. Indeed, the struggles are often about their history: about the connections that can be and will be made between past, present, and impending future.

In this context of choice and necessity, history is claimed through a people's own ways and their own experiences, necessarily both from and against outsiders' claims. The tensions of this process can create a deep and often bitter factionalism – a factionalism that develops and becomes rooted in diverse historical visions.

These history-invoking factional splits occur not only in specifically political contexts, as in the struggles of D. F. Lowery and his allies against James Chavis and Joseph Brooks and their supporters, but they also emerge, at times strongly, within families, kin groups, and churches. Brothers and sisters, for example, split apart over the Lumbee–Tuscarora identity issue, one "becoming" Tuscarora, the other remaining Lumbee.

The wreckage such historical identity splits can cause, whether on the level of the Lumbee–Tuscarora turmoil of the 1970s or the Siouan–Cherokee conflicts of the 1930s, or within families and kin groups as brothers and sisters, parents and children turn against or away from one another – indeed, the wreckage that historical identity splits *must* cause: remember Preston Locklear turning against his own sister's children in order to build a Croatan school system – all this carnage comes precisely from an underlying *unity*, a unity or at the least a commonality of interest, of need, of hope. It is that most crucial issue of unity beneath the profound splits that brings us to Henry Berry Lowery, hero and founder for both Lumbee and Tuscarora, who was, in fact, D. F. Lowery's father's brother.

9

Henry Berry Lowery lives forever

I

For the Third Annual Homecoming Weekend festivities in July 1973, the Lumbee poverty program and economic development agency, Lumbee Regional Development Association (LRDA), printed and sold great quantities of a large shirt-pin button. The buttons had a picture of Henry Berry Lowery, and around the photograph the caption "HENRY BERRY LOWERY LIVES FOREVER."

He does, in many ways, starting with the fact that after he disappeared from Robeson County in 1872 without a trace he was rumored to have been seen in New Mexico, or other western places, well into the twentieth century. Other rumors had him accidentally killed by his own gun: no one else could have had the power to slay him, although the $12,000 reward for his body, dead or alive – the largest reward posted in the nineteenth century, as Lumbee proudly say, save for that on the outlaw Jesse James and Jefferson Davis, the Confederacy's president – certainly gave lots of people a motive for trying.

At the Second Annual Homecoming, in 1972, an awards ceremony and banquet was added to the Lumbee homecoming festivities. Over the years since then the number of different kinds of awards has grown: Distinguished Service Award, Business Person of the Year, Advancement of Education Award, and most recently, Farmer of the Year. But the first, and for three years the only award was the Henry Berry Lowery Award, for Outstanding Leadership in Indian affairs. Three men who have been especially influential in shaping Indian public identity were among those chosen: the Reverend D. F. Lowery was given the first award, James Chavis won it three years later, in 1975, and the Reverend Elias Rogers – who in addition to being involved in the Tuscarora struggle had been crucial in the reorganization and integration of the

157

Lumber River Electric Membership Cooperative – was honored in 1983. One woman has been given the award: Ruth Dial Woods, who has been active in advancing Indian education.

The awards and the pins are only part of an increasingly public commemoration of Henry Berry Lowery. In 1968 planning began for an outdoor drama, along the lines of the outdoor dramas presented both at Roanoke Island (one of the outer bank islands, where Raleigh planted what became the Lost Colony) and in the Blue Ridge Mountains, among the eastern Cherokee. Both these dramas depict Indian–White relations; both are substantial tourist attractions. The Lumbee show, *Strike at the Wind*, was first produced in 1976. It focuses on an eight-year period in Lowery's life, 1864–72, when he and his outlaw band were the Robin Hoods of Robeson County – although, unlike Robin Hood, they did in fact kill the high sheriff, and in addition the leader of every posse or militia detachment that was sent to hunt them down. They also killed several prominent White landlords with a reputation for brutalizing Indians beyond the customary indignities and exploitation, but in each case only after the person was warned to stop, or to cease hunting the Lowerys and their band.

Henry Berry Lowery's status came from far more than his heroic qualities and the crucial help he provided to a battered people in the post–Civil War turmoil. He was primarily a shape-changer: a hero who could not only change his own shape, as legends and contemporary accounts illustrate, but who changed the shape of a whole people. When Henry Berry Lowery began, in 1864, the ancestors of the present-day Lumbee and Tuscarora were legally regarded as "free persons of color," and often called "mulattoes," even though they themselves insisted that they were Indians. When he vanished they were, in the public eye, Indians. It was guerrilla warfare in the domain of culture as well as in the political economy.

A brief description of the formation and activities of the Lowery band will provide some of the event-context for a discussion of the cultural confrontations that came to center on his and his people's history.

During the Civil War the most important merchant port in the Upper South was at Wilmington, North Carolina, a major center for the shipment not only of cotton but of "naval stores": timber, turpentine, hemp, and pitch. Wilmington was about 70 miles east of the center of Robeson County's Indian settlement, then called Scuffletown, and they were directly connected to each other by the Wilmington, Charlotte, and Rutherford Railroad, which passed right through, and had several small stations within, the center of Indian settlement.

To protect this port during the war the Confederacy built an enormous sand and dirt fortification – Fort Fisher, one of the largest engineering projects ever undertaken at the time – at the pestilence-soaked mouth of the estuary, requisitioning slaves from surrounding plantations for the work. After the yellow fever epidemic of 1862–3 substantially increased the already high mortality of the fort's laborers, slave owners complained even more strongly about the use of their slaves for this work. Free persons of color were thus in serious trouble, being people who could be forced to work much like slaves and simultaneously people whose deaths were far less costly to the White elite.

Robeson County, with one of the largest "free colored" populations in the state, suffered the brunt of the labor impressment. (The other two places then with substantial numbers of people called "free colored" were Halifax and Warren counties, adjoining each other and the Virginia border, the home of the now state-recognized Haliwa Indians.) Substantial numbers of young Indian men in Robeson County took to hiding out in the swamps to avoid the recruiters. It was military service – military service for non-Whites – and so people who resisted or who fled could be and were summarily shot for such crimes as "desertion." So many young and adult Indian men were absent from their farms, hiding or in service, leaving women, children and the aged to till the heavy swamp soils, that in 1968 people still talked of this period as "the starving times."

Dragooning labor was only one of the major economic pressures upon the people of Scuffletown. The other was the rapidly intensifying loss of their land. This land loss, particularly for Scuffletown's larger landholders, began after the Revolutionary War and increased dramatically following the 1835 statewide disfranchisement of free persons of color, and the inclusion of the ancestors of the present-day Lumbee and Tuscarora in that category. Free persons of color lost the right to keep and bear arms, to vote, to testify against Whites in court, to sit on any jury, to attend state-supported schools, and to select ministers for their churches. Most of these are rights that turned out to be directly related to maintaining land ownership, although the possession of property by free persons of color did not come under direct legislative assault.

The "tied mule" stories I was told in 1968 illustrate one form of a more general process of land loss suffered by disfranchised people: A neighboring White farmer would tie his mule on an Indian's land, or put a fresh-killed hog in an Indian-owned smokehouse, raise the sheriff and claim theft; then a locally convened all-White jury would force a land sale for payment of the fine.

However they arrived at the condition, increasingly landless Indians provided an inexpensive labor supply for ditching and draining the land of expanding White-owned plantations. Indeed, it was precisely the Indians' increasing landlessness and powerlessness, along with the expanding railroads, that made their swampland increasingly valuable.

In the midst of the starving times, by early 1864, Scuffletonians were actually plundering White plantation smokehouses and storage bins for food and taking enough so that it could be widely shared among kin and neighbors, Black and poor White included. Some Robeson County plantations were substantial enterprises and were well stocked: after the Union army, under General William T. Sherman, smashed and looted its way through the county in the spring of 1865, Dr. Hector McLean claimed he lost

> *4 mules, 6 horses, 6 cattle, 124 hogs, 2,000 bushels of corn, 600 bushels of potatoes, 300 bushels of peas, 100 bushels of wheat, 20 bushels of rice, 6,500 pounds of fodder, 7,000 pounds of bacon* [pork], *60 gallons of syrup, 100 chickens, and some 25,000 fat lightwood fence rails which were used for campfires and for corduroying muddy roads.*

By contrast, Mary Normant, a lifetime resident of the county, described the living conditions of "free persons of color" by the end of the Civil War:

> *If a traveler wishes to visit a Scuffletown shanty he will be compelled to leave the public road and take a foot-path leading through the woods, across branches* [creeks] *and swamps, until he reaches a worm fence made of pine rails, inclosing a half-cleared patch of land containing three or four acres, in the centre of which generally stands the mulatto cabin, constructed of pine poles about five or six inches in diameter, notched one above the other until it reaches the height of eight feet and then covered* [roofed] *with pine boards; the chimney . . . of poles and clay as far up as the body of the house goes, and the balance of the chimney of sticks and clay . . .; a door is cut on the front side and the chinks stopped with clay; no windows generally. . . . The two or three acres cleared are ploughed and planted in corn, potatoes and rice, which come up* puny, *grow* puny, *and mature* puny. . . . *The bed is made on the floor (generally a clay floor); two or three stools to sit on; no division in the cabin, one apartment* [room] *comprising the whole establishment.* (Emphasis in the original)

G. A. Townsend, a reporter from the *New York Herald* sent to investigate Henry Berry Lowery, gives essentially the same description in his edited volume of reports, adding at the end, "the Scuffletowners go out to work as ditchers for the neighboring farmers, who pay them the magnanimous wages of $6 a month."

II

The first person that Henry Berry Lowery killed was James Barnes, on Christmas Eve day in 1864. The second, three weeks later, was J. Brantley Harris. Barnes owned a neighboring plantation, had threatened the Lowerys about their presumed plundering of his stock, and was steering the labor-recruitment officers to the Lowery homestead, which contained ten brothers.

Harris, the second victim, was reputedly the most vicious recruitment officer. He had recently killed three of Henry Berry's father's brother's sons, one in a direct murder that concerned Harris's desire to get access to a Scuffletonian woman Henry's cousin was courting, the other two, who might well be suspected of planning revenge, while he was taking them with their hands tied behind their backs to the train for the labor battalion at Fort Fisher. Both Barnes and Harris were shot in broad daylight on the open road.

Less than three weeks after Harris's death, the Home Guard invaded the Lowery homestead and shot his father and an older brother, even though his father at least was clearly innocent. The Home Guard then tied his mother to a post, blindfolded her, and shot a volley over her head in a mock execution, trying to get her to reveal where the Lowerys hid their guns – legally denied to free persons of color. Henry Berry and a group of followers almost immediately raided the courthouse in Lumberton, seizing for themselves and their community a large supply of modern – breech-loading – rifles destined for the local militia, and the war was on.

It was a strange war, with obvious enmities but surprising intimacies. For example, before the year was out Henry Berry married Rhoda Strong. He was just seventeen, she was sixteen. Pastoring the wedding was not Henry Berry's brother Patrick, who was a Methodist minister, but a White squire and a member of the Home Guard, Hector McLean, himself present at the murder of Henry's father and brother, but who tried to stop it, and who did prevent two of Henry's other brothers from being shot. In the midst of the wedding feast, held in Henry's mother's yard, despite the fact that he was a hunted man and the wedding widely discussed, Henry Berry was taken prisoner by the local militia, although McLean attempted to protect him through his rank and influence.

Henry Berry soon escaped from jail. The "band" that quickly formed around his leadership was composed of "Boss" Strong, Henry's wife's brother, who was fourteen when he joined but one of the key leaders; Calvin and Henderson Oxendine, Henry's first cousins, whose brother Hector had just been killed; George Applewhite, a Black stoneworker and former slave, who was married to one of the Oxendines' sisters and was one of the main leaders of the band – and the only one known to die of old age. These were the leaders and the core. In addition the band included as long-term regular members, John Dial, also joining at about age fourteen, whose father was tortured by the Home Guard; Stephen and Thomas Lowery, Henry's brothers, "Shoemaker John," another Black ex-slave, and Zack McLaughlin, a poor – or as they were locally called, from what the elite saw as their closeness to "Indian" lifestyles – "buckskin" Scot.

By the middle of 1865 the band was engaged in an almost constant stream of plantation robberies. Although the breakup of many plantations in the years following the Civil War gradually reduced the possibilities for plunder, they still found many places with large stockpiles of food, clothes, and other supplies: "to list them all would be almost to list the citizenry [used as a synonym for Whites] of one section of Robeson." In fact, there were so many armed raids and robberies, some more than a dozen miles apart in the same evening, that we must assume that a substantial part of what happened was done by "plain folks" and attributed to the heroic band.

Central to the impact of the band itself was the style of its operations – elegant, simple, apparently fearless – confronting the White upper classes both with their crudity and with their terrified helplessness. The band often showed up to plunder in the early evening and, posting a guard, would politely dine with their hosts before taking the goods. If they took a mule and wagon to carry the plunder off, these were sent back after the goods were distributed. Nine years this continued, while posse after posse, Home Guard, sheriff's deputies, federal troops, and bounty hunters searched the area.

Henry Berry, coming down Drowning Creek (as the Lumber River was then called) alone in a little boat, was once ambushed by a detachment of eighteen men from the county militia. He advanced on them, firing; they fled. He and his band stole the safe out of the sheriff's office, and another from a large merchant firm, leaving them open and empty on the main street in Lumberton, the county seat. He once joined a posse that was searching the swamps for him. The Whites were being plundered of their arrogant sense of superiority as well as their goods, and mocked in the process. It was not, however, a game.

Men who came to hunt the Lowery band and men who used their position in the White hierarchy to harm Scuffletonians excessively stood a good chance of being killed. Following the murder of Barnes and Harris, they were always first warned to stop. Henry Berry and his band killed Owen C. Norment, Murdock McLean, Hugh McLean, John Taylor, Archibald McMillan, Hector McNeil, Alexander Brown, Col. F. M. Wishart, John Sanders, High Sheriff Rueben King, Daniel Baker – the last two in their own homes, all the others out in the open, and usually in daylight. It takes a knowledge of what the local upper classes call Robeson County's "social history" to appreciate the magnitude of this list.

First, all these men are White, and all but two were members of the Conservative (proslavery, anti-Reconstruction) party.

Second, the roster includes almost every one of the "important" family names in the county, then and now. McLeans have been state senators and bank presidents and included a governor; McMillans and McNeils are what are locally called "first families"; Wishart, as in Wishart Township; Rueben King was, in addition to having been the high sheriff, the wealthiest man in the county; Owen Norment captained the local militia, and his grandfather headed the county court – and so forth.

The band's victims, in addition to the leaders of all the posses sent out to hunt them down, included the members of the Home Guard that murdered Henry's father and brother, and the bounty hunters who came looking for the rewards. The ease with which the band afterward eluded pursuit showed that the swamps were social as well as physical presences – not merely densely woven mats of undergrowth, through which only local people could easily move, but equally densely woven walls of communal silence, through which information flowed in only one direction.

During these years Henry Berry escaped from jail twice and was active in helping several of his band in their escapes. The sheriff once arrested four of the band members' wives, hoping to get the men to turn themselves in. They forced a local planter to write and deliver this note to the sheriff:

> *Robeson County, N.C. July 14, 1871*
> *To the Sheriff of Robeson County & C L Sinclair:*
> *We make a request, that our wives who were arrested a few days ago, and placed in Jail, be released to come home to their families by Monday Morning, and if not the Bloodiest times will be here that ever was before – the life of every man will be in Jeopardy.*
> *Henry B. Lowery Stephen Lowery Andrew Strong Boss Strong*

That is what the note actually said. The way it was reported, shortly after it happened, and the way it is remembered now, the note ended "if not we will commence to drench the county in blood and ashes."

However it made its impression, the wives were sent home with an armed guard, to make sure that nothing happened to them on the way.

Only one member of the band was ever caught and executed during its operations, and only two or three were ever shot and killed until the end. Despite being outlawed in 1868 – which meant that he and his band were literally outside the protection of the law and could be killed by anyone, anytime, under any circumstances for the reward – Henry Berry was never taken, and disappeared in 1872. Indians say he escaped to the west; local Whites say he was killed by an accidental discharge of his own gun. In either case, the end of it all came within a year of Henry Berry's disappearance, when his brother Stephen, who had been the first leader of the band, was shot in a surprise attack.

III

By the time Henry Berry's band came to an end, local Whites were engaged in an intense debate that reached to the core of the dominant culture's understanding of "race" and racial differences: trying to explain how it could have happened. One major part of this attempt to explain turned Henry Berry into a superman, endowing him with impossible superhuman qualities. These mythical descriptions by contemporary Whites have become widely accepted by Indian people throughout the twentieth century, and they have had the important effect of minimizing the crucial social basis both of his attacks and of his ability to evade pursuit.

More significantly, the center of the *White* attempt to explain the abilities of the band dealt with the "race" of the people involved, and entailed a public, albeit tentative, transformation of Scuffletonians from "mulatto" to "Indian," including imposed images from the dominant society about what it meant to be an Indian.

We will call two people as witnesses and exponents of this cultural struggle within the dominant White society to create and impose meaning: Mary C. Norment and Giles Leitch. Mary Mormant's husband, Owen, was captain of the local militia that hunted the band and was killed by Henry Berry. She subsequently wrote the most detailed of the contemporary local accounts: *The Lowrie History, as acted in part by Henry Berry Lowrie, the Great North Carolina Bandit, With Biographical Sketches of His Associates. By Mrs. Mary C. Norment, Whose Husband was Killed by the Outlaws* (1875).

Giles Leitch was a prominent Conservative county lawyer. Leitch successfully defended the Home Guard members who killed Henry

Berry's father and brother, getting them off without any sentence whatever. In 1872 he was called to Washington to testify to Congress about the situation in Robeson County. Congress was investigating the Ku Klux Klan's violent suppression of Blacks during Reconstruction; Leitch was called by Conservatives in Congress who wanted to demonstrate that without Klan violence there would be an outpouring of what congressmen might well regard as an even more dangerous assault on the social order. His statements come from the transcript of that investigation: *Report of the Joint Select Committee to Investigate the Conditions of Affairs in the Late Insurrectionary States* (1872).

Mary Normant's description of Henry Berry Lowery brings forward and interweaves the issues of his superhuman qualities and his racial identity:

> *Henry Berry Lowrie . . . is of mixed blood, strangely commingled, having coursing in his veins the blood of the Tuscarora Indian, the Cavalier blood of England and also that of the descendants of Ham in Africa, his great-great grandmother being a copper-colored negress, raised on the banks of the James River in Virginia. . . . The color of his skin is of a mixed white and yellow, partaking of an admixture, resembling copper, the Indian color however, still predominating, though the white and black remain apparent. Such a skin is affected very little by heat or cold . . . or by exposure, or good housing. . . . [T]he color of his eyes is a grayish hazel . . . his hair was straight and black like an Indian's. He is 26 years old, five feet ten inches high, and weighs about one hundred and fifty pounds. . . .*
>
> *In regard to his arms: a belt around his waist keeps in place five six barrelled revolvers . . . behind, slinging style, a Henry rifle, which carries the extraordinary number of sixteen cartridges. In addition . . . he carries a long bladed knife and a double-barrelled shot gun, his whole equipment weighing not less than eighty pounds. . . . With all his armor on he could run, swim, stand weeks of exposure in the swamps, walk day and night and take sleep by little snatches, which in a few days would tire out white or negro. Being fond of blood he has waged for the past ten years a savage and predatory war . . . without fear, without hope, defying society. . . .*
>
> *Occasionally his blood and inclinations will crop out, and his three natures of white, Indian and negro will come forward and show themselves to the close observer. . . . In his love for rude music may be discovered the negro trace. He plays on the banjo, and accompanies the playing with singing. This banjo, together with the Juba beating and dancing of the mulatto girls, has on several occasions come near to betraying him to his pursuers. His Indian nature may be traced in his*

character, by his using mulatto women as an auxiliary to war and plunder. . . . He sleeps on his arms and never seems tired; ever active, ever vigilant, he is never taken by surprise. His cavalier [i.e. White] scrupulousness may also be observed in the matter of a promise or a treaty. Those most robbed and outraged by this bandit give him credit for complying strictly to his word. Like the rattlesnake, he generally warned before he struck. Two things he has never done – he has never committed arson, nor offered to insult white females. In these two things may be traced his cavalier blood.

Giles Leitch wrestles with the same issues – White, Black, or Indian? – but does so, while no less irrationally, on the level of community:

Giles Leitch sworn & examined

By Mr. Blair:

[The questions that answers make obvious are here omitted.]

A. I am a native of Robeson county; I was born about twenty-one miles from the county seat, where I now live; I have been living at Lumberton since 1851. . . . My profession is the practice of law.

A. The county of Robeson had about one thousand five hundred white voting population before the close of the war. Since then, since the colored population has been enfranchised, there are about three thousand voters in the county; of that one thousand five hundred additional voting population, about half were formerly slaves, and the other half are composed of a population that existed there and were never slaves and are not white, but who since 1835 have had no right of suffrage. . . .

Q. What are they; are they negroes?

A. Well sir, I desire to tell you the truth as near as I can; but I do not know what they are; I think they are a mixture of Spanish, Portuguese and Indian. About half of them have straight black hair, and many of the characteristics of the Cherokee Indians in our State; then, as they amalgamate and mix, the hair becomes curly and kinky, and from that down to real woolen hair.

Q. You think they are mixed negroes and Indians?

A. I think they are mixed Portuguese, Spaniards and Indians; I mean to class the Spaniards and Portuguese as one class, and the Indians as another. I do not think that in that class of population there is much negro blood at all; about half of the colored population that I have attempted to describe all have always been free; I was born among them and I reckon I know them perfectly well. They are a thriftless, lazy, thievish and indolent population. They are called "mulattoes"; that is the name they are known by, as contradistinguished from negroes. There is a family of them by the name of Lowry, that seems to have more

Indian characteristics than any of the rest of that population....
By the Chairman, Mr. Poole:
Q. You have reference now to the Lowry family?
A. Yes, sir ... at the close of the [Revolutionary] *war they were rich,*
their riches consisting mostly in slaves. They were colored themselves
and they owned slaves.... They ... wasted their substance in that
county in litigation.... I do not think they have owned slaves within
about thirty years. Well, then, the men of those families became mechan-
ics; they had a sort of cunning about them that was different from the
negro. They had an address about them....During the confederate
war ... they were classed with ordinary negroes....
By the Chairman, Mr. Poole: [following a long discussion of how
many people Henry Berry Lowery killed, and why; his ability
to flout authority, his support of the pro-Reconstruction Re-
publicans] *Q. I understand you to say that these seven or eight*
hundred persons that you designate as mulattoes are not Negroes, but
are a mixture of Portuguese and Spanish, white blood and Indian
blood; you think they are not generally negroes?
A. I do not think that the negro blood predominates.
Q. The word "mulatto" means a cross between the white and negro?
A. Yes, sir.
Q. You do not mean that work to be understood in that sense when
applied to these people?
A. I really do not know exactly how to describe these people. The most
of them have bushy, kinky hair, and they are about the color of a cross
between the white and the negro; but they do not exactly partake of the
characteristics of such a cross.

Several questions follow about Lowry's father and brother being shot
by the Home Guard and the outrages upon the women of the family,
as the probable origin of the troubles. The chairman is a Republican,
and he is trying to turn the issue back to retaliation for brutalities
practiced upon non-Whites and poor Whites, and to raise the issue of
the special situation of Indian people in all this.

Q. Is there any white blood in that Lowery family?
A. I really do not know. I think the father was Indian; I think the
family has about the characteristics of the Cherokees of our State. The
mother was named Cumbo, and I think it is likely that there may have
been some white blood in the Cumbo family....
Q. Is there a considerable portion of territory in the western part of
North Carolina set apart for the Cherokee Indians? You have been a
member of the legislature, and perhaps you know how that is.
A. Yes, sir; I believe there is.

Q. Do you recollect whether, by law, white men are excluded from purchasing land in that territory set apart for the Cherokee Indians?
A. I do not remember about that.
Q. You recollect that the Cherokee Indians are congregated within a certain territory of country in the western part of the State, and that with the permission of the State they occupy that territory?
A. Yes, sir.
Q. Was this ten or twelve square miles of territory [actually much larger; Leitch had minimized the area of Scuffletown and the surrounding swamps] *in Robeson County, by common consent, left somewhat in the same way to this Lowry set of people?*
A. No, sir.
Q. Are they main portions of the inhabitants in that section of the county?
A. No, sir. . . .
Q. Who lives in Scuffletown besides them?
A. The Lowry family is Indian; then there are Locklears, Oxendines, Hunts, Joneses and Grayboys [the actual name is the more Indian "Braveboy"; he transforms it to a Black/White metaphor]; *I do not recollect how many other negro names there are. There are a dozen different families there. Some of the Lowry and Oxendine families are related by marriage. But Lowry is Indian; the balance of them are not understood to be Indian – they are mulatto; I mean colored people.*

Leitch is, however, talking about a community, however much he may want to segment this community according to his fantasies about race, granting the most Indianness to the most violent.

Mary Norment, near the beginning of her history, describes how she believes the area called Scuffletown was given its name. In doing this, she is firm and clear that the inhabitants are, all together, either Blacks or mulattoes, a position she will soon have to abandon:

Col. Vick, then merchandising at Fair Bluff, in Robeson county, (Vicksburg in Mississippi being named after him) Christened (to use a Scotch phrase) all that region lying East of Drowning Creek and extending one or two miles East of Bear Swamp with the euphonious soubriquet of Scuffletown, *from the act of the mulattoes inhabiting that region congregating in Lowrie's grocery and after imbibing pretty freely of whiskey, in engaging in the* broad shuffle [Blacks are supposed to "shuffle"], *and also from the fact that it was generally a scuffle with the mulattoes to live – "to keep body and soul together," owing to their improvident habits. This portion of Robeson county no respectable, enterprising white man will live in, owing to the fact that it is not productive, lying too low to be drained and improved, being interspersed with bogs and swamps, which are covered with an almost impenetrable under-growth, together with a more potent reason that the white race do not believe in the intermingling of different races.*

This is a strange interpretation for her to assert, considering her attempt to account for Henry Berry Lowery's actions by his different "bloods." But all the local Whites' interpretations of him and his band show a profound and constantly shifting confusion and a continuing series of identity transformations. Whites were forced to make these transformations in perceived identity by the demands of their own world view, in which it was inadmissible for Blacks to *successfully* challenge Whites. The most powerful and revealing statement to that effect comes in Mary Norment's summary of the band's assaults:

> *It was by* ambuscading *that they succeeded in killing J. Brantly Harris, James P. Barnes, Owen C. Norment, Murdoch A. McLean and his brother Hugh, John Taylor, Archibald A. McMillan, Hector McNeil, Alexander Brown, Col F. M. Wishart, and Giles Innman. All these most excellent citizens of Robeson county met their sad fate at the hands of these modern Robeson county Apaches – these North Carolina Modocs; not in civilized warfare – not in accordance with modern military tactics, but by the bullet of the high-way robber and midnight assassin. Even ex-Sheriff King . . . came unfortunately to the end of his earthly career through the Indian stealthiness of these subtle villains, who blackened their faces and hands to disguise their identity and race, and then crept up slyly and pushed the door open as easily as possible and demanded him to surrender.*

"The Indian stealthiness of the subtle villains, who blackened their faces and hands to disguise their identity and race." What an extraordinary statement! In fact they walked up to King's porch without any blackening of their faces and hands, and it was George Applewhite who shot Sheriff King, when King made the mistake of drawing a gun on Henry Berry. But what Norment is saying is that these people, who fooled us all these years into thinking they were "colored," by "blackening their faces and hands," are really Indians, and wild, savage, sneaky Indians at that. So endures the culture of domination, while the world it was rooted in crumbles and is rebuilt – with both the opposition and the labors of its victims.

The ancestors of the present-day Indian people of Robeson County had themselves been claiming they were Indian – firmly but quietly. In 1867, with Union control of the South consolidated, there was some pressure, particularly by Lieutenant Birney, head of the Lumberton office of the Bureau of Refugees, Freedmen and Abandoned Lands, to bring the killers of Henry Berry's father and brother to trial. Seeking to defend and explain the actions of the Home Guard, Birney was written a letter by "H. Coble, Pastor of Center Church, and L. McKinnin, Minister of the Gospel." Their letter opens:

> *Sir, In accordance with your request we submit the following state-*
> *ment of facts and circumstances connected with the killing of Allen*
> *Lowry and his son William in the early part of March 1865.*
>
> *We would premise, in the first place, that the Lowrys are free from*
> *all taint of Negro blood. They are said to be descended from the Tuscarora*
> *Indians. They have always claimed to be Indian & disdained the idea*
> *that they are in any way connected with the African race.*

But they did not publicly always insist on an Indian identity, and indeed at times referred to themselves as "melungeons." Part of the reason for their lack of insistent specificity has to do with the politics of racial identity for non-Whites in the early nineteenth century southeast, a period that witnessed, very quietly, the forcible and brutal removal of Indians westward and, at the same time and with almost equally brutal consequences, revisions of state constitutions that disfranchised free persons of color.

Both this "Indian removal" and the disfranchisement of free persons of color happened in a context where one's "racial" identity played a crucial role in the reproduction, over time, of the social relations of production. To be Black, or Indian, or White – or less specifically but no less significantly, one of the multiple different socially recognized mixes: a *mustee* (mixed Indian and Black); a *mulatto* (mixed Black and White); a *mestizo*, or more commonly a "half-breed" or "half-blood" (mixed Indian and White); or *melungeon* (mixed Indian, White, and Black) plus the legal categories free person of color (which included all the above and more) and free negro – all meant a great deal, not just in terms of political rights and protections, but in terms of the kinds of positions one could and could not have in the processes of production and the kinds of returns for one's labor one might reasonably expect.

When the people of Robeson County became publicly recognized as Indians, they did so in a context where most of them, along with many Whites and African-Americans, became sharecroppers. Once a person is a sharecropper, they and their children and their grandchildren will be sharecroppers until they either migrate out of the area or until the whole system collapses. What we call "racial" or "ethnic" identity does not matter as much as it did in the colonial and early federal periods for the *reproduction* of a brutally unequal social division of labor. People can call themselves and be called anything – Black or Indian or even

Martian – and they will still sharecrop, year after year after year, although they would have some different political rights, perhaps a few more economic possibilities, and perhaps a few different illusions were they recognized as White.

V

Just across the state line in South Carolina are many people with the same family names as those prominent among the Indian people of Robeson County; moreover, many family histories speak about people moving back and forth from North to South Carolina, and of kinship, social, and religious-associational ties (some of which have been discussed in Chapter 5, in the context of the school cases). In 1859, the Chavis and Jones families in Edgefield County, South Carolina (Chavis being a name that in Robeson County always indicates an Indian; Jones a family name for Indians, Whites, and Blacks), sent the following petition to their State Legislature:

> *To the Honorable the Legislature of the said State The humble petition of Frederick Chavis, Lewis Chavis, Durany Chavis, James Jones, Bartley Jones, Mary Jones, Jonathan Williams & Polly Dunn, respectfully sheweth*
>
> *That the first six petitioners above named, to wit, the Chavis and Jones families, are free persons of color being descendants of Indian ancestors. The other two, to wit, Jonathan Williams and Polly Dunn are free colored persons alleged to be descended from, or mixed with the blood of, the negro race.*
>
> *That the tax collector of Edgefield District, during the month of May or June last, issued executions against each of your petitioners for the Capitation or poll tax imposed on free persons of color, for the sum of $8 each, on the ground – as your petitioners are informed – that the Comptroller General had directed the tax collector of that district to collect back tax for 4 years next before issuing the executions.*
>
> *Your petitioner Polly Dunn is only 16 years of age, and Bartley Jones is only 17 years old.*
>
> *Your petitioners of the Indian blood, that is to say, Frederick, Lewis and Durany Chavis, James Bartley and Mary Jones, pray your Honorable body to say whether by free persons of color they mean to include descendants of Indians, or only those who are mixed with negro blood, in order that they may know whether they are liable for this tax or not.*
>
> *And if they were not intended to be included, they pray that said taxes may be refunded to them.*
>
> *[signed (for them)], Dec. 9th, 1859*

"Root hog or die"

Two years earlier, in 1857, a man named William Chavers was indicted, in North Carolina, under the law against free negroes carrying
guns. The case reached the state supreme court (50 NC 27), upon
Chaver's appeal, and wound up focusing on whether a free person of
color could be charged under laws against free negroes; the decision
was no. The fluidity of claim and counterclaim that this case reveals is
also important to note:

> *An indictment charging the defendant, as a "free person of color"
> with carrying arms, cannot be sustained; for the act (Rev. Code, ch 107
> sec 66) is confined to "free negroes."*

[Statement of the case:]

> *The defendant was charged, as a free person of color, with carrying
> a shotgun. . . .*
>
> *A Mr. Green proved that he and the defendant, with others, came to
> this court* [for the original case, in Brunswick] *upon a steamboat
> from Wilmington, and that the price of a passage for white persons was
> one dollar; that while on the way the defendant handed him one dollar,
> and requested him to pay the fare of himself and his brother with that
> sum, saying he understood that the fare of white persons was one dollar
> and colored persons half price, and that he and his brother were colored
> persons, and that the witness accordingly paid the fare of both of them
> with one dollar.*
>
> *The defendant's counsel insisted, in his argument, that his client
> was a white man, and called upon the jury to inspect him and judge
> for themselves. . . .*

[upon appeal:]

> *The motion for a new trial being denied him, the defendant, through
> his counsel, moves here* [in the state supreme court] *in arrest of
> judgment, because he is charged, in the indictment, as a "free person
> of color," whereas the section of the act, under which he is indicted,
> makes it penal for any "free negro" to carry arms about his person. The
> counsel contends that, although the terms "free negro" and "free person
> of color" are often used in chapter 107, Rev. Code, as synonymous, yet
> it is not always the case, and that therefore the indictment . . . cannot
> be sustained in substituting the latter description of the person or the
> former.*
>
> *There can be no doubt that the two terms are sometimes used in the
> act to which the counsel refers, as synonymous; as, for instance, in
> sections 11 and 13, which prohibit free negroes from working in certain
> swamps without a certificate; and we also think, with the counsel, that
> there is at least one instance (and one is sufficient for his purpose), in
> which the terms cannot be so regarded. The 44th section declares that*

> *"any slave or free negro, or free person of color convicted by due course*
> *of law, of an assault with intent to commit rape upon the body of a*
> *white female, shall suffer death." Here three classes of persons seem to*
> *be included, to-wit, slaves, free negroes, and free persons of color. The*
> *last section of the act . . . defines who shall be deemed free negroes and*
> *persons of mixed blood, but does not declare who shall be embraced*
> *under the term "free person of color." . . . Free persons of color may be,*
> *then, for all we can see, persons colored by Indian blood, or persons*
> *descended from negro ancestors beyond the fourth degree. . . . Judgement*
> *arrested.*

By 1857, White people in and around Robeson County were calling the people with what are now Indian surnames "mulattoes": mixed White and Black. In 1795, the same people were often called "mustee," mixed Indian and Black. In each instance, and although the particular people being labeled were semi-enslaved indentured servants, it was recognized that in order to describe them one had to describe their kin relations:

> Fayetteville North Carolinian, *December 3, 1857*
> *I Will Give TWENTY FIVE DOLLARS reward for the apprehension*
> *and lodgement in jail so that I may get him, of Willie Revels, whom*
> *I bought in Fayetteville for 5 years, about 12 months since. He is a tall,*
> *slim young mulatto, usually accompanied by a dog. Had with him*
> *when he left two dogs, one brindle, the other black. He is probably*
> *lurking about the Locklayers in Robeson County, or may endeavor to*
> *make his way to Marion district S.C. where he has relations. He has*
> *a wife, Matilda Locklayer, in Robeson, and is probably in that neigh-*
> *borhood. . . . John T. Wright*

> The North Carolina Sentinel & Fayetteville Gazette, *June 4, 1795*
> *Ten dollars REWARD will be paid to any person who will deliver to*
> *the subscriber, in Georgetown [SC], a mustie servant woman named*
> *Nancy Oxendine. She is a stout wench, of a light complexion, and*
> *appears to be about 30 years of age. . . . It is supposed she has been*
> *enticed away by her brother & sister, who were here in February last.*

In 1840, five years after disfranchisement, White citizens of Robeson County were complaining about their inability to control the unruliness of the whole community. While doing so, and while calling them "free colored," they indicated that they knew this was a community – which did not yet have a collective name – that had its own collective, separate, and special history:

> *Robeson County, Nov. 28, 1840*
> *To the Honorable the General Assembly of the State of North Carolina:*

> The memorial of the undersigned respectfully represents:
>
> The County of Robeson is cursed with a free-colored population that migrated originally from the districts round about the Roanoke and Neuse rivers. They are generally indolent, roguish, improvident and dissipated. Having no regard for character, they are under no restraint but what the law imposes. They are great topers, and so long as they can procure the exhilarating drought seem to forget entirely the comfort of their families. . . . We think that a law restricting them in the sale of that article would benefit them and the community at large.
>
> [36 signatures]

While the community as a whole, in some contexts at least, was referred to as "free colored," individuals within it were specified differently. A surviving, partial "list of taxables" for the county shows that many people with Indian surnames – Lowery, Oxendine, Chavis, Locklear, Revels – are listed as paying the White poll tax in 1837 (including Allen Lowry, and a Mary Cumboe, who owned 400 acres but paid no poll tax); a few with the same names are listed as paying the Black poll tax. By 1845 many of these same people were registered as paying the Black poll tax. As a *community*, they were increasingly seen as "free colored"; as *individuals* in the category of citizens – which is what the poll tax indicated – they could be either White or Black, and they were rapidly and increasingly becoming categorized as Black. This changing designation, in the context of the changing political economy, was an act of violence.

Throughout the South there had been, particularly in the decades before the Civil War, substantial political tensions between the piedmont region with its small farms and manufactories, and the plantation-dominated coastal plain. As the population of the piedmont increased and came to equal or outnumber the White population on the coastal plain, their political demands became more insistent. To simplify, for purposes here: the piedmont inhabitants wanted roads and railroads and bridges and dams and post offices – a whole economic infrastructure – and it was the coastal plain plantations that were generating the wealth that could finance this, were they taxed sufficiently. West Virginia seceded from Virginia over such tensions; in North Carolina a compromise was reached, expressed in the 1835 revision of the state constitution. The piedmont was given more political power in the state legislature and over the selection of the governor, which meant they could more easily realize their economic ambitions; the planters were given much tighter control over free people of color and other actual and potential laborers, which meant that they could more easily secure and expand their wealth.

The disfranchisement of free people of color was thus not only an act of violence upon individual political rights, but by making individuals more insecure in their rights and liberties and more dependent on protection and "benevolence" from powerful Whites, it was also an assault upon community – the web of relations that had grown up between free people of color, Black or Indian, as the number of people in this category increased and their settlements developed into communities.

Against this violence, the Scuffletonian's own violence, from the origin of their community onward, was central to their survival as a people. Consider two texts, by way of illustration:

In 1773, when North Carolina was still a colony, the government issued a proclamation against several people of this community for protecting their own. The proclamation indicates that they possessed their lands, at this late date, still without what was earlier called "patent, deed or quit rent" – that is, without the authority of the state:

> *A List of the Mob Railously Assembled together in Bladen County* [Robeson was then part of Bladen], *Oct 13, 1773,* [The names marked with * are common Indian names now] *Harbourers of the Rogues as follows: Major Lockelear*, Becker Groom, Ester Carsey Capt. James Ivey, Joseph Ivey, Iphraim Sweat*, William Chavours* Clark*, commonly called Boson Chavers, Benjman Dees*, Willm Sweat*, George Sweat*, Wm Groom Sr, Wm Groom Jr Gideon Grant, Thos Groom, James Trace, Isaac Vaun, Job Stapbleton, Edward Locklear*, July Locklear**
>
> *The Above List of Rogus is all free Negors and Mullatus living upon the Kings Land*

The first written description of this people, a 1753 survey of the military situation made in the context of the French and Indian War, shows the seeds of the same dynamic – land, identity, and social isolation or partial autonomy both challenged and reproduced in episodes of violence:

> *Drowning Creek on the head of the Little Peedee 50 families a mixt breed [or crew; the word is unclear] a lawless People possess the Lands without Patent or paying quit Rents. Shot a surveyr for Coming to view their lands being inclosed in great Swamps. . . .*

Henry Berry Lowery has indeed lived forever, for he was the crystallization into one brief historical moment of social processes that have been occurring among the Lumbee from colonial times to the present. There has almost always been, whether Indian peoples wanted it or not, an intimate and specific connection between violence and being Indian – a much different connection than that between violence and being

175

Black. The specific ways that violence became part both of the *autonomy* of Indian peoples and also of their *integration* into an expanding colonial political economy brings us to the core of large-scale processes that transformed pre-contact aboriginal peoples into different kinds of post-contact Indian societies and simultaneously into distinctive, separate groups within each kind.

The brutality in and of these early transformative processes is still influential in shaping the current situation of Indian people. It underlies some of the most profound ambiguities in the relations of inequality and cultural differentiation within and between Native American societies, and between Native American peoples and the dominant society and state. We turn next to these colonial processes, and then to show how these processes live within, and are invoked by, the present.

PART FOUR

"Now our inmates":
Colonial formations and formation's heritage

Prologue

In 1769 a committee of the Council of South Carolina, seeking permission from the Crown to expand the colony's areas of settlement and governance, reported on conditions in the northwestern interior of the colony – the central piedmont. Two important issues were at stake: primarily the boundary between South and North Carolina and secondarily the location of the "line of settlement" – the boundary line that divided White settlement areas from Indian lands. The Crown, concerned that Indians near the settlers would become so alienated by the depredations upon them that they would cease to ally themselves with the English, sought to constrain expansion across the line. The colonists were, of course, constantly pressing the Crown to shift the line inland, and continually settling across the line, wherever it was.

Both back-country settlers and Indians played crucial roles in the colonial economy, producing commodities and helping to hold slaves in place. In the reproduction of the slave system, Indians had an especially important and multifaceted role. The export tax on Indian-produced deerskins helped subsidize the importation of White indentured servants, who were seen as allies of the planters in case of Black insurrection. Moreover, Indians, often desperate to acquire guns, powder, and shot, entered the business of pursuing runaway slaves much more readily than did poor or back-country Whites – particularly Indian peoples on the piedmont, increasingly trapped between the English to their east and the militarized native confederacies to their west.

Colonial elites tried, in multiple ways, to expand inland and to keep control over both sides of their expanding frontier, although expansion made control over native peoples much more difficult. And the colonists continually argued with the Crown, which sought to constrain expansion within the line of settlement, seeking to explain the importance of an expanding frontier and to show that the settlers on or across the line were crucial to the continuity, success, prosperity, and stability of the colony.

Among the claims that were made about the importance of the whole 'back-country' region is that the settlers there volunteered to help suppress Blacks. From the colonial records, these folks seem to have "volunteered" rather more often than they actually appeared. The colonial elites actually depended heavily on the very Indians they were displacing for this aid, and they sought simultaneously to resolve and to explain this contradiction.

The whole fabric of the political and cultural economy of the colonial frontier appears in vivid color in the following report from the Council of South Carolina. For a political document it is stunningly clear and straightforward, starting with the admission that White prosperity was founded on Black misery and continuing on to describe how domination over Blacks, Indians, and back-country Whites was organized:

> *The staple commodities of South Carolina being Rice, Indigo and Naval Stores and lately Hemp. . . . These kinds of produce cannot be raised and extended but by the labor of Slaves. . . . But the number of such laborers their condition of slavery being apt to raise in them ideas of an Interest opposite to their Master becomes dangerous to the public safety where the number of White Men is over balanced by a superior number of Negroes wherefore it had been the Policy of South Carolina at great charge to give encouragement to the importation of Europeans as a Counterpoise thereto, this measure tho very constantly pursued has not been adequate to the growing evil which is the natural consequence of the growing prosperity of the province, it is therefore very expedient to include in this Province all those Settlers who have lived on Rivers whose Streams arise to the Westward of the Line of 1764 down which the Hemp Flour and Lumber begin to be brought to market at Charles Town at a less expensive carriage than the present general means of waggons. Bounties are given by South Carolina to Hemp raised in this Province and many living North of where the West line proposed by Governor Tyron have received our Bounties accordingly and it is but justice to mention the readiness which many of the Back Settlers expressed to have marched down to assist in Suppressing the general Insurrection of our Negroes which was apprehended in 1766 and here let it be remembered that North Carolina is secure from this danger of Negroes the white men are vastly superior to the number of Slaves in that Province.*
>
> *We Humbly conceive there are also many reasons why this Province should be strengthend by alloting this body of land now pretty well*

178

> settled with white men to South Carolina because during the Cherokee
> War in 1760 and 1761 many of the Inhabitants near those parts at
> the first consternation and ravages of the Indians incursions fled into
> the northern Provinces but several who ventured to defend themselves
> in Stockad'd Forts were enabled to maintain their posts by the assistance
> of Arms Ammunition Provisions and Clothing received from this
> Province. . . .
>
> As the Settlers imported at the expense of this Province are not now
> confined to townships but are allowed to choose lands where they are
> most suitable to their minds many have settled up the Broad river whose
> upper branches will be cut off from this Province by this continuation
> of the line of 1764 in a West course and several Settlers imported at the
> expense of this Province thrown into North Carolina.
>
> It would be convenient and reasonable that the Catawba Indians
> should be comprehended in the proposed boundary as a very usefull
> Body of Men to keep our Negroes in some awe. The year 1766 afforded
> a very strong proof of their Utility on such services for about Christmas
> 1765 many Negroes having fled into Large Swamps and other circum-
> stances concurring there was great room to apprehend that some dan-
> gerous conspiracy and Insurrection was intended and tho the Militia
> was ordered on Duty and were very alert on this occasion the Governor
> thought it right to invite a number of the Catawba Indians to come
> down and hunt the Negroes in their different recesses almost impervious
> to White Men at that season of the year the Indians immediately came
> down and partly by the terrour of their Name their diligence and sin-
> gular sagacity in pursuing Enemies thro such Thickets soon dispersed
> the runaway Negroes apprehended several and the most of the rest of
> them chose to surrender themselves to their Masters and return to their
> duty rather than expose themselves to the attack of an Enemy so dreaded
> and so difficult to be resisted or evaded for which good service the
> Indians were amply rewarded. . . . this province hath acquired a power-
> ful influence over this tribe of Indians now our inmates.

We have three issues before us here in Part Four: first, the formation
of different *kinds* of Native American societies in the early contact and
colonial periods, and simultaneously the formation of specific named
groups within each general kind of native society; second, how the
development of different kinds of native societies throughout the colonial
period incorporated within the social organizations and cultures of
increasingly separate native peoples the conflicts, confrontations, and
alliances of the colonial frontier; and, third, the historical claims that
were then and are now made by and upon these emergent Native
American peoples.

179

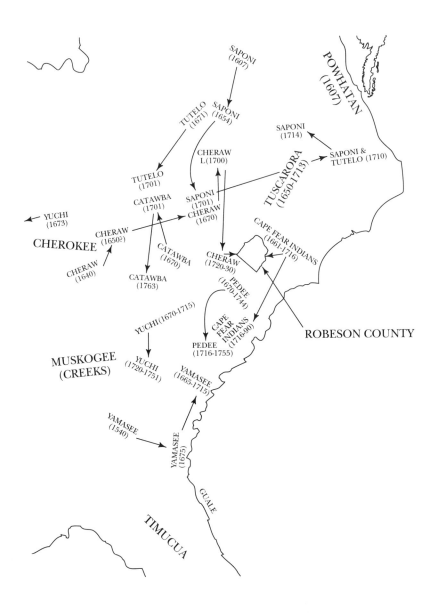

Map 2. Native peoples of the colonial southeast, with schematic indication of native population movements. Adapted from John R. Swanton, *The Indians of the Southeastern United States* (USGPO, 1946).

10

Six pounds of paint to encourage the Indians: Colonial political-cultural formations, part one
The origins of native vulnerability

William Thompson . . . was obliged to distribute out the Ammunition I left with him, amongst our friend Indians, and other Goods to encourage them to fight their Enemies, for they were very much dispirited, there being no Ammunition or Paint in their Nation but what I had left . . . . Upon the War breaking out I returned back to the Chickesaws and gave 6 lb. Paint to the Indians to carry to our Friends to encourage them.

John Highrider to Gov. Glen, 1750

A Nation of Indians called the Catabas living within the Limits of this Government have a long time been at War with the Tuscororas of North Carolina, and it is always the maxim of our Governm't upon the continent to promote war between Indians of different nations with whom we trade and are at peace with ourselves for in that consists our safety. Being at war with one another prevents them from uniting against us.

Robert Johnson to the Board of Trade, 1732

I

Indian societies in the colonial southeast were formed in the matrix of five processes of differentiation – five processes of antagonistic separation:

1. *A rapidly emerging, fundamental separation between the historical dynamics of pre- and post-contact native social systems.* The dynamics both of change and of stability that characterized pre-contact native social systems were rapidly shattered in the contact period, and different dynamics of development and social reproduction, with completely separate and distinct internal logics, emerged.

2. *The post-contact development of increasingly different, increasingly divergent kinds or "forms" of native societies.* Three fundamental forms of native society emerged in the post-contact period: (a) large, powerful, militarized trading confederacies, such as the Cherokee, Choctaw, and Creek; (b) small "settlement" and "tributary" groups, integrated into the colonial political economy in profoundly different ways from the confederacies;

181

(c) autonomous native communities with a post-contact historical dynamic substantially different from either the confederacies or the settlement groups.

These three social forms are not simply categories or a typology. Rather, the range of variation within each form and the mutually antagonistic separation between them illuminate the transformations occurring at the intersections of the expanding, incorporative frontier and changing native claims upon the land, each other, the Euro-American colonies, and slave and free Blacks. At the center of these transformations are issues of *use* and of *claim*: how native peoples (and others) were used, and the claims they made upon and within the processes of use.

3. *The emergence of increasingly separate and distinct native societies, each with increasingly firm and fixed boundaries within each general form of native society.* This process was interwoven with the simultaneous increasing (but never complete) separation of leaders from the matrix of kinship and daily life in their communities. The same processes that, for example, welded the Cherokee into an increasingly distinct and separate people – a "nation" or a "tribe" against other native nations or tribes – transformed their leaders from "beloved elders" to "chiefs."

4. *The increasing intensification of internal, "factional" differentiation within post-contact native political communities* ("nations," "tribes" or "towns"), which often led either to civil war within the political community or to the formation of separate, "new" political and cultural entities. For example, the Seminole emerged from a segment of the Creek nation – a segment that formed over irresolvable differences in strategies for coping with White domination. There was little other social or material basis for this separation, yet the Seminole soon were regarded as, and became, a distinct people. Indeed, the term "faction" minimizes the characteristic profundity of internal splits even when they do *not* lead to episodic tidal waves of assassinations, civil war, or the formation of distinct groups.

5. *The increasing separation of "Indians" from "Whites" and "Negroes"* on the level of ideas about different kinds of people, and simultaneously in the social organization of daily life and work. Most U.S. schoolchildren have heard the story of the "Boston tea party," at the onset of the American revolution, when Yankee patriots dressed "like Indians." John Highrider, with his 6 pounds of paint, and Governor Glen, with his frequent insistence that Indians fight rather than farm, add another dimension to this: they are forcibly dressing, in paint and in the political economy, the native peoples as Indians as well.

These five forms of increasing differentiation swept across the whole

range of Indian social life from political economy to culture and ceremony. All were imposed "from above," as part of the process of
domination, and all were claimed by the people themselves as part of
processes of asserting their own interests and of resisting – and collud-
ing with, evading, and accommodating to – domination.

The intense elaboration of native cultural forms that characterized
the incorporation of native peoples into an expanding Euro-American
colonial political economy can be understood only in the context of
these forms of differentiation: Aboriginal peoples became "Indians"
in ways that made them both more different from the Europeans than
they were at point of contact and simultaneously more an integral part
of a complex colonial social formation, a formation that was constructing
different kinds of Euro-Americans, African-Americans, and Indians.

The dramatically elaborate feather headdress of the plains Indians in
the early and mid-nineteenth century is but one forceful instance of
this long-continuing process – a complex interweaving of incorporation, distancing, and antagonistic divergence in the context of native
cultural embellishment. The headdress celebrated a range of new possibilities and new social lives for plains native peoples, brought by their
increasing acquisition of horses and guns, including the increased ability
to acquire substantial quantities of eagle feathers. The separation of
horse-mounted "nomads" from both their own forest-farming ancestors
of the Canadian north woods and from the Native American village
agriculturalists living on the plains; the separation of Indian warriors
from Indian farmers (who also fought, but on different, more defensive,
terms); the separation of warriors and chiefs from other ranks and
statuses within the same society (along with increasingly antagonistic
gender differentiation); all this and more was flaunted by the headdress,
which at least some Indians knew made them appear more dramatically
powerful while mounted, and covered their increasingly weak aggressive
and defensive potential with a mystificatory flair. The headdress thus
covered not only the head (scalp?) and back, but also helped conceal
the imposed militarism, the *unavoidable* need to war against both other
native peoples and Whites, and, as a growing but still substantially ig-
nored body of evidence indicates, the native people's own fear, terror
and dismay about the violence of their situation.

Perhaps for the same reasons that have led the dominant society –
and native people as well – to *not* see the headdress as a symbol of native
incorporation into a larger and dominant social system, a system that
was antagonistic to native needs and interests, as well as a symbol both
of native flair and force, and of native *Indianness*, neither anthropology

nor history has addressed the evidence which indicates that a substantial number of nineteenth century plains Indians owned, rode, and traded mules, not horses. Mules make Native Americans seem more like us, and even more clearly our victims, as opposed to the culturally charged, morally blinding fantasy of native peoples on the plains as the nearly total "other" – horse-mounted, "nomadic" warrior-hunters. This fantasy ignores not only the native people mounted on mules but the substantial numbers of settled Indian village farmers hoeing their mudflats along the rivers. Similarly, the issue of the intensity of native peoples' fears, and how they coped with them – which strongly indicts not Indians but those who imposed such conditions – remains quiet, among both Indians and other Americans, silencing the intimacy and the co-involvement of dominators and dominated that resides in the midst of the more spectacular differences.

Native American societies on the Great Plains are only the most dramatic and revealing example of a general case. Largely populated by relatively small groups of farmers along the river edges before the advent of the horse and the gun, and doomed after the end of the Civil War, the whole florescent native cultural forms that have come to stereotype "Indians" lasted – from the downward expansion of forest-dwellers out of the Canadian forests, who became mounted on horses and mules bred in northern Mexico for the Spanish mines, to the onslaught of White settlers and the confinement of surviving native peoples on reservations – one hundred and fifty years, more or less. Similarly, if even less frequently recognized, the whole period from the formation of the major native confederacies in the southeast (Cherokee, Choctaw, Creek, Chickasaw, Tuscarora) through their flourishing to their devastation – both individually and as a social form – was also about one hundred and fifty years, more or less – from the late 1600s to the early 1800s.

[As an aside: the supposedly pre-contact "Powhatan Confederacy," as the partly politically allied native towns were called by the English who settled in their midst at Jamestown, in 1607, is a complex and somewhat special case. It may have been partly a development from the pressures of Caribbean-based slave raids and wars, along the coast to the south. It may also have been partly a pre-contact, aboriginal development, as native towns sought to situate themselves between and against the political-economic reach of the southern chiefdoms and the coastal and riverine settlements that were producing both for their own subsistence and for the interregional, long-distance trade. Either as an aboriginal or a post-contact phenomenon, or both, the Powhatan Confederacy was more intensely elaborated and undermined in the context of dealing with the Jamestown settlement.]

The point here, in the comparison between the plains and the southeast, is not the similarity (mostly superficial) of time span, but the more basic similarity of the emergence and rapid, intense florescence of fundamentally new native social forms, forms that expressed the destructiveness of the imposed situation in part through an intense cultural and social-organizational elaboration of the differences between dominated and dominators, and in part through destructive assault upon other native peoples.

All of these developments were suddenly and violently transformed by Indian "removal" – removal of the southeastern Indians westward; the plains Indians to reservations – along trails drenched with tears and imprinted, on this softened ground, with long-continuing images and symbols of lost grandeur, lost grandiosity, and continually reborn terror and despair. The grandeur and the grandiosity of the briefly militarized native societies' former ways then became embedded in images and symbols shared by the descendants of these societies with substantial segments of the dominant culture, and also with many of the impoverished and marginal *native* victims of native militarism and brutality. The continuity of these militaristic symbols, such as the headdress-wearing horse-mounted warrior, as important and partly effective emblems of self-assertion, dignity, and continuing resistance to domination is thus deeply paradoxical, for such symbols also convey other, more destructive lessons as well.

If the paradoxes could not, and still cannot be reduced or resolved, they can at least here perhaps be clarified. They go beyond the issue of native peoples' continuing use, in the context of continuing resistance, of an "arsenal of symbols" created in the context of imposed domination. These symbols range from the specific, such as the long feather headdress, to the equally important but more general and diffuse notion that "real" Indians were people like the Iroquois, Cherokee, Sioux, and so on: peoples whose social and cultural organization, created in the colonial context, made them able not only to fight back against White domination but also to brutalize other Indians. The paradoxes go beyond this "arsenal of symbols" to at least two further, more fundamental, questions: How do people who have almost always, almost inevitably, lost almost every struggle against domination continue to struggle? What views of history, of past, present and future, can sustain such true grandeur of hope and of action?

We must also ask: Who pays what price for such views; who gains what? This is a particularly painful question, in part because it is so difficult to address without seeming to confront and undermine hope. But having seen, for example, Indian prejudice against African-Americans, and some

185

of the appalling price *both* pay for this, the question must be raised. It will be addressed, if not fully answered, in this and the next chapters.

II

We may begin analysis of the transformation of southeastern native peoples in the colonial period by a brief examination of the uses to which native peoples were then put. In this sketch we distinguish three broadly defined periods: *aboriginal, contact,* and *colonial.*

"Aboriginal" refers to native peoples before European contact. In any analysis that focused on the pre-contact southeast a number of crucial sub-regional and short-term temporal distinctions would have to be made, even for the few centuries before contact that will be the focus here. But in order to indicate some of the major changes in a *native* pre-contact historical dynamic brought about by the European invasion of America, only a few distinctions between different pre-contact social forms will be necessary.

The "contact" period is marked as the period of devastation – by disease, by Indian slave-raiding warfare, by forced and induced migrations – by all the effects of the European presence in North America (and the Caribbean, whose island colonies extensively used Indian slaves from North America) that preceded the regular, if episodic, presence of Europeans themselves on the landscape of any particular subregion. The "colonial" period refers to the predominance of processes of incorporation of native peoples into a Euro-American political and cultural economy, from the first use of Indians to the point where the Indians became "useless" to the colonists – or useful in much different ways – and were intentionally destroyed or removed.

When long-term historical processes are being discussed, the term "post-contact" is used to refer to both the contact and the colonial periods, taken together. Ordinarily, however, the distinction between a contact and colonial period is important to make. The proportional duration of these two periods varied widely from one locale to another. In a few places near the early European coastal settlements there was hardly any contact period at all; in other, more sheltered or isolated areas, such as the swamps of Robeson County, the contact period was long – indeed, centuries – and the colonial period lasted only a few decades.

In this chapter and the next we look first to the colonial period and the issue of use and transformation, and then to the contact period, and then quite briefly (considering the range of issues that need to be at least mentioned) a few points are introduced about the historical dynamics of aboriginal (pre-contact) native social systems and how the European onslaught altered the social dynamics of aboriginal societies. On the basis of this preliminary discussion of colonial, contact, and pre-contact native historical processes we shall be able to look again, but more closely, at the colonial period, in order to highlight both the vulnerabilities and the contradictions within emergent native social systems in the colonial and post-colonial periods.

These fundamental vulnerabilities and contradictions endure from colonial times to the present, taking on a limited variety of surface appearances. *The specific forms of Native American vulnerability and the specific contradictions within native social systems actively shaped the formation of very different kinds of Indian societies, with very different historical trajectories and very different appearances within the larger American culture.* When this is seen it also reveals the present requirements for Indian "status recognition" by the federal government (the subject of the final chapter) as a fantasy of domination, which, under imposed requirements for asking Indian people to provide the history of their political organization and to describe their "Indian culture," serves to conceal both.

III

The most effective introduction to the transformations of native societies in the colonial period, and the emerging contradictions embedded in these transformations – both of which are difficult to see in a simple chronology, for they are highlighted by looking simultaneously at the multiplicity of linkages to "before" and "after" – is to grasp the scale of *use*; to start by seeing just how intensely, and then in what diverse ways, native people were used.

Charles Town (Charleston after 1783), in the center of the coast of what is now South Carolina, was founded in 1670. By the early 1690s a deerskin trade with the people of the southern Appalachians – people the colonists came to know as Cherokee – was beginning to flourish. Some statistics on the magnitude of the trade with the Cherokee and neighboring groups have survived and were collected by Verner Crane. Crane, whose book *The Southern Frontier* is crucial to understanding southeastern colonial native societies, points out that the statistics represent an unknowable portion, but far from the whole, of the deerskin trade. A count was recorded of the deerskins shipped from the port of Charles Town to England; these were the skins that were taxed. The numbers sent to New England, to Germany, to the West Indies, the amount the merchants wiggled through the smaller ports to avoid the export duties, the number of skins the colony itself used, the number that went southwestward to the French: all uncounted and unknown. Shall we say, as a guess, that somewhat more than half the Indian-procured skins were counted?

What we know is that many of the larger and heavier skins went to England, and that these skins came more from the mountains than from the piedmont, where deer were smaller and lighter. The following trade figures, for only that portion of the deerskin trade that was re-corded, *might* generally approximate the numbers of skins shipped through Charles Town from the Appalachian region alone:

> *From 1699 to 1715 the average* annual *importation into England from Carolina was nearly 54,000 deerskins.* [This comes to 864,000 prepared skins.] *The greatest number purchased by the English mer-chants was 121,355 skins from Christmas, 1706 to Christmas 1707. . . . In 1748 the province shipped off over seven hundred hogsheads, con-taining approximately 160,000 deerskins . . . each hogshead being worth Fifty Guineas in Charles Town* [in 1746]; *and to this must be added the Duty, Freight, Insurance and Merchants' Gains which make alto-gether a considerable sum.*

The whole image of the "naked savage," "roaming" or "wandering" about in the forest with bow and arrow, collapses totally with these statistics, and this is just the beginning.

We are dealing here with highly organized forms of production. The fact that production was so intensely organized through – by means of – the *developing* "Indianness" of the native peoples must be taken to reveal, rather than to conceal, the dynamics of native peoples' *integration* into the colonial political economy *as Indians.* Their Indianness was, indeed, their *otherness*; simultaneously, and equally fundamentally, it was the form of their *inclusion.*

To make this crucial point clearer: "Capitalism," as it is ordinarily if somewhat simplistically understood, emerged in Europe on the basis of alienating people from direct possession of the material bases of pro-duction, and massing the dispossessed people together in new forms of production. One of the key features of capitalist production is that the product passes out of the control of the people who work on it, and into the hands of others, at the point of production. Factory workers do not make shoes or textiles and then sell them. Rather, in return for their wage, what they produce at any point in their work process does not belong to them but to those who possess the means of production and who organize the work processes.

In the southeast, the export trade in deerskins and other pelts was a major factor in the early colonial economy, and the Europeans pos-sessed neither effective means of production nor, more crucially, the capacity to organize and mobilize labor on the scale required. Native peoples had both; European colonists sought to possess and control *them*. They did this, however, through processes that secured this control while simultaneously underwriting a substantial amount of native social and cultural autonomy.

Sidney Mintz has shown, in his book *Sweetness and Power*, that key forms of labor discipline and mobilization crucial to the development of large-scale European capitalism were developed and refined not in England (or even Europe in general) but on the sugar-producing slave plantations of the West Indies. Here a related but different point is being made: very large pools of Indian labor were being channeled and put to use specifically through *changing and developing forms of native social organization*, including forms of political and economic leadership through which labor came to be organized, the village and clan-based forms of access to land, the kin and village-based forms of cooperation in the work of producing deerskins, and even the forms of native militarism that were invariably a part of the trade in pelts.

The developing Indian social, cultural, and productive systems in the colonial period thus not only expressed native peoples' interests, claims, intentions, and histories but were also, intensely, forms of integration into the colonial political economy. This economy was of course not yet "capitalist," but the forms of wealth extraction and domination central to the development of capitalism were emerging, and the seeds of capitalism were forming in processes of social and cultural – that is, "ethnic" – differentiation and interconnection. The creation of "Indians" and Indian societies through the transformation of aboriginal social systems – a process that *increased* the cultural and social-organizational differences between ordinary Native American village farmers and ordinary European village farmers over the two hundred years from, say, 1550 to 1750 – played a key role in the social, political, and economic processes of accumulation that were the precondition for the emergence of capitalism.

The deerskin trade was crucial to both Indians and Euro-Americans. The export tax on Indian deerskins subsidized the importation of White indentured servants to help hold down Black slaves; more generally, the returns on the trade brought to southern colonies a substantial amount of the actual currency – the coins and bills – that greatly facilitated moving slave-grown crops to port. On the other side, for the English-allied Indians, the deerskin trade was ordinarily the main source for a continuing supply of guns, powder, and shot, without which the Indians would have been even more defenseless and vulnerable.

"Now our inmates"

The English colonists not only needed the deerskin trade, they needed *Indians* as the procurers of the skins for this trade. This need came from a variety of reasons, including a general shortage of Euro-American labor in the colony, the existence of more appealing options for colonists than deer hunting (options that included, for those who were attracted or driven to the margins of the frontier, herding forest-foraging cattle and hogs on the same sort of land that Indians would have used to get deer). Most of all, the English colonists were probably incapable of mobilizing free labor on a scale and with the high level of organization necessary for commercial deer hunting and skin preparation. Nor, of course, could they have armed slaves and sent them into the woods. In contrast to the usual way of thinking about "civilized" and "primitive," "modern" and "backward," it was precisely the Indians who had the ability to put together large-scale, flexible, and adaptive forms of labor organization to meet the newly emergent needs. Indeed, this was one of the *central* features of a developing "Indianness" – and this ability was absolutely crucial to the European colonists: for deerskins, for colonial wars, for slave procurement, and for a host of other reasons that we shall review.

IV

Alongside the deerskin trade, but starting much earlier, southeastern Indians were extremely active in the slave trade, at times financing their wars against each other – just as the Europeans financed many assaults upon native people – by the sale of captives. As Charles Hudson put it: "This became so prevalent that in contemporary documents the statement that Indians had gone to war is virtually synonymous with saying that they had gone to capture slaves."

Indian people were not extensively used as slaves in the mainland colonies, but were "transported" to the West Indies. The relative ease of escape on the mainland and the fear that after escape they might return for vengeance diminished the demand for native slave labor. But the most effective obstacle to the extensive use of Indian slaves within the South Carolina colony, by the early 1700s, was the fear of an Indian–Black alliance. From about 1710 to 1775, South Carolina had a population of approximately one-third more Blacks than Whites; counting the major Indian groups around the colony, which is the way South Carolinians saw it, there were many more Indians than Whites or Blacks. In the context of White fears of an Indian–Black alliance, and the possibility not only of a joint attack but an attack by either with the other standing aside, the colonial government took a variety of measures

190

to separate Indians and Blacks as antagonistically and as far as possible, including shipping native captives far away.

For this reason – and as it rubs against the grain of subsequent stereotypes – the magnitude of the trade in Indian slaves is still not widely recognized (here I join a continuing list of scholarly reminders on this point), nor is its organization, nor the transformative impact it had on native societies.

For the Indians on the piedmont in the early 1700s, slavery, and deaths in the wars to take slaves, probably represented as great a threat as disease. Piedmont Indians were almost completely trapped between the expanding coastal Euro-American settlements to their east and the European-armed Indians of their western and northwestern mountain regions. These more western Indians became, by the late 1600s, somewhat protected from enslavement owing to the crucial role they were beginning to play in the skin trade and in the colonial wars, Armed with guns for these purposes, and facing nearly equally well armed native peoples to their west and southwest, they fell upon the piedmont peoples – and when they could, each other – with devastating effect. As Charles Hudson put it:

> *When the French arranged for a truce between the Chickasaws and the Choctaws in 1702, they estimated that at the instigation of the Charleston traders the Chickasaws had enslaved five hundred Choctaws and had killed 1,800 of them. . . . In 1708, when the total population of South Carolina was 9,580 . . . there were also 1,400 Indian slaves.*
> [There were, in 1708, 4,080 Whites and 4,100 Black slaves; for the first time more Blacks than Whites.]

The 1690s seemed to be a turning point in the organization of the trade in Indian slaves: before, the Europeans had been arming coastal native peoples – or more precisely some of them – and setting them against others; after, the material and social-relational bases of power flowed to the emerging inland confederacies.

The Spanish set the pattern for Indian enslavement in Florida and Georgia; it seems to have been followed rather closely by the English. Columbus, as is well known, arrived in the Americas in 1492. What is much less well known is that he returned to Hispaniola in 1493 with 1,200 colonists: by 1497 about one-third of the substantial native population of that island were dead; by 1507 the entire native population, at least several hundred thousand people, were all gone – dead from disease, killed in the "wars" to take slaves or land, or enslaved. In 1523 the Spanish Crown gave Lucas Vasquez de Ayllon a patent for the exploration of the southeastern coast of mainland North America, which also established the terms for taking Indians as slaves:

"Now our inmates"

> *I give to you permission and control so that if in any part of the said*
> *land that you may thus discover are found in possession of the native*
> *Indians slaves, of those they took in wars . . . and if they be truly and*
> *justly slaves, when you have bought them by agreement with the In-*
> *dians, you may take them freely to the island Espanola or to any part*
> *of the other islands to put them on our plantations or dispose of them*
> *as you wish.*

Thus Indian slaves were not to be taken directly, but only if they were captives of other Indians. This had a particularly devastating effect on the native population. It may, in fact, have been the central dynamic of the *contact* period, for the coastal natives carried not only their armed assaults to the interior but, more destructively, a substantial number of deadly European diseases. This policy, moreover, clearly established the principle that what small chance of survival there was depended almost entirely on alliance with one or another of the European colonies. Native peoples were driven to embrace such alliances under circumstances that even the Europeans themselves admitted were destructive.

For example, the English were made welcome when they came to settle at Charles Town in 1670. The local Cusabo Indians were hard-pressed by the Spanish Indian allies at Guale to their south, and the Westo, who had moved into the region as a group and settled on the Savannah River inland from the Cusabo. The Westo had guns from the trade with Virginia; other native people in the area did not. When Robert Sanford surveyed the area in 1666, looking for a place to found a settlement, he noted: "The Westoes, a ranging sort of people reputed to be man eaters had ruinated that place, killed sev'all of those Indians destroyed and burnt their Habitations and they had come as far as Keyawah doing the like there."

The Westoes at this point were the long arm of the Virginia colony; it was Virginians that were devouring the natives of the region in their hunger for slaves and for the profits of the slave trade. But the colonists that Sanford represented had been doing just as much damage as the Westoes, while trying to establish their settlement at Cape Fear (then called Clarendon), about 200 land miles north of the Cusabo – and the Cusabo knew it:

> *. . . indeed all along I observed a kind of emulacon* [competition]
> *amongst the three principall Indians of the Country . . . concerning us*
> *and our friendshipp, each contending to assure it to themselves and*
> *jealous of the other though all be allyed and this not with standing that*
> *they know wee were in actual warre with the Natives at Clarendon and*
> *had killed and sent away* [enslaved] *many of them, for they frequently*
> *discoursed with us concerning the warre, told us the natives* [at

192

> Clarendon] *were noughts, they land sandy and barren, their Country*
> *sickly, but if Wee would come amongst them Wee should find the*
> *Contrarie to all their Evills, and never any occasion of discharging our*
> *Gunns but in merryment and for pastime.*

The English did indeed come among them. By the end of 1671 the
Stono, one of the main Cusabo peoples, were reduced to "straggling
parties" having to rob English plantations for food. Governor West –
the English equivalent of the marauding Westo Indians – set a reward
for their capture and shipped all the survivors to the West Indies. This
was the beginning of the rapid elimination of the entire Cusabo, five
years after the first European arrived and one year after European
settlement. And the alliance the English formed with the Westo in 1674
was broken in 1680, when the English decided to go across them to the
inland tribes, eliminating the Westo's role as middlemen in the trade
in slaves and skins. They did this by direct and total assault, selling the
captives into slavery. Very early in the history of Indian relations with
English settlers, it was also established that neither alliance nor opposition were long-term effective strategies.

At this point – the 1670s – some coastal Indians were, along with the
colonists, raiding for slaves north, south, and west; others were marked
for victims. Twenty years later the tables turned for the western Indians:
no longer victims, they were to be agents.

V

One "text" – the description of a brief interchange between a party of
Creek Indians and a South Carolina trader among the "lower" Cherokee,
on the high piedmont east of the mountains – can center our understanding of the historical development of war between Indians and
colonists and between Indians and Indians. Even more significantly, it
shows us a profound divergence between Indians and colonists in how
that history was understood.

On November 14, 1724, W. Hatter, a trader to the Cherokee, wrote
the governor at Charles Town. A copy of his letter was forwarded to
England:

> *on Monday the 9th of this instant, by the first Cock Crow . . . A Party*
> *of the Creek Indians came to Toogelloo and No-You whee two towns*
> *adjoining on[ly] parted by a River, and by which Town's sides Mr*
> *Sharps trading house Stands. I happened to be then at a town called*
> *Timothy about twelve miles from my own house and twenty five from*
> *the towns aforsd when about noon came in The Warr-whoop, which*
> *gave an Account that Toogelloo was cut off. About two hours after*

come another and gave us an Account that the Enemy had not medled with the Indian Towns, but only fell upon Jno Sharps house and had Ransacked and Plundered the Same Carrying away all his Goods and had Shott him in the belly and that he was sent to call all the White People to come there. . . .

The next morning . . . we mustered up ten of us and went over to no-you-whee where we found Mr Sharp at an Indians house but not shot in the Belly as was told us, but Shot thro the Leg, and when we was all there he told us as followeth

That about first Cock Crowing in ye morning his dogs gave him Notice that some body was about ye house at which his Slave fellow got up to See what was the Matter and at his coming out he heard Gun fire and immediately One or two more at wch he wakes up his Master, and tels him the Enemy was about the house, upon wch Sharp gets up & opened the door, & lighted a Candle, and they all ye time pouering in whole volies of Shot into the house & yard, & then rushed in upon him & one of the Shot that came in thro the house went thro his leg. As soon as they Entered the house they began to Plunder it of all that was in it, & others was in his Store where he had his trading Goods, & took away every thing he had, both household Goods trading Goods & Skins & Provisions, he in the meantime made no resistance, but asked them to Smoak tobacco and intreated them not to use him after that rude manner telling them that the White People & they were friends & a great many friendly Arguments he used to them in English but all avail'd him nothing, neither would any of them Speak a Word of English, or if they could they would not let him know it, but when ever he spoke to them only laughed at him. One would come up to him & Shake him by ye hand & tell him he was a Tallepoosa, & take of his Coat, another would Cry out Euchee, and take of his Shirt & others two Egelluhs Cowealahs & Yomahitahs, till they had Stript him out of all his Clothes, leaving him nothing but his breeches on, they carried away all his Slaves except one which was his Slave man, who made his escape from them. In short they left him not a thread of Clothes to Cover him nor victuals to eat except a little Corn & Pumpkins which they could not carry off. Nay his very Pack Saddles they cut out the pads, & carried away . . . the House was like a Cullendar so full of Shot holes and ye Yard perfectly plowed up wth bullets by Computation there could be little less than a thousand Shott fired there, & a Miracle it was to me to See it, & Sharp in the House all the time & come to no more damage. And what does a little more Add to our Surprize is that they made no Attempt on ye Indians, or their Towns no not so much as to fire one Shott Against one house but pack'd up Sharp's Goods &

went off, but it was told me that they called over the River to the Cherokees [to the Creeks?: the document throughout blurs or confuses the colonists' usually firm distinction between Creeks and Cherokee, for reasons that will be seen], & asked them, why they fired away their Powder & Bullets wch does a little shock us to find no hostilities committed against each other.

While We was all at this Town talking wth Mr Sharp, the [Cherokee] headmen got together, & came to me to talk concerning this matter. I began wth them & asked them, how they could stand still and see their Enemy come to the White Mans, & shoot him & rob him wth carrying away all his Goods that he had taken so much Care & trouble to bring them, to Suply them with and not to go to Assist him, Altho they was at most within Gun Shot of them, & that if they would not help us at Such a time how could they expect that ever We should Assist them or bring Goods amongst them if they would not help to defend it.

They answered that their men was all out a hunting, & none but boys and old men at home & if they had been at home they should not have carried away ye Goods, but as soon as word was brought them they all left their hunting and came home & that they should not carry away ye Goods yet, but that in two days time when they dont expect them they would follow them and fetch back the Goods again, and asked us if we would not go with them, Since it was ye White man that Suffered and not them, for says they the papers you brought tell us that the Governmt Says, if the Creeks will not be good & mind what the Governmt Says to them [about not attacking the Cherokee] that they will Send us White men to joyn us and go within to fight them and Says they you see yourselves time after time, that they will not hear the Govern't but still persists in their Roguery not only Against us, but Against ye White People, mentioning all ye insolvencies they have been guilty of to the traders in ye Path & ye Killing of the three White men yt was kill'd at Norgoutchee, & telling us plainly that they saw no Order was taken wth them for their so doing & that they do believe that we are as much afraid of ye Creeks as they are, & that if they had been guilty of doing half so much to the White People as the Creeks had done they was Sure we should Soon come to Warr upon them & that they should expect no other.

In Answer to their asking us to go wth them after the Enemy, I told them it was true there was enough of us to follow them, & with a few Cherokees to fetch back what they had Carried away, & had we Chanced to been there when they came we would have defended Our Selves & them as long as we had lives, but to follow them into the Woods was

> *what we could not Answer, till Yr Excell'cy had given ye word, &*
> *besides that they must Consider there was a great many White men*
> *trading amongst [the Creeks] which doubtless would be kill'd, as soon*
> *as any of them got home to carry the News, that the White People came*
> *after them in Company with the Charokees.*
>
> *For my Part I could not tell what more to say to them on this, for*
> *they do not Stick to upbraid us wth Cowardice to Animate us Against*
> *ye Creeks as much as ever we have done them, but whither it be from*
> *their hearts or not We should joyn them for they Seem not displeased*
> *that they* [the Creeks] *did not offer to Sack their Towns, which I do*
> *not know but it given them some Prospect of Peace, which I hope may*
> *be Nipt in the bud, otherwise I fear* [it] *will Produce ill fruit.*

Throughout this extraordinary interchange the Indian people – both the Creeks who attacked Jonathan Sharp and, in a different way, the Cherokee – were confronting the Europeans with the history of their wars and raids, and were also themselves confronting, and distancing themselves from, their own history.

To begin, the names the Creeks called Sharp, as they shook his hand, stripped him of his clothes, and plundered his food and his goods, were names of piedmont and coastal plain tribes (or towns) that the Europeans had attacked or destroyed, or had provoked the larger and more powerful Indian confederacies into destroying. Over and over again in the colonial documents, as Indian headmen were brought or came to Charles Town to negotiate with the governor and council for trade or for peace – negotiations that often entailed agreeing to assault other Indian peoples for European purposes, in order to secure the essential trade for themselves – the Europeans mentioned in the documents their ritual of "shaking hands" with the assembled headmen at the start of the negotiations. Over and over and over again the same documents mention a characteristic warning to the assembled Indians: those Indians who oppose the Europeans will be left "naked and starving." The colonists continually threaten to "cut them off" – to deny "enemy Indians" the crucial ammunition and trade in clothes, blankets, guns, axes, and knives, leaving them defenseless and exposed. Moreover, colonial military tactics against native towns often entailed burning standing and stored crops as well as houses. (Epidemics among native Americans, as in Europe, often had their most lethal effects in areas devastated by hunger and famine. However substantial the biological susceptibility of native Americans to unusual, imported diseases, to ignore the role of imposed famine in the history of the great Native American epidemics is to "naturalize" what was often in significant part an outcome of political policy.)

The Creeks, in sum, did to Sharp exactly what had been done to and through them; they showed the Europeans in the most dramatic way possible the history of the militarized engagements between them. They did this with an extraordinary "waste" of their supply of ammunition and completely avoiding any assault upon the Cherokee. In the utter disregard of their practical need for ammunition, and in their avoidance of (or respect for) Cherokee people and their property – whom the French had been openly encouraging them to destroy and the English subtly encouraging them to diminish – they were demonstrating their autonomy and their distance from their own history.

The most subtle and complex indication of the Creek assertion of autonomy that this text conveys is the author's pervasive confusion of Cherokee and Creek. Indeed, I have never read a colonial text where it was so difficult to figure out who was doing what to whom. This may be because for the colonists one of the primary distinctions between Creek and Cherokee (or between any other "different" native groups) was the manipulable hostility between them; when this collapsed, at least temporarily, so did the Europeans' distinction between the two.

The Cherokee picked up these themes of autonomy and of what we might call the theater of historical knowledge, taunting the Europeans with their cowardice and showing a very detailed awareness of how the Creeks had treated the English traders both by direct assaults and by defaulting on debts. The Cherokee invoked a history of treaties and offers of friendship and mutual aid from the English, even laying before the Europeans the honest admission of their own fears of the Creeks, perhaps seeking to prod the Europeans into a more straightforward response, perhaps subtly taunting the Europeans into confronting the transparency of their own deceptions. They offered, further on in this text, to have their best runners carry the letter to the governor, requesting permission for the Europeans to attack the Creek, but Hatter, its author, noted in a postscript that reasons of personal business delayed his finishing the letter for four more days.

None of what the Creeks or Cherokee did seemed to have any effect on the Europeans' conception of their relation to the Indians. The English never seemed to notice what the Creeks were "saying" to them, nor could the Creeks, for all their bravery and bravado, materially distance themselves from the history that was being imposed on them. And the English literally "stuck to their guns" with the Cherokee, remaining concerned primarily about the dangerous effects of peace between Cherokees and Creeks. Native American peoples' own understanding of history simply did not matter to the Europeans, save as a partial obstacle to using them. This, I think, was a central aspect of the increasingly totalizing progress of domination, and a mirror to native peoples for seeing their own vulnerability.

This document was written in 1724, at the culmination of a decade-long turning point in the relations between English colonists and southeastern native peoples. The turn began with the substantial destruction of the Tuscarora and Yamasee peoples in wars between 1711 and 1715, and the concurrent "utter extirpation" of many of the smaller native groups on the coastal plain and piedmont.

Until sometime after the Tuscarora and Yamasee wars, the English colonists at Charles Town – the most exposed and least densely settled of the continental English colonies – were afraid of Indians' power and, more to the point, were *using* native peoples, at least some of whom they feared, intensely needed, or both. After the wars they were still using native peoples but feared them less and needed them in ways that were still significant, but increasingly less crucial.

This turn is both complex and particularly revealing of characteristic contradictions across which domination was and is continually reorganized. It is worth a book in its own right; some of its main features will be schematically indicated here.

Between 1703 and 1708 there was a rapid increase in the number of Indian slaves taken in the Carolinas, which decimated many of the coastal peoples. As and after this was happening, Tuscarora, located on the interior of the coastal plain, south of Virginia, were coming under increasing pressure from the southward-expanding English settlers, who had moved south of the Tuscarora's Neuse River in 1706. Tuscarora were also increasingly devastated by the ravages of smallpox, which was particularly virulent among them in 1707 and for several years afterward.

In addition, they were increasingly angry about the way they were treated by the traders. Until after the Yamasee war in 1715, when the colonial governments somewhat restrained the worst brutalities (such as kidnapping people for enslavement) traders often dealt brutally with native peoples. The colonial governments, while mumbling against such practices, engaged in more organized, quieter, and more insistent forms of domination. In 1712, for example, the South Carolina government instructed its Indian agents that the value of the return presents given to Indians should not exceed one-half the value of the presents that the Indians had given: a policy that had serious cultural and political-economic effects on native "allies." Virginia's most serious provocation, from the testimony of Indian complaints, was its almost unrestricted expansion directly within Indian lands.

In 1710 a substantial portion of the Tuscarora peoples tried to reset-
tle in Pennsylvania and were rebuffed. In the fall of 1711 some Tuscarora,
mostly in the southeast regions of their territory, rose up with their
native allies against the English. Tuscarora living more to the northwest
stayed neutral or even helped the English.

South Carolina quickly sent aid to the newly formed colony of North
Carolina, in the person of Col. John Barnwell and 528 men, 495 of
whom were Yamasee and other Indian peoples. They did a lot of damage
to Tuscarora and their allies, but not enough to keep them from rising
again in 1712. In response, South Carolina sent Colonel Moore with
approximately 900 Indian troops, including a large contingent of
Yamasee, and 33 White soldiers. In the spring of 1713 they killed about
1,400 Tuscarora and enslaved a further 1,000. Soon after they finished
their work together, slaughtering and enslaving Tuscarora, South
Carolina turned on the Yamasee.

Since the late 1600s the Charles Town colony had exceedingly ambivalent relations with the people they called the Yamasee. As early as
1684 Scots settlers were going on illicit slave raids with Yamasee. The
Yamasee became significant trading partners with the colony in the
early 1700s, at first especially in the trade for Indian slaves and then in
a two-way trade, capturing Black slaves from the English and selling or
transporting them to the Spanish at St. Augustine, while selling Black
slaves or recaptured runaways from the Spanish settlements back to the
English. English traders seemed to deal with Yamasee with particular
brutality, despite – or perhaps because – the English were particularly
afraid of both Yamasee strength and autonomy. This autonomy was
materially sustained by Spanish and French sources for Yamasee guns.

After about 1710 the Yamasee themselves became the victims of slave
raids, traders were pressing hard against them, and they seemed to be
having increasing difficulty making a relatively secure place for themselves along and between the colonial frontiers of the Spanish, English,
and French. After they contributed substantially to the war against
Tuscarora (and profited handsomely from the sale of captured
Tuscarora), they themselves rose up against the English, who then
brought Tuscarora survivors down to fight, and quickly destroy, the
Yamasee. On their way down the coastal plain, the Tuscarora also
wreaked havoc on coastal Indian peoples who the English had just
finished using against them – particularly the Cape Fear and Waccamaw
Indians.

The South Carolina colonial government seemed to have learned two
crucial lessons from these wars: first, that they could continually and

effectively use Indian peoples that they were treating very destructively – Yamasee against Tuscarora, and even more surprisingly, Tuscarora against Yamasee; second, Indian people probably could or would not effectively unite against the colonists.

This second "lesson" was not, for quite some time, completely learned or trusted, for the English continued to be concerned with the issue of pan-Indian unity throughout most of their eighteenth-century colonial presence, and they continued to take steps against this possibility. But they were increasingly more concerned about combinations of Indian peoples against their useful Indian allies than the direct threat of such combinations against the English themselves.

In 1717 South Carolina, just over its war against the Yamasee and facing hostile, well-armed Creeks, complained to the Crown:

> *I am now to inform you of melancholy news in relation to our Indian Warr, we have two white men Lately come from the Creeke Indians that brings acct. that the Senecas or Mohocks are Joined wth them and resolve to fall on the Charachees & Cuttabaws that are now our friends, we also understand that the french Indians will help the Creeks, if so, our friendly Indians will be Intirely cut off in all humane probability, and then any may judg the Consequence what will become of us next.*
>
> *I cannot see how it is possible such a handfull of men tired out wth this Warr can much longer keep this Country without a relief from our native Country England. . . .*
>
> *The Creek Indians . . . pretend they will not hurt the English, but as for the Charakees and Cuttabas they will have no peace wth them, presume this pt. of policy is acted by them on purpose that we may not assist the sd. Charachees nor Cuttabas, we are in Such a streight that we know not what to do, nor how to turn . . . I cannot see what will become of poor Carolina at Last.*

While the tone of this document is a bit more extreme than circumstances warranted, it marked nearly the end-point of serious English fears that they would be overwhelmed by native peoples acting in consort. To the contrary, by 1715 the Indian peoples of the coastal plain and piedmont were finding Virginia and the Carolinas allied against them, and their situation and possibilities for survival and for living-space deteriorating rapidly. They were forced into "peaceful" relations with the colonists completely on the colonists' terms, and often under threat of devastation by the Cherokee, who had become South Carolina's principal trading partner and ally after the Yamasee war.

Shortly after the Cherokee became allied with South Carolina, two crucial processual developments strongly, and almost simultaneously, intensified.

First, Cherokee people went into a serious decline in numbers, in their productive capabilities for farming and for commercial hunting, and in their military power. By 1720 South Carolina's traders and Indian agents were observing that Cherokee were having few children. They were not replenishing their losses, save partly by the subsequent incorporation of other native people moving to join them, and the losses were severe. In January of 1719–20 Governor Robert Johnson of South Carolina wrote the Board of Trade:

> *By the within Account of the Number of Indians Subject to the Government of South Carolina in the year 1715 Yr. Lordships will find upwards of Eight and twenty thousand Souls of which there was Nine thousand Men, which traded for above 10,000 £. Stirling Yearly in Cloth Guns Powder Bullets and Iron ware & made return in Buck Skins, Doe Skins, Furs & other Peltry, and there was one way or other near 200 English Indians Traders Imployed as Factors by ye Merchants of Carolina Amongst them; But in ye Said Year 1715 most of them Rose in Rebellion and Murdered ye Said Traders and Severall of the Planters & their Familys that lay most exposed to them but before ye end of the said Year we recovered the Charokees and the Northward Indians after Severall Slaughters and Blood Sheddings which has Lessened their Numbers and utterly Extirpating some little Tribes as the Congarees Santees Seawees Pedees Waxaws & some Corsaboys so that by Warr Pestilence & Civill Warr Amongst themselves the Charokees may be computed reduced to abt 10,000 Souls & the Northern Indians to 2,500 Souls. . . .* [The Cherokee were computed by the Colony to be 11,500 people in 1715.]

The second development, beginning shortly after the onset of this period of precipitous decline, was the substantial intensification of processes of effective – if never complete – political, military and, to an extent, economic consolidation of diverse peoples known to the European colonists as Cherokee. "Cherokee" more effectively became "*the* Cherokee" – a functioning, if factionalized, confederacy – while suffering substantial decline. This double process of population decline and confederacy formation was, in fact, a characteristic feature in the formation of all the southeastern Indian confederacies, and although it is crucial to understanding these formative processes from a native perspective it remains poorly understood, nor can it be properly examined here.

The colonial governments had a long-standing, active interest in welding cohesive Indian groups together and in strengthening native leaders' control over these groups – creating leaders the English first called "kings" and later "chiefs" (and a variety of other names, including emperor and variants of the Spanish *cacique*). Virginia did this in the mid-seventeenth century with the defeated Powhatan Confederacy and other nearby groups; South Carolina actively pursued this policy throughout the eighteenth century, instructing its Indian agents, for example, in 1712:

> *That in all Places where you come you shall strictly charge the Indians to be honest, loving and assistant, kind and obedient in all reasonable Demands to the white Men living and trading among them, and att the same Time to aquaint yourself with their Custom, Usage &c., giving the King and Head Men Advice in Relation to the managing their People the better to keep them in Subjection, and with Example and Arguments drawn from a Parralell with our Government, and always as much as in you layes, keep in Favour with the Cheif Men, advising and assisting them to maintain the Authority given them by this Government.*

In sum: To a considerable extent European colonial domination created the Cherokee as a separate, named people, pressured for the transformation of their Beloved Elders into "chiefs," and forced the chiefs and the people off their farms and into the forest as hunters and warriors (hunters for European profits and warriors in imposed, senseless, and unwinnable wars). The authority-creating policies of the English colonists did not, however, seem to have nearly as much effect in shaping native leadership as did the pressures of trade, war, land seizures, retaliatory campaigns by colonists and by other native peoples, all in the context of severely declining populations. Such pressures increasingly consolidated Indian confederacies, enhanced the power of chiefs (and the turmoil between contenders for power) and, as often the case when power is consolidating among a dominated people, changed the relations between men and women, diminishing the status and well-being of women.

At the center of the double process of population decline and confederacy formation is a point that is crucial for understanding the situation of native peoples in the southeast: processes of confederacy formation made native peoples stronger, politically and militarily, made them more effective in claiming a space and a place for themselves, and contributed substantially to the survival and well-being of the native peoples in confederacies. But the webs of strength were fully interwoven, strand for strand, with warps of intense vulnerability, a vulnerability that had, as its inner fibers, the Indians' continuing need to be *used* – used even in the midst of their autonomy and their florescent assertiveness – in order to survive. The vulnerability of native peoples, along with their strength, profoundly affected their social relations within and between their communities.

VI

Indian people were very vulnerable to the European onslaught in so many brutally direct ways – from disease, from warfare, from enslavement, from colonial military tactics designed to create famine by burning crops – that it is difficult to see the *logic* of Indian vulnerability (how it was structured into the whole colonial political economy), and even more difficult to see why the logic of vulnerability is important. But this logic is crucial to the subsequent history of the survivors – to shaping the forms of Indian social systems that emerged within, and from, the colonial period – and it is also crucial to how subsequent "historical" understandings of the colonial period were formed and used.

The logic of Indian vulnerability is an integral part of a broader logic of early capitalist (and merchant capital) forms of alienation and incorporation, and of the expansion and consolidation of a state's power to reshape daily lives and productive possibilities for large numbers of people. Emerging capitalism, as we noted above, initially accumulated a substantial part of its labor supply in Europe, by alienating people from their direct control over the material means of production – land, raw materials, tools. To do this it was not necessary to seize people's land, or to break down the doors of their cottages and carry away their spinning wheels and hand looms. It was "only" necessary, for example, to develop the mechanical spinning jenny and the power loom to make the cottagers' spinning wheels and hand looms an alien presence within their own homes; large-scale farming and the removal of tariff barriers to imported grains made a mockery of the ownership of small plots of farmland and eventually also to the attempt to combine small-scale farming and cottage industry.

In Europe the increasing irrelevance of widespread forms of small-scale rural ownership (small plots of land, with markedly diminished or no access to commons resources; the possession of a hand loom, or later a spinning wheel, which all rapidly became increasingly useless as a basis for social survival) became dramatically apparent in the late eighteenth and early nineteenth centuries. The wounds of uselessness were carved deeply into the bodies of people already scarred by the massive dislocations of the European population in the late seventeenth and early to mid-eighteenth centuries.

In central Europe, starting shortly after the brutal devastations of the Thirty Years' War (1618–48) – a war that was probably one of the most destructive of villagers and villages of any war until aerial bombardment was invented – there was a massive population dislocation: 350,000 Germans migrated to the southwest, another 300,000 went from the southeast to Prussia, another 100,000 fled to Spain, to Poland, to America. Hundreds of thousands of Russians went south or east; Scots, Irish, and English were dislocated and relocated by the tens of thousands, over and over again. The "capitalization" of agriculture, which largely followed these massive dislocations and which preceded manufacturing and industrial capitalism in Great Britain, the Low Countries, and northern Europe, triggered further population dislocations.

This transformation of agriculture was the basis for two centuries of intense and widespread misery in Europe, and it culminated in the more or less complete alienation of large numbers of people from their own means of producing a living. In Europe, however, this process occurred in the midst of complex counter currents emerging from the population dislocations, which allowed many people not only to survive but at least temporarily to prosper, or to take relatively long-term advantage of the opportunities that others' misfortunes created: getting hold of land and goods left behind by migrants, for one example; or finding a place to migrate where there were long-lasting chances for at least comparatively modest prosperity; or taking advantage of the new productive possibilities created in the midst of the losses engendered by the growth of capitalism. Native Americans, suffering proportionately more massive dislocations, had far fewer opportunities and suffered an even more profound alienation from their own resources.

While the early power looms in Europe quickly made the cottagers' hand looms useless as a source of livelihood, they also created an enormous demand, in some places at least, for hand-spun thread produced on cottagers' spinning wheels. Destruction of one possible form of earning a livelihood came together with the rapid emergence of other forms. When spinning was mechanized, however, cottagers were not so lucky: hand spinning, for hundreds of thousands, was replaced by starvation.

Among Indians, the whole process of dislocation and alienation took a partly similar, partly different and even more intense form, with few if any long-term escapes possible, while short-term "solutions" (for example, success in the fur trade) usually *required* brutalizing neighboring native peoples.

As the power loom and spinning jenny made the European cottagers' tools productively useless, so also the gun made the bow and arrow increasingly irrelevant as a means either of defense or of food-procurement (since the commercial hunt thinned out the ranks of the deer to the point where the limited effective range of arrows became increasingly problematic). More than irrelevant, to have only a bow and arrow was increasingly to hold your doom in your own hands and, most likely, to know it, just as the cottage spinners and weavers of early industrial Europe came to realize that no matter how hard and long and cleverly and intensely they worked with their hand tools, driving their families and themselves to ever greater and more painful exertions, they would still starve – starve themselves and watch each other starve.

Two differences between the Indian and the handloom weavers' situation are important to note. Whereas the weavers confronted powerloom mills owned by *others*, in many cases the Indians themselves, in their own communities, quickly came to own the guns that made their bows and arrows an alien presence. And not just their bows and arrows: the gun also made the deer in the forest, and the forest itself, alien.

Moreover, for the European cottage-industry population, as their own tools and productive equipment became increasingly trivialized, increasingly irrelevant to survival, the social relations of kin and community through which people acquired these tools, learned to use them, and organized their work, also became increasingly – if never totally – irrelevant for social survival. For most native groups, in contrast, their social relations to each other became more crucial while the usual material basis for these social relations collapsed.

This is a complex and difficult set of points, but no less significant for being so. Consider first a modern, more simple example: Indian people in the bitterly cold forests of northeastern Canada, who through much of the twentieth century have lived by hunting furs for trade, almost *never* in this period wore fur coats or parkas, but usually the cheapest industrially produced cloth. To hunt beaver as a key component of earning a living is to be in a situation where one could never afford to wear beaver skins. Although it is your intimate knowledge of the forest that is crucial to procuring the pelts, this intimacy substantially serves others' ends. Whatever joys and rewards and social living you get from this intimate connection to the land comes in the midst of, and despite, the use of this intimacy by and for others.

We must extend the illustration further, for much more is at stake. Intimacy with the forest, and the ways of the animals within it, which makes it possible to procure beaver or deer, and which also makes it possible to live through the rigors and difficulties of this kind of work, is ultimately and intensely an intimacy with people and not, to put it bluntly, with trees. I have walked traplines in northern forests with people who sustain themselves by this kind of work; the amount of knowledge it takes to live in such fashion is almost overwhelming. Such knowledge is intensely social, which is to say that it depends crucially on social relations capable not only of conveying but of producing this knowledge – a knowledge that must be continually created, continually developed, continually extended and transformed, owing to the extraordinary variability of the presence of animals on the landscape. Moreover, mistakes in conception or judgment can rapidly bring both substantial suffering and intense need for short- or long-term help. As the fur trade rapidly became increasingly important for access to the basic means of survival, native peoples' intimacy with the forest – and with each other – just as quickly became used to serve the purposes of others. All the social relations through which the necessary pelts were found, caught, cured, transported, and traded became permeated by the influence of alien, usually antagonistic, others. Friendship, kinship, alliances, enmities: all these relationships and more, for native peoples, simultaneously were, and were not, their own.

The point of the illustration of the gun, and the social and productive relations that went with it, making the bow and arrow irrelevant is that the Indian peoples of the colonial period were in a situation where, in order to survive – in order to continually and increasingly produce from a diminishing base the deerskins and wars and slaves and other goods and services for which they were needed, and from which they secured what quickly became the necessities of their survival, particularly guns – they had to continually develop and elaborate and refine their relations to each other: the social relations that created and conveyed the essential knowledge and skills and forms of cooperation. But they had to do this in a context in which the historical roots and material basis for their social relations were continually destroyed, continually undermined, continually trivialized. A bow and a quiver of arrows is not just a set of tools but the product of a history-pregnant set of social relations that convey how to make them and how to use them; relations that contain and reexpress the forms of respect and alliance and involvement with each other that engender, and are engendered by, the forms of cooperation crucial to creating the effectiveness of such limited tools as bows and arrows. Deer run exceedingly fast and seem to have a well-developed sense of self-interest: without specific and fundamental kinds of social relations, a bow and arrow are just two sticks of wood and a piece of string.

What makes a bow and arrow work is cooperation; specifically, the hunters' knowledge of each other and their commitment to coordinated endeavors. To lose the bow and arrow at the point where one *must* procure ever more deer in ever more difficult circumstances threatens to undermine the social relations that make continued survival possible. The enhanced individualism that the greater range of effectiveness of the gun makes possible is not exactly a substitute.

The outcome of this situation was that native societies quickly became exceptionally "fluid" – capable of, and experiencing, extremely rapid and fundamental changes in forms of organization and mobilization. It would be a serious mistake to see this fluidity as simply an adaptation to rapidly changing circumstances, although it was indeed adaptive in some important ways. It was also, at times, extremely destructive – self-destructive.

This destructiveness took many forms: the intensity of factional warfare within colonial Indian societies; the frequent murder of people advocating different modes of adaptation – each mode of adaptation also being an intensely threatening opening to loss – of land, of their limited autonomy – and each mode of adaptation an opening, from within native societies, to a destructive penetration by the colonial powers.

Vengeance for the death of a clan or town member was so frequently mentioned to contemporary Europeans as the purpose of Indian wars and raids upon each other that today's scholars now usually assume that some intrinsic or historically long-standing hunger for retribution was more responsible for native warfare than was maneuvering for position in the fur trade. Both were important, although rather superficial, reasons. The intensity of kin- and village-based vengeance activities and commitments may have been not so much an aboriginal "essence" as an expression of the desperation to find a new basis for unity and co-involvement precisely within the imposed and growing violence of their situation: All this in addition, of course, to the frequent European insistence that native peoples take revenge on one another, usually in response to interference with the Europeans' trade or expansion.

One of the primary entailments of an intensifying commitment to vengeance is an intensified commitment to the unity of the vengeance-seeking or vengeance-victimized group. The social core of the process of organizing around issues of vengeance is expressed in the characteristic assertion of the fundamental unity – in fact, the identity – both among the vengeance-seeking group and among its potential victims. *All* the members of the kin group, clan (or town) of the injured were morally responsible for pursuing vengeance; *any* of the kin, clan (or town) members would be an appropriate target. This double unity that vengeance developed was probably the major counterweight to the increasingly shattering pressures of the European onslaught.

The unity of native peoples in the colonial period is an extremely complex issue, an arena of multiple, intersecting, and diverging developments. The gun, we are suggesting, alienated native people from their own history, their own material culture, and their historically and materially rooted social relations. Even more, it was part of the processes that alienated native peoples from their lands and resources *even while* they still possessed their lands and still had significant resources on their lands. Guns made deer alien, transforming the deer still in the forest from objects of Indian use to objects primarily for European use, and made native peoples major agents of this new use.

"Indians" became intensely and specially responsible for procuring deer both to secure what they themselves needed from Europeans and to serve European needs. The simultaneity of these diverse ends introduced a profound disunity into native societies – a disunity not simply manifest as factional struggles at any one time but also expressed temporally as a profound and fundamental need on the part of native peoples to turn against their own history in order to find what future they could by serving other histories. An example of this process, which continues to the present, will clarify the issue.

During the period of the Vietnam war, when I worked with Indian people in North Carolina, it was an intense heartbreak to talk with young Indian boys, seventeen and eighteen years old, who were planning to enlist in the U.S. Army, often to be scouts. Along with second lieutenants (combat officers who lead assaults and cover retreats), scouts generally have the highest mortality rates in field combat, and in Vietnam in particular they died like flies or survived with their limbs and minds shattered. What these Indian children often said, before they went off to their doom, was a pack of self-assertive, self-destructive, imposed and claimed lies: We Indians have special abilities to move silently through the forest; we Indians have special skills as scouts and as hunters – we Indians will show them. As the long quotation used to open Part IV has shown, this was the European colonists' useful image of the Indian. The native societies upon whom this image was imposed, and whose own prior history was thus increasingly erased, were not at all focused on the forest.

When the Europeans came, Indian people in the southeast were primarily *farmers* who also used deer for meat and for skins. I am not at all sure that it makes sense to say that pre-contact native people *hunted* deer for these purposes, not with any of the meanings "hunting" now has. Since about A.D. 1200 native people in the southeast had been regularly burning the forests in the vicinity of their villages to create browsing-grounds. The deer herd, so managed, became enormous:

Thomas Ashe, in 1682, wrote: "There is such infinite herds that the whole country seems but one continual [Royal] park."

In this context we might better think of native peoples as *collecting* deer, which were, by the contact period, a semidomesticated (controlled, managed) population of animals. It is crucial to realize that native people became forest hunters *not at all* because of any special native abilities to move around the forest, and not even as the most obvious way to enter into what became necessary trade relations with the Europeans. Native peoples taught the Europeans how to grow both corn (maize) and tobacco. Corn was one of the most profitable crops the colonists grew for the domestic market; tobacco was especially profitable for the international market. Did the Indians not produce these crops commercially because they did not know how? Did they not produce these crops commercially because they were not commercially oriented? All such reasons are transparent nonsense, the colonists' self-serving lies that concealed and still conceal the histories that the colonial encounter created; imposed lies for which young Indian boys, and others as well, still pay the price.

It was, to the contrary of such explanations, inconceivable for the Europeans to allow native peoples to produce for these rapidly growing and very profitable markets. Not only would native people have competed with European settlers, but the whole structure of managing the native population depended intensely upon conjoining native people with diminishing resources. Native people could sell deer, or beaver, or themselves as mercenaries, or their land, or each other for slaves – whatever would, from the moment it became a commodity for trade, begin to completely and totally decline. The deer and beaver trades, the mercenary wars, the slave trade – all of these may have been, for substantial periods of time, generally expanding sectors of the economy, but in any one place the resources declined drastically and the center of procurement shifted westward from the very moment the trade began: precisely what was supposed to happen to the native people themselves. In a controlled and managed fashion, neither too quickly nor too slowly, native people were supposed to decline and die out, and the center of native population to shift westward.

This was not just their imposed fate but also, as we shall later see, their use: the frontier expanded westward in a way that maintained the inequalities between different classes of Whites, and between Whites and African-Americans, precisely because of the way Indian societies, on the moving edge of the frontier, were used. There were times when Indian resources gave out on the far edge of the frontier, or the native people in these places died out, from one epidemic or another, and the colonists would lure, or force, groups of more western Indians to relocate *eastward*:

> *The Yamasees, who had once lived near the Spanish mission in Guale [now coastal Georgia], had been induced by the Spanish to move to St. Augustine. There they had become embroiled with the local Timucas and had between 1680 and 1685 marched off to the Creek country [Georgia and Alabama]. Lord Cardross, leader of the Scottish settlers at Port Royal, lured the Yamasees to settle between Port Royal and the Savannah River where they could be supplied [with guns] by the English while they warred on the Timucas and held the Spanish allied Indians at bay. Cardross was suspected of having made this move in order to use the Yamasee as slave hunters in Florida.*

Native peoples, in sum, became commercial deer-hunting Indians, rather than commercial tobacco or corn farmers, *more because of the logic of European domination than for any reasons whatsoever within native social systems*, other than their ability to organize themselves to do this kind of work. It was not only the specific structure of political-economic domination, just outlined, that made native peoples into what the Europeans called "forest rovers," but also both colonial military tactics that emphasized crop destruction and the colonists' seizing or purchasing "Indian old fields" – cleared agricultural land. Added to these pressures were the inducements of preferential markets for native forest products, mercenary soldiers, and slaves. In addition, the English used an ideological rationale for their seizure of native land that created the reality it invoked: that *they*, the Europeans, were farmers who followed the Biblical injunction to subdue the land and make it multiply, whereas Indians were merely creatures of the forest who used the land but had no divinely sanctioned claim to it. All of this was capped by a European need for *savages* to their west, partly to keep the White indentured servants and the Black slaves from fleeing westward.

So for an Indian youth in the twentieth century to find his dignity and his life – and simultaneously lose both – in a claim to a noble and skillful forest past, is not only to participate in creating an appallingly destructive misunderstanding about history, it is also to be an Indian by participating in what was and is a Euro-American fantasy about an Indian past and an Indian "essence." Thus fundamental resistance to destructive domination through the self-assertion of a proud past becomes fused with collusion with this same domination.

The fantasy history of Indians as people of the forest was not, perhaps, entirely imposed. Were that the case, I doubt that it would be so widely accepted. There were also, I suggest, important countercurrents.

210

One such countercurrent emerges from the well-springs of alienation and its whirlpools of vulnerability: Indian peoples were alienated from their direct access to the *products* of their fields and forests, and had this access, and the social relations that made access effective, increasingly mediated by the increasingly dominant Euro-American society. And they then quickly and nearly totally lost their fields and forests. To reconstitute some access to what they once had within the domain of culture – from specific acts such as unifying their connections to one another for purposes of "vengeance" to more general and diffuse claims to special knowledge of the forest – can thus be seen as also a claim to continue their own history on their own terms.

I suspect, moreover (although the evidence is exceedingly scant) that this same process of resistance and collusion, rooted within a created historical vision, became – necessarily – an aspect of Indian culture in the colonial period itself. It is haunting how the Cherokee, for instance, could shift so quickly in the early 1690s from being the victims of coastal and piedmont Indian slave raids to procuring slaves from the same region. One might call this revenge; one might also call it a denial or transformation of their past. The point here, however, is not at all to criticize native peoples – that is neither my purpose nor my place – but to show that a significant part of the structure of domination over native peoples in the colonial period was rooted in their imposed alienation from their environment, from their social relations to one another, and from their own history. The social relations, environmental connectedness, and historical visions that native peoples then themselves developed were all built within, *and also simultaneously in opposition to,* this general situation – this vulnerability, this radical rupture between past and present.

211

11

Distinguishing the headmen: Colonial political-cultural formations, part two
The history of local histories

As I know you Abraham to be a good friend and the Young Twin and the Young Lieutenant's Brother are come down to see me I shall distinguish you three with presents accordingly, and I will distinguish the other Headmen your followers also, although many of them come only to see this great Town and the great ships, yet as you tell me they bring English hearts with them they shall receive some tokens of English kindness. Even those who are not here are sensible and will feel the advantage of enjoying a friendship with us, as thereby they will have a full and plentiful supply of goods carried up in their Nation to exchange for their skins, which their industry in hunting procures to supply their wants of cloathing and ammunition, which wants alone as you know, do now greatly distress the Cherokees, even if we had not such an army among them which can hinder their planting; and let the known distress of the Cherokees show to your young men the folly and vanity of such boasts as are made by a naked starving Cherokee, who is naked and starving because at war with the English.

The South Carolina Lieut. Governor's talk
to the Creek Indians, 1761

King Blount Chief man of the Tuscaroroes representing to this Board that some of his people are disorderly and are throwing off their Obedience to him as their Ruler and praying the Protection of this Governm't and this Board being fully Satisfyed of the faithfulness and Fidelity of the said Blount desired . . . the Governor to grant a new Commission to the said Blount and to Issue a proclamation Commanding all the Tuscaroras to render the said Blount Obedience otherwise they will be looked upon as Enemies to the Government.

North Carolina Council, October 1725

Gentlemen,
We lately received the agreable news that the King and great men of the Cherrikee Indians had been amongst you and were very willing and ready to Imbrace such offers of peace as were made to them . . . by the friendly assistance of those powerful Nations an end may be put to . . . the Yammasee Indians . . . [they] may be dispersed and entirely driven from their Towns and Settlements . . . the intention of our Board here [in England] is that Tract of

212

Land commonly known by the name of the Yammasee Settlement be parcelled out.

Carteret, P., M. Ashley . . . March 3, 1716

To distinguish the headmen was simultaneously to bestow honors upon them, in ways that bound them to Europeans' intentions while making them victims of these intents; to separate the headmen, antagonistically, from their followers – distinguishing them from their followers – while binding their followers to them; and to separate and distinguish headmen from one another, antagonistically, while enmeshing them in each other's struggles against the Europeans. These three interwoven processes, which together fragmented and localized native peoples' history, began in the early post-contact transformations of native societies.

I

Francis Jennings has produced a mind-shaking reassessment of the European conquest of North America. However controversial and subject to revision his interpretations may be, he has changed completely the framework for understanding both conquest and the transformation of native societies in the context of conquest.

Jennings starts by leading us through what he calls "the gate of numbers": an analysis of the native peoples' situation which begins through an understanding, and a rough approximation, of the *size* of the aboriginal population at the point of contact. Quoting Henry Dobyns that "the idea that social scientists hold of the size of the aboriginal population of the Americas directly affects their interpretation of New World civilizations and cultures," Jennings proceeds to reveal the existing demographic estimates of the native North American population as so appallingly low as to preclude a realistic understanding of native social organization. His study is widely available and thus the main points may be briefly summarized.

Jennings starts with the history of the demographic interpretation of native North America – not the history of population size, but the history of the population estimate. Two points emerge: (1) without any basis for such revisions, the estimates of the size of the native population at contact keep being reduced; (2) the original estimates of the post-contact population – the hunches and estimates and counts by early European travelers and colonists – were almost always made after a century or more of contact, of epidemic diseases and other disruptions that ravaged native peoples, and are thus far from being evidence of

213

the size of the pre-contact population. Indeed, estimates by archaeologists suggest a very much larger population.

In North America almost no data for contact-point population estimates are available. For the Valley of Mexico, primarily the Aztec domain, where the Catholic church made and kept much more substantial if far from good records, the studies of Borah and Cook have shown a probable 95 percent decline in the native population in the first one hundred years. The pressures on native people were radically different in the valley of Mexico from those along the Atlantic coast of North America, but resistance to European-induced epidemics, the major killer of native people at this time, was not likely to have been substantially different.

The lowest population estimate for the southeastern native populations is by A. L. Kroeber: 150,000. By modern standards of interpretation it is simply ridiculous. The most conservative of the useful reinterpretations of the data suggests a population three times this figure; but evidence has also been interpreted to suggest that it may have been at least ten times Kroeber's estimate – 1.5 million. At stake is not only the issue of aboriginal social organization but the magnitude of the European-precipitated genocide: the issue is very controversial. My own understanding of the date leads me to think that after all the protests and objections to Jennings are worked through, and on the basis of increasingly more sophisticated archaeology, along with a better grasp of the productivity of so-called simpler societies and a more developed view of the magnitude of the European onslaught, here and elsewhere, the population estimates will come to center on a figure substantially larger than the largest of present estimates, that is, more than two million native people in the southeast alone. Even this figure may turn out to be embarrassingly low.

There is no need here to call for unnecessary controversy. For the argument to be made it will suffice to accept a figure halfway, or a bit more, between the lowest and the highest of the current estimates: a population six to seven times Kroeber's figure, or about one million people.

The basic point is that with such a figure the whole notion of clearly demarcated and separated "tribes" at the point of contact, with substantial empty space between them, collapses. In its place, we can come to see a social landscape in the pre-contact southeast that was constituted by networks of native villages and towns with multiple and diverse kinds of connections between them.

Understanding native social organization at contact is intertwined not only with issues of scale but also with conceptualizing an aboriginal social dynamic. Particularly when we are seeking to understand the

214

social system and social integration of a region, it is crucial to see process simultaneously with mass.

The starting point for understanding southeastern aboriginal historical processes is the fact that in the immediate pre-contact period there were two basic types of native social organization (although of course a broader range existed): small, relatively egalitarian social groups that archaeologists have labeled "hill tribes," although they extended far beyond the piedmont and were not necessarily "tribes," and larger, more powerful and more internally stratified groups that have been labeled "southern chiefdoms." After the European onslaught, in the early colonial period, there were also two basic kinds of native social organization: small, relatively egalitarian hamlets and settlements, and the large, powerful, militarized confederacies, increasingly unequal in their internal organization. Moreover, the major post-contact confederacies were in the same general region as were the pre-contact southern chiefdoms; the post-contact small Indian settlements were in the same general region as were the pre-contact hill tribes. Not only was there *no* connection between the two superficially similar forms of diversity, pre- and post-contact, but the lack of connection is the starting point for delineating both pre- and post-contact native historical processes.

II

Along the Gulf Coast west from northern Florida, northward up the Mississippi River to the Ohio River, northeastward up the Ohio and then eastward along its tributaries into the southern Appalachian mountains, there was an immense arc of easily tilled river-bottom lands, with travel along the waterways facilitating trade. Cultivation came to this region between 1,000 and 500 B.C.: first gourds, then squash, and then by about 300 B.C. maize. After these plants were established – and they were most likely imports from Central America – native cultigens came, or came back, into prominence: sunflower, pigweed, goosefoot, marsh elder, and perhaps others.

Several locales in this region, shifting from place to place over time, practiced comparatively intense forms of cultivation and were also the centers of a far-flung trade: copper coming southeastward from west of the Great Lakes; marine shells from the Gulf Coast moving north and west; flint, obsidian, and pipestone circulating from the Atlantic and the Great Lakes to the Rockies, and more perishable goods probably being traded as well. Raw materials, semifinished, and finished utilitarian objects and elaborate works of art were traded in substantial quantities. Agriculture and trade together provided the basis for the

215

more stratified and densely settled societies that flourished – each only briefly – in this region.

Starting about 1000 B.C., along with agriculture, differential burial practices for people of the same town begin to be distinguishable. Some of the inhabitants were buried in earthen mound tombs, increasingly provided with elaborate grave goods, eventually including sacrificed people; others were given much less special and "costly" treatment. Over the next thousand years burial mounds became larger and more elaborate, massive earthen temple-plaza mounds began being assembled, and peoples of the region started building geometrically patterned earth-works, outlining a variety of figure-shapes across or enclosing tens to hundreds of acres. Some of the stratified, ceremonially expressive trading towns were fortified with wooden palisades, and some had a substantial raised central plaza, with temples and "meeting halls" surrounding the plaza. In the vicinity of some of these towns, smaller and much less elaborate contemporaneous hamlets have been found, evidence for social stratification not only within but also between settlements.

When cultivation became widespread – indeed, nearly universal – in the southeast, about A.D. 1200, it only rarely developed into a major agricultural dependence. When it did, it was usually associated with the major towns. More commonly, plant cultivation was integrated into the continuing pursuit of "wild," or more specifically, semidomesticated, foods (for example, deer, pigweed, sunflower). Among these groups that did not intensify plant cultivation the social unit remained – or became again – the small, relatively egalitarian village.

These villages are difficult to label categorically. I would call them farming and collecting villages, but they were not completely agricultural. They farmed their fields, and to the extent that they managed the surrounding forests to enable themselves to maintain their settled life, they "farmed" the woods as well. The stratified towns were agriculturally based; here *agriculture* refers not just to planting and tending crops, but also to the organization of agrarian production, including the regularized extraction of a substantial "surplus" from this production, to generate and reproduce fundamental social inequalities. Farming villages, such as those among the Cherokee in the early colonial period, had political and religious leaders who lived in the same kinds of houses, wore the same kinds of clothes, and themselves did the same kinds of productive work as all the other people in the community of the same age and gender. By the time the Cherokee were removed in the 1830s, agriculture, while far from universal, had been well established: some Cherokee went west with their substantial holdings of African-American slaves, their wagons and farm implements, and in one case, on their own steamboat; others were forced by the United States to trudge west through the winter half naked and starving, dying as they went. Agricultural villages, far more so than farming and collecting villages, materialize inequalities in rather brutal ways.

North American archaeology has shown a pervasive ideological preference for the more complex and socially stratified pre-contact agriculturally based locales. This preference has fueled and funded a substantial amount of research on these sites but simultaneously constitutes a serious obstacle to understanding such places and the historical dynamics of the regionally based social systems in which they were embedded.

Many studies of the pre-contact southeast take an almost apologetic stance when dealing with the fact that "our" Indians did not form into great states or empires as did the Inca, Maya, or Aztec. They point with some pride to the enormous earthwork mounds of the Mississippi Valley, and talk of simple village sites as "dull." S. Winckler, to take only a recent example, an author of one of the *Smithsonian Guides to Historic America*, wrote in the *New York Times* about the Native American city called Cahokia, which had a population of about 30,000 and a temple mound (named Monks Mound) one hundred feet high, built near the meeting point of the Missouri, Mississippi, and Illinois rivers between A.D. 900 and 1200:

> *Despite its history, Monks Mound might disappoint an eager pilgrim on a first visit. The heap of earth lacks the obvious elegance and craftsmanship of works engendered by the Mayas, Aztecs and Incas. It is grown over with unkempt grass and weeds. It looks not exotic, but of this world, like tailing from a surface mine or the misbegotten foundation of an unfinished overpass.*

Such comments comparing Native North Americans to the by-products of our "progress" are particularly revealing in the unstated context that Aztec and to a lesser extent, Maya ruins were reconstructed from rubble not just as tourist attractions but as illustrations of particular, then-current visions of history. Their "reconstruction" did not always or only follow from what could be seen of their original design but was also organized to present a mid-twentieth-century Mexican vision of an Indian past. Cahokia mound, as it presently exists for display, is another kind of presentation of a past, perhaps deliberately left in a crumbling, semi-wild state as befits what we want to define as *the bypassed*, the by-products of our "development."

To continue the quoted presentation of Cahokia-Monks Mound:

> *Monks Mound is, however, an eminence, a hulking reminder that the human race so loves prospects that where none avails itself it creates*

> *one. The beauty of the place lies on the summit. Here a person can feel the millennial tingle in the rib cage that accompanies a broad view from a high place. In its prime Monks Mound was reserved for the elite. It kept them on a higher rung, at a healthy remove from the masses.*

It is a serious mistake to assume, as does our pervasive conceptual propaganda for "civilization," that the people who lived at that time actually preferred hauling millions of baskets of earth to build a massive temple mound or someone else's tomb, or having their sisters and daughters stuffed into the sides of burial mounds to commemorate the death of some elevated ruler, or hoeing the quantities of corn needed to feed the mound-builders, to living their own village life. Such might have been the case, but we must look at events at least with the opposite possibility in mind.

The pre-contact stratified social systems in the southeast were, in any one place, relatively short-lived. There were substantial periods of time – the longest being from A.D. 300 to 700 – when few if any significantly stratified native societies occupied the region. When the stratified societies disappear, so usually does the archaeological evidence for maize cultivation, indicating a correlation between intensified agriculture and intensified inequality. This association between intensification of agriculture and of inequality is widely found in the development of archaic states. The southeastern region of North America is, however, unusual in *not* having two other characteristic features of early states: an increasingly well-developed centralized storage of foodstuffs, and geographic or socially constructed boundaries that "contain" a population within the state-building area.

Among the most important components in the emergence of stratified societies are boundary-enhancing and boundary-maintaining processes that contain, centralize, and aid in organizing a population sufficient for such activities as war, extensive trade, monumental building projects, and elite-appropriated craft production. All this ordinarily rests on the backs of an agrarian-production populace, harnessed to an increasingly intensified, increasingly specialized agriculture, from whom surplus foods are extracted.

Centralized storage of this extracted "surplus" is perhaps often substantially rooted in the irregularity of agrarian output in archaic states and "protostates" (using protostate as a label, without implying a necessary developmental sequence). The Biblical story, in Genesis, of Pharaoh's dream of seven fat cows, and seven fat ears of grain, followed by seven lean and paltry ones, and Joseph's advice – build granaries, famine is coming – is only the most widely known case study, as it were, of a recurrent phenomenon in state formation: the increasingly intense need, as agriculture is intensified, for centralized management of storage and distribution to cope with increasingly serious variations in output. Much less widely remembered from this story of Joseph in Egypt, but of substantial significance for illustration here, is that the story of building and stocking the granaries, and the use of the granaries in the ensuing famine, is a story of the elaboration and consolidation of pharaonic domination over the Egyptian countryside. Centralized storage and powerful elites are logically connected processual developments in early agrarian states. The comparative absence of centralized storage in precontact native North America must have substantially constrained elite power, shifting it from the systemic regularities of agrarian surplus extraction to the more fluid grounds of trade and war.

State-formative processes are, further, ordinarily associated with social or physical barriers to an outward flow of people – people moving away from the grasp of emergent state power, from the extraction of surplus, from the militaristic demands, from the labor-service impositions. Often there are physical boundaries to dispersal, such as the deserts on either side of the Nile valley, or beyond the Tigris and Euphrates river basin. Sometimes the barriers to moving away are social – for example, the ferocity and regularity of Aztec military assaults on neighboring peoples. One of the most extreme and thus most revealing cases is the Great Wall of China, laced together and raised from prior smaller walls in the period 400–200 B.C. Owen Lattimore has suggested that the wall was built more, at first, to keep people who were becoming peasants *in* rather than the "barbarians" *out*. Only when an agrarian population could be effectively contained and reshaped into a rent-paying peasantry with a substantial surplus being extracted from them, did the peoples outside the wall – who, as Lattimore shows, in many ways only became "barbarians" with the construction of the wall – have reasons to want to climb over it to get their hands on what was inside.

Not being able to constrain or contain a population for the substantial development of classes, and not having the resources of major food storage to secure elite domination within the realm of the material necessities of ordinary daily life, the rituals and panoplies of power and the substantial inequalities of these pre-contact stratified societies had but a slender material basis. Native American stratified towns were capable of growing in ways that intensely elaborated internal inequalities: one-fifth of all the pre-contact copper found in the state of Ohio has been found in one grave. These stratified towns have proved, however, to be durationally fragile, constantly disappearing, constantly emerging anew. I suspect that a more developed archaeology will show that people simply moved away, moved out of the reach of these places – a population flow from protostate to settlement – and the declining towns deintensified agricultural production.

The rapidity of their emergence and their durational fragility indicates that such centers were more nodal points in trade networks than production point for this trade. Production of many trade items, indeed, seemed to stay in the hands of relatively egalitarian villages, generating flint, seashells, copper, and so on, which meant that despite the extensive trade it was primarily a production of use-values rather than commodities, *for it is domination at or over the point of production, not trade, that makes commodities.* ("Commodities" here is used in the most general sense of the term – goods produced for exchange and for the material rewards exchange brings, without necessarily entailing a monetized exchange.)

The fragility of each of the stratified towns in this trade network, and the special elasticity of the regional social system as a whole, was substantially rooted in just this noncommodification of trade items. If domination was absent at or over the point of production, then while the transfer-nodes in the networks of exchange might have been able to momentarily skim off a surprisingly large amount of goods, they ultimately had no enduring basis, no materially rooted set of regional social relations, for reproducing their position.

This fragility in the social position of the large stratified towns and of the elite within these towns was thus derived from three main factors:

1. The low level of development of centralized food storage, which kept the subordinate population from being dependent on the elite at the material core of daily life and, by extension, in the work process to produce this material core. Centralized storage *always* comes with elite domination over either some aspects or some moments of the work process to produce what is stored.

2. The relative autonomy of communities that produced most of the goods for the long-distance trade. Although some of the items in this trade were craft goods generated within the large, stratified towns, more seem to have been the products of village producers.

3. The lack of significant physical or social barriers to moving away, particularly for the subordinate population – the people who might otherwise end their lives stuffed in graves on the sides of the elite burial-mound tombs. This mobility seems to have been rooted in a structural "openness" to substantial population flow, which was part of the basic social organization of the matrix of more egalitarian societies

surrounding the stratified towns. This openness, still to be found in the post-contact period, had several social-organizational bases, including a flow of people between towns and hamlets due to changing postmarital residence; the continual emergence of small satellite hamlets connected to more densely settled towns, but at some distance from them; towns splitting and recombining; and far-reaching lines of common clan membership and trade relations, along which lines people could be residentially mobile.

One of the major, if unintended, impacts of the European invasion was a profound alteration of the flow of people across the social land-scape. While in pre-contact aboriginal societies the flow of population was probably away from the major centers of power and domination, in the post-contact period a very substantial part – perhaps the great majority – of the migrations of native people were *toward* and into the newly emerging centers of native power, trade, and militarism: the confederacies that formed in the colonial period and offered what little hope of survival or "success" that could be had.

Native people in the colonial period flowed into the emerging con-federacies in very substantial numbers; without this influx the major confederacies would likely have collapsed from the ravages of war and disease long before the colonial period ended. Seen from the perspec-tive of the people who were moving into the emerging confederacies, rather than from that of the confederacies seeking to survive: when people run toward power, rather than away from it, their world has, indeed, been turned upside-down.

III

The post-contact southeastern natives' migrations reveal – in their scope, in the different forms the migrations took, and in the changing points of origin, routes, and terminal locales – the magnitude of the assault on native peoples and the emergent forms of response to this assault. To conceptualize these migration patterns we must first sketch a social geography of the southeast, from the Appalachian Mountains to the coast: the basic land forms and how Europeans and native peoples situated themselves upon, and used, diverse kinds of lands.

Along the region bounded by the Savannah River in what is now Georgia to the James River in southern Virginia, the coastal plain is exceedingly flat, primarily sand or clay soils, and about 70 to 80 miles wide. West of the coastal plain, stretching inland a further 100–150 miles, lies the piedmont – low, rolling, sometimes rocky hills and uplands.

At its western edge the piedmont rises increasingly sharply into the Appalachians.

The "fall line," where the piedmont rivers drop off the hard-rock interior onto the coastal plain, although not a dramatic feature of the physical landscape, was nonetheless a crucial zone for the organization of Indian–White relations.

In some areas the fall line is a specific break in the landscape, marked by waterfalls and sharp changes in the local ecology. The Great Falls of the Potomac River, just above Washington, D.C., is probably the best-known of such points. In other areas, including Robeson County, the fall line is more of a transitional zone, 10 to 20 miles wide, and between the piedmont and the coastal plain there is a belt of sand hills and pine forests.

The fall line is also marked by regions of extensive swamps. On summer afternoons the offshore winds pile clouds against the piedmont updrafts, and for a few hours almost every day the rain pours down, flooding fields and swamps alike. Even in the relatively drier winters the rivers, flowing rapidly down through the piedmont and the sand hills onto the flat coastal plain, slow abruptly and spread out into huge sheets of water, depositing their silt and moving slowly through innumerable channels, marshes, pocosins, bays – and now drainage ditches. As the rivers wander down toward the coast they are often bordered by extensive riverine swamps. Just where the land meets the sea it often rises slightly, creating a series of substantial coastal swamps. These different kinds of swamps, all far more extensive in the seventeenth and eighteenth centuries than they are now, shaped the patterns of early European settlement and trade, and for a time provided areas of shelter and relative safety for the coastal native peoples.

The area that is now Robeson County lies on the inland edge of the coastal plain, abutting the fall line and edging the boundary with South Carolina. South of Robeson County the coastal plain swamps are mostly riverine, winding from the fall line to the sea; north of Robeson County the rivers are clearer and the swamps are primarily coastal. Robeson County not only has extensive fall line swamps, but the rivers flowing through it southeastward through South Carolina are swampy for long stretches toward the sea. Traveling directly westward from the sea toward Robeson County one would encounter large coastal swamps: in the colonial period this was probably the area most sheltered from European settlement and the European onslaught.

European settlement in the area of Robeson County indeed occurred later than in any other coastal or eastern piedmont area between Charles Town, South Carolina, and Jamestown, Virginia. This subregion was, until the late 1700s, the main "blank spot" on the English manuscript maps: there is nothing comparable east of the Appalachians. European colonists for long had much less use for this area than did the native peoples, who settled it long before the Europeans arrived and who continued to migrate to it throughout the eighteenth and early nineteenth centuries.

For the colonists, the fall line between plain and piedmont came to mark a break between two different kinds of social and economic organization that emerged in the eighteenth century. The "low country," as they called regions in the coastal plain, came to be an area of relatively intense export agriculture, relatively densely settled, and increasingly organized into plantations. The "back country," as the piedmont was called, was settled as an area of small farms, with a less commercialized and more various agriculture, and increasingly with small-scale manufacturing. The fall line itself – a point at which the rivers often become unnavigable to even rather small freight-carrying boats – was generally not a zone of settlement for the colonial Europeans until much later, when towns and cities grew up on the river falls to take advantage of water power and the trade between the interior and the coast.

For native peoples, to the contrary, as Charles Hudson points out:

> The territory lying immediately to either side of the fall line was an important region in itself. Some of the most populous societies in the southeast lay alongside this line, the reason being that from this vantage point the Indians could exploit the natural resources of the coastal plain, the piedmont, and the fall line itself. The best freshwater fishing in the southeast was at the fall line, where in certain seasons fish could be taken in vast numbers.

The kinds of native societies that developed along the fall line in the contact and colonial periods took a substantially different form from the kinds developing on the coastal plain, the piedmont, and in the mountains, although in the pre-contact period the geographically based regional differences in social organization were apparently not as sharp. The post-contact emergent differentiation had three main sources: differential patterns of incorporation into the expanding colonial frontier, changing patterns of migration, and, under these pressures, the way aboriginal social-organizational forms were shattered and rebuilt.

To conceptualize the subregion that is now the North Carolina piedmont – from north-central South Carolina to southern Virginia, actually – we must see, in our mind's eye, a gradually closing pincers, increasingly squeezing the native peoples over a period that lasted from the 1620s to the 1780s. The main components of this squeeze were the spread of European settlement, the patterns of trade, and the forms of incorporation of native societies. What follows is far from a history of this increasing squeeze and the transformations it brought; rather, some of the main elements are outlined in order to depict the processes that engendered both different kinds of native societies and enduring contradictions within these societies.

The two anchors of early European settlement in this region were the Jamestown colony, founded in 1607 and spreading down to the Albermarle Sound region of northern North Carolina over the next fifty years, and the Charles Town colony, founded in 1670. Each quickly came to make different kinds of demands on native peoples, and a major part of the trap that closed on the piedmont Indians came from the differences in these demands.

The productive core of the early Virginia colony was tobacco, and the dynamic of the colony quickly became the process of growing ever-increasing quantities of the "sot weed." In 1612 John Rolf began to develop a more palatable and productive Virginia tobacco, capable of competing with the West Indian product. The market for this crop rose rapidly and the prices were high enough to make the settlers reluctant to waste their cleared land or their energy growing food. In 1616 Governor Thomas Dale imposed a regulation controlling the amount of each settler's land that had to be used for food crops rather than tobacco, in an attempt to lessen the dependence of the settlers on native supplies. In 1618 the colony shipped about 20,000 pounds of tobacco; the following year a better cure was developed, by an African slave, which made the weed less sickening to use; by 1622 exports had risen to 60,000 pounds and would increase eightfold in the next five years.

The Virginia colonists, who began their historical career wanting and depending on native peoples for a supply of foodstuffs, shifted quickly and decisively to wanting land, particularly cleared land. And the light, sandy soils preferred for tobacco cultivation were precisely the same kind of land that native peoples themselves used to grow food crops. The colonists' hunger for land, and their continuing demands for food and other supplies led to their rapid geographic expansion and their relentless pressure on the surrounding peoples.

The Powhatan Confederacy, as the native peoples around the Jamestown colony were called, rose in rebellion twice: in 1622 and in 1644. Although the 1644 rising was quickly broken, native people were pursued, hunted, and butchered for two further years. The peace that was granted in 1646 had two significant long-term effects: it established the status of "tributary Indians," and it imposed on them a new kind of internal unity that enhanced their usefulness to the colonists. It also enabled colonists, with coastal Indians either in support or as bystanders, to turn against some of their former Indian allies on the piedmont. Then, having subdued their native neighbors, the colonists could either ignore or use them to reorganize the piedmont. As Wesley Craven explained it:

> *The distinguishing feature of the peace of 1646 . . . was a provision making the defeated Indians tributary to the government of the Colony. It was not a new idea. Such a proposal had been made as early as 1609, but with a significant difference. The thought then had been to destroy Powhatten's authority by making the tribes* [of his "confederacy"] *individually dependent upon the English, who would rely for discipline of the tributary Indians on an alliance with their enemies* [the native peoples of the piedmont]. *Now* [in 1646] *the decision was made to preserve at least some semblance of the old union as a device for giving effect to the new tributary status and to an alliance with the tributary Indians against their foes* [on the piedmont]. *Hence the distinction between "neighboring" or "friendly" Indians and "foreign" Indians that runs through virtually all discussion of the Indian problem for the remainder of the century.*

Although the colonists may have initially intended to "preserve some semblance" of older forms of political organization among their tributary Indians, they quickly sought to introduce new forms of control over, and within, these societies. This process was part of a further crucial outcome of the peace of 1646: establishing a boundary line between areas of European and Indian settlement.

Before the 1644 uprising settlers lived interspersed with native groups. The peace of 1646 established the first boundary line between settlers and Indians. Settlers had exclusive possession of the land on one side, Indians – supposedly – of the other. Forts were built to secure the line, and the Indian trade legislatively reorganized to run through, and so to finance, these forts.

But as this "local" trade rapidly shifted away from world-market commodities (pelts and slaves) to local-market goods and services, the trade increasingly devolved to individual natives who came within the English line of settlement to barter and to sell. This was soon regulated by colonial statutes that also invested local native leaders with new sorts of authority. For example, in 1661, in the Virginia colony:

> *An Act to Regulate the Entrance of Indians into the Settlements*
> . . . *Be it therefore enacted for the prevention thereof and to the end*

> that the Nations may be distinguished and soe if they are taken in the
> manner of doing injuries, the sufferers know to what King to address
> themselves for remedy, that badges, silver plates, and copper plates with
> the name of the town graved upon them, be given to all the adjacent
> Kings within our protection. And that all the said Kings give it in
> charge to their people that none of them presume upon what occasion
> soever to come within the English bounds without those badges or one
> with a badge in their midst.

Such regulations not only strengthened the position of "kings" by enhancing their control over trade and traders, they probably also worked to give these kings more clearly bounded groups to rule. The colonists kept trying to enhance their control over these rulers and their groups: a statute of 1665 authorized the colonial governor to select, rather than simply confirm, local native leaders, and also gave him the authority to punish native "disobedience" by native leaders.

But the tributary Indians did not remain significant to the Virginia colonists for very long. By 1670 Virginia traders began regularly bypassing local Indian groups to trade for fur, deerskin, and slaves with the more distant Tuscarora and on down south along and across the fall line to the Catawba. In 1677 Jamestown signed a treaty with the bypassed Nottoway in which the Nottoway were given protection from enslavement and, no longer threatening, were allowed to come into the English settlements to sell food, craft items, and by 1700, hogs and peaches that they raised for sale to the settlers. They, and others increasingly like them, also sold a variety of petty services: hunting game, carrying messages, guiding traders and travelers, and working as porters in the deerskin trade.

In 1705 the Virginia House of Burgesses opened the land south of the Blackwater River for colonial settlement. The Nottoway, who had been shunted about for more than thirty years, stayed put. In lieu of a boundary between Indians and Euro-Americans, the House of Burgesses defined blocks of land for Indian use. The Nottoway were now living within the English line of settlement: this, plus perhaps the fact that they were "settled" as a group, made them what was then called "settlement" Indians.

"Tributary" and "settlement" Indians were, in the terms of the Virginia legislature, two distinct categories of native peoples. Elsewhere in the southeast (for example, in South Carolina), these might not have been legislatively delineated, separate categories, but there was much the same social reality, if under different local names: tributary Indians were resident outside the line and paid tribute in admission of fealty; settlement Indians lived within the line. Tributary Indians tended to be used as mercenaries and as a shield against the increasingly militarized inland confederacies somewhat more than were settlement Indians. As both the line of settlement and the native peoples frequently moved, any particular native group could, as long as it survived, shift back and forth from one category to another. But both were decimated at a staggering rate – by disease, by war, by alcoholism, and in a variety of other ways.

The death rate among such peoples may or may not have been higher than among the native confederacies, but the confederacies were replenishing their numbers by the constant and substantial addition of native people – as individuals or as whole groups fleeing for sanctuary, by war captives, by runaway slaves and by intermarriage with frontier Whites and Blacks. Settlement and tributary Indians did not attract in-migrants of any kind in any numbers, and the colonial records are replete with instances of such groups fragmenting, moving off in different directions.

By 1700 the Indian trade had moved quickly and decisively inland, largely bypassing the piedmont, and was centered in and near the southern Appalachians. There were several reasons for this, but primarily it was the desire of the colonists not to strengthen nearby Indians, either by trading with them directly or by using them as middlemen, for their strength might be dangerous to the settlers. Moreover, the English colonial policy makers were increasingly interested in using their Indian trade to gain allies in strategically crucial frontier positions between themselves and the Spanish in Florida and the French on the Mississippi (and the Great Lakes). As William Willis summed up the situation:

> The colonial South was an arena for an unremitting struggle for empire and trade among the White colonies, and the Indian tribes were caught in the middle of the struggle. Whites competed for their allegiance, for their trade, and for their warriors. Success in the empire struggle depended upon success in the Indian country.

Further, as the eighteenth century naturalist William Bartram noted, "a buckskin of the Cherokee will weigh twice as much as one bred in the low, flat country of Carolina," and the larger skins were much more desirable. As the centers of trade came to skip across the piedmont to the mountains, a space was left between the settlers, still fairly close to the coast in the early 1700s, and the confederacies that were consolidating their positions in and near the mountains. It was a dangerous space, but a space nonetheless.

To understand what happened to native peoples in this space we must first briefly look at the confederacies. During the colonial period

227

the confederacies on the one side, and the English on the other, shaped the kinds of native groups that formed and survived on the piedmont. Even after Indian removal, in the 1830s, what happened within the large and powerful native confederacies left long-lasting cultural traces across the piedmont, markedly influencing historical developments among piedmont Indians throughout the nineteenth century and on into the present.

IV

Shifting the main centers of Indian trade and the main Indian–colonial alliances westward beyond the piedmont was a crucial factor in creating the dominant Indian confederacies. This shift was, simultaneously, the doom of the piedmont native peoples, particularly as "Indians," and the matrix in which new kinds of native groups, not as clearly socially recognized as Indians, emerged on the piedmont and along the fall line.

The shared framework of native social life on the coastal plain and the piedmont, and in and beyond the mountains as well, on which all these diverging developments were based, was the native *town*. Throughout the entire southeast, through and beyond the end of the contact period, the town and the clan were the basic units of native social life, and the emergence of Indian confederacies – which from the native perspective were confederacies of towns, not "tribes" – took place through an imposed and increasingly necessary transformation of the relations between native towns.

In the pre-contact period we have distinguished two kinds of towns amidst a broad array of social forms. One, associated with the southern chiefdoms, was based on agriculture and trade and often, from evidence of enclosing palisades, on war as well. Characteristically, such towns had substantial internal status and class differentiation and an array of physically massive cultural embellishments, including temple mounds and elaborate tombs. The other form of town, characteristic of the more egalitarian mixed farming and collecting groups, was a politically, religiously, and residentially organized clustering of people. Materially, these towns also expressed their social life in a variety of public buildings and ceremonial ball courts, as well as dwellings, but were far more egalitarian in their physical design.

Owing primarily to the ravages of disease, compounded by the far-reaching disruptions of war and enslavement upon a relatively fragile social form, most of the highly stratified towns were gone by the early contact period, leaving a variety of the more egalitarian form as the most widespread and characteristic feature of native social organization. Interwoven networks of such egalitarian towns were the social basis for the whole range of subsequent transformative developments.

In 1711, on the eve of the Tuscarora War, Catechna – a Tuscarora town – captured two European explorers: John Lawson and Christoph von Graffenreid, and two African-American slaves traveling with them. The slaves were freed; Graffenreid, who survived, closely witnessed and described how his and Lawson's fates were decided. Two councils were called. The first convened in Catechna town and was attended by its householders. The second council was broader, for it brought in the headmen of the nearby Indian villages, both Tuscarora and non-Tuscarora (by the Europeans' categories), including Shakori and Chicahomini. The councils decided to kill Lawson and spare Graffenreid.

The town was, here as elsewhere among native peoples, the basic political unit. Between towns there were a number of alliances and relationships of different kinds, and these alliances almost always included, at least until confederacy formation was much further developed, peoples that the colonists regarded as separate tribes or nations. Some of these "different" groups were, however, partly tied together by each having members who belonged to the same clans.

Even when specific native peoples – specific peoples as the colonists saw them – were under severe military pressure, the native town, complexly connected to diverse other towns, remained the basic political unit. In 1707, for example, trade was cut off between Virginia and the people they regarded as Tuscarora, because one town refused to deliver up to Virginia several of its members for trial. Other towns wanted the trade restored, but had no power to force the town in question to do what Virginia wanted.

In the genocidal Tuscarora Wars of 1711–13, which ended in the Carolina colony shattering the Tuscarora, "*the* Tuscarora" never once met all together, but were split into two groups, each of which included people regarded as non-Tuscarora. The "hostile" Tuscarora included, in addition to several Tuscarora towns, the villages of Coree, Neusiok, Woccon, Pamlico, Bear River, and Machapunga. The "neutral" Tuscarora, who sided with the English, included towns of people called Shakori, Chicahomini, Meherrin, and Nottoway. Does this mean that there was no such entity as "the Tuscarora" (or "the Cherokee" or "the Choctaw")? Yes, and then in the progress of events, no.

"The Tuscarora" were not at all unique in having this two-level political structure of towns and open alliances that changed composition with changing circumstances. A similar situation was found among native peoples throughout the southeast, lasting at least through the first several decades of their dealings with Europeans. Among the people who came to be known as the Cherokee, the town was also the basic political unit. James Adair, who began trading with the Cherokee in 1735, wrote that towns were governed by councils and by men he called "chiefs" – although they had no formal rank or titles, no inheritable status, and no power to enforce their decisions beyond persuasion, reason, and negotiation. At this point in colonial Indian history they were still more properly "beloved elders" than chiefs, and their influence still only rarely and inconclusively reached beyond their own towns.

In 1755 Edmond Atkin, South Carolina's Indian agent, wrote: *"The upper and lower Cherokee differ from each other, as much almost as two different Nations. . . . They seldom take part even in each others Wars, which is the case also with the upper and lower Creeks."*

Several scholars have pointed to the centrality of towns in southeastern native political organization. John P. Reid, for example, in this recent review of Cherokee political and legal history during the colonial period, notes:

> *Fragmentation was the essence of Cherokee government and is still the most useful component for reconstructing the course of Cherokee history, especially when considering foreign affairs – the nation's dealings with other southern Indians, not merely with European powers. The governance of the Cherokee, it must be borne in mind, was in the towns. There was no semblance of national government save in times of great emergencies. . . .*
>
> *Cherokee military weakness lay in their divisions, for they were spread through sixty independent towns. . . . Their language was subdivided into at least three distinct dialects, and their nation was segregated into five regional groups, often competing with one another. . . . There was little feeling of unity and more than a touch of animosity between the five regions. . . . The Lower Cherokee called their Overhill brethren "pipemakers" and "frog eaters."*

Reid at this point is referring primarily to the Cherokee of the early 1700s. His notion that the Cherokee were a *"nation" at that point in their history* is not supported by any evidence, and, as Reid himself notes, they did not, in fact, have any formal – or even informal – unifying political organization, nor any cross-cutting social institutions, including clan relations, that bound together all and only "Cherokee." Their name itself seems to have been derived from a Powhatan-confederacy term, which the English once transcribed as "Rehachehacarean," which meant something like "enemies who live in the hills."

While it is unclear to what native social and political "reality" the

English term "Cherokee" refers, *if indeed any*, it is clear that the Europeans, particularly the colonial government at Charles Town, increasingly treated them as a nation, and later as a "tribe." Through treaties, trade pressures, military assaults or trade restrictions on one or more towns as "vengeance" for the acts of another, they were increasingly pressured toward becoming a single and separate political entity. Fred Gearing, in his brilliant study of Cherokee state formation, sums up this process especially well, although still incorporating a doubtful assumption: that there was a preexisting Cherokee entity that became politically unified, rather than that the process of political unification was simultaneously the process of their creation as a social and cultural entity:

> *A Cherokee state was created because, beginning in 1730, that became increasingly necessary. South Carolina could cut off trade; from 1730 on, whenever Cherokee villages lost their constant supply of ammunition, they were left exposed to armed enemy tribes. Many villages were repeatedly to suffer from such exposure. South Carolina demanded that all Cherokee be restrained from violence against traders and against the colonial frontier, and threatened reprisal. From this point forward, the act of a Cherokee individual could tangibly hurt many other Cherokee, most of whom would not know him, and some of whom might live a hundred miles from him. As Cherokees recurrently experienced this social fact they responded by creating a tribal state. In effect, South Carolina, by virtue of her power, was able to ascribe to the aggregate of Cherokee villages a political unity. The tribe could become a political unit in fact, or suffer. . . . The Cherokee priest state was some thirty years building.*

Even when the Cherokee state was fairly well consolidated, individual towns held on to much of their autonomous political organization and orientations. State formation – or, more broadly speaking, the formation of the southeastern Indian confederacies predominant in the middle and late colonial period (Cherokee, Choctaw, "Lower" and "Upper" Creek, and Chickasaw; the Catawba and Tuscarora, among other, had similar beginnings but did not "develop" this far) – fundamentally changed the relations between native towns.

Before the consolidation of these confederacies as great trading, warring, slaving, and slaveholding regional empires, the core feature of their social organization was that their constituent towns seem to have been widely connected to other native towns in a diverse array of non-coterminous ties – ties that had substantially different boundaries, substantially different "maps."

Each town was connected to an array of other towns through ties of common clan membership, marriage relations, trade, religious customs, shared language, as "jural communities" (in Gearing's phrase: clusters of towns that sought to work out disputes by negotiation), through ties to common ceremonial centers called "mother" towns, military alliances, and in a variety of other ways. The most important point about these ties is that starting from any one town the map of its ties to other towns, for any one of these kinds of connections, would *not* be likely to have boundaries similar to the boundaries of its other kinds of connections. Clanship, for example, would tie together one cluster of towns, military alliances a different cluster, shared language dialect still another cluster, and so forth. What European domination did was to reorganize many of these ties in the direction of one coordinated package, transforming the fundamental basis of regional native social organization – these non-overlapping ties – by welding together, in the heat and pressure of domination, much more sharply demarcated groups, one set antagonistically against the other. This imposed unification was never completely successful, for the emergent entities were often racked by bitter cleavages, but the unification was sufficiently powerful to shape the emergent cleavages.

These cleavages took a wide variety of forms, and had an equally wide variety of causes: between elder and younger men over the issue of fighting the Europeans, as among the Cherokee in the early 1700s and the Creeks by midcentury; equally bitter but differently structured splits over whether to return runaway slaves; between different factions of a confederacy over agreement to land-cession treaties, or whether to give up "White" ways and return to "traditional" orientations, as did the Creek "Red Stick" faction in the early nineteenth century; the clusters that formed around war leaders or "prophets" such as Tecumsah and Pontiac; the splits in confederacies over alliances with the British, French, or Americans, as with the Creeks and the Iroquois in the last half of the eighteenth century. The well-known but poorly understood fact that Indian peoples often sided with the Whites to attack and destroy each other and their own is but one indication of the profundity of the splits *within* emergent native societies.

The various "confederacies," "nations," and "tribes" that attacked each other were often more closely interwoven with one another than the defective, ultimately inapplicable concepts of "confederacy," "nation," or "tribe" permit us to see, and the problem is compounded by the heritage of European colonial policies and practices interwoven in our historical concepts. To understand native social systems – both their tensions and their unity – during the colonial period, it is crucial to grasp the historical specificity and historical dynamics of the labeling *concepts*: particularly "confederacy" and "nation."

The notion that the great colonial Indian confederacies (Cherokee, Upper and Lower Creek, Choctaw, Chickasaw, and so on) were ordinarily unitary entities, episodically shaken apart by tensions and cleavages, misses a fundamental point. All these social groups were created as one form of native response to the pressures of domination and incorporation, but they were never fully consolidated into completely separate and distinctive peoples except in the fantasies and policies of the Europeans, who had the brute power to give these fantasies some social reality. To the extent that the European colonists made war upon and treaties and trade agreements with, acquired land from, encouraged attacks between, and relocated "*the* Cherokee," "*the* Choctaw," "*the* Lower Creeks," – there came to be entities such as the Cherokee and the Choctaw. These entities became further materialized as they came to be the social, political, and cultural framework for native peoples' own attempts to make their way through the maze of domination's conflicting and antagonistic demands and impositions. But these confederacies – this emergent social reality – never fully replaced nor completely subordinated the underlying town and clan matrix of social relations, relations far more widespread and complex than could be contained within the boundaries of the emergent confederacies. To ask, in sum, for a history or an anthropology of "*the* Cherokee," or "*the* Creek" or "*the* Tuscarora" – or "*the* Lumbee" – is to miss, from the outset, some of the most fundamental features of native social life and historical process.

V

"Towns" were social entities formed in the domains of politics and of culture; they were not – or not necessarily – residential communities. A brief clarification of this point will help develop an understanding of the antagonisms that emerged within and between towns as the relations between them were reorganized and consolidated.

Among the Cherokee in the early to mid-eighteenth century, for example, several towns' councils – the meetings of collective self-governance – were in fact attended by members of physically distinct residential communities, who regarded themselves as members of a common "town." Some residential communities had two distinct and separate town councils, meeting separately and independently, each governing the affairs of its own members. The Creek had the same pattern, and in both cases the town was centered on more than simply its council meetings, but also included the physical structures of a town meeting place for their religious-political gatherings and a ball yard, where religiously and politically significant "games" were played. Charles Hudson describes the situation for the Creeks, using "chiefdom" to refer to the same entities that here are called towns. He calls them chiefdoms precisely to avoid the association between "town" and residential community; the problem his terminology raises, however, is that these entities were not governed by "chiefs" until relatively late in the colonial period:

> *The Creek chiefdom was a group of people who had their own ceremonial center with a town house, square ground and chunky yard. The chiefdom might include only one town or settlement of people, or it might include several, along with individual households scattered up and down the river. Some Creek chiefdoms were relatively autonomous, while others were connected to one another in various ways. Some chiefdoms, said to be mother and daughter, were formed by segmentation. . . . The process could also work in reverse. That is, if a chiefdom became too small to be viable . . . it could fuse with another. . . .* [Referring to the Cherokee towns of Great Tellico and Chatuga, in the early 1700s: they] *occupied the same areas with their populations intermixed, but they maintained two separate councils in two separate town houses. They lived in the same community, but they were separate corporate entities.*

Perhaps the most conceptually complex issue for developing an understanding of these great trading and warring Indian confederacies of the colonial period is the issue of their internal unity and their internal tensions. The power of these confederacies, evidenced by their attractiveness to Europeans as partners in trade and allies in war, the respect they won from the colonial powers, and their ability to organize the countryside – all this lay in their size, their massed force and their potential for coordinated action, buttressed by the diplomatic and negotiating skills of their powerful and influential leaders. On the other hand, they constantly split, siding with different colonial powers, and worse: at times they engaged in bloody civil war against themselves. There seem to have been much deeper causes for this simultaneity of unity and opposition than differences in strategy for coping with their situation, and some of these deeper causes, with new and changing surface expressions, persist to the present.

Indian confederacies were intensely *used* by the colonial powers: used as procurers of skins and pelts, used as allies and mercenaries in colonial wars, used as sources of native slaves, used as an inland wall to keep slaves and indentured servants from running west, used as troops to assault other native peoples for settlers' purposes – used. In the context

234

of this multiplicity of uses, of competition between diverse sectors of the colonial elite over how to use Indians, and the competition between diverse colonial powers for Indians to use, native people had a lot of room to maneuver and to negotiate. But ultimately they had to do one thing or another, for one European power or another, first in order to procure the necessary arms and ammunition, and then to repay the colonists' "gifts," made to and distributed through the emergent and newly powerful native leaders. These distributions were a central part of the new power and control of these leaders.

In this context of use, "unity" became the fundamental site of the contradictions in native peoples' situation. For their own sake, and in pursuit of their own goals and interests, native people had to unify, for without unity they were even more vulnerable. Even though the European colonial governments sought to impose unity on discrete clusters of natives – in part to simplify processes of trade and treaty negotiations, land cessions, and control of native retaliatory and aggressive assault – the same unity also served native needs. But it was a unity that facilitated use by dominant others, a use that was, in any form, often collectively self-destructive. Such unity was thus deeply paradoxical, and it inevitably brought with it fundamental and intense opposition, either to the use or to the unity itself.

VI

Throughout the colonial period the most predominant, intense and regular use of native people, particularly in the large confederacies, was as sources of supply for "the Indian trade." In the southeast this was primarily a trade in deerskins, but slaves, other pelts, and war against other natives were purchased by the colonists. In all these forms of trade the usual exchanges were based on credit – goods advanced to native people a season or more before they delivered what was wanted – rather than payment at point of delivery. Credit relations massively intensified the penetration of European domination within native societies, and also massively intensified the contradictions in the native peoples' situation. It was, indeed, far more destructive of native people's autonomy than were on-the-spot payments.

Trade for payment at the point of transfer meant that each transaction, each use, could be negotiated, even if between unequals, and that no more or less than what was exchanged could be claimed or given. Credit, however, bound time into the relationship between native and agent, transforming both native leadership and native kinship. Credit pressured native people, often by a very high penalty for failure, to

235

organize themselves to meet, in the future, an external demand. When the advance was not repayable in the agreed-upon goods – when there were, for example, not enough deerskins to satisfy the debt – other demands could be unilaterally imposed, and land or mercenary service were the usual new demands.

When traders advanced substantial quantities of goods – kettles, axes, knives, blankets, cloth, guns, powder, shot, alcohol and more – in the spring, against delivery in the fall or the following spring, they ordinarily did so not directly to native people, but by working through native leaders. These leaders then had to distribute these goods in ways that committed people to do the work to produce the requisite goods. Although it has been so labeled, this was absolutely *not* "redistribution," a form of political economy where native leaders collected goods from their followers and redistributed them. Redistributive systems have built-in forms of control over leadership – the goods initially must come from ordinary people to their own leaders – that this new distributive system did not have.

The credit system, not based on one-time transactions but on continuing, and usually deepening, relationships, gave new kinds of native leaders new kinds of power and forced them to use it. They often had to use this power in ways that harmed their own people, for example, by ceding land or agreeing to fight costly wars, whether they wanted to do these things or not. Nor was there much that could be done by their followers to control them, other than assassination.

Credit seems also to have had a substantial impact on native kinship, although here the interpretation must be tentative: suggestions that further research *may* be able to demonstrate or deny. There are two kinds of evidence for this. In the early period of trade between South Carolina and native peoples, from about 1685 to 1720, we can find quite a few instances in which the South Carolina council, or its commissioners of the Indian trade, protested traders collecting debts from the kin of those who contracted them. The president of the commissioners of Indian trade, speaking to the Yamasee, July 11, 1711:

> *Mr. President acquainted the Indians yt ye agents had Orders to inform them yt they were not obliged to pay their relations Debts wch they had not Ingaged for And also advised ye Indians to use yr utmost indevor to pay their Just debts and for ye future to take Care not to run in debt wth the Traders The Indians Answer'd thy were preparing to go to war and a hunting to pay ther Debts.*

It is quite likely that the wars the Yamasee were planning were in fact slave raids, but it is unclear if the commissioners wanted the Indians to know that they were not responsible for their relations' debts to

236

constrain the sale of rum to the Indians, to support emergent, more controllable native leaders (against the countervailing claims of kinship) by centering the trade, and trade debts, on the leaders, or to keep individual English traders from gaining too much power and influence over Indian affairs. I suspect that the latter was often a significant factor in any combination of reasons.

By the middle of the eighteenth century another kind of evidence about kin and credit emerges. There are several instances in which, under the stress of domination, native "prophets" emerged with calls for new ways of life and protests against current practices. Often these prophets protested the native practice of men having several wives. The Delaware Prophet, as he is called, in 1762 – shortly after the unification of the Delaware – announced the displeasure of the Great Spirit with wars between Indians, with alcohol, with the making of magic by sorcerers and witches, and with polygamy. Now this can be understood as a form of syncretism, incorporating some of the beliefs and practices of the dominant society in a movement partly designed to separate its adherents from the dominant society. But I do not think that this is the most insightful reading of his message. The Delaware Prophet was not very syncretic: he emphasized getting rid of the Whites and bringing back the deer by purification through emetics, sexual abstention, abandoning firearms and European imports, and stopping the use of flint and steel to light fires.

Rather, I think it more likely that the deerskin trade in particular had intensified certain kinds of kinship relations at the expense of other forms of social relations. In the context of producing prepared ("tanned") deerskins for the trade, men usually hunted and women usually stretched, cleaned, and cured the skins. Having several wives, accumulated at the expense of other men in the area, was a way of accumulating a labor force for work in the production of trade goods. It was far from easy work: this form of "polygamy" was often so much at the expense of the women who were used that it is not clear that it is appropriate to call their connection to the hunters "marriage," although this was the framework in which the demands on their labor were organized. Credit, and its distribution within native society, probably provided both the material means and the strong incentives to intensify some kinds of "kinship" demands on one another – both men on their subordinate "wives" and men on other men for such wives – and to make these demands increasingly unequal, diminishing other kinds of more open relationships, such as co-villager, co-participant in religious rituals, and co-equal spouse. The anthropological notion that "tribal" societies are organized primarily around kinship relations may express a historically specific situation far more than is usually realized.

Guns, powder, shot, blankets, knives, axes, hoes – all these trade items became an increasingly necessary part of the forces of production and of the processes of social reproduction for native peoples in the colonial period. Thus native people could only obtain access to some of the basic necessities of their lives through their relations to Europeans; more specifically, through their ability to satisfy European demands. Simultaneously, their access to labor and support within their own community depended on their ability to invoke, and at least partly satisfy, their kin, clan, and co-villagers' claims and needs. Because the Europeans had little if any interest in the general well-being of their Indian trading partners, and because many of the Europeans' demands were antagonistic to the well-being of native peoples, any native position of power, influence or responsibility – in the town, in the clan, or in the family – was riven with profound, destructive, and irresolvable contradictions.

Towns, as we have pointed out, were not simple physical entities, not simply relatively densely settled places of common residence. They were, rather, cultural and social constructs: ideas of belonging, of commonality, of unity that were materially and ceremonially expressed in the town house, ball court and the intertwined customs of political consensus, ritual cleanliness, and religious celebration.

As the paradoxes and contradictions of imposed domination ricocheted within native culture, they struck deeply within the fundamental frameworks of native political and social organization. Several diverse developments seemed to have preserved a fragile unity in the face of these destructive challenges.

Perhaps the embellishment of native culture, characteristic of the early colonial period, was an antidote to disintegrative pressures. The unity demanded by mobilization for vengeance and for restitution seems more definitely to have been one of the major forces for cohesion. The intensification of leadership and kinship also seems to have served to hold emergent forms of Indian social organization together. The growing class formation within native societies provided, in the midst of the tensions and bitterness it engendered, a further centralizing thrust, pulling people around an emergent elite. Lastly, and most strangely, there seems to have emerged a unity within these emergent native confederacies that was more solid and more effective in their dealings with and – unfortunately – their assaults upon other native peoples than in their dealings with the European colonies. This observation is an impression that emerges from reading in and through the colonial records and from attempting to reconstruct the perspective of native peoples of the piedmont and fall line, who suffered intensely from the destructive power of the confederacies and whose colonial cultural and social organization was forged in the vise between the colonists on their east and the confederacies to their west.

VI

From the last quarter of the seventeenth century through the middle of the eighteenth, native peoples on the piedmont and along the fall line sought to cope with the growing power of the settlers and the Indian confederacies by migration, but this strategy intersected with the expansion and the expanding reach of the peoples they were trying to avoid, shifting the center of their coping strategies from physical movement to social organizational and cultural change – changes that were rooted in patterns of population movement.

In the contact and colonial periods four interconnected kinds of migrations in particular directly shaped the formation and transformations of native societies on the piedmont and fall line:

1. The intrusive movement of substantial groups of native peoples, who came into an area already occupied by other Native Americans and held their new ground by force. This movement was primarily northwestward and southeastward along the larger rivers.

2. The movement of European settlers to the west, south, and southwest from their early Virginia and northern Carolina settlements at Jamestown and Albemarle, and to the west and northwest from the settlement at Charles Town.

3. The forcible relocation of Native American societies by the colonists, either westward, away from areas of colonial settlement, or eastward toward the settlements.

4. The movement of native peoples north and then south along the piedmont and the fall line, from South Carolina to Virginia and back, in search of a place to maintain themselves. This northward and southward movement on the piedmont was particularly influential in the formation of new kinds of social systems. Its dynamics can be clarified by a brief look at some aspects of the other forms of migration.

1. The intrusive movement of large groups of native peoples, who came in force to an already settled area, was primarily a feature of the contact and very early colonial periods. Some of these early movements, such as that of the Peedee in the 1540s, seem to be coastal peoples moving onto or across the fall line in response to coastal slaving; other

migrations, somewhat later, such as the Susquehannock, seem to be movements by inland peoples eastward, which contributed to the turmoil and warfare on the piedmont. At first this pressured other native peoples to seek the protection of the English, and then to move away when this protection diminished or was withdrawn.

2. The movement of Europeans onto the piedmont – southwestward from Virginia; northwestward from Charles Town – was not at first an expansion of farmers. As Frank Owsley has shown, the agriculturalists were preceded along the southern colonial frontier by Euro-American herdsmen, often tending large herds of cattle and swine. These animals were pastured in forests or on ranges across the "unsettled" lands, on much the same kinds of feed that deer used, and driven to market once a year. These herdsmen, who also hunted deer and trapped for their own food, sought out the piney woods of the piedmont and the mountain valleys of Appalachia to gain an extra source of income and to eliminate the wild competitors for the forage their herds needed. Their presence had two major effects on the native peoples of the piedmont: it contributed to the rapid demise of deerskin trading as an economic option, and as the herdsmen took over the drier, upland areas of the piney woods, it left the swampy regions more open to continued native occupation than the piedmont highlands, even before the Euro-American farmers arrived and settled the drier lands.

3. The third form of population movement, the specific relocation of native peoples by Europeans, has already been briefly discussed. A few additional points: The pressure on some Indian people, such as the Yamasee, to move eastward toward the line of settlement was also a pressure to become more tightly incorporated into the colonial system of use. This pressure fell heavily on the peoples of the piedmont, particularly as native population in the vicinity of the settlements declined rapidly from the effects of epidemics, from enslavement, and from warfare. To become more tightly incorporated, particularly for the smaller piedmont groups, was to quickly incur the same fate.

4. In the last quarter of the seventeenth century, starting shortly after the founding of Charles Town (a colony that soon became much more intensely involved in the large-scale Indian trade than was Virginia), there was a major northward shift of the piedmont native population. From central South Carolina, northern South Carolina, and the southern and central portions of what became North Carolina, native peoples moved quickly and in large numbers northward, many settling near what became the Virginia–North Carolina border: that is, at the southern reaches of the Virginia colony.

They did not last long in their new locales. The defeat of the Tuscarora in 1713 opened the coastal plain and eastern piedmont to an outpouring of European settlement. In 1718 Virginia closed Fort Christiana, built on the colony's southwestern piedmont margin, after the defeat of the Tuscarora, as a gathering point for the smaller groups of native peoples and a focal point for the Indian trade. After the fort was closed, native peoples of the area were left without protection or incentive to stay. With increasing momentum in the 1710s and 1720s they migrated back southward, although after peace was established in 1722 between the Iroquois Confederacy and the Virginia Indians, some went north to join the Iroquois.

In the migrations northward and back south, native peoples regarded as separate and distinct by the colonists combined, split, and recombined. What seems to have happened in this region is that the town, a social and cultural construct, gave way to the settlement under the pressures of migration, fragmentation, and recombination. These settlements were rural villages or hamlets, populated by Indian people, that were culturally and economically organized by cross-cutting lines of kinship and affinity, by local cultural practices, and *by a necessary social and cultural isolation from an increasingly dangerous milieu.*

The native peoples in this southward migration stream, some of whom went as far south as southern South Carolina and then turned back north again, came to a stop by the mid-1700s, primarily in one of three locales: among the Catawba, who held the inland region on the northern boundary of South Carolina, approximately at the east-west midpoint of the piedmont; among the Cheraw, on the easternmost edge of the piedmont just south of the North Carolina–South Carolina border, and in Robeson County, on the inland edge of the coastal plain, just north of the border with South Carolina. From the Catawba to the Cheraw is about 80 miles; from Cheraw to Robeson County less than 30. This whole border region, contested between North and South Carolina from the founding of the North Carolina colony in 1711 and for at least the next fifty years, was unsettled, open country, ineffectively governed by anyone, and inhabited by peoples who were not easy to see or engage.

After the war between the Yamasee and South Carolina, in 1715–16, the Catawba's autonomy and freedom to negotiate trade and alliance began to deteriorate rapidly. By the 1730s they were reduced to impoverished dependency on South Carolina. Of the three "collecting points" for settlement by southward moving Indians, the Catawba – the furthest inland and most "developed" of the three in the direction of forming a native confederacy, which was a smaller-scale version of the Cherokee – were the most vulnerable. There could no longer be a small-scale version of the Cherokee: colonists had no need for or interest in such formations, and the Cherokee, who literally and figuratively held the high ground, would not or could not risk the competition.

By the 1740s the Catawba were taking English surnames: they could survive as a people but there was no longer any future for them as colonial "Indians" – as people who did what "Indians" were encouraged or allowed to do, or could themselves claim, on the colonial frontier. As the Catawba position became untenable, the piedmont native migrations came to rest among the Cheraw or in Robeson County. The Cheraw position weakened next, soon after the Catawba, under the pressure of Welsh and Huguenot settlers moving up the Peedee River basin to northwestern South Carolina. In the 1730s the Cheraw fragmented, some moving west to join the Catawba – but to join them in their increasing impoverishment, which by the middle of the century had become extreme, even in comparison with other Native Americans – and others moving into the area that is now Robeson County.

VII

After the mid-1600s native people who survived on the inland edge of the coastal plain, the fall line, and the eastern piedmont often did so by distancing themselves from integration as Indians into the colonial political economy. One of the earliest instances of this as an apparently conscious and deliberate strategy was among the Wanoake of southern Virginia. After their "king" was killed, in 1665, they split – some going to live among the English, some going to the swamps. Soon, those in the swamps left to join the others, with the English, but after two years all were expelled. They went back to their old towns for a further two years, but were afraid to plant corn and were afraid of the Tuscarora. They then returned to the English where, for a brief while, they lived in cabins in the midst of orchards, finally returning to the swamps, living in cabins as small-scale, ordinary farmers, their autonomy and their survival as a people partly preserved by their social, cultural, and physical invisibility.

The Nottoway and Meherrin, as well as other native peoples in this area, had similar responses. In 1680–1 they moved out of their towns on the fall line, which lay across what had become primary Virginia trading path, to a settlement secluded in the midst of swamps. Starting about this time, several of the smaller native groups began to cultivate fruit trees. The diminished possibilities for hunting encouraged a more diverse agriculture, and with orchards they could have a small-scale trade with the settlers and other peoples of the region.

242

Fruit-tree cultivation by the small Indian groups represents, I think, the material embodiment of both a settled community life and a diminishing presence as culturally visible Indians on a larger social landscape and field of forces. Fruit trees take several years to come to productive maturity, cannot be shifted to a new locale as readily as corn, and are particularly vulnerable, with long-term consequences, to military assault. To cultivate orchards is, in many ways, to hide one's presence within them more effectively than can be done in forests.

We can see a partial blurring of the cultural-symbolic distinctions between Indians and Whites – a blurring of their customary positions in the colonial political and cultural economy – in a letter from Governor and Council president Thomas Pollock of Virginia to Mr. Drinkwater in New Bern, North Carolina, commenting on provisioning troops, *who were almost all Indian*, for the continuing war with Tuscarora. The letter was written in the early spring of 1713: "*We have a sloop with 800 bushels corn, 32 barrels meat and some tobacco* [for the Indians!] *now coming round, . . . which might be sufficient to maintain the forces now with you till August next . . . with what new corn and peaches may be had at the Indian towns . . . would last until our new corn is gathered.*"

What we find, in sum, is the emergence and consolidation of groups of native peoples along the eastern piedmont, the fall line, and the coastal plain, and their development of a complexly based isolation – and more than isolation: a substantial, if incomplete, autonomy. Native peoples were moving into relatively isolated regions, especially swamps in the borderlands between different colonies, and taking up, at least superficially, Euro-American characteristics: European names; usually the English language; cabins of Euro-American design, with horizontal, rather than vertical logs; and some components of European agriculture, at first especially orchards and hog raising. This Europeanization of native peoples was *not* simply acculturation but the framework for *social* isolation – for being left alone, for being seen as neither Black nor Indian nor, in some profoundly ambiguous ways, White – an isolation revealed by the long-lasting, continuing separateness of many of these peoples, who have endured as distinct groups until the present.

It was a relatively successful strategy. The whole coastal plain and eastern piedmont, from New Jersey southward to northern Florida and westward around the southern end of the Appalachians, is dotted with these semi-separate, semi-isolated groups, semi-hidden by their social and cultural quietness to all but local eyes. The Lumbee, in the most favorable location for this adaptation, are but the most populous representatives of this general social form.

VIII

Basic problems with this adaptation emerged in the early mid-nineteenth century, after the destruction of the native confederacies and the removal of the survivors westward to Indian territory. From the vantage point of the small, semiautonomous settlement groups in the southeast, the process of "Indian removal" was interwoven with increasing pressure against all free persons of color, and both were part of a cultural and social reduction in the number of different "kinds" of people that were socially and legislatively allowed space to exist in the new American states.

Their problems intensified in the last half of the nineteenth century, as major transportation arteries were extended throughout the piedmont and coastal plain. With the collapse of Reconstruction and the rapid growth and imposition of "Jim Crow" laws at the turn of the century, all non-White people were exposed to increasingly severe economic, political, and social pressures, pressures that intensified even further with the post–World War II mechanization of agriculture and the increasing failure of small-scale farms from the 1960s onward.

By the mid-twentieth century the pressures on these surviving small groups came to have an increasing, differential impact *within* these groups. Previously, fate and circumstance had been widely shared, despite some substantial differences in material well-being. But by the early 1960s the increasing loss of social separateness – or, more precisely, the changing and expanding range of economic integrations – became embedded in an intensifying class differentiation among southeastern native peoples in the coastal areas.

In this context of increasing internal class differentiation, in the context of the flourishing African-American civil rights struggles of the 1960s, which native peoples wanted, ambivalently, both to join and to remain separate from or within, and in the context of growing struggles for recognition – not just the federal recognition whose procedures were formalized in 1978, but a broad social and cultural recognition of Indian rights, Indian needs, and Indian ways – there was and is a dramatic elaboration of public Indian cultural identity by a great many such groups throughout the entire region.

Over these struggles for identity, rights, honor, and benefits – for an Indianness that is more than poverty and oppression – hangs the weight of the fantasy image of "real" Indians. The Chrysler Corporation may market a "jeep" with the appalling and culturally imperializing name "Cherokee Chief" (less prone to roll over than the usual jeep, designed more to be driven on ordinary roads and marketed to middle-class Whites as a compensatory illusion of autonomy, freedom, and security: precisely the qualities we sought to destroy among the people who came to be known as the Cherokee), but Chrysler would, of course, never try to peddle their wares with names such as "Lumbee (or Tuscarora) Sharecropper."

So the Lumbee and Tuscarora have had to try to establish their rights and their existence as Indians with such images as evoked by the "Cherokee Chief" before them – images often dressed up in plains Indian eagle feathers, not weeding farm fields or wiping their toddler's urine from their laps. "Cherokee Chiefs" are fantasies embedded in the dominant society's brutality and illusions, not symbols of any real human beings ever or anywhere. And most destructive of all, many Indian people – both descendants of the great confederacies and descendants of their colonial native victims – have come to share (although also to confront) some aspects of these violent images, and to use such images to help meet current needs.

The descendants of "real" Indians – people so regarded in the dominant society – have at times vigorously opposed attempts of the descendants of some piedmont and coastal plain native peoples to gain legal recognition as Indians under the 1978 Federal Acknowledgment Program. Indian benefits from the federal government are an exceedingly small pie, and they do not want to share it, particularly with people they do not think of as fully Indian. Moreover, even if the image of the native warrior of the great confederacies is an image emerging from, and dear to, the dominant society, dear because it makes our own militaristic brutalities seem more "natural" and gives us a special historical past within the present, such images have become important to many native people as well, including some of the descendants of the confederacies and some of the descendants of their victims. Such images are also about resistance to, and separation from, the dominant society, and this can make them appealing both to native people and to members of the dominant society.

"Unrecognized" native peoples are often judged by the dominant society and by other native Americans in terms of a cultural, legal, and social-organizational heritage of the colonial onslaught that they are now pressured to live up to, but were from colonial times to the present forced to claim their own lives against. The fact that some native American Indian associations have been more willing to recognize the validity of the Robeson County Tuscarora Indian identity than the claims of their full brothers and sisters and cousins the Lumbee, measures the still-living heritage of the dominant society's imposed history of "Indians," with its attendant fantasies. While the history of what was done to native peoples in the formation of different kinds of Indian societies is itself fully brutal enough, the distorted sense of history – particularly what is now glorified and commemorated and what is now silenced and denied – makes it even worse.

12

"This isn't Burger King" vs. "31 pages of unalphabetized Locklears"

I

The weight of multiple layers of Lumbee and Tuscarora history, and the unavoidable necessity to shape social life both within and against this history can be seen, pressed into a dense confrontation, in a sign that was prominently displayed in the Robeson County jail in the mid-1980s:

> THIS ISN'T BURGER KING
> WE DON'T DO IT YOUR WAY
> YOU DO IT OUR WAY

Superficially this is reasonable: jail is punishment; punishment plus, supposedly, "correction" of the inmates' ways. No longer commonly called penitentiaries, that is, places that held penitents (people regarded as having souls, who had sinned and must, and can, now *themselves* atone for their evil ways), jails are now usually called "correctional facilities," places where inmates are controlled and "corrected" by authority. The older name (which once carried at least a hint of the irreducible humanity of the prisoners) survives with an entirely new meaning in the prisoners' and guards' slang: "pen," a cage for animals.

The sign was not simply reasonable, it was, like the notion "correctional facility," also arrogant. More than defining the jail, it was specifically and assertively a sign of the times: "Burger King," a chain of fast-food eateries only recently spreading through the small-town rural south, has slightly mitigated its conveyor-belt food production by offering customers the option of having their food the way they wish – "we do it your way" – provided that such wishes and ways fall within a certain narrow range.

247

The worldview behind the concept "correctional facilities," rooted in an Enlightenment confidence in the "improving," progress-inducing power of reason, is similar to Burger King's options: there is a very narrow range of variation in what constitutes "reason," what kinds of ways and wishes could be met or even allowed voice.

Eddy Hatcher and Timothy Jacobs, two young Tuscarora men, did time in that jail, under that sign. Soon after they came out, on February 1, 1988, they armed themselves with sawed-off shotguns and seized the offices of the *Robesonian*, taking seventeen people working there as "hostages." They wanted an official hearing; they wanted the public's attention; they wanted an investigation. The most pressing issue they were calling forth onto the public stage was the death of a sick Black man in the county jail; asthmatic, he had been allowed to die despite his pleas for medical help. They were also outraged that an Indian man had been shot to death – shot in the head and killed instantly – by Deputy Sheriff Kevin Stone. Kevin Stone was the son of the high sheriff, Hubert Stone. The man he killed had been stopped while driving, in a search for narcotics. He was armed with an empty plastic bucket. The coroner's inquest accepted both of Kevin Stone's explanations: that it was an accident; that it was self-defense.

Three interwoven issues characterize the two decades following the early 1970s collapse of the dreams for an effective Indian–Black political alliance. Each is a focused search, an arena of struggle and a domain of loss and victory. These three fundamental issues are: recognition, Indian rights, and "living." All three are deeply interconnected, although each has its own momentum, its own forces, its own problems. "Living" is the most complex, the most diffuse, the most pervasive, and the most important of the three; it is the one that unites the other two struggles at the deepest and most profound level.

To begin, "living" is about "earning a living"; not a wage, and not simply a "living wage," as the union slogans put it, but earning a wage and simultaneously the space and the dignity and the social relations to live with and from the wage you earn. Living is also literally just that: it is not dying in jail for want of medical attention, or being shot by cops because in their necessarily hasty judgment and in their cultural world you seem too dangerous. Living as a human person, not as a "nigger" or a "savage," is also having at least some things your way, including the right to be one's self and Black, or African-American, or Indian: the space and the recognition and the resources to respond to the world more or less on one's own terms.

Gavin Smith, in his book *Livelihood and Resistance*, sees "living" in much

248

the same way, and it is his understanding of the connection between earning a livelihood and the necessity of resistance, among people who have been driven down, together, over and over, that informs the connection called into view here: rights, recognition, living. What he argues, in a study of Peruvian peasants' struggles against the fading dominance of the local hacienda system, is that in order to earn even a minimum living peasants are forced to struggle within and against a field of dominant forces, whether they want to or not. This field of forces, which includes the state, the army, and different kinds of local elites, including the hacienda owners, is internally discordant, with conflicting, contradictory, and, at times, impossible or incomprehensible demands. Few of these demands would enhance the well-being of peasants; most are directly oppressive. In the spaces, gaps and conflicts between different kinds of imposed demands and pressures, and from their own diverse and divergent needs and claims, peasants are forced into opposition to get what they need to have. Having a few sheep, for example, makes a crucial difference in a family's physical well-being; to keep these animals alive it is usually necessary to pasture them on lands the hacienda more or less effectively claims. To live is thus necessarily to resist – not usually in dramatic confrontations, and not necessarily from any particular ideology, but just as an ordinary part of ordinary daily life: because you and your family and neighbors want to eat. This same conjunction of livelihood and resistance has been, in subtle and pervasive ways, a central feature of the lives of Indian and African-American peoples in the rural south – both in politics and daily life.

The rapid and widespread advent of fast-food stores across the landscape of Robeson County is one highly visible expression of an increasing "proletarianization" of the population. Between 1960 and 1970, agriculture and manufacturing changed places, nearly equivalently, as the largest source of employment in the county. In 1960 there were 11,178 people in agriculture (and forestry, counted by the census in the same category but not particularly significant at this time), and 3,851 in manufacturing; in 1970 there were 4,000 people employed in agriculture and 9,604 in manufacturing.

For well over a century Robeson County has been fully and deeply embedded in a "capitalist" system of production, and in this perspective its working people have long been a rural proletariat. But this is not the most useful perspective here. The transition from agricultural to industrial predominance has largely been a transition away from working in and around the house for a return that was only in small part and episodically in cash. The rest of the recompense, even for day laborers, was the house itself, some foodstuff or a place to grow food, and a range of barter, sharing, and mutual-aid relationships with neighbors and kin. Manufacturing jobs are commuting jobs with weekly cash wages. This is, in the narrow sense of the term, "proletarianization," but the key point for understanding the whole process is that the whole range of social relations that come with low-waged proletarianization are very difficult to shape into a living.

The people of Robeson County have dealt with this problem by recourse to, and perhaps an intensification of, the social relations of an earlier time: the kin, neighborhood, and church co-involvements that were part of the farming communities. But these relationships no longer have the same material and social basis or the same reinforcements that they once had. They no longer come so densely packed together: kin, neighbors, congregants in the same church, people who share farm equipment and meals, planting and harvest help – all, or many, of these lines of mutual involvement continue to and through the present, but increasingly reach out in different directions. Low wages often turn relatively small, recurrent incidents – a broken car or well-pump, a doctor bill, a stretch of unemployment – into crises. What has increasingly come to be needed in these crises is cash, not a borrowed farm machine or some help with the harvest. Communities and churches still respond admirably well to disasters: a trailer blown over in a hurricane, a house fire, a collection for major surgery, particularly for children. But the routine vulnerabilities of ordinary daily life are both overwhelming and substantially unaddressed. And larger needs, such as increased education for the children, often stay out of reach as families are pressed down by the weight of daily life.

Low wages, even more so than poorly recompensed farming, invariably entail increasing dependence on state programs: unemployment insurance, Social Security and disability pensions, medical clinics, free school programs, college scholarships and loans, and so forth, so that one's children have a chance for a better life, or just to keep up with the increasing prerequisites for employment. Those who have continued farming, especially those on increasingly useless small plots of land, or as sharecroppers facing increasing mechanization, are in a similar situation as low wage workers: increasingly vulnerable, and directly or indirectly increasingly dependent upon state policies and programs, including crop supports, technical advice, and loans. In this context of increasing vulnerability, increasing needs, and diminishing local ability to meet these needs, rights and benefits – Indian rights and Indian benefits – become increasingly important. And their importance is far from simply material. A new framework for living an Indian life is emerging, shifting from the local community to much larger political and social arenas.

But many of the emerging needs of the people in Robeson County are unlikely to be met by any government program. Factory workers, for example, most of whom are without pension plans of any sort beyond the desperately inadequate returns from the federal Social Security program, now live by the thousands in mobile homes – flimsy structures that blow over in strong winds, burn like torches and, most crucially, that will rot into leaky, decrepit slum housing in twenty or at most thirty years – just about at the point when the working days of the families now in them are finished.

It is, for both wage workers and farmers, a new kind of vulnerability, more abstract and impersonal than before, because the needs that shape this vulnerability are not addressable through one's personal social relations. Deference to the landlord or the boss is no longer nearly as relevant as it once was: machines displace the deferential and the assertive alike. Nor are family ties quite as crucial as once they were: a great many wage workers and small farmers now will grow old without a working family farm, or without even a solid frame house, large enough to hold a married child and their family and with enough land for a garden plot, to shelter them. *Being Indian or Black in communities of Indians or Blacks, with "your own" church, "your own" schools, and "your own" people having some kind of power or influence, thus comes to matter not less in this process of "modernization" and rural proletarianization, but more: increasingly, but not yet conclusively, such identities are all that is left as a social matrix to people who have come to live alongside and between the conveyor belts of factory production, mechanized agriculture, and history.*

In this context of increasingly abstract and increasingly generalized domination, most fully expressed by the bureaucracies that administer state programs, increasingly abstract and generalized forms of identity and alliance – being Indian, rather than being a resident of Prospect, or Back Swamp, or Union Chapel – are given more importance, more weight. The pressures for these generalized ethnic identities come also from above, for example, in the form of federal state grants for housing, for the elderly, for minority scholarships, granted to Indian or African-American focused "poverty programs," or directly to Indian or African-American people. The struggle against domination and for Indian rights and benefits is thus joined at a level where new kinds of more abstract histories must be formed and lived: histories that are less about such things as kinship and family and church and more about being Indian or Black. This transition has been particularly problematic for the Tuscarora and for the poorer Lumbee.

251

II

Both new and enduring Indian issues are contested and conjoined through an intense intimacy with history, an intimacy that enables people, by a single word or two, to call to the foreground a specific prior struggle and to tie that past struggle to current claim.

Vermon Locklear – his name alone pointing back to an intensely rural, intensely poor swamp Indian past – through most of the 1970s and 1980s the chief of one of the major Tuscarora groups in Robeson County, issued the following statement in the course of his attempts to wrest Indian benefits from the federal government:

> *The Hatteras Tuscarora Indian Nation of North Carolina*
> *Vermon Locklear, the spokesman along with the historian Benny Locklear, the request with all the remaining 22 individuals along with the descendants have requested this too be taking care of*
> *1. Federal recognition as a tribe*
> *2. Rome [Home] base and the lands that adjoin it that was set up in 36 and 37 as the 22 individuals request here today.*
> *3. The funds that was set aside that we were entitled to 37 and 38*
> *4. And all the benefits that are entitled us as indians, such as our schools, hunting rights, fishing rights, such as requested by the individuals as requested here today.*
> *This is to certify that we are requesting that under section 19 of the xxxxxxxxx [erased] 984. On the Home Base we wont money propriation to build there build on the Home Base with we are ask 200,750.00 thousand to build ther build. We are ask for 100,50.00 thousand to organize our people under Re-originally into Tribe Hatteras Tuscarora Indian Tribe or Nation.*
> *Members* [seven names listed]

He writes as he talks: note one hundred fifty thousand. Moreover, he writes directly in the terms in which he thinks, with no need for amplification or explanation, because he thinks in terms that are historically meaningful, with references to the past that lives, openly, in the present. Everyone knows what "22" means, what "the 22 individuals request here today" implies. The numbers 36, 37, 38 are a more complex reference. They refer to claims for land and for rights that people think were granted or are due and have not been fulfilled; to the swirl of events around the founding of the Red Banks Mutual Association and Pembroke Farms; to a complex and conceptually open boundary between land for Indians (land that Indian people will or do own), Indian lands (land that Indians, together, control), and a reservation (land that is held in trust for Indians by the U.S. government). Because of the way history is, and must be, invoked in present struggles, both the Tuscarora struggle for land and for rights and the Lumbee struggle for full recognition hold the potential for "making history" in the double sense of that term: for changing what is happening in the present in basic ways, and for connecting an emerging present to *a* past in ways that give people's sense of *the* past new forms of meaning and of meaninglessness.

Tuscarora claims for their rights have called forth the most extraordinary range of history-invoking responses, both ideological and legal. There is no law that says one has to be literate or articulate by the rules of the dominant society to gain one's rights, but not playing by the usual rules the Tuscarora are frequently mocked – almost toyed with – by the government, by some of the more articulate Lumbee, and by many people in the local White "power elite." But they win, sometimes a lot, often a little: their intense insistence; the passion and the work they commit to their cause – including traveling to Washington to look for and study documents, and to confront "the BIA" with their claims; the allies they draw, including sophisticated Indian attorneys from the Native American Rights Fund and support from the National Congress of American Indians; and, importantly, support from some powerful and influential Lumbee – all these come together in ways that lead them, over and over again, to win at least some of what they claim, only to see other people ride to power and secure crucial rights on the basis of their victories.

III

After the Federal Acknowledgment Program (FAP) began, in 1978, in the Bureau of Indian Affairs, allowing federally unrecognized Indian peoples to "petition" for acknowledgment or recognition (the two terms are used interchangeably), the Lumbee, several Tuscarora groups, and a few tiny and socially insignificant other Robeson County Indian groups (including the "Cherokee Indians of Robeson and Adjoining Counties" and the "Hattadare [Cape Hatteras + Virginia Dare] Indian Nation") began to mobilize for producing petitions, beginning with a letter to the BIA announcing their intent to petition. The county Tuscarora groups – the most prominent being the Hatteras Tuscarora under the leadership of Vermon and Leola Locklear, the Eastern Carolina Tuscarora led by Keever Locklear, and the Drowning Creek Tuscarora, with a changing leadership – kept coming together to submit one petition and then separating again, each to make their own case.

I was hired in 1980 by Lumbee River Legal Services (acting under the general direction and authority of Lumbee Regional Development Association) as a consultant to help with their petition; the Hatteras Tuscarora hired Wesley White. We each had different strengths and different faults; we each had our own agendas, which interwove both supportively and antagonistically with the agendas of the people who hired us; we each had deeply ambivalent relations with the people for whom we worked, causing us to be hired and to be turned out or to withdraw repeatedly. Both of us, in one way or another, worked for and tried to work for, both Lumbee and Tuscarora. Wes White is an extraordinary document researcher, a man with the patience and skill to find key documents in an extremely large pool of mostly irrelevant data. He had difficulty assembling these documents into the kind of argument that would satisfy the BIA. He also found some interesting evidence tying ancestors of the Tuscarora into a native people that at some point in the colonial context were called "Saponi," an origin that the current Robeson County Tuscarora found offensive – perhaps because the Saponi were not a very militant people, perhaps because Henry Berry Lowery, traceable kin to Leola Locklear (Vermon Locklear's wife and a significant Tuscarora leader in her own right) was identified, very much as they saw it, simply with the Tuscarora. I took much longer to find relevant information, worked frighteningly more in the domain of analytical argument, and had my own agendas, both theoretical and political, which were often embedded, on both sides, in complex love-respect-anger-dismay relationships. Moreover, I could come to the county only episodically, for midterm and holiday breaks in the midst of teaching, which created massive problems all around.

I was particularly concerned in the first few years of my work with the Lumbee – until it became clearly impossible – that the Lumbee petition, which was a more substantially financed and well-organized endeavor, not leave the Tuscarora out. I tried desperately to pull people together under an umbrella petition for "The Indian People of Robeson County," represented by Lumbee and Tuscarora tribal councils. Many Lumbee took the position that the Tuscarora were welcome to sign on the Lumbee tribal roll – as Lumbee, of course – if they did not want to be left out. The Tuscarora had their own claims on the future, the present, and the past, and after several intense meetings the whole unifying effort collapsed. Lumbee and Tuscarora, as well as other Indian peoples in the petitioning process, were partly dependent on who they could get to help them, and had to work within the BIA's imposed guidelines, which made it almost essential to get technical help from people trained in historical anthropology. In the midst of all this, however, they managed to strongly and effectively insist on their own agendas. By the mid

1980s I was no longer working for the Lumbee on their petition. Dr. Jack Campesi, who had already worked successfully on several acknowledgment cases, did the bulk of the writing and document-organizing work, with Wes White doing a substantial amount of the crucial archival research.

The Tuscarora petition went in first, in 1984. Soon after the BIA receive a petition, they complete a first reading and reply with what has come to be called "the O.D. letter": an initial response that lists "obvious deficiencies and significant omissions." The idea – which on the BIA's part is regarded as friendly and helpful, but which many native people think of as harsh, unreasonable, and designed to chase them away – is to comment on areas of the petition that seem likely to be problematic in the subsequent full review, in order to provide an opportunity to amend the petition before the formal review begins.

On June 11, 1985, the BIA wrote their O.D. letter to Vermon Locklear, from which the following excerpts are drawn:

> *Dear Mr. Locklear:*
>
> *. . . the Hatteras Tuscarora petition for Federal acknowledgment . . . reflects a great deal of effort, time and expense. However, as a result of this review, considerable additional information is needed. . . .*
>
> *. . . we feel it is important that we make clear a distinction between the terms "individual" and "group" as defined in Part 83.1 of the regulations. A group is a number of people having some unifying relationship. A large number of unconnected people does not necessarily constitute a group. . . . The unifying element may include . . . common interests and kinship. Groups can be formal, that is they can have a written governing document, or informal, without a governing document. Political power in a group resides in its membership. The members may delegate all and/or part of their power to a governing body by ratifying a governing document.*
>
> *For acknowledgement purposes a tribe must be a formal group and not a collection of individuals. A tribe must be distinct from non-Indians as well other Indian groups in its area. The group must be able to trace a tribal history and not just the history of particular individuals.*
>
> Membership Lists
>
> *Your membership lists were difficult to review and we are not sure we understand them. We will be happy to work with you. . . . One of our problems in the review was that some of the material had been alphabetized while other sections had not. . . .*
>
> *Two lists were submitted with the petition: one dated June 1980 entitled "Membership Roll of the Tuscarora Indian Tribe" (hereinafter*

the *"1980 roll"); the other, an undated 8 ¹/₂ × 14 list which begins with 31 pages of unalphabetized Locklears (hereinafter the "undated roll")* . . . [which] *appears to have been prepared some time in the late 1970s.* . . .

The 1980 roll contains 2,326 members. It is divided into three separate sections which are described below:

1. The first section, containing 23 pages, is paginated A to W. The format provides for the member's name; his address (though city and state are frequently omitted); and the names of the member's parents. Generally, no other information is provided.

2. The second section contains approximately 80 pages which are paginated I to LXXX. Here members appear to be grouped into families. Full dates of birth and addresses have been provided for most members of this section.

3. The third and final section appears to have been reproduced from 3 × 5 cards. Pages are numbered 1 to 274. Information provided varies widely from card to card. What is the significance of each of the three separate and distinct sections of this roll? Why are they in different formats? Is it, perhaps, that one section represents the Drowning Creek members enrolled with your group?

. . . the fact that of 2,322 members listed on the undated roll, 927 have the same surname of Locklear, adds significantly to our problems in analyzing the membership. . . .

. . . The new list [which the BIA is asking for] *will need a formal letter of certification . . . which states . . . that it* [is current and] *. . . contains all persons who not only consider themselves to be members but are considered to be members by the group. This means that the Drowning Creek Tuscaroras currently on the roll will have to be removed unless they have provided you with written indication that they have joined with and want to remain on the Hatteras Tuscarora membership roll.* . . .

History

The history of the Hatteras Tuscarora that has been provided does not focus on the requirement of 25 CFR 83.7. One of the problems is the confusion between individual and group history. For example, the emphasis in the history is placed on showing that certain individuals were identified as Indian, especially in the pre-1885 period. There is very little showing that a group existed and was identified as Indian.

On page 35 of the petition, mention is made of the "Long Swamp Locklear settlement" around the year 1796, but no description of this settlement is provided. Please submit a description of this settlement, including the names of the inhabitants and any reference to the settlement as being an Indian settlement. . . .

In many places throughout the petition, excerpts from photocopies of historical documents have been edited with blanked out portions – in some cases with hand-written alternative words inserted – thus altering the meaning of the text in question. This occurs specifically on pages 211, 353, 354, 414, 426 and 428. Please provide copies of the original and unedited versions of all the altered texts in question.

The petition does not adequately focus on the history of the governing structure within the past and present Hatteras Tuscarora group. Certain brief biographical accounts of given individuals are provided, but no connection is made between these individuals and a continuous governing or political body within the group. Therefore . . . provide a statement regarding the historical record of the governing structure of the Tuscarora community prior to 1885, with supporting documentation; and give a general overview of the history of the governing system of the Tuscaroras from the first continuous contact with non-Indians to the present. . . .

Current Community and Governance

Please provide a comprehensive description of the current community or communities of the Hatteras Tuscaroras. Include information and any documentation you might have to demonstrate how the group maintains its social cohesion or unity. A detailed map showing the location of the community or communities and the number of members in each location would be helpful. . . .

Describe the activities your group engages in to maintain its social cohesiveness or unity. Are there, for example, periodic (annual, semi-annual, or quarterly) events which bring your members together? If so, please describe them. Perhaps your group's cohesiveness resides in kinship ties and social events such as weddings, funerals, church, etc. . . . Article XIII [of the Constitution and By Laws of the Tuscarora Indians in Southeastern Carolinas], Tribal Marriage, states "No member of the tribe, be married out of this tribe. It shall be felony against the rules of the nation." Do the group's members adhere to this provision against marrying out?. . . .

In your description of the current community, it well be extremely important for you to differentiate your group from other groups, both Indian and non-Indian, in your region. Recent censuses . . . for Robeson County and adjacent areas give the Indian population as well over 30,000. Some of these people include both petitioners and non-petitioners. Petitioning groups include the Cherokee Indians of Hoke County, Drowning Creek Tuscarora, Cherokee Indians of Robeson County, and *the Lumbee Regional Development Association. Many of the members of these groups have surnames in common with the members of your group which would suggest that they may also be descendants of the same early families in the area. Further, some newspaper accounts do not always differentiate between these various groups and frequently refer to them as Robeson County Indians or Lumbees, Please provide any newspaper articles that refer to the Hatteras Tuscarora. . . .*

The group is referred to throughout the petition by a variety of similar but different names. Please discuss each of the following names, their origin and period of use. Hatteras Tuscarora Indians (initial petition), Tuscarora Indians in the Southeastern Carolinas (governing document)

Tuscarora Indians of North Carolina (1980 roll, section 1)

The Hateis Tuscarora Tribe Indian (1980 roll, section 2)

Tuscarora Tribe Indian (1980 roll, section 3)

Tuscarora Indian Tribe (undated roll)

What name does your group wish to be known by in the Federal Records?

Sincerely, . . .

Deputy Director, Office of Indian Services

Tribal membership rolls are a more complex issue than may first appear. One of the few bits of "sovereignty" actually remaining in Native American hands as "domestic dependent nations" (in the famous words of Chief Justice John Marshall, in 1831) is the right to determine their own membership. The BIA, however, feels that it cannot simply accede to this right, but must exercise some control over the principles by which the membership list is assembled, and over the people on it, at the very least for the initial lists of the petitioning tribes and, as they hope and plan, for longer.

Tribes that have always been recognized, and tribes that successfully petition for recognition, have what the BIA describes as a "government to government" relationship with the United States. It is a strange relationship, full of equalities and inequalities woven together into a morass of irresolvable paradoxes. The simplest problems emerge from the gross inequalities of power; the United States ultimately decides – or continually tries to decide – what (and how much) Indian governments will be allowed to govern.

When Indian peoples try to insist on their autonomy and rights the situation often becomes more complex, for while the native peoples may be simply exercising their own "legal" rights, this can also challenge power and authority. Indian peoples have rights as Indians within the United States, rights that are claims against the U.S. government, claims that have real costs – for health care, for schools, for tax abatements and so forth. The BIA takes what it considers a reasonable position: it does not want a core group of "real" Indians granting tribal member- ship to people indiscriminately, for by so doing the Indian government is binding the U.S. government to provide "Indian services" and "Indian rights" to these people. Yet who is and is not a member is a proper part of the sovereign rights of Indian governments.

The people at the BIA who will review the petition include an anthro- pologist responsible for reviewing the sections on community organiza- tion, a historian who reviews the historical origins section, and a genealogist who checks the tribal roll, or a sample of it, to make sure that the individuals listed are indeed of "Indian descent." The BIA challenged several aspects of the Tuscarora roll, including "31 pages of unalphabetized Locklears." The BIA also firmly and repeatedly asked the Tuscarora to demonstrate that they were a group, not just a collec- tion of individuals. The two complaints subtly but powerfully oppose each other, at least as people such as Tuscarora understand their rela- tionships to one another.

How do you alphabetize thirty-one pages of Locklears? One quick answer is to do it exactly as the telephone directory does: last name, first name, middle name or initial. But this abstract ordering brings its own confusions and, moreover, its own domineering intrusions. How do you group families: by the adult father, or by his elderly or deceased father, still socially present? What about women, who are simultaneously daughters, wives, mothers, and individuals in their own right? Take the case of a mature man we shall call John P. Locklear, Jr., whose deceased father was John R. Locklear, and who was raised by his grandfather, his mother's father, after whom he was named, John P. Locklear. Locklears can marry Locklears: while many are "related," many know of no relation whatever between them. Everyone calls John P. Locklear, Jr. "John Junior," and he most likely signs documents and endorses his checks "John Jr. Locklear." Do you alphabetize him as John Paul, his "legal" name but the name people use to refer to his grandfather? Do you alphabetize him as, or under, John Robert, his father's name, because if you ask people in a conversation "which John Junior?" almost everyone would answer "John Robert's Junior," identifying him by his father. What about his wife, whom everyone knows as "Miss Ruth" – the title of respect *always* going with the name; she earned it by a lifetime of hard work, good mothering, and constant church attendance. Do you alphabetize her by her own name, or include her "under" her husband's name, or "under" her father's or mother's name, for if you ask "which Miss Ruth?" you are more or as likely to be given her father's or mother's name as her husband's. To alphabetize is to deny the very social organization and the family history that the BIA is asking the Indians to provide – but to provide on the BIA's terms, with BIA concepts. The BIA staff has been willing to consider informal political organization, but they in turn have to justify their decisions "upward." Could the Tuscarora ever go to court and claim that their social organization – or at least the fact that they have a social organization, interwoven with their customs and worldview, and most fully expressed in the flexibility that permits people to refer to John Jr. and Miss Ruth in any one of several different, all perfectly clear ways – begins to be evident from their submitting a list of "31 pages of unalphabetized Locklears"? This isn't Burger King, although people now have to compete for that kind of livelihood.

IV

In the winter of 1967–8 three Lumbee men – Bruce Jones, Horace Locklear, and Rod Locklear – and I worked together to incorporate an Indian "poverty program" agency that we first called "Regional Development Association." Our idea was to develop programs with federal funding that would better serve poor people in the county than the existing programs: poor people that would be primarily Indians, but would also include some Blacks. There was an existing poverty program agency, Tri-County Community Action Agency, Inc., dominated by Whites, spread over a three-county area and, to us, seemingly a "bandaid" operation. We wanted more; we wanted it special for Robeson County; and we wanted to do something for and with Indians in and just outside the county, for in the larger three-county context Indian needs seemed to be even less well met than those of Blacks. All of us worked, or had worked, for an innovative, Black-led statewide poverty program, and we wanted to bring the possibility of innovation home.

There was a political agenda as well, a substantial part of which was expressed through the intersection of the growing voter registration drive in the county and my intense efforts to re-create, of all things, my grandmother's history. As she and my family told the stories, my grandmother came to New York from the Jewish ghetto in Vilnius, in 1902. She was met on the docks, when she landed, by a worker from the remnants of Tammany Hall – the Democratic party machine – who spoke her language (Yiddish) and who helped her to find an apartment and a job. When my grandfather was in the hospital for a long stay, Tammany Hall sent a basket of food to her and flowers for him. When there was no heat in the apartment and banging on the steam pipes did not help, it was the neighborhood party worker that she called. What

I remember most vividly was that when my grandmother was so old and senile that she could not recall my name she still went downstairs from her New York tenement apartment and voted straight Democratic, every two years, as regularly as clockwork.

Over and over I told this story to the Indian people I worked with, while we were registering voters, discussing strategy and planning change, making the point explicit: the future did not lay in our talking about injustice but in our ability to organize ourselves to do things for people in need. We never wanted a close integration between a political movement and a service agency. Even if we had wanted it, our plans were formed in the midst of all sorts of scare stories about how difficult it was to pass through "401.C.3" – the section of the tax code that required a totally apolitical organization to qualify for the essential non-profit, tax exempt status. What we did want, in some unclear and un-specified way, was a "movement" that would, at one end, help people with new kinds of programs, that would provide direct assistance, for-mal and informal, and that would, at the other end, bring people to the polls to vote, we hoped, for new kinds of local officials.

There was a deeper, more diffusely grasped political agenda, where-in my own experiences more closely intertwined with the experiences and hopes of the people with whom I worked. Before coming to Robeson County in the spring of 1967, I had worked in a contract-research company in Washington, D.C., for a year and a half, most of that time working on a project to study the "War on Poverty" in six midwestern and southwestern Indian reservations under contract to the "Indian desk" of the Office of Economic Opportunity.

Federal poverty programs on Indian reservations had a unique form of organization. In an ordinary, non-Indian poverty program in cities and rural areas of the United States, the program was funded through a "community action agency" set up specially to administer poverty programs. Liberal politicians in Washington did not want to pour federal funds into the usual power structures of cities and counties, regarded as corrupt, inefficient, and fundamentally uninterested in helping the poor, so community action agencies were established, with substantial autonomy – at least at first – from "city hall." This set the stage for a rapidly intensifying struggle between city halls and poverty agencies, and in places where political machines were well entrenched the agencies lost quickly and completely, usually much to the detriment of the poor.

But on Indian reservations the tribal councils became, or directly administered, the community action agencies. Because tribal councils had no power of taxation (save some usually paltry mining and timber royalties, and even these were usually set and administered, on behalf of the Indians, by the BIA) they were completely dependent on the federal government for their operating funds. The poverty programs, while also based on federal funding, were much more loosely controlled and constrained than other programs, giving tribal councils "their own" funds and a substantial amount of autonomy for the first time since the tribal councils were created, in their "modern" form, by the 1934 Indian Reorganization Act. (In some cases, such as among the Navajo, tribal councils were created a decade or so before the act, primarily and explicitly to sign over oil and mining rights.)

None of us in those days knew how this autonomy and the new kinds of tribal council power on many reservations – particularly on the plains and in the southwest – would merge with a growing class formation within the reservation, often permitting a rising local Indian elite to consolidate political and economic power at the expense of the needs of their poorer cousins. I told the stories of poverty programs and newly effective tribal councils as I then knew them, they told me their stories – mostly histories of a people trying to deal with domination – and their hopes for a better future, and we "went for it": not exactly a tribal council; nothing that specific or that organized, for it was all just starting, although Horace Locklear and Rod Locklear kept raising the idea for the future. We "went for" a chance to do something about poverty, illiteracy, and the declining possibilities in agriculture – and more: a more secure, more autonomous, and more expressive life for Indian people and – at first at least – for their local African-American allies as well.

We sought all this in the necessary context of federal and state programs and laws we only dimly understood. There were no Indian or Black lawyers in the county at that time, and no local White lawyers we felt we could either trust or afford, so I was delegated to write the incorporation papers of the new organization. I had not the slightest idea what I was doing – I went to the law library at the University of North Carolina and asked to see some incorporation papers for non-profit organizations, got a few samples, and copied them out. There was one provision in several of them: "This corporation shall have no members." None of us could figure out what that meant, but we put it in our charter because that was what charters of incorporation said. We laughed a lot; we met in strange places – Bruce Jones and I rewrote the charter late one joyful, optimistic night on the trunk of a parked car under a streetlight on the outskirts of Durham; and as part of the mood of the late 1960s, amidst what still seemed like the productive, engaging turmoil of civil rights and poverty programs we had the strong sense of together helping to make a new world. We did, a tiny bit, and of course we didn't, and most of what happened we never planned.

V

Regional Development Association (along with a government-financed poverty law program with a substantial Lumbee clientele, Lumber River Legal Services, Inc.) became the center of the Lumbee struggle for rights and for recognition within and then against the practices and claims of the federal government. As it developed, it quickly transformed into *Lumbee* Regional Development Association (LRDA), with an all-Indian board of directors and a specific Lumbee focus. The board of directors was continually expanded in the early 1970s and a majority of its members came to be Lumbee whose parents, grandparents, and great-grandparents were active leaders in struggles reaching all the way back to the founding of the school system in the 1880s.

While rooted in long-standing Lumbee forms of political leadership, it came increasingly to assume new kinds of powers in dealing with, and at times confronting, the federal government and other native Americans. In both these contexts there were surprising, unanticipated, and serious controversies, and equally surprising forms of support. LRDA began to get several million dollars a year of federal program funds set aside for Indian peoples, which brought both substantial benefits and substantial troubles as the stakes of claim and counterclaim increased.

In the negotiations that led to the funding of LRDA and the gains this brought, and in the conflicts that emerged, new claims on histories and history were often invoked and at times even forcefully imposed.

For about a year after it was founded, Regional Development Association (RDA) was a shell of an organization: a charter, a board of directors and little else. But there was a lot else to do, and RDA did not much matter. The spring of 1968 was the culmination of the intense voter registration drive, and the Democratic primary election in May the center of hope and attention. The political alliance of Indians and Blacks was supposed to win, and to win it all. Instead, it lost everything. While plans were being made to try again in 1970, not yet realizing that all would again be lost, RDA began to grow, and to grow outside the usual channels for Lumbee hopes and claims.

In 1969 Helen Scheirbeck, a Lumbee Indian residing in Washington, D.C., and employed as a staff assistant to Senator Sam Ervin, helped the National Congress of American Indians (NCAI) obtain a substantial grant for Indian adult literacy and saw that NCAI funneled some of the money to RDA for such a program in Robeson County. At the same time, Brantly Blue, a Lumbee Indian who had gone to Tennessee for a law degree and stayed there to practice law and to become active in Republican party politics, was appointed to the Federal Indian Claims Commission. He used his growing knowledge of how national Indian affairs "worked" to inform influential Lumbee about how they might get various kinds of federal government assistance and he continually prodded Lumbee to apply.

In 1970 RDA reorganized, changing its name to the Lumbee Regional Development Association (LRDA), dropping me from the board of directors and expanding the board from four to nine members, all Indian. By 1971 LRDA had five programs with an annual combined budget of $440,000; two years later there were two more programs and an annual budget of $790,000; two years after that, in 1975, LRDA had tied into the Comprehensive Employment and Training Act, which reflected a national shift in poverty-program priorities to job training and development, and their budget jumped to $2.5 million. Money on this scale brought substantial opposition to the Lumbee getting federal funds for Indians.

Funding for LRDA came, in part, from the Office of Economic Opportunity (OEO) and, increasingly, from the Department of Health, Education and Welfare (HEW) and the Department of Labor. Most of the money LRDA received came through Indian "set-aside" budgets, and this quickly became a major issue.

Starting in the early 1970s, HEW set aside a small portion of some of its program funds to use for nonreservation Indians. This was done through a division of HEW called the Office of Native American Programs (ONAP). The general idea behind ONAP was that reservation Indians would be served by the BIA but that a substantial portion of Native Americans (and Alaskan and Hawaiian native peoples) lived "off reservation" and many were in desperate straits. Some of these Native Americans had moved from reservations to other rural or urban areas and were enrolled members of recognized tribes; some were Indians whose people were not recognized and did not have a reservation as a base.

In 1970 the Lumbee were denied funding from the Indian desk of OEO, on the grounds that they were not federally recognized, but OEO helped them get regular (non-Indian) OEO funds. The preexisting tricounty poverty program in Robeson and two adjoining counties protested vigorously, for its own funding was reduced. The Lumbee's successful response was that they were serving Indians with an all-Indian staff and program. The potential contradictions of this situation – they were receiving non-Indian funds for Indian programs (but were, on the other hand, serving people who might otherwise be bypassed) – were only the inauguration of the troubles and the successes to come.

In 1975 the United Southeastern Tribes, Inc. (USET) – an organization of federally recognized tribes in the southeast, including principally the Eastern Band of Cherokee, the Mississippi Choctaw, and the Seminole of Florida – submitted an application to the U.S. Department of Health, Education and Welfare to provide technical training and assistance to forty Indian tribes that were receiving Native American program funds. USET refused, however, to include the Lumbee in its training plans. HEW, in reply, made the award of their grant ($390,000) conditional upon their providing assistance to Lumbee; USET refused again and were denied the contract.

The United Southeastern Tribes then filed a complaint with the Comptroller General's office (a branch of the General Accounting Office, with oversight responsibilities), claiming in essence that since the Lumbee were not federally recognized as Indians, the rejection of their application had been arbitrary and capricious; further, they asserted, the Lumbee were not entitled to receive Indian funds from HEW. Once again the Lumbee Recognition Act of 1956 (Public Law 84–570) was invoked, with USET claiming that the final sentence of the act,

> Nothing in this Act shall make such Indians eligible for any services performed by the United States for Indians because of their status as Indians, and none of the statutes of the United States which affect Indians because of their status as Indians shall be applicable to the Lumbee Indians

precluded any Indian funds from going to the Lumbee.

While this was happening, the case of *Maynor* v. *Morton* – Lawrence Maynor, one of the "original twenty-two," and still seeking his rights, suing Rogers C. B. Morton, secretary of the interior – was working its way through the courts. In April 1975 the court of appeals held that Maynor's rights as an Indian, granted in 1936, were not terminated by the 1956 Lumbee act. Leaning heavily on this decision – the outcome of a case brought by the Tuscarora – the comptroller general, at first ignoring the dispute while programs continued to come to the Lumbee, eventually decided against the United Southeastern Tribes and in favor of the Lumbee continuing to receive Indian funds (Comptroller General's Office, File B-185659 Aug 1, 1979):

> USET, among others, believes that the statute denies any and all benefits to the Lumbees which would be conferred because of their status as Indians.

> *We believe, however, that there is a different and better interpretation of this Act . . . set forth by the U.S. Court of Appeals for the District of Columbia Circuit in* Maynor *v.* Morton, *510 F 2d 1254 (1975), [which] holds that*
>
> > *"The whole purpose of this final clause . . . was simply to leave the rights of the 'Lumbee Indians' unchanged. . . . The limited purpose of the legislation appears to be to designate this group of Indians as 'Lumbee Indians' and to recognize them as a specific group. Moreover, Congress was very careful not to confer,* by this legislation, *any special benefits on these people so designated. . . . But we do not see that Congress manifested any intention to take away any rights conferred on any individuals by any* previous *legislation. . . . The whole purpose of the clause . . . was simply to make sure that a simple statute granting the name 'Lumbee Indians' to a group of Indians, which hitherto had not had such designation legally, was not used in and of itself to acquire benefits from the United States Government."* [emphasis in the original]

The comptroller general commented: "*[The Lumbee Act] constitutes neither congressional recognition of the Lumbees as Indians . . . nor congressional direction that they be denied benefits if otherwise entitled.*"

At the end of his review of the issues, the comptroller general referred to the practices of the Department of the Interior, and in so doing distinguished between an Indian "tribe" and Indians as a "racial entity":

> *The practice of extending Federal recognition to Indian tribes arises from the unique legal status of those tribes under Federal law and from the plenary authority of Congress to legislate specifically for Indians. Federal legislation relating to Indians as such is not based upon racial classifications, but rather reflects the power of Congress "to regulate Commerce . . . with the Indian tribes." . . . The Department of the Interior declined to comment on the eligibility of the Lumbee for . . . benefits. However, the Acting Commissioner of Indian Affairs noted that Congress has from time-to-time provided benefits for groups with special social and/or economic needs. He stated that "in some such instances, it seems likely that Congress intended that Indian people, as a racial entity, be among the special beneficiaries."*

This decision was based on a wide range of opinions invited and collected by the comptroller general. It came as the result both of the Tuscarora suit against Morton and from a lot of hard work and political pressure on the state and federal governments by Lumbee associated with LRDA, and a continuing, intense, and partly successful effort to enlist the support of other Native American peoples. But the decision

266

characterizes the current and continuing situation of the Lumbee. Even their major victories – here, that they could receive funding as Indians – come in a form that, although supporting their needs and interests, simultaneously threatens and challenges them in ways that often have surprising consequences.

VI

In 1970 Lumbee became very active in organizing federally unrecognized tribes in North Carolina. They pressured the governor to establish a state commission of Indian affairs, which was begun in 1971 with Lumbee, Coharie, Haliwa, and Waccamaw-Siouan tribal members: the Cherokee were invited but declined to attend. Aside from the Cherokee, the Lumbee and the Haliwa were the only state-recognized tribes; with help from the commission and LRDA, the Coharie and Waccamaw–Siouan peoples became recognized by the state, and several smaller groups and urban Indian associations acquired state incorporation papers – "charters" – making them eligible for program funding.

The success of the Lumbee on the state level was based on a growing alliance with state Republican leaders, including Jim Holshouser, who in 1970 was the chairman of the state Republican party, and in 1972 became governor. With Republican support and with their own organizational sophistication, the Lumbee easily dominated the state's Commission on Indian Affairs, providing eleven of the eighteen members and the director. The Lumbee were seriously committed to helping other Indian people in the state, deeply hurt by the opposition of the Cherokee, and concerned also to use their organizational abilities and connections to meet their own needs, including making sure that the Tuscarora did not become a threat to their power but remained a useful supplement. As LRDA's 1985 "History of LRDA" put it:

> Although the Tuscaroras may not have achieved much as a group, from 1970 to 1975 they focused much attention and publicity on Indian issues of Robeson County. State and federal officials were put under greater pressure to help resolve Indian problems in Robeson County. These same state and federal officials found it much easier to fund a moderate, well established organization like LRDA to deal with problems that the Tuscarora were publicizing so vividly.
>
> From 1975 to 1980, the Tuscarora leadership was fragmented. . . . In 1980 to 1985, the Tuscarora received assistance from younger leaders who had experience in government programs. The Tuscaroras have received funding from federal agencies and are providing services to

> Indian people. They have begun a new Tuscarora tribal roll and are
> still remaining critical of the LRDA and Lumbee leadership.
> The LRDA leadership has effectively blocked the Tuscaroras from
> being recognized as a valid tribal organization by the state. Tuscarora
> leaders have been able to get positions of leadership at the national level
> and assistance from other Indian tribes outside of North Carolina.

At the same time that the Lumbee were so heavily engaged in securing their position within the state they were also trying to turn events
more in their favor, building a broad base of support by using their
skills and connections to help smaller Indian groups throughout the
eastern United States.

In 1971, the same year that the state Commission on Indian affairs
was founded, two Lumbee Indians, Helen Scheirbeck and W. J.
Strickland, founded the Coalition of Eastern Native Americans (CENA).
CENA was soon helping sixty small Indian tribes from Maine to
Louisiana: helping them in specific, material ways, including obtaining
grants to run poverty programs and technical advice on administering
such programs. It also helped some, such as the Poarch Band of Creek
Indians in Alabama, mobilize themselves and obtain grants to pursue
recognition, eventually successfully.

The National Congress of American Indians – the largest and most
powerful of the federally recognized tribes' political and lobbying organizations – had accepted the Lumbee as members in 1972 and 1973.
Later they would say that this was because they were broke and needed
the dues, but indeed they had included individual Lumbee as members
as far back as the 1930s. In 1975, under the influence of the United
Southeastern Tribes, NCAI excluded the Lumbee and adopted a
resolution asking government agencies not to fund the Lumbee as
Indians – a resolution that was passed again in 1976. In 1979 NCAI got
a new director, more sympathetic to the Lumbee. The Lumbee went
to the 1980 convention in force, with a delegation led by LRDA, and
in the voting for southeastern area vice-president of NCAI, they organized
the defeat of the incumbent, John Taylor, from the Eastern Band of
Cherokee, and his replacement by Eddie Tullis, of the Poarch Band of
Creeks. In 1983 Tullis moved up in NCAI and his place as area vice-
president was taken by Bruce Jones, a board member of LRDA. Starting
in 1980, NCAI firmly supported the Lumbee – at least until 1984, when
a new national director was elected.

While the Lumbee were engaged in regional and national Indian
politics, the Tuscarora were doing the same, and having an easier time
of it. They were admitted to NCAI in 1979 – finding it easier to be fully
accepted as Indians by other Indians than the Lumbee, although they

268

have had, for much of their "history," exactly the same history as the Lumbee. In August 1980, just before the NCAI convention that the Lumbee went to in force, Leola Locklear (on behalf of herself, her husband Vermon, and their people) wrote a letter to the Lumbee newspaper:

> *Dear Sir,*
>
> *The National Congress of American Indians adopted and accepted the Tuscarora Tribe of Indians of Maxton, North Carolina given by hand seal on the 12th day of November 1979.*
>
> *The National Congress of American Indians had a part and recognized the Tribe and all of the Tuscarora members, to the Federal acknowledgement for federal recognition. We are historical, and constitutional, we can prove our ancestors back over two hundred years. We give our thanks highly to the historian Wes White and the other historians who gave their help toward Tuscarora Tribe in helping getting Federal recognition* [which they have not yet gotten].
>
> *We, the Tribe, have been organizing since 1969. We have enrolled 2,000 and some few hundred members. The floor rug is almost ready to be spread in North Carolina on the banks of Lumbee River. The Tuscaroras are proud to say, that we can stand up for our American heritage. The enrolled members are just before getting their hunting and fishing rights. They are also getting ready to stop paying taxes. The secretary of the tribe, Ruth Helen Locklear is proud that the Tribe is on their way toward reaching their goal which our back parents have always worked for, and something which we hope that will be successful for our children that are behind us. Hello. I, Leola Locklear am proud to say that I know, and can prove that my great-grandfather, Henry Berry Lowry had the blood of the Tuscarora, and was not a Lumbee. This is what makes me angry when I look at the history. This is why I want to stand up, and fight for what I believe in, that Henry Berry's ancestors was indeed the Tuscarora blood. This is why I want the truth to come out for one time for our people in Robeson County and adjoining counties. We highly appreciate each of our members who have helped us through this struggle. For any information concerning the Tribe, contact the Tribal Counseling Board of the Tribe at. . . . Or contact . . . , Secretary. . . .*

Why did the Tuscarora have – at least at this moment in their history – an easier time being accepted by other Indians than did the Lumbee?

The Tuscarora struggle for rights and recognition appears, on the surface, to be more outside some of the shared meanings of the dominant society than does the Lumbee struggle. Both use the courts, both petition the BIA, both appeal to Congress, but with a difference in

269

language, appearance, comportment, style, in the kinds of issues that are raised, the ways these issues are rooted in the past, and the claims that are made.

There are probably far more Navajo in business suits on any given day than Lumbee, and this does not lead anyone to question the Indian identity of the Navajo. There may, however, be something about "being Indian" that calls for more of a separation from the dominant culture than many Lumbee *seem* to present, although a substantial part of what is called for may in fact be more about intense poverty and the ways of life that go with such poverty than about being Indian.

"Indianness" in the contemporary United States is deeply paradoxical, for reasons that only partly originate among native peoples themselves. Consider the horrible murders and arson and general mayhem on the Mohawk Indian reservation at Akwesasne in the spring of 1990. The center of the dispute was the advent of gambling casinos and high-stakes bingo halls on the reservation, operating in the shelter of the semiautonomous legal status of the reservation where, in essence, U.S. criminal codes prevail, but not civil regulations. *Some* of the supporters of high-stakes gambling define themselves as "traditionalists" who want to be Indian and not poor, although they are finding their small reservation swamped with tourists and their land given over to commercial buildings and parking lots. On the other side are also "traditionalists," who want to get rid of the gambling halls as being profoundly antithetical to any conceivable "Indian" way of life. Although my heart and my thoughts are completely on the side of the people who want to get rid of gambling, I can understand and sympathize with the claim that in the political-economic situation they are in, the people who oppose gambling are consigning themselves to an Indian way of life that whatever its spiritual and interpersonal rewards materially is corn soup and not much more, and often necessitates leaving for work in a distant city for a substantial part of the year even to afford that.

Both sides in this horrendous, murderous dispute are racked with internal contradictions, compounding the tensions between them. Unfortunately – very unfortunately – it does not help to resolve the situation to realize that in almost every instance of such intense factionalism the underlying problem substantially originated in the destructive use and manipulation of reservation lands and peoples by the dominant society, in this instance the polluting, land-destroying effects both of the St. Lawrence seaway and of the kinds of heavy industry that have grown up in the region.

In the midst of this general, widespread, conflict-laden conjunction of Indianness, poverty, and assertiveness is the fact that Tuscarora have been able, some times at least, to have their Indian identity more accepted by other Indians than the Lumbee. This illustrates some basic, underlying paradoxes of Indian identity, for the Tuscarora and the Lumbee are one people in fundamental ways: but as long as the frameworks for forming Indian identities and the criteria by which Indian identities are judged are continually reshaped by the violence of the larger society, then to be an Indian is to have one's own social identity formed and judged both within and against that violence.

VII

The 1970s and 1980s brought dramatic and substantial political and economic gains and were a special time for many people so recently at least partly out from under the heavy thumb of a local White agrarian-based elite and a system of sharecropping, merchants' crop liens, and White domination of all the county offices and programs, and the courts as well. People whose childhood was spent playing in the swept-dirt yards of simple wooden houses, houses perched on cinder or wooden blocks, in the classic southern poor rural style, were now driving big, almost new cars and drawing salaries administering and staffing "programs."

There were more and more programs, and more and more victories. In 1979 Lumbee River Legal Services was founded, with an Indian director – the brilliant lawyer Julian Pierce – and it began to provide effective legal aid to the elderly, to poor people in need of help (Black, White, and Indian), and to take on and successfully prosecute class action suits. Lumbee River Legal Services organized the bulk of the investigative work on the Lumbee recognition petition, entailing a substantial commitment of time, money, and resources, and helped other North Carolina tribes as well. LRDA assembled the tribal roll, increasingly in terms of the BIA's standards. When the petition was submitted, in 1986, the roll included over 36,000 Lumbee, almost all with family ancestry charts.

But all the growth, all the power, all the gains were built on a base that through the 1980s became increasingly fragile. Not that the gains will be completely lost – though some may be – but less controllable events are now bringing the possibility of new kinds of suffering and of the resurgence of old problems.

On April 1, 1986, the *New York Times* reported the opening public move of new and continuing struggles: U.S. Ecology, Inc., planned to build the nation's first commercial incinerator for low-level radioactive waste near the Robeson County town of St. Pauls. In addition:

> *Near Laurinburg, 35 miles from the incinerator site, another company, the GSX Services Corporation, plans to build a large treatment plant for hazardous waste. It would process half a million gallons of toxic waste from 10 states every day, pumping the treated water into the local municipal water treatment plant that empties into the Lumber river.*
>
> *The placement of these two waste-treatment plants, bracketing the boundaries of Robeson County . . . has fueled a dispute between the companies and residents who say they are resisting the plants in an effort to protect their health, the surrounding environment, and their civil rights.*
>
> *The residents contend that their area was selected for the plants because it has a median family income about half the national average and has historically wielded little political power, and because more than half the people are black or American Indian.*
>
> *. . . Spokesmen for GSX and US Ecology . . . categorically deny that the sites were political choices.*
>
> *. . . Dan Jones, director of administrative and public affairs for GSX, said: "We were brought here by the North Carolina Department of Commerce. We selected this spot because it had the proper facilities, including the ability to discharge into a publicly owned waste-water treatment plant.*

Burning nuclear waste on land surrounded by Indian people is new: usually the United States *buries* its radioactive wastes there. As the Lumbee were increasingly recognized as Indians they increasingly came to share directly the situation of other Native Americans. Less than three weeks later the Menominee were in Washington, D.C., to protest using their lands for a nuclear dump. The *New York Times* on April 18, 1986, revealed how the government argues from statistics when Indian well-being is at issue:

> *A delegation of Menominee Indians from Wisconsin is protesting the inclusion of their reservation among a dozen proposed sites for nuclear waste. . . . The timberland of the 7,000 members of the tribe has become one of five Indian reservations under consideration as a subterranean radioactive dump.*
>
> *. . . The other Indians lands on the list are the neighboring Stockbridge-Munsee reservation in Wisconsin and the reservations of the Penobscot and Passamaquoddy in Maine and the Winnebago in Nebraska. Mr. Rusche [director of the Department of Energy's Office of Civilian Radioactive Waste Management] said it was a geological coincidence*

> *that five of the twelve proposed nuclear dump sites were on Indian land.*

These were *proposed* nuclear dumps; eleven of the sixteen present dumps are on or near reservations. The whole intense struggle of the Lumbee and Tuscarora to publicly claim their Indian history and to have this history legally acknowledged is no less intense, and no less heartbreaking in its setbacks, for the fact that claiming their history is also joining the ongoing history of a people who are continually used in destructive ways.

Other kinds of "economic development" were also taking place in Robeson County. In the mid-1970s lumber and paper companies began buying land in the county on a massive scale. By 1986 the Georgia Pacific Corporation owned 12,707 acres, Canal Industries 8,391, Federal Paper Board 5,711, Darlington Veneer 5,412. While land prices soared and smaller farmers were driven out, the old merchant supply houses also intensified their investments in land: McNair Investment Corp. holdings grew to 16,319 acres, Biggs, Inc., to 12,966 acres, Pates Supply 5,500; these supply houses were joined by prosperous White farmers and a few Indians. Altogether, by the mid-1980s less than 250 landholding corporations and individuals owned 257,000 acres of Robeson County: almost half the total land, and well over half the farmable land and accessible timber.

This loss of productive land to corporate interests has brought with it, as usual, a worsening situation for the rural poor: In 1986 several farmers told me that they were demechanizing at least some of their crop production: they said it had become much cheaper to use hand labor than to "bulk" tobacco with machines. For those who are too old, or illiterate, or without a car, or unable for one reason or another to get a factory job, and for whom there is no more land left to tenant farm, there are few choices other than occasional farm "day labor" work at any pay offered.

VIII

By the spring of 1989 the Lumbee were increasingly concerned about the fate of their petition for recognition. The petition had been at the BIA for nearly three years – two large volumes, the massive tribal roll, and a truckload of supporting documents – and the BIA had not yet even responded with the "O.D." letter from an initial review. The BIA has a small staff in its acknowledgment office (two anthropologists, two

273

historians, and two genealogists), and a lot of petitions to process. The Lumbee case was highly charged, not the least because so many Indians were involved. A few hundred native people more or less does not make much difference to Indian Affairs budgets; 36,000 or more Lumbee are another issue completely.

Out of fear that their recognition petition would be tied up at the BIA for years, perhaps a decade or more, that their programs would thus wither, and most crucially, that all the hopes and social momentum generated in the context of enrolling 36,000 people for recognition would be dissipated, Lumbee leaders tried a different strategy. In the summers of 1988 and 1989 they decided to bypass the BIA recognition process – a process called "executive recognition" from the fact that the BIA is part of the executive branch of the federal government – and seek legislative recognition in Congress.

Since 1975 Lumbee had been trying, now with the active assistance of their congressional representative, Charlie Rose, to have the last sentence of the Lumbee act removed. This is the sentence that begins "Nothing in this Act shall make such Indians eligible for any services performed by the United States for Indians. . . ." Twice between 1975 and 1989 a bill to drop this last sentence passed the House of Representatives but failed in the Senate; now they would try again. This time, with their petition resting at the BIA, the stakes were much higher.

In fact the Lumbee were pressured to make the stakes for victory or defeat in Congress very much higher. Concerned that there would be objections to taking the issue to Congress while their petition was at the BIA, and equally concerned that the whole recognition effort would languish at the BIA, the Lumbee themselves took the position, in their testimony to Congress, that the final sentence of the 1956 act precluded the BIA from acting on their petition, so Congress must act.

At the hearings on the bill the Cherokee testified against the Lumbee, as did the Tuscarora; the bill died in committee, and in the turmoil of the attempt the Solicitor General of the United States wrote to the BIA:

> *Oct. 23, 1989 (BIA.IA 0929)*
>
> *To: Deputy to the Assistant Secretary – Indian Affairs (Tribal Services)*
> *From: Associate Solicitor, Indian Affairs*
> *Subject: Lumbee Recognition legislation*
>
> *This responds to your request for assistance in interpreting the Act of July 7, 1956 . . . the "Lumbee Act," in connection with developing a Departmental position on proposed legislation which would extend Federal recognition to the Lumbee Indians of North Carolina as a tribe. . . . Your acknowledgment regulations . . . do not apply "to groups which are, or the members of which are, subject to congressional*

legislation terminating or forbidding the Federal relationship."... Thus the first issue is whether the ... Lumbee Act is legislation "terminating or forbidding the Federal relationship"....

If the Lumbee Act is such legislation, your staff has no authority under your current regulations to act on the extensive petition submitted by the Lumbees. Moreover, even if your regulations were changed, absent Congressional action removing or clarifying the language ... [of] the Lumbee Act, the Federal government would be precluded from providing services or acknowledging a government-to-government relationship based solely on an administrative determination if the Lumbee Act is such legislation.

For the reasons briefly described below, we have concluded that the Department would be exposed to substantial risks of litigation if it provided services or acknowledged a government-to-government relationship with the Lumbee Indians. ... I do not believe that you as a prudent trustee for those Indian tribes which have been acknowledged would be justified in committing the resources at your disposal to reviewing and making an administrative determination on the Lumbee petition knowing that there are unique circumstances surrounding the Lumbees as a result of the prior legislation which make a serious challenge to your determination inevitable. ...

For all the above reasons, I am constrained to advise you that the [Lumbee] Act ... is legislation terminating or forbidding the Federal relationship ... and that, therefore, you are precluded from considering the application of the Lumbees for recognition. ...

Congress, under a variety of pressures, refused to act on this Lumbee Recognition Bill; the BIA, ordered not to act, accordingly shelved the Lumbee petition and the Tuscarora petition as well.

In the spring of 1991 the Lumbee tried again – their energy and optimism surprisingly undiminished, their hopes embedded in hours, days, weeks, and months of detailed planning. With the help of Representative Charlie Rose and Senator Terry Sanford, a pair of bills were introduced "to provide for the recognition of the Lumbee Tribe of Cheraw Indians of North Carolina, and for other purposes" (H.R. 1426 and S. 1036). The "Cheraw" designation was added to this bill partly to satisfy the Federal Acknowledgment Program's requirement for descent from a specific "historic" tribe. The petition for recognition, shelved at the BIA, also used this designation. Cheraw was also the historical identity attributed by the government anthropologist and major scholar of Indian history, John Swanton, in the 1930s – when the Lumbee were on the edge of federal recognition as Siouan Indians of the Lumber River: more specifically, the Siouan-speaking Cheraw.

The label "Cheraw" refers to people who were, before they were largely exterminated by White Carolinians, as fully and completely Indian as any other Native Americans; it also is the name for an eighteenth- and nineteenth-century fantasy in the dominant American society about who or what constituted a Native American people – and the Lumbee are being pressured to claim their historical identity as much in terms of the dominant society's self-serving fantasies as in terms of their own past. For while the Lumbee (and their congeners the Tuscarora) are substantially the descendants of the people known as Cheraw, the Cheraw are more properly understood as a manifestation (of the more complex reality) of the people now largely known as Lumbee.

In an unusual move, designed to speed up and simplify the whole legislative process (which was taken by the Lumbee as a positive sign), Congress condensed the Senate and House hearings on this pair of bills into a "Joint Hearing of the House Committee on Interior and Insular Affairs and the Senate Select Committee on Indian Affairs." The hearings took place August 1, 1991. LRDA brought a large delegation to testify and to witness, and they mobilized warmly supportive testimony from the North Carolina governor's office, the Menominee (who had suffered termination and could testify with sensitivity and passion about the importance of federal government support), the Oneida Indian tribe of Wisconsin, and the Tunica-Biloxi of Louisiana. Arlinda Locklear, the tribal attorney, made such a powerful statement that she was especially recognized and applauded by the committee, and she was buttressed and supported by Ruth Locklear, the director of Lumbee Tribal Enrollment, Dr. Jack Campesi, and by dignified and moving statements from Mr. Adolph Blue, chairman of the Board of Directors of LRDA, Dr. Welton Lowery, chairman of the Lumbee Elders Review Committee, and the very special and very old Rev. Johnnie Bullard, who spent much of the night before, after the long trip to Washington, praying for guidance.

The Lumbee were opposed in testimony by Mr. Vermon Locklear, chairman of the Hatteras Tuscarora Tribe – and his famous, but not very hardworking pro-bono lawyer – and Mr. Waters, an attorney and lobbyist representing the Eastern Band of Cherokee Indians, who put a great deal of work into opposing the Lumbee, insisting that they be referred back to the BIA. Cherokee opposition included invoking Lumbee legislative defeats with somewhat similar bills in 1989 and 1990, and among other objections they pointed out (erroneously) that recognition would cost the federal government 106 million dollars annually for Indian services, and that these funds were not likely to come out of the Pentagon's budget.

The Lumbee were also opposed by the BIA, insisting that Congress only pass a bill that allowed the Lumbee to be considered by the regular BIA acknowledgment channels – and further insisting, under aggressive and disbelieving questioning by several senators and congresspeople, that they would and could do a competent and quick review. The BIA also asserted, strongly and repeatedly and to the obvious anger of several senators, who did not like being confronted on such grounds, that they would recommend, through the secretary of the interior, that the president veto any legislation that Congress might pass on behalf of the Lumbee other than legislation allowing the BIA to proceed with its review of the petition.

On September 26, 1991, the House of Representatives voted for the Lumbee Recognition Bill, 263 to 154. The Senate Select Committee reported the Senate version of the same bill to the full Senate on November 20, with a vote of 9 to 5 recommending Senate passage. One senator requested, successfully, that the Senate consideration be delayed until the next session, in the spring of 1992.

It is not at all clear what then will happen. Individual senators who object to legislation can be more effectively disruptive than can representatives; North Carolina's senior senator, the agressively conservative Jesse Helms, has not publicly announced either support or opposition, and the fear is that he will oppose, being more inclined to favor the Cherokee than the Lumbee. The Lumbee are not waiting quietly to see what the outcome will be. LRDA sent a substantial delegation to the December 1991 meetings of the National Congress of American Indians, seeking support, and is also seeking to consolidate support in the Senate and to diminish opposition from the BIA and thus the possibility, in the event of Senate passage, of presidential veto. Hope dances – with its breath held – across an unpredictably turning balance beam.

The Lumbee may or may not win this round or the next. If they lose they will clearly fight again, on the same terrain or in the courts, either for direct recognition or to be allowed to go through the BIA acknowledgment process. Meanwhile the BIA, during the fall of 1991 – partly under congressional pressure, which was in evidence in the Lumbee hearings, and partly under pressure from both recognized Indian groups (who generally want the procedures tightened), and a number of petitioners (who want the procedures and criteria clarified) – has begun a substantial revision in the whole recognition process. If the Lumbee win – both Senate passage and presidential assent – they will instantly be confronted with other necessary struggles that have important consequences and uncertain outcomes. In order to deal with the fears of some Native American peoples that such a large group as the Lumbee would, if recognized, greatly reduce their portion of the federal funds for Native Americans, the Lumbee added to this recognition legislation a proviso that they would make no claims on existing federal Indian funds, but would tie all their future claims to federal budgetary increases for the Bureau of Indian Affairs and the Indian Health Service – not likely candidates for congressional largesse.

Conclusions
Living Indian history – With "heretofore unquestioned" rights

I

The most haunting issue I have faced in the quarter-century that I have worked with and thought about Native American peoples is the question: How do people who have lost so many struggles manage to keep struggling?

The whole of their situation makes this a question about history, or more precisely about ethnohistory: What is there in their relations to each other and to the dominant society that enables Native Americans to build and rebuild understandings of the past and of the future in ways that permit or encourage them to continue to try to take hold of both? In this question lies the most generally relevant lesson to be learned by an anthropology of and for ethnic peoples, and also the most general sense of respect for the peoples whose continuing struggles such an anthropology must be witness to, and at times, within.

No simple or single explanation can be given; at best I can put forward what seem to me to be some useful components for understanding this issue.

To begin, Native American peoples have had to continue to struggle just to continue to exist. Across the entire gamut of their distinctiveness within the dominant society – and for much of their history during and since the colonial period, also their distinctiveness from one another – native peoples have been continually and inescapably challenged. These challenges have been particularly forceful where distinctiveness is a foundation for, or emerges from, any kind of substantial social autonomy, including the collective possession of land, self-governance, and different religious practices.

While such challenges, it must be stressed, are pervasive, unavoidable, and for very high stakes, they are *not at all* the basis or the framework for the struggles between native peoples and the dominant society. To claim such would be to simplify native histories, to reduce the complexities of the problem to superficiality, and most of all to fail to grasp the multiple ways that internal struggles within native societies – or indeed within any dominated ethnic people – take their shape and their significance.

The core of the situation is that the social, cultural, and political distinctiveness of native peoples, so intensely a focus of contestation with the larger society, is and has long been insisted upon, indeed generated, by the very social forces that seek to undermine or destroy it. While it is often claimed that the expansion and consolidation of state power, and also the origin, expansion, and consolidation of capitalist relations of production, undermine, trivialize, and ultimately erase the social variation they encounter, they also, and simultaneously, depend upon and create such variation.

We have seen, particularly in the discussion of the colonial encounters, that processes of domination and the use of native peoples developed, elaborated, and embellished a wide range of differences between native and colonial societies and between increasingly divergent kinds of native societies. We have also seen the multiple ways that such differences were appropriated – how the dominant society sought to incorporate this emergent differentiation into its own political and economic schemes, using it and destroying it at the same time; and how native peoples sought to use and develop, in their own ways and for their own purposes, this same emergent differentiation – in opposition, in collusion, in alliances of many diverse kinds and in assault: in multiple ways that were necessarily various, necessarily fluid, and necessarily associated with intensifying and changing internal antagonisms and alliances.

The first point, in sum – which does not at all answer our question, but only leads us toward an answer – is that native peoples must continue to struggle and that these struggles must continue to divide native peoples, partly antagonistically, from one another. One reason why this is so is that none of the available strategies for coping with domination can possibly be very effective, or effective for very long. Isolation, confrontation, accommodation, opposition: all have their partial successes and their costs, their adherents and their opponents.

Moreover, and more to the point here, it is not clear that unity is an unambiguous benefit. Without at all denying or minimizing the pain that internal disunity and internal antagonism cause, nor minimizing the point that internal disunity weakens a people and can make them

280

even more vulnerable, we must still address the issue that unity facilitates use.

In the late 1960s, when I was working with Indian people in the voter registration and civil rights drives, we were desperate for some financial and legal-political support. At that point in time, still opposed by the local "White power structure" (as the Indian activists called it) and by the traditional Indian locality leaders, we were running ourselves ragged in the voter registration drive alone. One weekend Mr. Thadis Oxendine and I drove over 300 miles and brought fifteen people to be registered; thousands more were still unregistered. Mr. Thadis went to see some state politicians he knew, looking for aid (both funds and some easing of the registration procedures), but got disappointingly small support. When he returned and came to an Indian strategy meeting, he said to us that he was told: "Go home and get yourselves together. *As long as you're not together no one can use you.*" So people tried, intensely and unsuccessfully, to get together. Only much later did any of us, myself included, realize the deep ambiguity and danger that resides within being used. It seemed, and it was in fact the case, that so much was lost in not being together, in not being useable, that it was at first hard to see the whole issue clearly.

People do not choose unity or disunity in order to make themselves useful or to distance themselves from use; they split and combine from other causes and with other outcomes in the balance. One of the pressures on native peoples that often engenders splits is the *changing* ways that ethnic otherness is integrated into, used, and also marginalized and made useless by the larger society, and the changing opportunities and costs this creates for native people. The emergence, resolution, and reemergence of internal divisions among native peoples, in the context and as an aspect of changing relations to the larger society, brings "history" to the foreground – especially "history" as the uncertain, problematic, negotiable, and necessarily contestable connections to be made or denied between past, present, and impending future.

II

Native American peoples have long confronted situations where the denial of their history – particularly the history of their relations with the larger society – plays a crucial role in the assault on their autonomy. One particular form of deniable and denied history is legal precedent, and both the directness and the consequences of such denials are often stunning. Indeed, the denial of precedent and history forms the core of the legal decision that has shaped much of the situation of Native Americans in the United States: the famous decision of John Marshall, chief justice of the Supreme Court, in *Cherokee Nation* v. *The State of Georgia*, 1831. This decision established the devastating notion of Indian societies as "domestic dependent nations" (in this case used to deny the Cherokee standing to pursue their rights in the Supreme Court, open to direct appeal only by *foreign* nations). The same decision also held that Indians were wards of the state: in some sense, to be treated as perpetual children who could not grow up; who could generate no historical process among and for themselves. The judgment stated:

> *This bill* [the suit] *is brought by the Cherokee Nation, praying an injunction to restrain the state of Georgia from the execution of certain laws of that state, which, as is alleged, go directly to annihilate the Cherokees as a political society. . . .*
>
> *If courts were permitted to indulge their sympathies, a case better calculated to excite them can scarcely be imagined. A people once numerous, powerful, and truly independent, found by our ancestors in the quiet and uncontrolled* [a truly revealing "slip": the usual legal phrase is "quiet and uncontested"] *possession of an ample domain, gradually sinking beneath our superior policy, our arts and our arms, have yielded their lands by successive treaties, each of which contains a solemn guarantee of the residue, until they retain no more of their formerly extensive territory than is deemed necessary to their comfortable subsistence. . . .*
>
> *. . . So much of the argument as was intended to prove the character of the Cherokees as a state, as a distinct political society, separated from others, capable of managing its own affairs and governing itself, has, in the opinion of a majority of the judges, been completely successful. They have uniformly been treated as a state from the settlement of our country. The numerous treaties made with them by the United States recognize them as a people capable. . . .*
>
> *Though the Indians are acknowledged to have an unquestionable, and, heretofore unquestioned right to the lands they occupy. . . yet it may well be doubted whether those tribes which reside within the acknowledged boundaries of the United States can, with strict accuracy, be denominated foreign nations. They may more correctly be denominated domestic dependent nations. They occupy a territory to which we assert a title independent of their will, which must take effect in point of possession when their right of possession ceases. Meanwhile, they are in a state of pupilage. Their relation to the United States resembles that of a ward to his guardian.*

> *They look to our government for protection; rely upon its kindness and its power; appeal to it for relief to their wants; and address the president as their great father. . . .*
>
> *The court has bestowed its best attention on this question, and, after mature deliberation, the majority is of the opinion that . . .*
>
> *The motion for an injunction is denied.*

This is far from a unique instance, and far from restricted to the Cherokee. The Lumbee, to recall a point from Chapter 12, were held eligible to receive special Indian funds by the comptroller general. On August 1, 1979, he wrote that the Lumbee act "constitutes neither Congressional recognition of the Lumbee as Indians . . . nor Congressional direction that they be denied benefits." This opinion was consistent with the opinion in the case of Maynor v. *Morton*, where the federal courts held that the Lumbee act did not terminate the relationship of Indian people of Robeson County, as Indians, to the federal government. Yet ten years later the associate solicitor of Indian Affairs, in an opinion for the solicitor general, asserted that the Lumbee act is "legislation terminating or forbidding the Federal relationship," and so prevented the BIA from even considering the Lumbee petition (or the Tuscarora, caught up in the same net).

Denying precedent loosens some of the constraints on power, making it even more arbitrary and total. There are times and places where precedent is denied – as in the Supreme Court, or when Congress unilaterally abrogated both Indian treaties and the treaty-making process – and the denial seems irreversible. There are other instances when it seems as if a direct challenge to the rejection of precedent might be possible, as in the case of the Lumbee petition and the blocking opinion of an associate solicitor. I find it surprising that in these cases at least such direct challenges are not more often made – just as it was surprising that no one challenged the declaration that single-shot voting would no longer be allowed.

Although there may at times be good strategic reasons for not pursuing such challenges – in the case of the petition, for instance, it helped bring the issue directly before Congress – the failure to develop such confrontations points toward a more general, underlying process that should be raised to the foreground for at least brief consideration.

Ethnic histories are inevitably histories of ruptures, from the origin of ethnic groups either in major population dislocations or in a usually brutal and relatively sudden incorporation into the political and cultural economies of an expanding state. Further, the more vulnerable ethnic peoples, such as Native Americans or African-Americans, have

283

histories that characteristically are marked by continuing sudden and substantial changes in their circumstances and situation. Behind these continuing ruptures and breaks are often found long-term trends that have to do with how minority ethnic peoples are incorporated into and simultaneously marginalized by the larger society – for instance the violent confinement of Native Americans to reservations and the subsequent brutal reduction of native social life on the reservations by land-allotment policies and intensified missionary control, or the more or less forced exodus of African-Americans from the rural south into, and then relatively quickly out of, northern urban industrial and manufacturing employment. From such continuing pressures, manifest in continuing, imposed ruptures (and the internal divisiveness that constantly accompanies such events), vulnerable ethnic peoples are constantly forced to learn and relearn how to situate themselves historically across, rather than impossibly against, the breaks that power imposes. Often this seems to be accomplished by encapsulating histories within intensely local social forms (such as families or church associations) and simultaneously by developing diffuse historical visions of internally unantagonistic ethnic collectivities (we Lumbee, we Indians, we Blacks). But what matters most are not the solutions to the tensions that continuing ruptures create, but rather the point that people's senses of the possible, of the relation between hopes and accommodations, are necessarily formed both within and against continuing ruptures, breaks and imposed denials of relevant and meaningful pasts. The legal or legislative denial of precedent, in sum, is a significant part of what it means to be a Native American in the United States – and a significant part of how this meaning is taught to, and opposed by, Native Americans.

The whole Federal Acknowledgment Program is, in important ways, another expression of the deniability of Native American histories, for native peoples are required to coordinate (and to document) their past experiences with the conceptions and perceptions of Indian "tribal" histories that are held by the dominant society. This acknowledgment process, on the surface about entitlement and acceptance, is also both subtly and pervasively demeaning. Thus, perhaps, people come to turn away from, rather than confront, the denials they encounter.

But they turn away and yet continue to struggle. No sooner was the petition shelved than the Lumbee were before Congress, the Tuscarora right after them; while they were losing one battle before Congress they were mobilizing for the next. Such powers of regeneration are themselves a victory. That brings us back to the question that opened these conclusions, which was a question about people's relations to one another, and how these relations become a well-spring for active and continuing engagement with the production of history.

The continuity of this struggle in the midst of continuing, partial defeats should call our attention to some fundamental problems in the anthropological concept of culture. The notion of culture as "shared values" should not be taken to be a simple fact of social life; rather, it delineates a terrain of necessary struggle. Just as the notion of class is historically meaningless unless it is understood to point toward processes of struggle and change, so also the notion of culture, of shared values, must be understood to be about who is going to share what sorts of values, in what ways, why, and with what effects.

III

The two features of Lumbee and Tuscarora social life that have most forcefully imprinted themselves on my mind are the intensity with which they express respect for one another in daily life and ordinary discourse – the continual use, even among friends and close acquaintances, of the titles Miss and Mr., along with first names – and on the other side, the violence to one another; the killings in particular.

The two are *not* directly connected. Mutual respect does not come from fear of violence, although some respect from the dominant society, or at least caution, may be so derived; nor does respect seem, in any way, an antidote for violence. What connections there are between respect and violence come from the origin of both in the wide range of oppression and abuses continually endured.

Yet complex connections between respect and violence do exist, and are strategically significant. "Violence" names but one form of a long-standing problem among oppressed peoples. The broadest and most general sense of the term points toward the way oppressed people are led to do harm to one another – to abuse, destroy, dominate, oppress, and exploit one another in the same or in similarly situated groups. This ordinarily happens from a surprisingly large range of motivations and causes, including collusion with larger dominant and oppressive social forces; in the context of resistance to these larger forces of domination; in the context of the self-hatred and collective self-destruction that so often comes to characterize aspects of oppressed people's sense of self and their relations to each other; from other causes as well.

Mutual respect and mutual violence are both forms and ways of living histories. Histories of abuse, of fear, of hope, of struggle, of reward – all permeate both relations of respect and of rage. Of the two, respect is probably the more historically conscious and the more explicit in its invocation of certain kinds of history; especially the recognition of each other's life histories in the context of a shared, larger history. To call a friend Mr. or Miss is to silently name the contexts in which people are rarely called by their titles, to mutually separate yourselves from these contexts, and to partly heal the wounds. Mutual respect is a central form of autonomous precedent, of bringing people's past within the present as a worthy model for the future, for respect is earned, not automatic.

Thus I have come to understand that a crucial component of helping people to organize to claim control of their history entails helping people build the kinds of social relations that solidify their ongoing forms of respect for one another.

But two problems emerge with this strategy. First, respect is often interwoven with being "respectable" by the values of the larger society, and *respectful* of these values – values that can be very destructive to the poor and the needy, the even more vulnerable among one's own people. Second, respect is often accorded to "success," including success at the kinds of economic "development" that enhances the inequality – the class formation processes – among ethnic people. Such class-formative internal inequalities are ordinarily tightly interwoven with the increased integration of an ethnic people into larger structures of domination, exploitation and humiliation.

The paradoxes of mutual respect, simultaneously and in specific ways enhancing the dignity and autonomy of a people and yet – especially if framed within the values of a larger social order – making them more vulnerable to outside pressures, constitute one of the central, current, history-shaping contradictions of ethnic peoples' political situation, and one of the central strategic problems before us.

To suggest approaches for the further development of effective strategies: to begin, we must call into question the anthropological notion of culture as "shared values." This concept is simplistic, for people (especially here Native Americans and African Americans) must – just in their ordinary lives and not as an explicitly "political" act – struggle against and learn *not* to share some of the values of the dominant society and of each other. Further, the notion of culture as shared values implicitly takes the point of view of the powerful and particularly of the state, which operate both on this assumption and toward this end. We should thus pay more attention to culture both as an arena of struggle not just between but within ethnic groups and classes, and as a wholly integral part of other transformative projects. Since culture does not float in a space of its own, but is rooted in social relations, this entails developing forms and processes of opposition to domination and exploitation that are rooted in, and confront, the tensions and antagonisms *among* an ethnic people or – equally – *within* a working class.

287

Sources and perspectives

In discussing the sources and perspectives for this work I have sought to accomplish two goals: to identify the location of relevant quotations and specific data and to indicate the contexts from which my interpretations emerged. I have not usually cited widely known sources when I took no specific point from them directly, except when discussing the background for the more general interpretations. The discussion of sources is organized by chapter; Roman numerals refer to chapter sections.

A few abbreviations are used:

BIA	Bureau of Indian Affairs, U.S. Department of the Interior.
BPRO	British Public Record Office.
BT	Board of Trade, Great Britain.
Col Rec NC	*The Colonial Records of North Carolina*, William L. Saunders, ed., Raleigh 1886–90. Subsequent editions are often cataloged as North Carolina, the State Records; there is now a second series, continuing Saunders, published by the North Carolina State Department of Cultural Affairs, Division of Archives and History, 1974–.
CSSH	*Comparative Studies in Society and History*.
LRDA	Lumbee Regional Development Association.
SC DAH	South Carolina, Department of Archives and History.
USGPO	Washington, D.C., U.S. Government Printing Office.

The source for the first epigraph is Frederick Binder, *The Color Problem in Early National America* (The Hague, Mouton, 1968). The second epigraph is from James Mooney, *The Ghost Dance Religion and the Sioux Outbreak of 1890*, pt. 2, Fourteenth Annual Report of the Bureau of American Ethnology to the Secretary of the Smithsonian Institution, 1892–93 (USGPO, 1896).

Preface

Most of the issues raised in the preface are more fully discussed below, and will be referenced in those contexts. A few introductory notes are more appropriate here.

I My writing about the Lumbee began with my Ph.D. dissertation, "The Political History of the Lumbee Indians of Robeson County, North Carolina: A Case Study of Ethnic Political Affiliations" (New School for Social Research,

288

1971). Little from the dissertation remains here, save the attempt to come to grips with the history of identity that power insists must be contestable. The dissertation that Karen Blu began while we were in the field, and the book it became – *The Lumbee Problem: The Making of an American Indian people* (New York, Cambridge University Press, 1980) – is an insightful study of the Lumbee, although crafted out of a different approach to explanation.

The issue of the formation and transformation of ethnic groups and identities is condensed from my essay, "Wenn Papagaein Sprechen Lernen," in Alf Lüdtke, ed., *Herrschaft als Sozial Praxis* (Göttingen, Vandenhoeck & Ruprecht, 1991). A condensed version of this study, in English, has been published as "When Parrots Learn to Talk, and Why They Can't: Domination, Deception and Self-Deception in Indian–White Relations" *CSSH*, 29 (January 1987): 3–23. In brief, at the center of processes of ethnic group formation are two interwoven contradictions: for the colonizers "the impossibility and the necessity of creating the other as the other – the different, the alien – and incorporating the other within a single social and cultural system of domination"; for the colonized it is the contradiction between "distancing oneself from domination and engaging with domination to struggle against it" (1987, p. 7). All of this takes shape and form on a terrain of *use* – of the multiple and competing uses to which diverse kinds of colonists tried to bind Native Americans, as "Indians" of particular kinds – and the negotiations and contestations within and between Native Americans over the kinds and purposes of alliances and oppositions they would engage, especially when the material basis of their autonomy depended upon what they could secure through one kind of alliance or another.

Morton Fried, *The Notion of Tribe* (Menlo Park, Calif., Cummings, 1975), remains one of the most important works of historical anthropology for this perspective. Jeremy Beckett, *Torres Strait Islanders: Custom and Colonialism* (Cambridge, Cambridge University Press, 1987), is particularly useful on the same processes in a different political-economic context. His argument is brought forward, and extended to mainland Australia, in his "Walter Newton's History of the World – or Australia," forthcoming, *American Ethnologist*.

The *necessary* creation and elaboration of the ambiguous and total otherness of the dominated is important to understand conceptually because it is so crucial politically. I have found the most useful general sources on this to be Owen Lattimore, "The Frontier in History," in *Studies in History* (London, Oxford University Press 1962); Jean-Paul Sartre, *Anti-Semite and Jew* [orig: *Reflexions sur la Question Juive*, Paris 1946] (New York, Grove, 1960); Franz Fanon, *The Wretched of the Earth* (New York, Grove, 1963); and for the multiple ways that fear, hate, rage, and use come together, with what effects, Joseph Conrad's *Heart of Darkness* is essential. For Native Americans four sources have been particularly helpful: Roy Harvey Pearce, *Savagism and Civilization: A Study of the Indian and the American Mind* (Berkeley, University of California Press, 1988; rev. ed. of *The Savages of America*, 1953); Perry Miller, "Nature and the National Ego," in *Errand into the Wilderness* (Cambridge, Mass., Harvard University Press, 1965); Michael Paul Rogin, "Liberal Society and the Indian Question," in *Fathers and Children* (New York, Random House, 1975); and William Christie MacLeod, "Celt and Indian: Britain's Old World Frontier in Relation to the New," in *The American Indian Frontier* (New York, Knopf, 1928). For a particularly revealing study of the way anthropology has taken the otherness of its usual subjects for granted, see Patrick Wolfe, "On Being Woken Up: The

Sources and perspectives

Dreamtime in Anthropology and Australian Settler Culture," *CSSH* 33 (April 1991): 197–224.

II The principal difference between the way the analysis of the political culture of ethnicity is developed here and the way it was approached in "When Parrots Learn to Talk . . ." centers on how history is conceptualized. The perspective on history and histories, and on history and anthropology that is presented here, was developed over the past several years in the context of a series of conferences on "the production of history: silences and commemorations" organized by the working group in anthropology and history at the Max Planck Institut für Geschichte, in Göttingen. (The papers from this conference series will be published under that title, edited by Gavin Smith and myself.) Particularly influential has been Hans Medick, " 'Missionaries in a Rowboat'?: Ethnological Ways of Knowing as a Challenge to Social History," *CSSH* 29 (January 1987): 76–98; Alf Lüdtke, "Flowers and Stones: Monuments to the Killed," a crucial study of histories and history, which will be published in the conference volume, as will David William Cohen's important background paper for the conference, "The Production of History."

The history of everyday life, particularly the way ordinary life is conjoined and disjoined from both the explicit and the quiet brutalities of power, has been a special concern for German historians, who have sought to develop a critical understanding of daily life, particularly in the contexts of early modern villages, proto-industrialization and Nazi power. They have raised issues that seem crucial for the development of anthropology. An excellent introduction to the development of "daily life history" in Germany, and to how it differs from what in England and America is called "social history," can be found in Geoff Eley, "Labor History, Social History, *Alltagsgeschichte*: Experience, Culture and the Politics of the Everyday – A New Direction for German Social History?" *J. Modern History* 61 (June 1989): 297–343. Less explicit methodological discussions, but with several useful and thought-provoking exemplars, can be found in Hans Medick and David W. Sabean, eds., *Interest and Emotion: Essays on the Study of Family and Kinship* (New York, Cambridge University Press, 1984). See also *Golden Ages, Dark Ages: Imagining the Past in Anthropology and History*, ed. Jay O'Brien and William Roseberry (Berkeley, University of California Press, 1991). The editors' "Introduction" offers an anthropological perspective that is both informed by, and partly divergent from, the "daily life history" approaches; further, they usefully address general issues for understanding the multiple ways that seemingly "natural" categories (race, gender, ethnicity) are historically specific. My essay in this volume, "House and History at the Margins of Life," seeks to clarify and refocus the range of methodological approaches that anthropologists have called "ethnohistory" by shifting the emphasis to how the people being studied produce and silence their own historical knowledge – their own histories of gender and ethnicity.

Part one Introductions

Chapter 1 Within and against history

I A general overview of the name changes of the Lumbee people can be found in my Ph.D. dissertation, "The Political History of The Lumbee Indians" and in Karen Blu, *Lumbee Problem.* Of special interest on this topic is Adolph Dial and David Eliades, *The Only Land I Know: A History of the Lumbee Indians* (San Francisco, Indian Historian Press, 1975). Professor Dial is a descendant of some of the people active in the identity struggles of the late nineteenth and early twentieth centuries.

The most detailed description of the legislation relevant to Lumbee legal identity and of the hearings surrounding this legislation is, unfortunately, not at the moment generally available. It is the petition for recognition, in two volumes, submitted in 1986 by Lumbee River Legal Services to the Branch of Acknowledgment and Research, the Bureau of Indian Affairs, 1986. *The Lumbee Petition, Prepared by Lumbee River Legal Services, Inc., in Cooperation with the Lumbee Tribal Enrollment Office, Lumbee Regional Development Association.* The authors are listed on the title page as Julian T. Pierce, Cynthia Hunt Locklear; Consultants Dr. Jack Campesi, Mr. Wesley White. The petition took more than six years of intense work by many people to produce, and Jack Campesi did very much more than consult; the title page reflects other concerns.

The Ickes quotation can be found in U.S. Senate, Committee on Indian Affairs, Rept. 204, 1934.

III The best introduction to the enslavement of Indians in the colonial southeast, for shipment to the Caribbean, is still Verner Crane, *The Southern Frontier* (Madison, University of Wisconsin Press, 1926; with various reprints); particularly useful are his citations, which form a guide to the original records. William Christie MacLeod's comparison of the conquest of the Scots highlands and islands, and Ireland as well, and the conquest of the Indians, plus his remarks on the enslavement of Irish and Indians, provides a stunning perspective on the creation and destruction of ethnic hinterlands: "Celt and Indian" in his *The American Indian Frontier.*

IV The starting point for an understanding of the political and historical dynamics of the practices that come to be regarded, by observers and by the people themselves, as "tradition" is Eric Hobsbawm and Terence Ranger, eds., *The Invention of Tradition* (New York, Cambridge University Press, 1983). The book has two strange omissions: it does not discuss the simultaneous developments in "the invention of tradition" and the formation of class; and does not address traditions that are invented "from below." Here part of this is engaged, but in the context of the formation of "racial" and ethnic identities, not class.

The distinction between the social relations of work and the social relations of production, and the dynamics of their connections, has been central to my studies of Newfoundland, except in the first essay, "Christmas Mumming in Outport Newfoundland" (*Past and Present* 1976), where it was not yet understood. The usefulness of the distinction is directly addressed in my *Culture and Class in Anthropology and History* (New York, Cambridge University Press, 1986), esp. chap. 5, "When Fishermen May Starve. . . ."

On "civil war" among native peoples: this painful, crucial subject has hardly been faced. The most direct starting point for further work is Richard White, *The Roots of Dependency* (Lincoln, University of Nebraska Press, 1983), especially the chapters on the Choctaw. For all its flaws, including a simplistic sense of the boundaries between "different" groups, George T. Hunt's *Wars of the Iroquois* (Madison, University of Wisconsin Press, 1967 [1940]) is important for perceiving the speed and the intensity with which tensions among and between native peoples developed.

Chapter 2 Toward and past recognition

I, II The regulations governing the recognition process were published in the *Federal Register* 43, no. 172 (Sept. 5, 1978): 39361–4. An overview of the history of federal laws regarding Indians is presented in Felix Cohen, *Handbook of Federal Indian Law*, Rennard Strickland, ed. (Charlottesville, Va., Michie, 1982). On the implications of the trade and intercourse acts, and Thomas Tureen's precedent-establishing cases, see Paul Brodeur, *Restitution: The Land Claims of the Mashpee, Passamaquoddy and Penobscot Indians of New England* (Boston, Northeastern University Press, 1985).

The discussion of participant observation benefited from the discussion of ambiguity in Kenneth Burke's "Introduction" to his *A Grammar of Motives and A Rhetoric of Motives* (Cleveland, World/Meridian, 1962), especially:

> *We take it for granted that insofar as men cannot themselves create the universe, there must remain something essentially enigmatic about the problem of motives. . . . What we want is not terms that avoid ambiguity, but terms that clearly reveal the strategic spots at which ambiguities necessarily arise. . . .*
>
> *We . . . consider it our task to study and clarify the resources of ambiguity. For in the course of this work, we shall deal with many kinds of transformation – and it is in the area of ambiguity that transformations take place.*

The critique of "subcultures" here is much influenced by Eleanor B. Leacock's dismay over the notion of a "culture of poverty." See in particular, her introduction to her edited volume, *The Culture of Poverty* (New York, Simon and Schuster, 1971). Eleanor Leacock was Kenneth Burke's daughter; this section is my tribute to that special family.

Chapter 3 Elements of the known

I This chapter comes directly from my own work in Robeson County; it seeks to capture what people tried to teach me in the context of our political organizing and what people assumed that any rational adult knew. There is an extended analysis of locality leaders in my "Political History," cited above, and a discussion of their collapse in my "Lumbee Indian Cultural Nationalism and Ethnogenesis," *Dialectical Anthropology*, vol. 1, no. 2 (1976): 161–72. On highly local linguistic variation, see Blu, *Lumbee Problem.*

II The organization of sectional politics in nineteenth- and early twentieth-century North Carolina is well introduced in V. O. Key, Jr., *Southern Politics* (New York, Knopf, 1949), esp. chap. 10, "North Carolina: Progressive Plutocracy." Also useful for a general overview, despite its organization as an apology for domination, is the standard "house" history: Hugh T. Lefler and Albert R. Newsome, *North Carolina: The History of a Southern State* (Chapel Hill, North Carolina University Press, 1963).

On town boundaries, town services, and African-American residential areas see, for example, the *Robesonian*, March 31, 1958, "Negro Civic Organization Asks about City Policies": "In the Negro residential areas of our city, long established parts, we find many streets without water. . . . [I]n the city of

Lumberton there is not one street in the Negro residential areas that has been paved. . . . Why can't we get sewage?" This is in the county seat, and refers only to areas within the town limits. In the smaller towns, African-American densely settled neighborhoods, at the end of the 1960s, still had water-well pumps in front of the house and outhouses in the back, about 10 meters distant.

III The population figures come from U.S., Bureau of the Census, *Census of Population: 1960, Final Report, Characteristics of the Population*, PC(1)-35 A,B,C,D (USGPO, 1961); and Census of Population, 1970, vol. 1, *Characteristics of Population*, pt. 35, North Carolina (USGPO, 1973).

IV The remarks here about integrated education benefit from my discussions, in the 1960s, with Dr. Peter Newcomer.

Part two The embers of hope

Chapter 4 Challenges to respect

The descriptions of the incidents come primarily from three sources: my own notes and two local newspapers: the *Carolina Indian Voice*, a weekly paper published by Lumbee in Pembroke, North Carolina, and *The Robesonian*, the newspaper published daily in Lumberton, the county seat. Both are on microfilm, with collections at the Pembroke State University library and the Robeson County library in Lumberton. Bruce Barton, the editor of the *Carolina Indian Voice* since the early 1970s, has published a compilation of his editorial columns, "As I See It": *An Indian Manifesto* (Pembroke, N.C., Carolina Indian Voice Publishers, 1983).

The analysis of how sharecropping and credit are organized was developed in the context of my work with the North Carolina Mobility Project. Horace Locklear, Roderick Locklear, Ronald Revels, Thadis Oxendine, and Mrs. Vera Lowery all spent many hours taking me into sharecroppers' homes, and Dr. Martin L. Brooks, whose patients included a large number of sharecroppers, alerted me to the manipulations of supply companies. James Agee and Walker Evans's book about sharecroppers, *Let Us Now Praise Famous Men: Three Tenant Families* (Boston, Houghton Mifflin, 1969 [1941]), taught me to look at fear with respect. Theodore Rosengarten's *All God's Dangers: The Life of Nate Shaw* (New York, Knopf, 1974) is a fine testimony to the capacity of people to claim their dignity and humanity in the midst of such systems as sharecropping and provides a good overview of how sharecropping was organized to control labor and lives; but the person Rosengarten calls "Nate Shaw" – Ned Cobb – and his family were special people, and my focus was more on people with fewer, more ordinary strengths and resources.

Chapter 5 The fires of race

I The description of Old Main burning is from the *Robesonian* (3/19/73), p. 1. The poem about this is from Adolph Dial and David Eliades, *The Only Land I Know*. Their discussion of the Save Old Main movement is on pp. 163–71; the poem at p. 170.

II The laws pertaining to education in Robeson County are all from North Carolina, *Public Laws*.

III The Goins case, central to the founding of the "Smilings," is excerpted from NC Supreme Court, Fall Term 1915, 296; Judgement and Record on Appeal. I owe most of my knowledge of the recent history of the Smilings to A. Bruce Jones, who began his professional career, shortly after graduating from Pembroke State College, as the principal of the two-room Smiling school, and the teacher of all the high school sciences in this school.

IV For the history of Robeson County education, see Clifton Oxendine, "A Social and Economic History of the Indians of Robeson County, N.C.," Master's thesis, George Peabody College for Teachers, Nashville, Tenn. (1934), pp. 26 ff. Oxendine became the Dean at Pembroke State College. Also Blu, *Lumbee Problem*, p. 245.

V C. Vann Woodward, *The Strange Career of Jim Crow* (New York, Oxford University Press, [2d rev. ed.] 1966), is a useful introduction to the institution-alization of segregation. Dated in its concepts and of limited depth, this book remains an important study of the speed at which basic social arrangements can change. The swirl of events around the names "Croatan" and "Cro" in the first decade of the twentieth century occurred in this same social context of the most intense and rapid institutionalization of "Jim Crow" legislation.

VI H. W. Guion's testimony is taken from U.S. Senate, Report of the Committee to Investigate the Condition of Affairs in the Late Insurrectionary States, 1872, vol. 2, pt. 2 (North Carolina), p. 245 (cited henceforth as *Condition of Affairs*). Albert Beveridge's Senate speech can be found in Richard N. Current et al., eds., *Words That Made American History*, 3d ed. (Boston, Little Brown, 1972), vol. 2, pp. 232–8.

VII I have been asked, by people resident in the community who have read this manuscript, not to cite the court case that is here called the Jacob Moll case in ways that would identify some of the participants.

The Croatan/Croatoan quotation from John White can be found in a number of anthologies of colonial documents, the earliest being Capt. John Smith, *The Generall Historie of Virginia, New-England and the Summer Isles. . .* , (London, 1624), p.15 This is one of a substantial number of early colonial texts photographically reprinted from the originals by University Microfilms in the 1960s, in the *March of America Facsimile Series* – an unfortunately too brief democratization of access to research source materials. This one is MAF 18, 1966.

McAllister's testimony on behalf of the Robeson County Board of Education is in the North Carolina State Archives, Supreme Court Records, 12 SE 330; 107 North Carolina 609; 10 LRA 823. I am much indebted to Wesley White, who found this trial record in the archives.

The most useful general overview of the early history of recognition, and the several origin traditions, is in O. M. McPherson, *Indians of North Carolina: A Report on the Conditions and Tribal Rights of the Indians of Robeson and Adjoining Counties of North Carolina*. U.S. Senate Document 667, 63d Cong., 3d sess. (USGPO, 1915). Most of this extensive report is composed of reprints of earlier documents and legislation relevant to the Indian people of Robeson County.

Chapter 6 The embers of Hope, Inc.

II The anti-single-shot regulations, and other formal procedures for elections, are in Henry W. Lewis, *Primary and General Election Law and Procedure 1968* (Chapel

Sources and perspectives

Hill, Institute of Government, University North Carolina, 1968), pp. 76–7. See also the *Robesonian*, where this regulation is publicly flaunted, despite its transparent probable illegality (e.g., May 1, 1970): "In the race for a seat on the board of education, the anti-single shot law will be in effect. In other words, in order for a voter's ballot to be counted, he must vote for three of the four candidates, since there are three vacancies." In fact, the issue of the *Robesonian* that announced, in front page headlines, "First Time Negro Has Been on City Ballot" (April 3, 1958) spent the bulk of the article explaining anti-single-shot voting. The exemplary figures on how this affects minority voting are the same ones I used at various strategy meetings of Indian and Black activists when I was asked to open this discussion.

III The voter registration figures are from the county board of elections, and were printed in the *Robesonian* a day or two after the registration books closed, three weeks before the May (Democratic) party primary elections.

IV "Hope" was actually incorporated in the state of North Carolina; from my work in organizing and incorporating the Lumbee Regional Development Association, I have copies of the incorporation papers of the Lumbee Citizens' Council and Hope, Inc., in my files; they are probably also on file with the North Carolina secretary of state.

A description of the Lumbee confrontation with the Klan can be found in two issues of *Life* magazine, Jan. 27 and Fed. 3, 1958; and in *The Only Land I Know*, pp. 158–61. A reading of the local, small-town papers for the winter and spring of 1958 helps to provide the context for this confrontation. For example, in the week following, the *Robesonian* (1/21/58) ran two stories on the front page: one a routine announcement about another Klan rally being scheduled, the second "11 Whites on Trial for Negro Flogging," which noted that six months earlier fifteen Whites, all acknowledging membership in the Klan (but four of whom were exonerated without trial), had flogged a fifty-eight-year-old man "a farmer, landowner and Baptist Deacon . . . as he and his wife cared for seven children of a white neighbor. The children's father was at a hospital with his wife, who was confined because of kidney trouble." The "offense" that the Black man had committed seems to have been friendship with a White neighbor. More than is usually understood, the Klan sought to prevent simple and ongoing egalitarian relations in ordinary daily life: the most total cultural assault on African-Americans possible, short of genocide.

VI The whole development of Indian and Black political claims in the South, and the thin line between respect and rage in the formation of these claims, can be more clearly understood in the context of the nonlegal arrangements power makes to quiet noise. Horace Stacy, of McLean and Stacy, wrote to Governor Clyde Hoey, May 13, 1938:

> *An Act of the General Assembly of 1917 provides that the Governor shall, on the first Monday of May of each year, appoint a mayor and four commissioners of the town of Pembroke. A majority of the voters . . . of Pembroke are indians, and ever since . . . 1917, there has been some feeling of resentment on the part of a great many indians. . . . This grew and grew until the issue had to be met by the white people of the town. . . . The town board with some of the leading white citizens and some of the leading indian citizens had a meeting and finally decided that they would agree to have a Primary Election in the town*

for the purpose of recommending to the Governor . . . the mayor, who should be
a white man, two white commissioners and two indian commissioners . . . [list
of nominees included].

We think it would be in the interest of peace and harmony . . . if you would
appoint the officers nominated in the town primary of May 10. Of course, you
understand, there is no law authorizing this town primary and it is merely a
plan worked out by the leading white and indian citizens.

Part three "Root hog or die"

Prologue

I am grateful to Wesley White, who found the newspaper article on Barbarous
Indians and called it to my attention.

The point at the end of the section about power creating chaos is specifically
a critique of the Weberian perspective on power, authority, and legitimation:
in a hundred different guises, all too familiar to students of sociology, the
notion that "charismatic," "traditional," and "rational-legal" legitimations give
power its order and coherence. Be that as it may – I think it is mostly nonsense
and an obstacle to understanding – it has diverted attention from examining
the chaos power characteristically engenders, and the crucial roles chaos has in
the reproduction and limitation of forms of domination.

Chapter 7 Prospect and loss

I The story of the FBI raid that recovered the documents quoted from the
Robesonian, April 9, 1973. The following day's paper has a dramatic photograph
of a large truck being loaded with boxes of documents. One month earlier,
March 7, 1973, the *Robesonian* headlined "28 Downtown Store Windows Broken
as 'Tuscaroras' Stage Demonstration"; and this was under the banner line,
printed in quotes, "In Support of Wounded Knee." The occupation of the
Bureau of Indian Affairs, from an Indian point of view, is best described in *BIA:
I'm Not Your Indian Any More – Trail of Broken Treaties* (Rooseveltown, N.Y.,
Akwesasne Notes, 2d ed., 1974).

II A quite detailed story about the confrontation with Tuscarora people in
front of Prospect school, under the banner "Numerous Weapons Seized," fills
the front page of the Sunday, March 25, edition of the *Robesonian*. The *Carolina
Indian Voice* and the *Robesonian*, for the spring of 1973, provide extensive descriptions of the events discussed here, and in the following sections.

VI Chief Howard Brooks's open letter on the Lumbee bill was not published.
I have a copy in my files.

Chapter 8 The original 22

I *Maynor v. Morton* (Lawrence Maynor v. Rogers C.B. Morton, Secretary, U.S.
Dept. of the Interior) U.S. Court of Appeals, District of Columbia, argued 21
Nov 1974, decided 4 April 1975 (510 F.2d 1254 [D.C. Circuit] 1975). The case
was filed in the U.S. District Court for the District of Columbia under the name
Vestia Locklear et al. v. Rogers C. B. Morton, on Feb. 23, 1973. The case was moved
to the Eastern District of North Carolina and Rogers Morton won on July 19,

296

1973. Lawrence Maynor, one of the original plaintiffs – and one of the original 22 – filed a notice of appeal on Sept. 12, 1973. This appeal provides the main source of data about the case.

The Indian Reorganization Act, Public Law 383, 73d Cong. (25 USC 479) can be found in vol. 25 of the U.S. Code. *United States Code, Annotated* (St. Paul, Minn., West, 1983). Section 19 of the act (479 in the code) covers eligibility. Commissioner John Collier's memorandum on how to deal with people of one-half or more blood is BIA document number 126839, Sept. 22, 1935. A copy of Carl Selzer's letter to Collier is in the files of Lumbee River Legal Services. The government sale of the Indians' community building is described in the correspondence of J. B. Slack, acting regional director of the Farm Security Administration, Raleigh, between 1943 and 1945. The culmination of the long process of development and destruction is described in William Zimmerman, Jr., assistant commissioner of Indian affairs, letter to Stott Noble, Farm Security Administration, Washington D.C., Oct. 25, 1945.

II The Red Banks and Pembroke Farms history in the Farm Security Administration hearings: Hearings before the Select Committee of the House Committee on Agriculture, to Investigate the Activities of the Farm Security Administration, Pursuant to House Res. 119, 78 Cong., 1st sess., pt. 3, pp. 1087 ff. (USGPO, 1944). John Pearmain's report, November 11, 1935, which details the living and farming conditions of the Indian people of Robeson County: "Report of John Pearmain, Assistant Regional Specialist, Indian Rehabilitation Division, Resettlement Administration, on the Condition of the Indians of Robeson County, North Carolina; Supplemental data to be attached to the Rural Resettlement Proposal being submitted by the Office of the Regional Director, Raleigh, N.C." (RR NC 22). A copy of this, and of most of the other substantial documentation on the history of Red Banks, is on file at Lumbee River Legal Services, in a collection that represents, in particular, the work of Geoff Mangum and Julian Pierce in reconstructing the history of this period, and Wesley White's archiving, and substantial additions to, the collection.

III The correspondence from E. J. Britt and D. F. Lowery to Sen. Josiah Bailey is presented and discussed in the Lumbee Petition; Lumbee River Legal Services has copies, from the Bailey Correspondence Series in the North Carolina State Archives.

IV Superintendent Fred Baker's report, July 9, 1935, is BIA Document 37889; National Archives Record Group 75, 36208–35–310, Siouan. Harold Ickes's comments on the Siouan and Cheraw recognition bills are presented and discussed in the Lumbee petition. John R. Swanton's influential report: "Probable Identity of the 'Croatan' Indians," in *Siouan Indians of Lumber River*, S. Rept. 204, 73d Cong., 2d sess. (USGPO, 1934).

V The plan and rationale for the first Back Swamp drainage project is described in Samuel McRorry, "The Back Swamp and Jacob Swamp Drainage District, N.C." U.S. Department of Agriculture, Experimental Station Bull. 246 (USGPO, 1912).

Chapter 9 Henry Berry Lowery lives forever

I, II For a review of the homecoming awards, including the Henry Berry Lowery Award winners, see Ben Jacobs, "The History of Lumbee Regional

Development Association, Inc, 1968–1985." This is unpublished, but copies are in the files of LRDA. It is an excellent history of a large range of processes and developments in the 1970s and early 1980s, including relations between Lumbee and Tuscarora, "double voting," and relations between Lumbee and national Indian associations.

The spelling of Lowery (Lowrie, Lowry) was not standardized in the nineteenth century, and a variety of forms appear. I use Lowery here, except for citations and quotation, which follow the author's usage. The central sources for the life and times of Henry Berry Lowery are: William McKee Evans, *To Die Game: The Story of the Lowry Band, Indian Guerrillas of Reconstruction* (Baton Rouge, Louisiana State University Press, 1971); Gary Lewis Barton, *The Life and Times of Henry Berry Lowry* (Pembroke, N.C., Lumbee Publishing, 1979); Mary C. Norment, *The Lowrie History* (Wilmington, N.C., Daily Journal Printers, 1875). Norment's book went through several editions, each with additions and some changes and deletions. See also the 4th ed. (Lumberton, N.C., Lumbee Publishing, 1909); and George Alfred Townsend, ed., *The Swamp Outlaws* (New York, Robert M. De Witt, 1872). There are so many different editions of Mary Norment's rather brief book, each with such restricted availability, that page references can be more confusing than helpful. The larger social and historical context of reconstruction in this region is well delineated in William McKee Evans, *Ballots and Fence Rails: Reconstruction on the Lower Cape Fear* (Chapel Hill, North Carolina University Press, 1967).

In my Ph.D. dissertation, *The Political History of the Lumbee Indians*, I invented several shorthand terms for kinds of events and in one case, kinds of people. As a way of grouping together the stories I was told about one process of land loss in the mid-nineteenth century, I made up the name "tied mule stories," for many of the stories were about mules. To describe the politically central Indians of a community, I coined the term "locality leader." And to distinguish between the political activism of the early 1950s and the voter registration group working in the 1960s, I started using "the Movement" and "the organization" with fixed referents, where a lot of politically active Indian people would use them interchangeably; as a favor to me, to help me follow their discussions and arguments, they started using them more specifically. These terms have now all entered into the local political and academic discourse: Dial and Eliades, for example, use the phrase "tied mule" stories in *The Only Land I Know* (p. 45), although hinting that the term is not local: "The Lumbees still refer with bitterness to what are called 'tied mule' incidents." William McKee Evans, in his "North Carolina Lumbees: From Assimilation to Revitalization," in Walter L. Williams, ed., *Southeastern Indians since the Removal Era* (Athens, University of Georgia Press, 1979), uses "tied mule," "locality leader," "the Movement," and so on.

There is an important point at issue here – complex, subtle, difficult for me to understand at first, but crucial: What this artificial naming process does is to distort a reality that is much more fluid and open; a reality that derives much of its power and force precisely from this fluidity and openness. Consider that in the 1960s, when I was living in the county, there were *no* group of "stories" called "tied mule" or any other label. People just told stories, some sad, some funny, or at least droll; some of them in response to questions I asked, some of them just telling me stories about how things were *and are* (at that time if not now). These were not a special group or a named type of stories that could be bounded, contained, labeled or categorized: they were still very much alive – they were about how things were and how things are, simultaneously. They were, in sum, living history, and if they come now to have a generic name it will be because they no longer have the same kind of presence they once had. I have only begun to understand this recently, through the influence of Gavin Smith's work on how Andean Indian people talk about their own history.

As I grasp the point, its implications grow. I think it matters that the people who lived in the Indian communities of Robeson County had no general name for their leaders. I called them "locality leaders"; the name caught on, and is now used occasionally in the county. They called these people by their given names: everyone knew who they were, and the lack of a categorical title was essential to understanding the basis of their influence. Actual communities of people, here and elsewhere as well, are often shaped by influential persons who, if they had a political title would lose it – lose the title and, more to the point, the kind of influence they once had. Political titles in small, locally focused communities are ordinarily created by the intrusion of externally based domination; their adoption marks a profound reshaping of the basis of local influence.

On the losses suffered by McLean during Sherman's march, see Evans, *To Die Game*, p. 48. The description of "Scuffletown" is from Norment, *Lowrie History* (1875 ed.), pp. 24–5. The two versions of the letter demanding release of their wives can be found, annotated, in *To Die Game*, p. 199.

III The different "bloods" of Henry Berry Lowery are described by Norment, *Lowrie History*, pp. 9–12. The Giles Leitch testimony is from the *Condition of Affairs*, vol. 2, pt. 2, p. 283.

IV Cobble's letter to Birney, on the Tuscarora ancestry of Henry Berry Lowery, in the U.S. War Department, Records of the Army Commands (Record Group 393, National Archives). My copy comes from Lumbee River Legal Services' Archives. The Bureau of Refugees, Freedmen and Abandoned Lands (Lumberton, N.C. Office), Record Group 105, National Archives, provides substantial further data about this area after the Civil War.

V The 1859 petition by the Chavis and Jones families to the state of South Carolina is in the South Carolina Archives, General Assembly papers, and was found by Wesley White, who also found the "railously assembled" proclamation in the Robeson County, Misc., collection at the North Carolina Archives. For an overview of European settlement in this area in the mid-eighteenth century, see Duane Meyer, *The Highland Scots of North Carolina, 1732–1776* (Chapel Hill, University North Carolina Press, 1961).

The William Chavers case is 50 NC 25 (1857), in the Supreme Court of North Carolina. The newspaper advertisements for runaway indentured servants can be found, with much other interesting material, in a report by Wesley White to Lumbee River Legal Services: "The American Indian Population in Robeson County, N.C. from 1837–1854" (Jan. 15, 1986). The "Drowning Creek on the Head of the Little Peedee" quotation which occurs in two different versions in the printed *Colonial Records of North Carolina*, is given here as I copied it from the original in the North Carolina State Archives. Record of the NC Militia, 1747–54, in record group: Troop Returns, 1747–1859, Military Records of NC Collection, shelf mark TR. 1–16. The printed version is NC Col. Rec., vol. 5, p. 161.

Part four "Now our inmates": Colonial formations and formation's heritage

Prologue

The "staple commodities of South Carolina . . ." quotation appears in the North Carolina and South Carolina Colonial Records, with small differences: NC Col. Rec., vol. 11, pp. 225–7; see there also (on p. 221) the letter introducing this document, which is missing from the Board of Trade records; or SC, Council Journals (Manuscript), April 4, 1769, pp. 604–6. The version here is taken from a South Carolina Department of Archives and History manuscript (and microfilmed) copy of *Records in the British Public Record Office relating to South Carolina, 1663–1782* (SC-AR M/1 Reel 2), pp. 57–61. This seems to be the most complete and accurate version of the original that is accessible outside the Public Record Office itself, when exact phrases are of interest.

Chapter 10 Six pounds of paint to encourage the Indians

The six pounds of paint quotation is from a letter by John Highrider to Governor Glen, Oct., 24, 1750. *Colonial Records of South Carolina, Documents Relating to Indian Affairs,* May 21, 1750–August 7, 1754. William L. McDowell, Jr., ed. (Columbia, S.C., S.C. Archives Department, 1958), p. 38. Robert Johnson, on promoting war between Indians who are friends to the English, BPRO, South Carolina, B.T., vol. 7, South Carolina DAH (SC-AR M/1, reel 4), p. 3, Dec. 15, 1732.

I, II On the florescence of plains Indian culture, see Preston Holder, *The Hoe and the Horse on the Plains* (Lincoln, University of Nebraska Press, 1970); Bernard Mishkin, *Rank and Warfare among the Plains Indians,* AES Monograph 3 (Seattle, University of Washington Press); Eric Wolf, *Europe and the People without History* (Berkeley, University of California Press, 1982), chap 6. On Indians and mules see, for example, *Athanese de Mezieres and the Louisiana-Texas Frontier,* vol. 2, pp. 120–1, "the Kiowa and Comanche traded to the French in the East 1,000 horses and the same number of mules. The Wichitas were the intermediaries." Cited in Mishkin, p. 6, n. 4.

III For the deerskin trade in the southeast, see Verner W. Crane, *The Southern Frontier* (Ann Arbor, University of Michigan Press, 1929 [rev. ed., 1956]); the quotation is at pp. 111–12. There is a fascinating census of the trade as a whole in 1715 in BPRO, BT, vol. 6, pp. 135–9.

Sidney W. Mintz, *Sweetness and Power* (New York, Viking, 1985). On the conjunction of war and the enslavement of Indians, see Charles Hudson, *The Catawba Nation* (Athens, University of Georgia Press, 1970), p. 29; on the rapid rise of Indian slaves in the early 1700s, see *Handbook of North American Indians* (Washington, D.C., Smithsonian Institution, 1988), vol. 4: *History of Indian-White Relations,* p. 408. William Willis, "Divide and Rule: Red, White and Black in the

Southeast," *J. Negro Hist.* 48 (July 1963): 157–176, is still an excellent overview, particularly of Indian–Black relations.

IV On the increasing squeeze of the piedmont Indians, the best starting point is Nancie O. Lurie, "Indian Cultural Adjustment to European Civilization," in James Morton Smith, ed., *Seventeenth-Century America: Essays in Colonial History* (New York, Norton, 1972 [1957]); John R. Swanton, *Indians of the Southeastern United States* (Washington D.C., Smithsonian Institution Press, [BAE Bulletin 137, 1946], repr. 1979).

The Spanish Crown's patent for enslaving natives: ms. Asiento y Capitulacion, trans. Paul Quattlebaum, *The Land Called Chicora* (Gainesville, University of Florida Press, 1956), pp. 138–40. On the Westoes "ruinating" the region, see Robert Sandford, quoted in Chapman Milling, *Red Carolinians* (Columbia, University of South Carolina Press, 1969), p. 47. On the Cusabo and the Westo, see ibid., pp. 47–8. Alexander S. Salley, Jr., *Narratives of Early Carolina* (New York, Barnes and Noble, 1939 [1911]), reprints the original: Robert Sandford, "Relation of a Voyage on the Coast of the Province of Carolina" (1666), pp. 75–108.

V W. Hatter's long, confusing, and amazing letter about the Creek and Cherokee confronting both each other and the European's sense of history, is from BPRO SC BT, vol. 2, Nov. 14, 1724, SC DAH(SC-AR M/1 Reel 3), pp. 270–9. On the spread of epidemics, Europeans, and general social turmoil, see Emmanuel Le Roy Ladurie, "A Concept: The Unification of the Globe by Disease (Fourteenth to Seventeenth centuries)," *The Mind and Method of the Historian* (Chicago, University of Chicago Press, 1981). The general situation between the South Carolina colony and the Indian peoples in the years surrounding the Tuscarora and Yamasee wars, in addition to being a central topic of the South Carolina Council Journals, is well illuminated by *Journals of the Commissioners of the Indian Trade*, September 20, 1710, to August 29, 1718, W. L. McDowell, ed. (Columbia, S.C., SC DAH, 1955). Presents to Indians at half the value of their gifts is here, at p. 33. A. S. Salley, Jr. has also republished excerpts from these journals; his volume is called *Journal of the Commissioners of the Indian Trade of South Carolina* (Columbia, S.C., 1926). The "poor Carolina" complaint, BPRO BT, vol. 10, June 8, 1717, SC DAH (SC-AR M/1 Reel 2), pp. 49–52. Governor Johnson's account of the subject Indians, the trade, and the "utter extirpation of Little Tribes," BPRO, BT, vol. 7, South Carolina DAH (SC-AR M/1 Reel 2), pp. 233–42. The instructions to Indian agents on keeping Indians subject to their own kings, in the *Journal of the Commissioners of the Indian Trade*, p. 32.

VI On the vulnerability of small producers in "proto-industrial" Europe, and only by way of an introduction to this complex subject, see Peter Kriedte, Hans Medick, and Jurgen Schlumbohm, *Industrialization before Industrialization* (New York, Cambridge University Press, 1981 [1977]); also Peter Kriedte, *Peasants, Landlords and Merchant Capitalists* (New York, Cambridge University Press, 1983 [1980]). For the way vulnerability transforms local culture, I am still indebted to Jane Schneider, "Peacocks and Penguins: The Political Economy of European Cloth and Colors," *American Ethnologist* 5 (1978): 413–47.

Barry Morris, *Domesticating Resistance: The Dhani-Gadi Aborigines and the Australian State* (Oxford, Berg, 1989); Jeremy Beckett, "Introduction" to his edited volume, *Past and Present: The Construction of Aboriginality* (Canberra, Aboriginal Studies, 1988); Jeffrey Gould, *To Lead as Equals: Rural Protest and Political*

Consciousness in Chinandega, Nicaragua, 1912–1979 (Chapel Hill, University of North Carolina Press, 1990), esp. chap. 3. These works extend the argument made here about vulnerability and cultural change into a far broader context and provide the basis for the development of a more general, and more multifaceted understanding. Georges Lefebvre, *The Great Fear of 1789: Rural Panic in Revolutionary France* (New York, Schocken, 1989 [1932]), also conveys a sense of the fears and desperations of nonrevolutionary times – times that we might call "ordinary."

Thomas Ashe, on the whole country like a royal park, in Crane, *Southern Frontier*, pp. 113–14. On the Yamasee being forced to relocate eastward see David H. Corkran, *The Carolina Indian Frontier* (Columbia, University of South Carolina Press, [for the Tricentennial Commission] 1970), p. 7. For a fuller discussion of native peoples being permitted to produce, for the colonial economy, only what were understood to be diminishing resources, see "When Parrots Learn to Talk."

Chapter 11 Distinguishing the headmen

The "talk" to the Creek, used as an epigraph, from the SC Council Journal, Sainsbury (manuscript) copy at South Carolina DAH, June 13, 1761. King Blount's commission from the North Carolina Council, it should be noted, follows well after the defeat of the Tuscarora and seems designed as an attempt not only to keep his followers loyal to him but to prevent them from moving away on their own: *Col Rec NC*, vol. 2, p. 573. On using the Cherokee to open Yamasee lands for European settlement, see BPRO, BT, vol. 6, March 3, 1716, SC DAH (SC-AR M/1 Reel 2), p. 151.

I Francis Jennings, *The Invasion of America: Indians, Colonialism and the Cant of Conquest* (New York, Norton, 1976 [1975]), esp. pt. 1, "Myths of the Marchlands." See also Wilbur R. Jacobs, "The Tip of an Iceberg: Pre Columbian Indian Demography," *William and Mary Quarterly* 31, 3d ser. (1974): 123–32. A. L. Kroeber's estimates in his "Native American Population," *Am. Anthrop.* NS 36 (1934): 1–25. A well-developed demographic history of native America, with an insightful reconceptualization of frontier processes in the context of more realistically conceptualized demographic processes, is given by Henry F. Dobyns in the first two essays of his *Their Number Became Thinned* (Knoxville, University of Tennessee Press, 1983). On "hill tribes" and "southern chiefdoms," see Joffre Lanning Coe, "The Cultural Sequence of the Carolina Piedmont" – one of the more useful articles in a generally useful, if dated, compendium: James B. Griffen, ed., *Archaeology of the Eastern United States* (Chicago, University of Chicago Press, 1952); with Griffen's own perspectives revised and summarized in "Eastern North American Archaeology, A Summary," *Science* 157 (1967).

II Coe further developed his analyses of pre-contact agriculture and social organization in *The Formative Cultures of the Carolina Piedmont* (Transactions of the American Philosophical Society, vol. 54, pt. 5, 1964); see also Charles M. Hudson, *Catawba Nation*, chap. 2; Christian Feest, "North Carolina Algonquins," and Douglas Boyce, "Iroquoian Tribes of the Virginia-North Carolina Coastal Plain," both in vol. 15 of the *Handbook of North American Indians* (1978), provide brief, focused, and more up-to-date surveys. Monks Mound (Cahokia) was discussed in the *New York Times,* September 10, 1989.

On the Chinese wall and the relations between states and hinterland peoples, see Owen Lattimore, "The Frontier in History," in his *Studies in Frontier History: Collected Papers, 1928–1958* (London, Oxford University Press, 1962). Morton Fried's *The Notion of Tribe* is one of the best and most important theoretical statements of this relationship; indeed, to my mind, it is one of the gems of modern anthropology. Its publication in an almost inaccessible source is an intellectual disaster. I was first alerted to the importance of seeing the flow of people across a landscape by a little-noticed but theoretically perceptive essay on the social organization of central highland New Guinea: James B. Watson, "Society as Organized Flow: The Tairora Case," *Southwestern J. Anthropology* 26 (Summer 1970).

III   Charles Hudson, *The Southeastern Indians* (Knoxville, University of Tennessee Press, 1976), has a focused and important discussion of the different uses native peoples and Europeans made of the fall line. The quotation from him on this is at p. 19.

The three general issues raised here – the relations between states and hinterland peoples, the different forms of population flow across a landscape, and to generalize the third, the different ways stratified and more egalitarian societies use ecological diversity – are all interwoven, most intensely in the domain of processes of cultural differentiation within and between societies. This topic will be directly addressed in my forthcoming essay, "Cultural Differentiation, Class Formation and the Logic of Subsistence Production: A Theoretical Perspective and an Andean Instance," and will also be one of the central issues in the third volume of this series on culture and class in anthropology and history. The discussion briefly introduced at the beginning of this chapter, concerning storage, commodification, and domination at the points of production and exchange, will be substantially amplified in volume three.

For the truce with the remainder of the Powhatan confederacy, and the ensuing growth of "tributary" and settlement Indians, see Wesley Frank Craven, *White, Red and Black: The Seventeenth Century Virginian* (Charlottesville, University Press of Virginia, 1971), p. 62; also his "Indian Policy in Early Virginia," *William and Mary Quarterly* 1 3d ser. (January 1944): 65–82. James H. Merrell, "Our Bond of Peace: Patterns of Intercultural Exchange in the Carolina Piedmont, 1650–1750," in Peter Wood et al., eds., *Powhatan's Mantle: Indians in the Colonial Southeast* (Lincoln, University of Nebraska Press, 1989). The act to regulate the entrance of Indians into the settlements, in William W. Hening, ed., *Virginia: The Statutes at Large, . . . [from] 1619. . .* (2d ed, New York, 1823), vol. 2, p. 141. Lewis Binford has a thought-provoking survey of the situation of the smaller groups, particularly good on their shifting status and situation in two articles: "An Ethnohistory of the Nottoway, Meherrin, and Weanoke Indians of Southeastern Virginia," *Ethnohistory* 14 (1967): 104–218; "Comments on the 'Siouan Problem'," *Ethnohistory* 6 (1959): 28–41.

William Willis on the struggle for empire and success in the Indian country, "Anthropology and Negroes in the Southern Colonial Frontier," in James Curtis, ed., *The Black Experience in America* (Austin, University of Texas Press, 1970), pp. 33-50; William Bartram on piedmont and mountain deerskin, from his "Observations on the Creek and Cherokee Indians, 1789," *Transactions of the Am. Ethnological Society* 3, pt. 1 (1853): pp. 1–81.

Sources and perspectives

The best sources for starting a reconceptualization of the linked processes of population decline and confederacy formation are James Merrell, *The Indians' New World: Catawbas and Their Neighbors from European Contact through the Era of Removal* (Chapel Hill, University of North Carolina Press, 1989); Charles Hudson, *Catawba Nation*; and Richard White, *Roots of Dependency*. Merrell, whose work is particularly insightful, and Hudson, who broke much new ground when his book was first done, both centered their analyses on a society that was even more decimated than usual. Richard White's book analyzes well a wide range of issues, including the topics of confederacy formation and population decline. He associates many of the links between such processes with ecological changes. Although this is a key aspect of the links, my suggestion is that it will also prove productive to analyze the social and cultural expressions of the interwoven processes of confederacy formation and population decline, particularly among the "stronger" confederacies, such as the Cherokee and the Creeks. For a particularly well-developed summary of a wide range of current research approaches to the ethnohistory of the colonial southeast (but with a different concept of ethnohistory than is presented here), see Peter H. Wood, Gregory Waselkov, and M. Thomas Hatley, eds., *Powhatan's Mantle: Indians in the Colonial Southeast* (Lincoln, University of Nebraska Press, 1989).

IV On chiefdoms and towns, see especially Charles Hudson, *Southeastern Indians*, pp. 233–4; Wilbur R. Jacobs, ed., *The Appalachian Indian Frontier: the Edmond Atkin Report and Plan of 1755* (Lincoln, University of Nebraska Press, 1967). For relations among people the colonists called Tuscarora, see Douglas Boyce, "Did a Tuscarora Confederacy Exist?" in Charles Hudson, ed., *Four Centuries of Southern Indians* (Athens, University of Georgia Press, 1975), pp. 28–45. On the internal relations of the Cherokee and the transition from Beloved Elder to Chief, see James Adair, *The History of the American Indians* (New York, Johnson Reprint, 1968 [1775]); Fred Gearing, *Priests and Warriors: Social Structures for Cherokee Politics in the 18th Century*, Am. Anthrop. Assn, Memoir 93 (vol. 64, no. 5, pt. 2), 1962; John Phillip Reid, *A Better Kind of Hatchet: Law, Trade and Diplomacy during the Early Years of European Contact* (University Park, Pa., Pennsylvania State University Press, 1976) – note here, in the light of my comment above on "locality leaders" among the Lumbee: "Headmen had no rank, no titles, no hereditary status" (p. 5). On Cherokee fragmentation and frog-eating, see Reid, pp. 2–4. The creation of the Cherokee priest-state, Gearing, *Priests and Warriors*, pp. 5–6. On Creek "chiefdoms" and the social basis of towns, including the point that two "towns" could coexist in the same physical community, see Hudson, *Southeastern Indians*, p. 205.

On the Yamasee not paying the debts of their relations, see *Journal of the Commissioners of Indian Trade*, A. S. Salley, ed., p. 13. The discussion of kinship and credit here was provoked by Arturo Warman, "An Interpretive Essay," in his *We Come to Object: The Peasants of Morelos and the National State* (Baltimore, Johns Hopkins University Press, 1980 [1976]).

VI, VII The topic of the diverse kinds of migrations of native people has a vast literature, for it is more a small piece of many works than a subject that has drawn much sustained or focused attention. It deserves more thought than it usually gets, for it can be of considerable help in understanding the formation of hopes and intentions in the midst of an intensifying squeeze. Nancy Lurie,

304

"Indian Cultural adjustment..." focuses on one small segment of the region and should be a model for other studies. Frank L. Owsley, "The Pattern of Migration and Settlement on the Southern Frontier," *J. Southern History* 11 (May 1945): pp. 147–76, helps to clarify the spread of colonial settlement, and hence the kinds of pressures native peoples were under. John Swanton, *The Indians of the Southeastern United States,* develops a good image, from innumerable small comments, of the flow of people.

For the closing of Fort Christiana, see Binford, "Ethnohistory of the Nottoway," p. 74. On native people growing corn and peaches for sale see *North Carolina Col Rec,* vol. 2, p. 28.

Chapter 12 "This isn't Burger King" vs. "31 Pages of Unalphabetized Locklears"

I The *Robesonian* did a special job of covering the taking of seventeen "hostages" by two Tuscarora Indians: the hostages were employees of, and taken and held at, the *Robesonian's* offices. The coverage begins on Feb. 1, 1988.

The discussion of livelihood and living is rooted in Gavin Smith, *Livelihood and Resistance: Peasants and the Politics of Land in Peru* (Berkeley, University of California Press, 1989).

Much of the data for this chapter comes directly from my own field research, and from various people giving me copies of letters, statements, and so forth. The chapter itself contains the identification of sources, with silences as requested concerning my access to sources. One imagines that copies of the quoted correspondence, for example, can be found in the originating office; that office and the date are indicated. For material that is not yet readily accessible, care was taken to quote exactly and extensively. Ben Jacob's unpublished *History of Lumbee Regional Development Association* (1985), on file at LRDA, is an excellent summary of many of the key political issues of the mid 1970s and the early 1980s. The Tuscarora open letters were published in the weekly Pembroke newspaper, the *Carolina Indian Voice.* Their statement about acceptance by NCAI published Aug. 28, 1980.

II, III Vermon Locklear's list of requests for the Hattaras Tuscarora tribe is unpublished and undated; it comes from the early 1980s. The published statements in the *Carolina Indian Voice* are on microfilm at Pembroke State University Library. The "O.D." letter to the Tuscarora is on file at the Branch of Acknowledgment and Research, BIA.

VI, VII The Mohawk controversy over gambling is best presented in the 1990 issues of *Akwesasne Notes.* The figures on changing land ownership and use in the 1970s and early 1980s were published in the *Robesonian,* Aug. 10, 1986, in a feature article entitled "Who Owns Land in Robeson County?"

VIII The Lumbee Recognition Act (HR 2335) hearings began on Sept. 26, 1989, before the House Committee on Interior and Insular Affairs. Ms. Angela McCoy, Secretary of the Committee's Indian Affairs Office, kindly provided me with information and testimony from these hearings. Through the courtesy and helpfulness of Ms. Ruth Locklear and the tribal attorney, Arlinda Locklear, I attended the 1991 hearings on SR 1426, and some of the preparatory and ensuing discussions.

Conclusions

II   The John Marshall decision: U.S. Supreme Court, *Reports* (30 US [5 Pet] 1), *Cherokee Nation v. Georgia.*

The issue raised in the conclusion, concerning the need to address the tensions and antagonisms among a dominated ethnic people (and within a working class) as a proper part of the process of confronting domination and exploitation, will be central to the third volume of this project. This issue, which in general terms is about the changing connections between culture and state power, turns out to be most productively understood by means of a fundamental reconsideration of kinship systems.

Index